SKILLS IN SEQUENCE

SKILLS IN SEQUENCE

THOMAS FRIEDMANN
Onondaga Community College of SUNY

with Tim Brown
Senior Writing Tutor, Writing Skills Center,
Onondaga Community College of SUNY

Diagnostic Tests by Wendy Demko Reynoso
Coordinator, Writing Skills Program, Student Academic Services,
California Polytechnic State University at San Luis Obispo

St. Martin's Press
New York

Executive Editor: Susan Anker
Director of Editing: Richard Steins
Production Supervisor: Julie Toth
Text design: Barbara Bert/North 7 Atelier, Ltd.
Cover design: Darby Downey
Cover photograph: David M. Grossman

Library of Congress Catalog Card Number: 87–060509
Copyright © 1988 by St. Martin's Press, Inc.
All rights reserved.
Manufactured in the United States of America.
21098
fedcba

For information, write to:
St. Martin's Press, Inc.
175 Fifth Avenue
New York, NY 10010

ISBN: 0-312-00291-2

To the Instructor

Skills in Sequence is a non-error–based text that teaches basic grammatical skills separately, sequentially, and within the context of paragraphs and short essays.

Because many students are unsure of correct forms, this text does *not* present them with errors to revise during the learning sequences. Instead, it offers exercises that require students to rewrite specific elements in the text from one correct form to another (past tense to present tense, for example). This process reinforces correct usage and avoids exposing students to forms that might confuse them. Only after students have become secure in their knowledge of correct forms are they asked to proofread for errors.

The grammatical and mechanical skills taught in *Skills in Sequence* have been focused by separating each problem into its own chapter, again to avoid confusing students whose sense of grammatical correctness is unsure. A student might have no general difficulties with subject-verb agreement yet consistently err when a verb precedes its subject. This text offers students a series of exercises carefully designed to deal with each specific situation separately.

Each chapter contains a sequence of exercises that proceeds from "Attention Focusing" to "Rewriting" to "Proofreading," with both initial and final "Writing Assignments." The "Attention Focusing" exercise focuses on the grammatical elements that will be manipulated in the chapter. The first "Rewriting Exercise" offers three to four paragraphs requiring students merely to write out the few words they need to change in each sentence. Subsequent "Rewriting Exercises" ask students to copy an entire short selection, even as they make the necessary changes. Although this requirement may elicit some groans from the students who must do the writing and the instructors who have to do the evaluating, the exercise is precisely what makes the practice of rewriting come close to the experience of writing. It shows students *how* grammar operates throughout a paragraph, and it demands the proofreading skills they must use in their own writing. Again, there are three to four "Rewriting Exercises" in each chapter, and supplementary exercises are available in the Instructor's Manual that accompanies the text.

To students who need not merely to learn but to make these grammatical skills second nature, a "word to the wise" is insufficient. They need repeated practice with particular mechanical skills if they are to build their grammatical muscles. In a sense, they learned their errors by repetition—by repeatedly misspelling a word or confusing a term, they made their errors automatic and habitual. Telling them to stop making errors cannot eliminate such fossilized behavior even when students are willing to do so. Instead, they must be given the opportunity to make correctness habitual, to reorient their "automatic pilot" to choose correct forms. Only a sequence of exercises will accomplish this end. Naturally, the extremely broad range of topics covered within each sequence will help maintain the interest of students.

Each chapter also offers ample opportunities to practice proofreading. Even after students habitually use correct forms, they will need to practice proofreading skills. These exercises are preceded by the innovative "Proofreading Strategies," a guide to successful identification, location, and correction of error.

Students who already habitually use correct forms but lack the ability to locate occasional errors in specific areas of grammar can move directly to the proofreading exercises. But prior to their attempting this part of the sequence, they should demonstrate through their writing that their sense of correct forms in a particular area of grammar is secure and that their errors are only occasional. They can do this by completing the diagnostic test, "Attention Focusing," and/or "Writing Assignment" in the particular area.

Whichever sequence instructors utilize, they can rest assured that this text, as recent work in writing research advises, does not attempt to teach grammatical or mechanical skills through isolated words or even isolated sentences. Rather, it offers throughout the context of paragraphs and short essays. After all, when students are asked to write an essay or theme, they must create sentences that show connected thought, rather than individual, unrelated sentences. If these practice assignments are to prepare students for the writing of their graded essays, they too must require organized and connected sentences.

The focus on grammatical skills is retained, however, even as students work on paragraphs. The writing topics are not random. In a process commonly called "controlled composition," each topic is carefully phrased to elicit the particular grammatical form discussed in the chapter. In addition to offering a particularly intriguing fusion of grammar and content, such essays can also serve as both diagnostic and mastery tests. For instructors who prefer formal diagnostic tests, Appendix 4 offers one for each Unit (I-VI) as well as one for the entire text. These tests, devised by Wendy Demko Reynoso, are also short paragraphs, though for the sake of convenience, the sentences are numbered individually.

Finally, Unit I and Unit IX provide an important framework for this grammar and proofreading text. They contain explanations and exercises for the writing of sentences on the one hand and of paragraphs within the essay on the other.

HOW TO USE THIS BOOK

Skills in Sequence is a "paper-specific" grammar text. That is, it contains a sequence of exercises for any errors a student's paper might have. Within the familiar but broad category of "subject-verb agreement," for example, a student may have errors only with indefinite pronouns or collective nouns.

As such, this text is a resource for all variations of grammar in student papers. You do not need to have students work their way through the text from beginning to end any more than you would have them read a handbook from front to back. Instead, as you read student essays (or use one of the many diagnostic tests available in the text or manual), and determine their problems with mechanics, you can assign chapters keyed to specific problems. The carefully designed and narrowly focused sequences in these chapters should lead toward mastery.

Should you wish to assign work sequentially, follow the chapters marked "Recommended." These chapters address the most common problems in grammar and proofreading. Chapters for less common errors are marked "Assign as Needed" and are on pages edged with black tabs in the upper corners.

Instructors may use their own specifications regarding organization and development, or they may utilize the approach to paragraph writing offered by Unit IX in *Skills in Sequence*. The "proposition—defense" method discussed in this Unit provides students with the equivalent of a thesis or lead sentence and a schema or format. The approach should prove useful for beginning writers, particularly when they attempt to write on a topic with which they are already somewhat familiar.

Also available are hundreds of topics, provided in two writing opportunities per chapter. These topics are of the "controlled composition" type, designed to elicit the particular grammatical constructions practiced in that chapter, and are thus useful both for diagnosis and reinforcement. Each of the eight chapters in Unit V (Sentence Boundaries) also contains at least two sentence-combining exercises, while the Instructor's Manual makes available supplementary exercises for each chapter in the text.

To help facilitate your review and evaluation of student work, *Skills in Sequence* contains elements of a "self-help" text. If circumstances prevent you from looking at a student's work immediately, you can direct the student to answers to the "Attention Focusing" exercise and the first "Rewriting Exercise" in each chapter (marked with asterisks in the text) available in Appendix 3 of the book. Also listed are the words to be changed for the second "Rewriting Exercise." As a result, students might be able to work their own way through a second rewriting and reach a proofreading exercise before requiring your specific attention. In addition, the answers to these exercises have been arranged in the Instructor's Manual on pages that can be reproduced or made into transparencies quite easily. This process will at times enable you to coordinate individualized instruction instead of forcing you to address the problem in a general way. Of course, you can teach any or all parts of this text to the class as a whole, or utilize it within collaborative learning situations. Students are particularly adept at proofreading each other's work for copying errors.

The diagnostic tests, keyed to the units in the text, are assembled in Appendix 4. For instructors who prefer holistic diagnosis, Part 1 of the Instructor's Manual offers selected topics designed to elicit essays in the present tense, third-person singular.

Finally, please note the other Appendix items. The list of principal parts of irregular verbs is no doubt familiar, but new is the section entitled "The Dictionary as Handbook," which calls students' attention to the grammatical and usage information available in dictionary entries.

Thomas Friedmann

Contents

UNIT V
PROBLEMS WITH SENTENCE BOUNDARIES: FRAGMENTS AND RUN-ONS 187

UNIT VI
PROBLEMS WITH MARKERS 255

UNIT VII
PROOFREADING FOR CONFUSING TERMS 327

UNIT VIII
PROOFREADING FOR SPELLING ERRORS 379

Recommended
Introduction
45. Common Spelling Patterns
Assign as Needed
46. *y* Endings
47. Doubled Consonants
48. Silent *e* Endings
49. Prefixes and Compounds

UNIT IX
THE PARAGRAPH WITHIN THE ESSAY:
A SHORT COURSE IN OPINION AND DEFENSE 401

Assign as Needed
50. The Organizing Proposition
51. The Two-Paragraph Defense

To the Student

WHAT YOU SHOULD KNOW ABOUT THIS BOOK

Answer these questions:

Where is the key for A on the typewriter?
Where on your face do you begin to shave?
How do you shift the gears of your standard transmission?
How do you put your earrings on?

Chances are that you could not respond to these questions without involuntarily moving your hands (and sometimes your feet). You cannot help but move your hands as you try to answer, because the knowledge for these activities—and for thousands more that we do each day, from getting dressed to walking to crossing the street—is automatic, not conscious. We have performed these activities so often that their knowledge has become a memory. Doing them is second nature. We can concentrate on other things and let our "automatic pilot" take care of such familiar activities.

Grammar, for many people, is also on automatic pilot. Just as your fingers can sign your name much more quickly than you could spell it aloud, successful writers can use basic rules of grammar and spelling without having to think about them. While they concentrate on content, organization, or style, their automatic pilots are taking care of spelling and grammar. Such people are not necessarily more intelligent than others. They have simply developed better habits. They have become so used to correct forms that they do not need to think about them.

This is your goal—to make basic grammar so habitual that you can use it without worrying unnecessarily about correctness, confident that in a great majority of instances your choices will be correct. You can accomplish this goal by working your way through a sequence of exercises. Even though a single rule of grammar makes sense to you, you will not be able to use it automatically until you have made it part of your nature. And that comes only through repeated practice.

This book thus helps you develop habits of correctness by offering you a new way of learning. At first, you will see only correct examples. You will not have to choose between "right" and "wrong" answers until you have become totally familiar with what is "right." Instead, you will be rewriting from one correct form to another—singulars to plurals, for example—without being exposed to incorrect forms. Second, you will be learning grammar one skill at a time, without confusing terminology or complicated exceptions. Third, you will learn these rules from short paragraphs and essays—never from isolated sentences. Finally, these short paragraphs and essays include headlines, recipes, fiction, pop culture, trivia, history, and other topics that will help retain your interest as you work your way through them.

Your success depends entirely on your willingness to practice. You will find that a particular rule seems reasonable and familiar. "I know that already," you might say. But you can demonstrate your knowledge of basic grammar only by using it accurately in your own essays. Knowing a rule is not the same as applying it correctly. Thus the text offers sequences of exercises, not one exercise, and asks you to work on them until you make no errors.

Once you have internalized your knowledge (made it second nature), you are likely to cut your errors in a particular area by 90 percent or more. Still, as you concentrate on content, organization, or style while writing your essay, you might make occasional errors in grammar or mechanics that can occur even among the best writers. At that point, your conscious mind can take over, using proofreading strategies to identify, locate, and correct the remaining errors. Never forget that no writer ever produces perfect writing the first time. All writers rethink, rewrite, and proofread, attempting to locate and correct any errors. Both good and bad writers make errors. The difference is that the good writer corrects those errors before handing in the work, but the less successful writer does not even realize the paper contains errors, much less know what they are or how to look for them. Using this text will move you into the ranks of successful writers and proofreaders in matters of basic skills.

HOW TO USE THIS BOOK

After your instructor has had a chance to read your first essay or evaluated a diagnostic test, he or she will probably list a number of grammatical areas where your paper has weaknesses. Each of those areas has a matching chapter in this text, available to help you learn the grammar and mechanics or the skills necessary to proofread for the kinds of errors you make. But before you begin doing the exercises in a chapter, you will have the opportunity to demonstrate that you really do have the skills to be covered. You can do this by completing an "Attention Focusing" exercise, writing a short paragraph that requires the particular skill, and correcting the errors in a proofreading exercise. If your own writing contains no errors of the type discussed in the chapter, and you can proofread for that type of error in the exercise, your instructor will no doubt let you move onto a new chapter.

If your instructor does require you to complete a chapter, follow this sequence:

1. Read the short "Review" segment in the chapter.
2. Do "Rewriting Exercise 1."

A rewriting exercise always requires you to decide first which words need to be changed or rewritten. Before actually rewriting a selection in "Rewriting Exercise 2," you can check in the back of the book to see if you have selected the right words.

3. Continue until you can hand in an error-free rewriting exercise.

Notice the words "hand in." The fact that you have handed in a correct final copy does not mean that you did not make any errors during the writing process. Rather, that final copy should always be the product of proofreading and correction. If you can locate and correct errors you might have made during drafting and revision before you submit your paper, you can consider the work error-free.

4. Read "Proofreading Strategies" in the chapter.
5. Choose a selection from "Practicing Proofreading" and complete it.

The easiest part of proofreading is correcting the error. You will be pleased to discover how successful you can be at correcting your errors *if* you have learned and applied two other guidelines: looking for only one type of error at a time and looking for it in a strategic way. If you can locate and correct all errors in the particular area discussed in the chapter, you can demonstrate your mastery in a number of different ways:

6. By writing on one of the topics in "Writing Assignment 2"

or

7. By passing the proofreading test at the end of the chapter

or

8. By passing the Mastery Test at the end of the Unit.

Your instructor may, of course, require a combination of these exercises.

Thomas Friedmann

SKILLS IN SEQUENCE

Unit One

THE SENTENCE
WITHIN
THE PARAGRAPH
(locating the verb and its subject)

Chapter **1**

LOCATING THE VERB

Because all English sentences contain a subject and a verb, the ability to recognize these basic units should help you write correct sentences. Even if you cannot produce correct sentences right away, your ability to identify the subject and the verb in a sentence you write will put you well on your way toward proofreading your sentences for correctness. The method that follows should help you locate the subject and the verb in a sentence. Although we may discuss many of the sample sentences individually, we will often present them within short paragraphs.

LOCATING THE VERB IN SIMPLE SENTENCES

Step 1: Think of the verb as the "time word" in the sentence.

The verb does, of course, show action, as your texts and teachers have been telling you for years. But, in addition to showing what the subject does or is, the verb carries information about **time** (usually called the **tense**). It is the time word in the sentence. The verb (with the help of attached letters, or "endings") tells you **when** the action is taking place.

    a. Halley's Comet **appears** in our solar system about once every 76 years.

The word **appears** informs us about the comet's action but also tells us that the action takes place habitually, currently, in the present: Halley's Comet appear**s**. The **s** attached to **appear** tells you that the action is habitual, in the present tense. (See also Chapter 14: Indicating the Present Tense.)

    b. Halley's Comet **appeared** over the skies of Julius Caesar's Rome in 87 B.C.

The word **appeared** certainly indicates the comet's action, but it also shows that the action took place in the past: it appear**ed**. The **ed** ending

3

attached to **appear** tells you that the time of the action is the past. (See also Chapter 15: Indicating the Past Tense of Regular Verbs.)

The past tense sometimes changes the entire form of the verb (see Chapter 16):

(the action takes place in the present) Halley's Comet **grows** daily.
(the action took place in the past) Halley's Comet **grew** daily.

c. Halley's Comet **will appear** next in the year 2061.

The word **will** with **appear** informs us that the time of the comet's action is in the future: Halley's comet **will appear.** The word **will** with **appear** tells you that the action will be in the future.

SUMMARY: The time indicators for the past, present, and future are attached to the **base** or **stem** of a verb—the verb in its simplest form, as it appears in dictionaries.

Step 2: Locate the verb in a sentence by changing the time of the sentence.

Just try different times for the sentence. By mentally adding one of the words below, you will be able more easily to change the time of the sentence.

in the past or **yesterday**
usually or **right now**
in the future or **tomorrow**

You can locate the time word (verb) in each sentence below by changing the time of the sentence. You need not rearrange words. Notice that one word in each sentence automatically changes to indicate the time. That word is your time word or verb.

a. I play basketball.

Rewrite to: (In the past) I **played** basketball. The word that changed—**play**→**played**—is the time word or verb.

b. My weight was over 180.

Rewrite to the present: (Usually) My weight **is** over 180. The word that changed—**was**→**is**—is the time word or verb.

or

Rewrite to the future: (use **tomorrow** and **will**).

Write here the word that changed: _____. It is the time word or verb.

The time change you make—to past, present, or future—will affect the time word in the sentence—the verb—but no other words in the sentence. It does not matter if you are not sure of the time in any particular sentence. Simply try adding one of those words (**usually, yesterday, tomorrow**) one at a time until a word in the sentence changes.

> **NOTE:** When you want to change the time of a verb, begin by returning it to its base or stem. Then add to that stem or base the new indicator for time. You might encounter some difficulty with verbs that change completely, such as **is** to **was** in the sample sentence earlier. If you do not know what the stem of a verb might be, look for the verb in your dictionary. Even a pocket dictionary will list different forms of verbs that change internally. Thus **went** is listed as the past tense form of **go.**

Step 2: (alternative) You can also locate the verb in a sentence by finding or adding a special time word.

When the time of a sentence is other than the simple past or present, there is an additional indicator of "time" in the sentence. The **complete verb** in such instances is an additional word (called a **helping** or **auxiliary verb)** plus the word to which it is attached.

a. I have managed to lose 10 pounds.

The word **have** is a special time word. The complete verb is the special time word plus the action word: **have managed.**

b. The coach will dismiss me.

The time word for the future is **will.** The complete verb is

_____.

If you are not sure where the verb is, try to insert a special time word and see where it would fit. It usually ends up just before the verb.

c. The weight loss inspired me.

Add **has:** _____. The word **has** fits best before _____. The complete verb in the rewritten sentence is **has** _____. The verb in the original sentence is

_____.

In the paragraph that follows, the words that carry more specific ideas about time—the **helping verbs**—are in **boldface.** The sentences are then listed separately to make working with them easier.

[1]Halley's Comet **has** worried people. [2]As predicted, it **had** appeared in 1986. [3]After its appearance in 2061, it **will have** been seen by billions. [4]It **is** carrying snow from the Oort cloud. [5]One space probe **was** studying it. [6]More **will be** studying it by 2061.

Tense	Helping Verb	Example within a Sentence	Complete Verb
(perfect) present:	has	Halley's Comet has worried people.	has worried
past:	had	As predicted, it had appeared in 1986.	had appeared
future:	will have	After its appearance in 2061, it will have been seen by billions.	will have been
(progressive) present:	am/is/are	It is carrying snow from the Oort cloud.	is carrying
past:	was, were	One space probe was studying it.	was studying
future:	will be	More will be studying it by 2061.	will be studying

PRACTICE 1: locating the verb in a sentence*

The short paragraph that follows contains 8 sentences, each with a subject and a verb. Find and circle the verb of each sentence either by changing the time of the sentence and noticing which word changes or by finding the auxiliary or helping verb attached to the action word. To make them easier to consider, the sentences are listed separately.

DRIVE-IN

1. Drive-in movies were invented by two New Jersey businessmen.

2. Hollingshead and Smith opened the first drive-in on June 6, 1933.

3. The huge screen measured forty by fifty feet, amazing the audience.

4. Watching from cars provided privacy along with entertainment.

5. It also kept small children from bothering other viewers.

6. The idea of drive-ins has taken hold in America.

7. Drive-in restaurants, banks, even churches have grown out of drive-in theaters.

8. American drivers will do anything to avoid leaving their cars.

LOCATING THE VERB IN MORE COMPLICATED SENTENCES

To every rule or principle there are exceptions; so too with the method you have just learned for locating verbs. Changing the time of the sentence and looking for the word that has changed should work with most sentences. But the sentences you write in a typical paragraph might be more complicated than the sample sentences with which you have been practicing, or your own sentences may contain unusual verbs. Locating the verb in such sentences requires knowing some additional principles about verbs.

How to Cope with the Unexpected (1)

Some verbs do not change even when the time of the sentences changes.

Written in the present: (Usually) I set the table for dinner.
Rewritten in the past: (Yesterday) I set the table for dinner.

The verb is **set,** but it does not change in the usual manner. In such instances, the use of **will** or another helping word reveals the verb because **will** takes its place right in front of a verb.

Rewritten in the future: (Tomorrow) I will set the table.

How to Cope with the Unexpected (2)

As you seek to find the verb by changing the time of the sentence, do not change any word that looks like an "action word" but has the word **to** before it. The word **to** plus a verb form the **infinitive** and do not indicate the time of the sentence. For example, **to eat, to sleep, to dream,** are all infinitives and thus contain no information about time. The "time word" in a sentence can never be the infinitive.

Written in the present: I like to watch the sun rise.
Rewritten in the past: I liked to watch the sun rise.

The infinitive **to watch** remains untouched. The "time word," or word that changes when the time of the sentence changes, is **like.**

PRACTICE 2: eliminating infinitives as possible verbs*

In the paragraph that follows, the word **to** appears 10 times. Underline each and circle the 8 instances when it is part of an infinitive.

HEALING THROUGH ZIPPING

[1]To Dr. H. Harlan Stone of the University of Maryland goes the convenience award. [2]He has pioneered the use of zippers instead of stitches. [3]Dr. Stone is now able to avoid repeated operations that were formerly

needed to change internal packing. [4]All Stone has to do is unzip the seven-inch skirt zipper which closed the incision. [5]He then changes the packing. [6]To finish, he has only to zip the wound. [7]Twenty-eight operations that previously took an hour or more are thus reduced to five-minute jobs. [8]The zipper bandage serves to decrease the time that a patient has to spend under anesthesia. [9]This enables acutely ill patients to recover faster.

How to Cope with the Unexpected (3)

Unless the sentence is a question, the main verb never appears after the words **who, that, which,** and **where.**

a. A man who indicated his love in an unusual way was William Randolph Hearst.

Rewritten in the present: (Today) A man who indicated his love in an unusual way **is** William Randolph Hearst.

The verb in this sentence is **was.** It cannot be **indicated** because **indicated** follows the word **who.** This is true even when the word following **who, that, which,** or **where** changes when the time changes:

b. He slipped Marion Davies a diamond watch that was worth a small fortune.

Rewritten in the future: (Tomorrow) He will slip Marion Davies a diamond watch that **will be** worth a small fortune.

The verb is **slipped.** It cannot be **will be worth,** because **will be worth** follows **that.**

PRACTICE 3: locating the main verb*

Consider "Healing through Zipping," the paragraph you read earlier. Rewrite below the four sentences in the paragraph that contain one of the relative pronouns **who, that, which,** or **where.** Circle the main verb in these sentences.

1. _____

2. _____

3. _____

4. _____

ADDITIONAL INFORMATION ABOUT VERBS

Using the verb **capture** as an example, the chart that follows identifies by name some verb forms, offers examples, and notes the chapters in which they are discussed in greater detail. Each of the **tenses**—present, past, future—has its own chapter, with the past tense separated into regular and irregular verbs.

form	example	explanation
stem or base	capture	the simplest form of a verb; nothing added
infinitive	to capture	**to** + the base form
present participle	capturing	base form + **ing** (Chapter 18)
past participle (regular verbs)	captured	same as the past tense (Chapter 19)
to be and irregular verbs	been	base + **n** or **en** (Chapter 19)

Chapter 2
LOCATING THE SUBJECT OF THE VERB

Once you can locate the verb in a sentence, you will have no difficulty identifying the subject of that verb.

> To find the subject of a verb, ask **who** or **what** before the verb and the part of the sentence after the verb.

    a. Halley's Comet **appeared** over the skies of Julius Caesar's Rome in 87 B.C.

The verb is **appeared.** Ask: Who or what appeared over the skies? Answer: Halley's Comet appeared. Your subject is therefore **Halley's Comet.**

    b. Halley's Comet **appears** in our solar system about once every 76 years.

The verb is **appears.** Ask: Who or what appears in our solar system? Answer: Halley's Comet appears in our solar system. Your subject: **Halley's Comet.**

Another way to find the subject: If the time word is an auxiliary or helping verb, use the complete verb with **who** or **what.**

    c. Halley's Comet **will appear** next in the year 2061.

The (complete) verb is **will appear.** Ask: Who or what will appear next? Answer: Halley's Comet will appear next. Your subject: **Halley's Comet.**

Most sentences have many nouns that are often mistaken for subjects. If you first locate the verb or time word in a sentence and use it to locate the subject, you will not be confused by those other nouns. Ask who or what with the verb (time word) and you will always find its subject.

PRACTICE 1: Use the verb (in boldface) in each sentence to locate its subject

sentence	who or what with verb	subject
1. My weight was over 180.	What **was** over 180?	*My weight*
2. I managed to lose 10 pounds.	Who **managed** to lose 10 pounds?	
3. The coach will dismiss me.	Who **will dismiss** me?	
4. **Losing weight** has become a problem.	_____?	*Losing weight*
5. I **think** of food all day.	_____?	

PRACTICE 2: locating the subject*

a. First locate and circle the verb in each sentence. (These sentences were used earlier. You should already know each verb.)
b. Ask **who** or **what** before the verb.
c. Underline the answer; it will be the subject.

DRIVE-IN

1. Drive-in movies were invented by two New Jersey businessmen.
2. Hollingshead and Smith opened the first drive-in on June 6, 1933.
3. The huge screen measured forty by fifty feet, amazing the audience.
4. Watching from cars provided privacy along with entertainment.
5. It also kept small children from bothering other viewers.
6. The idea of drive-ins has taken hold in America.
7. Drive-in restaurants, banks, even churches have grown out of drive-in theaters.
8. American drivers will do anything to avoid leaving their cars.

PRACTICE 3: locating the subject*

Circle verbs and underline subjects in the short paragraph that follows. To make it easier to locate verbs and subjects, the sentences are listed individually. Proceed by changing the time of each to locate the verb. After circling the verb, ask **who** or **what** before the verb to locate its subject. Underline the subject when you have located it.

AMERICA'S SONG

1. Our first patriotic song was written by a British physician.

2. Dr. Richard Shuckburg wrote "Yankee Doodle Dandy" in mockery.

3. He wanted to mock the simple tradesmen and townsfolk fighting the British.

4. The word "macaroni" in the song does not refer to the pasta.

5. It refers instead to a well-dressed member of the fashionable Macaroni Club.

6. Placing a feather in his cap made the Yankee into a fool, not a gentleman.

7. The colonists adopted the song despite its mockery.

8. They gleefully played "Yankee Doodle" during the surrender of the British.

LOCATING THE SUBJECT IN MORE COMPLICATED SENTENCES

The sentences you write in a typical paragraph may be more complicated than the sample sentences with which you have been practicing. You might use unusual subjects in your own sentences, place them in unfamiliar positions, or place other words between the subject and the verb. To identify the subjects of such sentences, you must become acquainted with some additional forms subjects can take and additional places in the sentence where subjects may be found.

How to Cope with the Unexpected (1)

People often equate the subject with a noun (name of a person, place, or thing). But the subject can also be an act or an activity. Some of the sentences used earlier have such subjects.

Losing more weight has become difficult.
verb: has become   subject: Losing more weight

PRACTICE 4: locating subjects that are actions*

One of the sentences in the paragraph "America's Song" contains subjects that name an action or an activity. Write it below, circling the subject in the sentence. Then make up a sentence in which the subject is an action or an activity.

1. _____

verb: _____   subject: _____

2. _____

verb: _____   subject: _____

How to Cope with the Unexpected (2)

When the subject appears right next to the verb, it is easy to find. But other words often come between the subject and the verb. In such cases, the subject is more difficult to locate. In the earlier example, **Losing** is the subject. The words **more weight** become part of the complete subject, but they merely add information about it. We illustrate a few such situations below. Chapter 11 discusses the most common types of words that come between the subject and the verb (called **intervening elements**) in greater detail.

a. A marriage proposal was sent to Antoinette de Pons.

The complete verb: **was sent.** Ask: What was sent? Answer: A marriage proposal.

b. A marriage proposal **in King Henry IV's blood** was sent to Antionette de Pons.

The phrase in **boldface** inserted between the subject and the verb does not alter the identity of the subject and verb.

The most frequent intervening expression is a **prepositional phrase,** easily recognizable because it begins with a relation word or **preposition,** such as **in, of, from, on, inside, outside, over, under.** In the sample sentence, the prepositional phrase is in **boldface.** The subject appears before it.

Watching **from cars** provides privacy along with entertainment.
verb: provides   subject: Watching   intervening phrase: **from cars**

PRACTICE 5: avoiding the prepositional phrase*

In each of the following sentences, circle the preposition and underline the prepositional phrase. You can best do this by first locating the verb and asking **who** or **what** with it to locate the subject. If the subject turns out to be a long phrase, see if you can lift a part (a **phrase** or a **clause**) out of it. Those intervening expressions simply give more detail about the subject. They do not contain the subject. Matching the right subject with the right verb is crucial when you are dealing with **agreement,** the subject in Unit III.

1. Placing a feather in his cap made the Yankee into a fool, not a gentleman.

verb: _____ subject: _____

intervening phrase: _____

2. The last album with all four of the Beatles was <u>Abbey Road</u>.

    verb: _____ subject: _____

    intervening phrase: _____

3. One song of the seventeen cuts on the album was "Octopus's Garden."

    verb: _____ subject: _____

    intervening phrase: _____

4. Ringo, who replaced the Beatles' original drummer, wrote the song.

    verb: _____ subject: _____

    intervening phrase: _____

How to Cope with the Unexpected (3)

In the sentences you have been practicing, the subject always appears before the verb. In some sentences, however, the verb appears before the subject, particularly in those that begin with **there** or **here.**

There is a horse in my driveway.

You can still locate the subject by asking **who** or **what** with the verb and placing the word **there** right after it. If you ask **Who or what is there?** you will answer **horse** and thus locate your subject. Make sure, of course, that the answer is sensible. (For more work with **there is/are**, see Chapter 12.)

ADDITIONAL INFORMATION ABOUT SUBJECTS

Some terms about subjects are used so often that it is important to recognize them. The summary explains and illustrates some of this terminology.

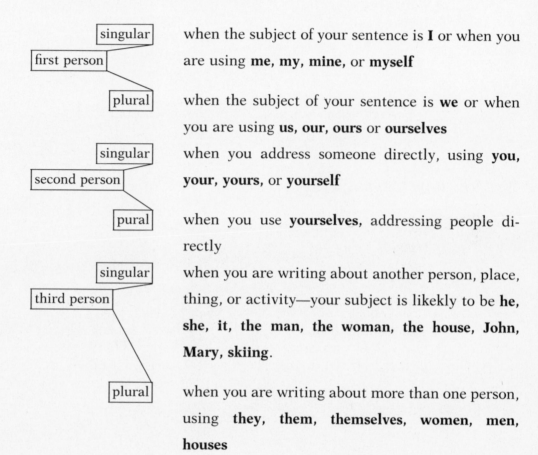

first person

singular — when the subject of your sentence is **I** or when you are using **me, my, mine,** or **myself**

plural — when the subject of your sentence is **we** or when you are using **us, our, ours** or **ourselves**

second person

singular — when you address someone directly, using **you, your, yours,** or **yourself**

pural — when you use **yourselves,** addressing people directly

third person

singular — when you are writing about another person, place, thing, or activity—your subject is likekly to be **he, she, it, the man, the woman, the house, John, Mary, skiing.**

plural — when you are writing about more than one person, using **they, them, themselves, women, men, houses**

Unit Two

PROBLEMS WITH NOUNS AND PRONOUNS
(number and reference)

Recommended

Assign as Needed

Chapter 3

USING THE ARTICLES
A OR AN

ATTENTION FOCUSING: the articles a/an*

Underline each **a** and **an** as well as the first letter of the next word. In the spaces below, write the words preceded by **a** in one column, the words preceded by **an** in another. The sentences are adapted from Leo Tolstoy's "The Three Hermits."

1. Once, when a fisherman was out fishing, he was stranded on an island.

2. In the morning, as he wandered about, he came to an earth hut, and met an old man standing near it.

3. He gave the fisherman a bite to eat and helped him mend his boat.

4. The islander was a small man, with a bent back.

5. He wore a priest's cassock; he had to be more than a hundred years old.

6. He was so old that the white of his beard was taking on a greenish tinge.

7. But he was always smiling, and his face was as bright as an angel's.

8. A second islander helped push the boat off.

9. He wore a tattered peasant's coat and his broad beard was a yellowish gray.

a + word	an + word
a fisherman	

19

WRITING ASSIGNMENT 1: the articles

Choose from the topics that follow. Write a short paragraph that includes a list of about 10 items. Choose **a/an** for each item.

a. What are the positions on a sports team? (**a q**uarterback)
b. Create an exotic fruit salad. (**a p**apaya)
c. Identify members of your family by occupation. (**a b**ricklayer, **an a**ccountant)

If you have made no errors in using *a/an*, you should try PRACTICING PROOFREADING 1 (p. 24) before asking your instructor to send you on to another chapter. If you did make some errors, read the REVIEW that follows.

REVIEW: the articles *a/an*

The article **a** precedes words that begin with consonants; **an** precedes words that begin with vowels. Because there are some exceptions, do not depend entirely on your eyes when you are selecting **a** or **an**. Sound out the first letter of the next word.

NOTE: See ADDITIONAL INFORMATION ABOUT ARTICLES, p. 23, for a discussion of the definite article **the**.

Use **a** before all **consonant sounds**

a **b**oy	a **c**old shower (the **k** sound)	a **s**afe landing
a **c**icada (the **s** sound)	a **l**over	a **t**ennis ball
a **c**hain	a **m**ajor general	a **th**ousand pardons
a **d**orm	a **n**ovelist	a **u**ser (a **y** sound)
a **f**anatic	a **o**ne-man show (a **w** sound)	a **v**ain fool
a **g**old coin	a **p**ainter	a **w**aiter
a **h**unter	a **p**honecall (the **f** sound)	a **y**oung girl
a **j**oker	a **q**uiet man	a **z**ookeeper
a **g**eneral (the **j** sound)	a **r**ough rider	
a **k**id	a **s**ure thing	

Use **an** before all **vowel sounds**.

an **a**nimal	an **oo**zing, slimy being	
an **a**mazing creature	an **u**gly thing	
an **e**agle	an **h**our-long wait	(you hear **our**)
an **i**deal specimen	an **F** on the report card	(you hear **ef**)
an **o**lder member		

> Continue by choosing a REWRITING exercise. It will provide practice in
> the use of the articles *a/an*. Work until you complete one without making
> any errors. Then, to practice your proofreading skills, go to the section
> on PROOFREADING, p. 23.

REWRITING EXERCISE 1: the articles*

Make the following changes in the use of articles:

  a. Underline the 16 **a/an** articles.
  b. Cross out any word that comes between **a/an** and a nationality.
  c. In the space above each line, make the 5 changes in **a/an** (**a daring American** becomes **an American**).

A TASTE OF HONEY

[1]A typical American does not think of them as food, but people from other nations consider insects to be quite nutritious. [2]A hungry Japanese will eat ants and silkworm pupae, while maguey worms have become such an export item that a Mexican is lucky to find them. [3]A modern Greek will eat cicadas, although Plutarch, because he considered them sacred, disapproved. [4]A snack of locusts (wings and legs removed) was a familiar treat in ancient Ethiopia and is enjoyed equally by a twentieth-century Iraqi. [5]The grasshopper is a treasured item in a vitamin-poor Angolan diet. [6]A tropical African tribe domesticates termites. [7]The famous David Livingston was not only an explorer but also an experimenter. [8]He is known as an adventurous Englishman who tried termites with apricots. [9]But with the single exception of honey—the regurgitation of bees—an average American will not consider insects as an item on his menu.

REWRITING EXERCISE 2: the articles

In the recipe that follows, substitute the article **a** or **an** for the number **1.** Write each **a/an** and the very next word that follows it in the spaces alongside. The starred (*) word is explained after the recipe.

Eight Cheese Enchiladas

sauce

1.	3 tablespoons olive oil	_____
2.	1 small onion, chopped	_____
3.	1 tiny garlic, crushed	_____
4.	1 ounce of diced green chilis (2 or 3 for hotter sauce)	_____
5.	1 pound cooked, peeled, and chopped tomatoes	_____
6.	1 cup tomato juice	_____
7.	1 quarter teaspoon powdered oregano	_____
8.	1 quarter teaspoon basil	_____
9.	1 *unit or cube of vegetable concentrate	_____
10.	1 tablespoon of cornstarch, dissolved in cold water	_____

filling

11.	grate 1 eight-ounce chunk of sharp Cheddar cheese	_____
12.	slice 1 half-cup of black olives	_____
13.	chop 1 young scallion (2 to 3 for hotter tastes)	_____
14.	chop a little parsley	_____

special utensils

15.	1 skillet	_____
16.	1 measuring cup	_____
17.	1 oblong baking dish	_____

How to Cope with the Unexpected (1)

The **1** before the starred [*] word **unit** changes to **a** because the **u** is sounded like **y**—a consonant. The **u** that begins **union** and **useful** also sounds like the consonant **y,** and the **o** in **one** or **once** sounds like **w.** The rule—use **a** before all consonant **sounds**—remains. REWRITING EXERCISE 3 contains an example of a vowel that sounds like a consonant.

REWRITING EXERCISE 3: the articles

Copy the entire essay, making the following changes regarding the articles:

a. Remove the words **Dallas** and **Owego** from the paragraph below.
b. Select **a** or **an** for each **the (the** unique becomes **a** unique**).**

A SURE-FIRE COLOR

[1]The Dallas, Texas, fire department has been searching for the

unique color that would make its engines noticeable. [2]The faction holding out for red feels that tradition must be upheld. [3]The opposing group argues that a red fire engine makes it appear that personnel are fire makers rather than fire fighters. [4]Both groups agree, however, that a solution is needed for the rash of collisions between fire-fighting equipment and other vehicles. [5]The alternative to red suggested by the optometrist-consultant Stephen Solomon was to repaint each truck lime yellow.[6] Solomon, the captain in the Owego, New York, fire department, explains that the lime yellow blend is an irritating and grating color. [7]An inattentive driver's eyes would be immediately attracted to it because they are very sensitive to yellows and greens. [8]Although people may initially consider it an unattractive color, they eventually accept it. [9]They certainly did in Detroit, Kansas City, and Newark.

> Proofread your rewritten paragraph by underlining each **a/an** and the first letter of the word following. You should have 7 new **a** and 3 new **an** articles.

ADDITIONAL INFORMATION ABOUT ARTICLES

The is the **definite** article; **a/an** are **indefinite** articles. Notice that, in the paragraph above, **the** refers to a specific or particular department, faction, and color. For the indefinite articles in REWRITING EXERCISE 3 to make sense, you had to eliminate the words—**Dallas, Owego**—that specified the areas. Substituting **a/an** for **the** changed the sense of the paragraph. In the original, there were two specific factions. Your rewritten version, containing **a/an**, makes no such claim. Note then that, although both types of articles might make sense grammatically, they can carry different information about the noun attached to them.

PROOFREADING STRATEGIES

Most people err by using **a** all the time. If this is also your error, you need to focus on the **a**. If you have used **an**, you have probably used it correctly. Proofread for correctness in the use of **a** by following these steps:

1. Circle each **a**.
2. Underline the word that follows each **a**.
3. Sound out the word; **a** precedes a consonant sound.

> Choose one of the PROOFREADING exercises. Work until you locate and correct all errors in the use of *a/an*. To demonstrate your mastery of *a/an*, try WRITING ASSIGNMENT 2 at the end of the chapter.

PRACTICING PROOFREADING 1

Circle the 23 instances of **a/an.** Correct the 5 errors.

THE STINGLESS SCORPIO

[1]An individual born under the sign of the scorpion is not necessarily a person to be feared. [2]In all likelihood, he or she is very different from a actual scorpion.

[3]The real scorpion is a night creature. [4]It has a long, curved tail that is useful for both defense and destruction. [5]It can paralyze either enemy or prey by injecting a quick-acting poison with that tail. [6]The astrological scorpion also shares with serpents an intensity, a steady gaze, a great deal of determination, and even a crackling, electric vitality.

[7]As for the Scorpio (a person born between Oct. 23 and Nov. 21), a similarity is claimed by astrologists to both a serpent and a eagle. [8]A Scorpio is thought to inherit from these creatures the stare which seems to penetrate an enemy's innermost secrets. [9]The Scorpio voice could be as smooth as soft cloth or as rough and sharp as a eagle's talons. [10]But as far as possessing a deadly nature is concerned, the Scorpio differs from the scorpion. [11]If the Scorpio has a sting at all, it is directed at enemies. [12]Friends may suffer a occasional hurt when the Scorpio insists on telling the truth, but they benefit greatly from an unique generosity and utter fearlessness so typical of an individual born under this sign.

[13]The typical Scorpio, like the scorpion, is fierce. [14]However, unlike the scorpion, that fierceness is a sign of extreme loyalty toward friends.

PRACTICING PROOFREADING 2

Circle the 26 instances of **a.** Correct the 4 errors.

THE "HARD" IN HARDBALL

[1]In most sports, success is measured by an efficiency of better than 50 percent. [2]In baseball, however, a batter is deemed a success even if he fails in seven out of ten attempts. [3]But consider the problems of a .300

hitter. [4]He stands next to a 17-inch-wide rubber mat called "the plate." [5]Barely more than a 60-foot distance separates him from a another athlete who hurls a tiny ball at speeds approaching 90 miles per hour. [6]It takes the ball only 41/100 of a second to travel from pitcher to catcher, and it takes the batter 28/100 of a second to swing. [7]This means that a hitter has only about 13/100 of a second to decide if he is going to swing the bat or not. [8]If he is an able batter, he may make contact yet still hit a pop-up or a grounder. [9]To hit a fair ball, the batter must make a accurate connection between a 4 × 1 inch strip in the middle of the bat and a spot about the size of a quarter at the center of a ball small enough to be hidden in a average-sized palm. [10]To hit a ordinary home run—285 feet—a batter must generate a force of 1,400 pounds. [11]With thirteen variables providing twenty-six possible ways to fail, it is a miracle a hitter ever connects, much less succeeds in three out of every ten attempts.

WRITING ASSIGNMENT 2: the articles *a/an*

Write a long paragraph according to your instructor's specifications on one of the following topics. Use each item repeatedly, placing descriptive words between the *a/an* and the noun. When you are satisfied with organization, development, and content, proofread for errors in *a/an*, using the strategies you have been practicing.

a. Compare the characteristics associated with **a Capricorn** and **an Arien,** or that of any other two astrological signs.
b. Discuss one major difference between **a home-cooked meal** and **a meal in a restaurant.**
c. Identify and discuss one difference in the way parents treat **a first-born** and **a middle or youngest child.**
d. Does a person behave differently in his or her own home state than outside of it? Use the words **individual** and **person.**
e. Compare **a painter's** approach to his or her material with **a photographer's.**

Chapter 4

USING SINGULAR PRONOUNS
(reference and agreement)

ATTENTION FOCUSING: singular personal pronouns*

   In the sentences below (adapted from Mario Vargas Llosa's The Scriptwriter), circle the 11 pronouns that refer to **Dr. Zaldivar** and draw lines from them to **Dr. Zaldivar.** Then circle the 6 pronouns that refer to **Sarita** and draw lines from the pronouns to **Sarita.**

1. Dr. Zaldivar was very tactful when he questioned minors.

2. He knew how to gain their confidence.

3. He was careful not to hurt their feelings.

4. By being gentle and patient, he easily led them around to talking.

5. But this time, his experience was of little use to him.

6. The moment he asked Sarita to speak, she began to talk in a steady stream.

7. Dr. Zaldivar tried to tell to her that she didn't need to tell him everything.

8. He found she could not stop herself.

9. She stopped only when he leaped from his chair and shouted "Enough!"

WRITING ASSIGNMENT 1: singular pronouns

   Write a short paragraph on one of the following topics. After naming a person, place, or thing, refer to it with pronouns.

a. Complain about or compliment the actions of a clerk who has served you.

b. Referring to a corporation, a college, or a manufacturer in your area as **it,** discuss its contributions to the community.

c. Say what you enjoyed about a magazine or newspaper you have read recently.

If you have made no errors using singular pronouns, try PRACTICING PROOFREADING 1 before asking your instructor to send you on to another chapter. If you did make errors, read the REVIEW. Chapter 4 also contains exercises on INDEFINITE PRONOUNS, on pp. 32–33.

REVIEW: singular pronouns

Here is a table of all singular pronouns. (Plural pronouns are discussed in Chapter 6.)

	Personal		Possessive		Reflexive
	Subjective	Objective	Subjective	Objective	
first person	I	me	my	mine	myself
second person	you	you	your	yours	yourself
third person	he/she/it	him/she/it	his/her/its	his/hers	himself/herself itself

Use a pronoun when you do not wish to repeat the name of a person, place, or thing.

Instead of:　Alice was beginning to get very tired of sitting by **Alice's** sister. Once or twice, **Alice** had peeped into the book **Alice's** sister was reading, but **the book** had no pictures or conversations in **the book.**

Write:　Alice was beginning to get very tired of sitting by **her** sister. Once or twice **she** had peeped into the book **her** sister was reading, but **it** had no pictures or conversations in **it.**

The pronouns **she** and **her** replace **Alice** and **Alice's,** and **it** replaces **the book.** Another way of saying this is that the pronouns **she** and **her** refer to Alice, and **it** refers to the **book.** The noun to which pronouns refer is called the **antecedent,** or the noun that "comes before."

Here are two important rules about using a pronoun:

1. The pronoun must refer clearly to its antecedent.
2. The pronoun must agree in number with its antecedent. If the antecedent is singular, the pronoun must also be singular. **Alice**

and **the book** are singular nouns. As a result, the pronouns that refer to them—**she, her,** and **it**—must also be singular.

REVIEW: indefinite pronouns

A group of words called **indefinite pronouns** are sometimes used instead of pronouns as well as with them. The singular indefinite pronouns that follow can thus be used only with singular nouns and singular pronouns.

no one	nobody	anything	each
anyone	anybody	everything	either
everyone	everybody	something	neither
someone	somebody	one	

See Chapter 13 for work on verb agreement with singular indefinite pronouns.

Continue with a REWRITING EXERCISE. After you complete one without making any errors, read PROOFREADING STRATEGIES and go on to PRACTICING PROOFREADING.

REWRITING EXERCISE 1: singular pronouns*

Write all changes in the space above each line.

a. Circle the 17 plural pronouns (in **boldface**) that refer to **pigs.**
b. Substitute **the first racing pig** each time you find the word **pigs.**
c. Because you now have a singular **antecedent**, you must replace all plural pronouns that referred to **pigs** with singular pronouns **(it/its/itself).**
d. Write the two starred (*) words as **pig's,** indicating possession with a singular.

THE FASTEST PIG BRINGS HOME THE BACON

[1]Pig racing originated in 1977. [2]Heinold Hog Market wanted to demonstrate hog intelligence. [3]Since then, pig racing has become popular at Heinold Downs.

[4]Heinold personnel trained the pigs for five weeks under the care of a veterinarian. [5]**Their** water was medicated to prevent common diseases. [6]**Their** food consisted of special feed fortified with vitamins and minerals.

[7]The intention was to keep **them** healthy but not as heavy as **they** would normally be. [8]**They** traveled to the races in specially constructed trailers. [9]The *pigs' air was changed every two minutes. [10]It was also cooled in hot weather. [11]The pigs even had **their** own water supply. [12]**They** learned to thrive on crowds and seemed to enjoy the cheers and applause **they** received.

[13]So that the crowd noise should not frighten **them,** a radio was played in **their** training barn 24 hours a day. [14]Each day **they** listened to country music and to broadcasts of Chicago White Sox baseball games. [15]To make sure **they** would not fight during the race, baby oil was rubbed all over **them.** [16]Any other pig racing against **them** was similarly smeared. [17]When **their** smell was the same, **they** behaved **themselves** and did not attack another pig.

[18]According to Mr. Roy Holding, trainer at Heinold Racing, 2.5 million people have bet at Heinold Downs since 1977. [19]He feels they have been astounded by the *pigs' cleanliness, speed, and intelligence.

REWRITING EXERCISE 2: singular pronouns

Copy the essay below, making the following changes:

   a. Circle **advertising people** and the plural pronouns referring to them.
   b. Cross out **advertising people** and the word **in** following the phrase.
   c. Because your new subjects are singular—the names of different agencies—make the pronouns that refer to each agency singular.

WENDY ATTACKS

[1]When Wendy's, the nation's third-largest hamburger chain, experienced sagging sales, it hired a new advertising agency, hoping to revive consumer interest with a new sales approach.

[2]From 1976 to 1979, Wendy's account was handled by advertising people in the Wells Rich Greene Agency. [3]They avoided humor in their ad campaigns. [4]They also believed that consumers were more interested in hamburgers then in other fast-food items. [5]They thus devised the "hot

and juicy" theme in their ads for Wendy's. [6]Folks from all walks of life were shown taking a bite and wiping their lips with a napkin. [7]The people in the Wells Rich Greene Agency made the so-called "bite and wipe" gesture their "signature."

[8]While the campaign brought Wendy's to national awareness, the chain, in an attempt to raise sales, turned to advertising people in the giant Dancer Fitzgerald Sample Agency. [9]They devised the famous "Where's the Beef?" series of ads. [10]Sales went up initially, but, by 1987, they were back down again, and Wendy's looked around for a new agency.

[11]It hired Dick Rich Advertising, formerly part of Wells Rich Green. [12]A one-man agency, Dick Rich revived the "hot and juicy" theme, including the "wipe."

REWRITING EXERCISE 3: singular pronouns

Copy the entire essay, making the following changes to use singular pronouns:

a. Circle the 20 plural pronouns that refer to **cowboys.**
b. For the first sentence of the second paragraph, substitute: **One famous black cowboy who won his spurs in those thickets was Henry Beckwith.** After that sentence, each time you see **black cowboys,** change it to the singular **black cowboy.**
c. Because your new subject is the singular **Henry Beckwith,** change all pronouns referring to him to the singular **he, him, his,** or **himself.**
d. The starred (*) word is explained after the essay.

OLD WEST, NEW HEROES

[1]Between three and five thousand black cowboys rode the Western ranges after the Civil War, according to Philip T. Drotning, in <u>Black Heroes in Our Nation's History</u>. [2]Hundreds worked as cowhands in Texas, but the most daring of the black men made a living searching the thickets of South Texas for stray cattle.

[3]Many of these cowboys won fame in those thickets. [4]Outsiders, however, knew little about them. [5]They had probably escaped from slavery

and had taken to the brush to avoid capture. [6]When the Emancipation Proclamation freed them, they just stayed on, hunting cattle that had grown up wild during the Civil war.

[7]The black cowboys spent their days in thickets so dense they could see only a few feet ahead of themselves. [8]They slept on the ground, covering themselves with a blanket spread over sticks. [9]They drank black coffee mixed with chili juice. [10]To sustain themselves, they ate jerked beef and cornbread. [11]They rode mostly at night, trusting their keen senses of smell and hearing to lead them to the meat–eating cattle they sought. [12]The night habits of the cowboys were such that Mexican cowboys joked they lived like coyotes.

[13]After rounding up enough of the longhorn cattle, they would drive them to big factories for tallow and hide located just outside brush country. [14]One day spent in civilization was usually enough to send them eagerly back to their beloved brush.

> Proofread your essay for accuracy in copying as well as in using singular pronouns. Underline the new pronouns.

How to Cope with the Unexpected (1)

Sentence 12 states that **they lived like coyotes.** When you change **they** to **he,** you must also change **coyotes** to **a coyote.** The word is a **subject complement,** meaning that it is "equal" to the subject. When the subject is singular, its complement also has to be singular. For example:

Lois Lane is a reporter. (**Lois Lane** and **a reporter** are both singular.)
He is a basketball star. (**He** and **a basketball star** are both singular.)
A house is not a home. (**A house** and **a home** are both singular.)

> The two exercises that follow deal with singular indefinite pronouns, such as *anyone, everyone,* etc. Review the material on INDEFINITE PRONOUNS, pp. 32–33.

ATTENTION FOCUSING: using singular pronouns (including indefinite)*

a. List all the pronouns that refer to Dr. Brouchard in sentences 1–2:

_____

b. List all the pronouns that refer to Dr. Brouchard in sentences 3–7:

_____

c. List all the pronouns that refer to Jim Springer in sentences 8–10:

_____

d. List all pronouns in sentences 4 and 13:

_____

GENES OR ENVIRONMENT?

[1]For his experiments to determine the power of genes, Dr. Brouchard of the U. of Minnesota needs twins who had been separated at birth. [2]He believes that any similarities between them are likely to be caused by genes, not environment.

[3]Dr. Brouchard learned of Jim Springer and Jim Lewis through a newspaper story. [4]Inviting each to the lab, Dr. Brouchard tested him extensively. [5]He found that both men enjoyed woodworking, liked math, and hated spelling. [6]Each weighed 180 pounds and stood six feet tall. [7]The two shared many other common aspects. [8]Jim Springer owned a dog named Toy. [9]He had married a girl named Betty, and he had a son named James Allan. [10]His twin brother, Jim Lewis, had also named his dog Toy. [11]He too had married a woman named Betty and had a son named Allan James. [12]Both men also crossed their legs in the same unusual way. [13]Each bit his fingernails, and each had eight cavities. [14]To Dr. Brouchard, these many similarities are more than mere coincidence.

REWRITING EXERCISE 4: indefinite singular pronouns

Copy the essay that follows, making the following changes to use indefinite pronouns:

a. Circle the 7 instances of **people.**
b. Underline the 10 plural pronouns that refer to **people.**
c. Substitute for **people** the singular indefinite pronoun **everybody.**
d. Once you replace the plural **people** with the singular indefinite pronoun, you must also substitute singular pronouns for the plural pronouns. Use the expressions **he or she, his or her,** and **himself or herself.**

(The expressions may sound awkward, but they will emphasize that the indefinite pronouns you are substituting are singular, requiring singular pronouns.)

THE TEA ISLAND

[1]People in England began their love affair with tea when Thomas Garway served it in 1667 in his coffeehouse. [2]Could people have expected this fragrant liquid from China to become their favorite drink? [3]In any case, people applauded when Prime Minister William Pitt, in 1784, decided that tea was a necessity, not a luxury, and lowered the taxes they had to pay on it. [4]And typically, they very much agreed with Rev. Sydney Smith, a nineteenth-century essayist, who wrote, "I am glad I was not born before tea."

[5]Each tea-drinking nation has its own story. [6]A Chinese dictionary in A.D. 350 attributes the origin of tea to Emperor Shen Nung (2737 B.C.). [7]Japanese mythology credits a Buddhist saint with the creation of a tea bush. [8]By A.D. 780, people in China, including the emperor, regularly drank tea in their shallow little bowls.

[9]People in the West thought tea to possess both beneficial and destructive qualities. [10]They believed that it worked as medicine. [11]They also believed that it could be harmful to their health. [12]One women's magazine quoted someone as saying that tea drinking kept his wife from doing her work.

[13]As for people in the United States, perhaps their memories of the Boston Tea Party remain too fresh. [14]Certainly people in the United States cannot surrender their hearts to tea the way people in England can.

PROOFREADING STRATEGIES

1. Know what kind of error you make and proofread for that specific error.
    a. You might not have matched the singular noun with a singular pronoun.

    b. You might not have provided your pronoun with an antecedent.

    c. You might have made an error from a HOW TO COPE WITH THE UNEXPECTED segment.

2. Look for errors of the type you make. Begin by circling the pronouns that you have used in your paragraph or essay. Then look backwards for their antecedents, making sure each pronoun has one. Also make sure singular pronouns agree with singular antecedents and plurals with plurals.

3. Correct errors in agreement by making antecedent and pronoun both singular or both plural. Correct for a missing antecedent by adding one.

How to Cope with the Unexpected (2)

Pronouns do not use the **'s** to indicate possession. If during proofreading you find an **'s** attached to a pronoun, you may be using a contraction such as **she's** for **she is,** or you may have an error. See Chapter 29 for work on contractions and Chapter 30 for work on the apostrophe.

After you correct all errors in a PRACTICING PROOFREADING exercise, demonstrate your mastery with WRITING ASSIGNMENT 2.

PRACTICING PROOFREADING 1

The 12 pronouns below belong to 4 different antecedents; 3 do not match their antecedents in number. Correct the errors. To aid your search, draw lines between pronouns and their antecedents.

DON'T SNACK ON CHALK

[1]An often dangerous habit of craving for non-food items is called "pica." [2]The millions of people who suffer from them consume chalk, clay, laundry starch, ice cubes, plaster, dirt, tinfoil, and paper. [3]Although it is not often a fatal habit, it is usually harmful. [4]It can cause vitamin deficiencies, ulcers, stomach upsets, and psychological problems. [5]A typical pica sufferer may crave their own hair, eating it by handfuls until it wads in their stomach and requires surgery. [6]Because pica is a habit, it can sometimes be broken, but its power can be very strong. [7]People in a Southern state were so used to eating a particular clay, that when they moved, they asked relatives for packages of the stuff. [8]The best way to

protect children from eating paint chips was to pass laws limiting the amount of lead in housepaint.

PRACTICING PROOFREADING 2

Of the 10 pronouns in the paragraph below, 6 are incorrect. Correct the errors.

MR. SECRETARY

[1]Although ninety-nine secretaries out of a hundred today are women, they did not always have a monopoly on the position. [2]Many early business tycoons, particularly railroad executives, preferred to hire a male as a secretary. [3]Often known as "an administrative assistant," they had to take dictation and transcribe. [4]They also had to cope with the hardships of travel. [5]A secretary was likely to spend long periods of time on the road, living and working in special railroad cars. [6]What they learned on the job often helped when they went to work elsewhere.[7] A president of the Santa Fe railroad was proud that he had once been a railroad secretary, while Chicago's late mayor, Richard Daley, claimed that he had learned his craft while working as a secretary to four different Cook County treasurers. [8]A man working today as a secretary might have graduated from a business school or received training in office work while they served in the Armed Forces. [9]They might even have an academic degree from a first-rate college.

WRITING ASSIGNMENT 2: singular pronouns

Write a long paragraph on one of the topics provided here, following your instructor's specifications for organization and development. Proofread for errors in pronoun reference and agreement.

a. Discuss the qualities of a pet you once had that somehow made him/her/it different from others of the kind. Identify it in the first sentence (dog, cat, parakeet, goldfish, alligator), referring to it afterward only with pronouns.
b. Describe the demands of some training program, physical fitness project, or diet that you once tried. Refer to the program as **it**.

c. Describe a friend who helped you out in a difficult situation. Refer to your friend only with pronouns after naming him/her.

d. Discuss a family dinner. Name people of both sexes. (Mention any pets that were around.) After the initial identification, refer to individuals with pronouns.

e. Think of a group that works as a unit: an audience, a band, a sports team, a family, a school board. Describe what the group does. After naming the group, refer to it subsequently by the singular pronoun **it.**

Chapter **5**
FORMING PLURALS

ATTENTION FOCUSING: plurals*

Underline the 8 nouns ending in **s.** (Do not count the title.) List them below and write **a** or **an** and the singular form of the noun alongside each.

SUPERSTITIOUS WARNINGS (ADAPTED FROM DEATH IN EARLY AMERICA)

1. Beware if your <u>roses</u> bloom twice in the same year.

2. If cows moo after midnight, something evil will happen.

3. White moths warn of impending death.

4. Footprints discovered in the fireplace speak of bad deeds.

5. Crossed knives foretell death.

6. When a rooster crows and other roosters join in, prepare for a funeral.

7. Diamond-shaped folds in the coverlet portend death.

roses	*a rose*		

WRITING ASSIGNMENT 1: plurals

Write a paragraph on one of the following topics.

a. Name some of the animals emerging two by two from Noah's Ark. (two bear**s**)

b. Name multiple items of clothing you own. (four pairs of black shoe**s**)

c. Name, by position, the personnel on a sports team. (three out-fielder**s**)

If you have made no errors in indicating plurals, go on to another skill. If you did make some errors, read the following REVIEW.

REVIEW: plurals

Plural means more than one. To indicate that most nouns are plural, you must add **s** to them. When a **singular** noun appears in a sentence, it is usually preceded by one of the articles (**a, an, the**) or by some other word. As you make the word **plural** by adding **-s**, you will have to drop or change the preceding article.

singular (one)			plural (more than one)	
a	tree	_____	**two**	trees
an	animal	_____	**these**	animal**s**
one	chicken	_____	**the**	chicken**s**
this	building	_____	**these**	building**s**
the	ballplayer	(**the** remains)	**the**	ballplayer**s**

Notice that, when plurals are formed, **a** and **an** disappear, and **one** and **this** change. Pay attention to these other words because words work together and often signal the reader or writer about other words. A single rule of grammar affects other words and often makes sense only as you consider the entire sentence.

ADDITIONAL INFORMATION ABOUT INDICATING PLURALS

Not all nouns indicate their plural state with an **s.** As you complete REWRITING EXERCISE 2, you will learn another way plurals are formed. You should become familiar with the types of words that indicate plurals in other than the most common way, but you do not necessarily need to memorize the rules for pluralization. Dictionaries indicate when the plural is not formed by the addition of **s.** If you develop the habit of checking your dictionary for unfamiliar situations *as they arise,* you will become a more successful writer. Exceptions are summarized just before the section on PROOFREADING STRATEGIES.

Continue with a REWRITING EXERCISE. After you complete one without making any errors, read PROOFREADING STRATEGIES and go on to PRACTICING PROOFREADING.

REWRITING EXERCISE 1*

Make the following changes regarding the use of plurals:

a. Cross out each indefinite article (**a** or **an**).
b. In the space above each line, write the plural form of each animal and all other plural nouns in the paragraph.
c. Look after the paragraph for an explanation of the starred (*) **cities.**

ANIMALS IN CITIES

[1]In addition to an occasional monkey, tiger, elephant, and cockatoo behind bars in city zoos, many other wild animals find homes in large *cities. [2]When lack of rain reduced food supplies, a nearby coyote headed right for Los Angeles, searching through garbage cans for sustenance. [3]A raccoon used the sewer system in downtown Washington, D.C., penetrating all the way to the White House. [4]Perhaps the most surprising visitors to the "urban jungles" are birds. [5]A peregrine falcon found a nesting place in Baltimore, Md. [6]The falcon treated high buildings as cliffs and each day feasted on a city pigeon.

How to Cope with the Unexpected (1)

The starred (*) word—**cities**—is a plural noun. In the singular, it was **city.** When the plural indicator **es** was added, the **y** became an **i.**

REWRITING EXERCISE 2: plurals

The recipe below serves 6 people. To serve 12, double each of the ingredients. Then, using the new amounts, rewrite the cooking instructions.

MEXICAN FRIED CHICKEN

1. 1 frying chicken
2. ½ cup flour
3. 1 pinch of salt
4. 1 cup water

½ cup cooking oil
1 tablespoon chili powder
1 cup canned tomatoes
1 onion, chopped

1 green pepper, chopped
1 pinch pepper
1 cup of rice

⁵Cut chicken into pieces. ⁶Mix a ½ cup of flour, a tablespoon of chili powder, a pinch of salt, and a *pinch of pepper. ⁷Dip the pieces of chicken into the mixture. ⁸Brown in fat. ⁹Remove chicken from skillet. ¹⁰Add an onion, a green pepper, one can of tomatoes, a cup of water, and the cup of rice. ¹¹Season with more salt, pepper, and chili powder if desired. ¹²Add chicken, cover skillet, and cook gently for 40 minutes.

> Proofread your rewritten paragraph for correctness in both copying and use of plural endings. Underline all plural nouns.

How to Cope with the Unexpected (2)

In the recipe above, the plural for the starred (*) word **pinch** is **pinches.** See p. 41 in this chapter for other special plural endings. REWRITING EXERCISE 3 contains nouns that indicate the plural other than by adding **s.** PRACTICING PROOFREADING 2 contains errors in such situations.

REWRITING EXERCISE 3: plurals

Copy the essay that follows, making each monster creature plural. (Check your dictionary for unusual plural indicators.) The plural form of the starred (*) word **grasshopper's** is **grasshoppers'.**

BUT THE GIANT LEECHES COULD LIVE IN THE WATER

¹Hollywood's monsters couldn't survive outside the movie screens, claims Michael LaBarbera, a professor of anatomy at the University of Chicago.

²Mammals radiate heat, which they need to dissipate. ³If called upon to do anything energetic, a 50-foot ape would simply pass out. ⁴Nor would such a huge ape risk leaping from tree to tree or off buildings.

⁵Similarly, no gigantic radioactive grasshopper could have marched into Chicago or anywhere else. ⁶A grasshopper that size would fall apart at the knees instantly. ⁷And instead of battling the insect-monster with flamethrowers, the defenders should have thrown bricks at the creature. ⁸The anthropod skeletons are soft as they are being regrown. ⁹The *grasshopper's skeleton would have kinked from well-thrown bricks.

[10]Nor could the fire-breathing lizard and the giant moth perform their acrobatic feats. [11]The lizard would be unable to bounce from mountain ranges, while a moth with a 200-foot wingspread could not breathe well enough to generate a breeze. [12]And an octopus wishing to embrace the Golden Gate Bridge would be unable to stretch the required 400 feet. [13]Lacking bones, the octopus would need to generate a hydraulic force that blood pressure cannot achieve.

A SUMMARY OF OTHER WAYS NOUNS INDICATE PLURALS

You have already encountered the special plural indicators with some nouns ending in **y (ies)** and with nouns ending in **ch.** You must also pay special attention to these other irregular plurals:

1. nouns that indicate the plural by changing in the middle: woman (wom**e**n), man (m**e**n), tooth (t**ee**th)
2. nouns that end in **-s, -sh, -ss, -x,** and **-z** (tax**es**)
3. nouns that end in **o:** potato (potato**es**), tomato (tomato**es**), hero (hero**es**)
4. nouns that end in **f:** knife (kni**ves**), wife (wi**ves**), leaf (lea**ves**)
5. hyphenated nouns: mother-in-law (mother**s**-in-law)
6. nouns with unusual indicators: child (child**ren**), focus (fo**ci**)

You do not need to memorize the rules for forming plurals in these situations. Try to remember instead what these special situations are. If you encounter one during proofreading, check your dictionary for the correct plural.

PROOFREADING STRATEGIES

1. Look only for errors in the use of plurals. The most common error is the omission of the **s** indicator or its incorrect use with certain special words. A noun ending in **y** is one such word.
2. Skim your essay quickly for such unusual words. Also, look for hints that English provides when singulars are present. The articles **a/an** (and sometimes **the**) precede the singular noun. The number **1** or the word **one**, as in the first REWRITING EXERCISE, as well as such words as **this** and **that**, similarly indicate the presence of a singular. Naturally, such words as **two, many, some, these, those** signal plurals. One way of proofreading, then, for the omission of plural endings is to search for articles. If there are no articles, there probably should be plural indicators at the end of your nouns. On the other hand, because **a/an** indicates a singular, a noun that follows one of those articles should not have a plural indicator.

3. If the noun lacks a plural ending, add **s** (or, when appropriate, **es**). If, on the other hand, clues in the sentence indicate that you are dealing with singulars, make sure your noun does not have a plural ending.

> Choose one of the proofreading exercises. Work until you locate and correct all errors in plural (s or es endings). To demonstrate mastery of plural endings, try WRITING ASSIGNMENT 2.

PRACTICING PROOFREADING 1

Of the 12 plural nouns in the paragraph that follows, 3 are incorrect. Correct the errors.

COLE SLAW

[1]The five members of the rock group NRBQ delighted audiences during a recent tour of Boston, Philadelphia, Washington, Los Angeles, and San Francisco by exploding Cabbage Patch Dolls on stage. [2]The group was so pleased by the favorable responses that it tarred and feathered doll during performances in New York City. [3]A member of the group, lead guitarist Al Anderson, announced that the group is opening a cemetery for the dolls. [4]He promised all dead doll decent burials, including headstones. [5]For a fee of 15 dollar, his group will even issue death certificates.

PRACTICING PROOFREADING 2

Locate and correct the 7 errors in forming plurals.

CANDIDATES FOR BLOOPERSTOWN

[1]Allan Zullo and Bruce Nash, the two author of The Baseball Hall of Shame, wrote their book because they think losers are more interesting than winners. [2]As a result, their book contains storys about some very entertaining flakes.

[3]One outstanding examples is Harry Heitman, a pitcher for the Brooklyn Dodgers, whose career lasted 1/3 of an inning. [4]He retired one batter, gave up two singles and two triple, and left the field, the ballpark, and the team, never to return.

[5]Outfielder Smead Jolley's career lasted three year filled with inept ball handling. [6]In a typical game, he allowed a ball to roll between his legs. [7]When the ball bounced off the wall, he let it roll between his legs again. [8]When he finally got his hands on it, he threw the ball ten feet over the third baseman's head. [9]The batter, of course, circled the four bases.

[10]To match these individual feat, the two authors offer the 1899 Cleveland Spiders. [11]This team lost 40 of its final 41 games, winning 20 and losing 134 game for the season.

WRITING ASSIGNMENT 2: plurals

Write a long paragraph on one of the following topics, following your instructor's specifications for organization and development. When you proofread, look for errors in plural endings.

a. Describe the interaction between trainers and animals at a circus.
b. Name some items that have superstitions attached to them. Explain and react to the beliefs associated with one of these items. Use the plural form of the item. (ladders, cats, crows)
c. Present a favorite recipe, doubling all proportions so that you will be using plural forms as often as possible.
d. Who are the outstanding players at various positions in a sport?

Chapter 6

USING PLURAL PRONOUNS
(reference and agreement)

ATTENTION FOCUSING: plural pronouns*

The sentences below, adapted from Mario Vargas Llosa's The Scriptwriter, contain both singular and plural pronouns. Draw lines from the 5 plural pronouns that refer to **minors** in sentence 1.

1. Dr. Zaldivar was very tactful when he questioned minors.

2. He knew how to gain their confidence.

3. He was careful not to hurt their feelings.

4. By being gentle and patient, he easily led them around to talking.

5. They would tell him everything about themselves.

6. But with Sarita, he was perhaps too effective.

7. She began to speak in a steady stream, using the most scandalous gestures.

8. Dr. Zaldivar tried to explain to her that they were unnecessary.

9. He found she would not stop using them.

10. It wasn't until he shouted "Enough!" that she stopped using them.

To which noun do the plural pronouns in sentences 8, 9, and 10 refer?

_____

WRITING ASSIGNMENT 1: plural pronouns

Write a short paragraph on one of the following topics. Establish clearly the plural **antecedents** or nouns to which the plural pronouns refer.

a. Talk about the actions of waiters or waitresses in a restaurant.
b. Say what you enjoyed about recent articles in a magazine or newspaper.
c. Evaluate some generalizations people make about nationalities, ethnic groups, or states in certain parts of the country. (Americans—they)

> If you have made no errors in the use of plural pronouns, try PRACTICING PROOFREADING 1 before asking your instructor to send you on to another chapter. If you did make errors, read the REVIEW. This chapter also contains work on INDEFINITE PRONOUNS, pp. 49–51.

REVIEW: plural pronouns

Here is a table of plural pronouns. (Compare to singulars shown in Chapter 4.)

	Personal		Possessive		Reflexive
	Subjective	Objective	Subjective	Objective	
first person	we	us	our	ours	ourselves
second person	you	you	your	yours	yourselves
third person	they	them	their	theirs	themselves

Pronouns take the place of nouns. When you do not wish to repeat the names of people, places, things, or activities, use plural pronouns.

Bonnie Parker and Clyde Barrow robbed banks in Texas, Louisiana, Oklahoma, and Arkansas in the 1930s. Sometimes **they** shared what **they** stole with the poor of the Ouachita Mountains in southwestern Oklahoma. Hearing of **their** actions, some people began to think of **them** as Robin Hood figures.

Without pronouns, this paragraph might read:

Bonnie Parker and Clyde Barrow robbed banks in Texas, Louisiana, Oklahoma, and Arkansas in the 1930s. Sometimes **Bonnie Parker and Clyde Barrow** shared what **Bonnie Parker and Clyde Barrow** stole with the poor of the Ouachita Mountains in southwestern Oklahoma. Hearing of **Bonnie and Clyde's** actions, some people began to think of **Bonnie and Clyde** as Robin Hood figures.

The pronouns **they, their,** and **them** replace the names of the two robbers. Another way of saying this is that these pronouns **refer** to Bonnie Parker and Clyde Barrow. The noun to which pronouns refer is called the **antecedent,** or the noun that "comes before."

Here are two important rules about using a pronoun:

1. The pronoun must refer clearly to the noun it replaces.
2. The pronoun must agree in number with its antecedent. **Bonnie Parker and Clyde Barrow,** taken together, would be considered plural. As a result, the pronouns referring to them must also be plural.

REVIEW: indefinite pronouns

The indefinite pronouns **both** and **many** are used with plural nouns and plural pronouns; **all, any,** and **some** accept singulars or plurals, depending on context. See also the discussion of singular indefinite pronouns in Chapter 4. Later in this chapter, you will find special exercises for indefinite pronouns.

Continue with a REWRITING EXERCISE. After you complete one without making any errors, read PROOFREADING STRATEGIES and go on to PRACTICING PROOFREADING.

REWRITING EXERCISE 1: plural pronouns*

Make the following changes in the essay that follows:

a. Circle the singular noun **sunbather** and the 16 pronouns referring to it.
b. Writing in the space above each line, replace the singular **a sunbather** with the plural **sunbathers.**
c. Replace all singular pronouns that refer to **a sunbather** with plural pronouns that agree with the plural **sunbathers.**
d. Starred (*) words are explained after the essay.

BURN BABY BURN?

[1]A sunbather eager for the perfect tan would do well to determine her skin type, according to Madhu Pathak, a research dermatologist at Harvard. [2]Basing his research on work with 100 women, he graded skin types I–VI, depending on the amount of protection they required. [3]A sunbather with fair skin and red hair would be designated Skin Type I. [4]She would always burn and never tan. [5]A sunbather with Type II would differ only in that if she exposed herself to sunlight for 45 minutes between 11 A.M. and 2 P.M., her skin would tan "minimally." [6]A sunbather graded

Skin Type III can get away with less protection. [7]She would still burn, but her burn would be moderate and her skin would tan uniformly to a light brown. [8]If her skin is graded Type IV, she would burn only a little and tan well. [9]If a *sunbather's grade for her skin is V, she would rarely burn, and she would turn dark brown. [10]Still, Pathak recommends sunscreens with various factors of protection for all sunbathers except those with Skin Type VI. [11]Such a sunbather would have ebony skin. [12]She would not burn at all, though even she might incur deep skin damage.

[13]A sunbather should also know some facts. [14]Using a solar reflector is like putting her face in a microwave oven. [15]And tanning is simply the *skin's initial attempt at protecting itself. [16]Instead of a *sunbather's skin cells embracing the heat, they are cringing from it.

How to Cope with the Unexpected (1)

The three instances of the **'s** are starred (*). Leave **skin's** as it is, but change the singular possessive **sunbather's** to the plural possessive **sunbathers'**. See Chapter 30 for work on the use of the **'s**.

REWRITING EXERCISE 2: plural pronouns

Copy the essay below, making the following changes to use plural pronouns:

a. Replace the words **the typical new video game** with the plural **new video games** each time you find them. Because of this change from the singular to the plural, you will have to change all pronouns referring to **new video games** to the plural.
b. Circle the 15 singular pronouns referring to **the typical video game.**
c. Replace them with plural pronouns.
d. Starred (*) words are explained after the essay.

JENNY ON THE PRAIRIE AND COLONIAL CONQUEST

[1]The typical new video game will be very different from those that pioneered the era.

[2]For one, it will be perhaps eight to ten times more complex. [3]It will require a great deal of strategy and brain power. [4]Because it will not be for solo use, as many of the early games were, it will provide opportuni-

ties for more complicated interaction among players. [5]Finally, it will not cut itself off with a flash as a spaceship is either rescued or destroyed. [6]Instead, it will likely end with resolutions that will be brought about through solutions rather than conquests.

[7]The typical new video game will also pay more attention to differences in personality. [8]It will allow aggressive people to compete with it by keeping one step ahead, but it will wait for less aggressive people to make their moves before it reacts. [9]Its additional attraction will be its ability to adapt itself for games only for girls or only for boys.

[10]Elizabeth Stott, a Richmond, Va., psychologist who designed such a typical video game, doubts that her creation will be labeled sexist. [11]She believes that it will be welcomed instead for enabling girls to use abilities such as creativity and planning that are natural to them.

> Proofread your rewritten essay for correctness in both copying and using plural pronouns. Underline each new plural pronoun.

How to Cope with the Unexpected (2)

Sentence 10 of the essay states that Elizabeth Stott doubts **her creation** will be labeled sexist. **Creation** is a singular noun. It agrees with **a typical video game** in the previous sentence. When you substitute the plural **games,** you must also change **creation** to the plural **creations.** The word is a **subject complement,** meaning that is is "equal" to the subject. When the subject is singular, its complement must also be singular. When the subject changes to the plural, its complement must also become plural.

A "cop" is also called a peace officer. ⟶ "Cops" are also called peace officers.

(When **"Cops"** changes to the plural, so does **peace officers.**)

Cobb was a great ballplayer. ⟶ Ruth and Cobb were great ballplayers.

(**Ruth** added to **Cobb** makes the subject plural; the complement also becomes plural.)

He was a lifetime .300 hitter. ⟶ They were lifetime .300 hitters.

(When **He** changes to **They, hitter** changes to the plural **hitters.**)

REWRITING EXERCISE 3: using plural pronouns

Rewrite the entire essay, substituting the plural **the du Ponts** for the singular **Irenee du Pont.** As you rewrite, you must change to the plural the nine pronouns that will be referring to **the du Ponts.** In sentence 4, the possessive **Irenee du Pont's** changes in the plural to **the du Ponts'.**

THE NYLON MASK

¹Did Irenee du Pont suppress a biography of his family written by Gerard C. Zilg in 1974?

²Mr. Zilg certainly believes that to be the case. ³The book, <u>Du Pont: Behind the Nylon Curtain</u>, received rave reviews and was selected by the Book-of-the-Month-Club. ⁴But, due to Irenee du Pont's influence (contended Mr. Zilg's lawsuit), the book flopped. ⁵The suit claimed that Irenee du Pont used his influence with the Book Club to cancel its contract with the book's publisher. ⁶He also convinced the publisher, Prentice-Hall, not to advertise the book. ⁷Zilg believes that Irenee du Pont's actions came after he failed to keep the book from ever going to press. ⁸Zilg claimed that, when du Pont read the book in manuscript, he tried to suppress it because he wanted to hide certain details of his life, such as his herd of attack iguanas and his many servants, said to outnumber those employed by the British royal family.

The two exercises that follow deal with plural indefinite pronouns. Review the brief discussion on p. 46.

ATTENTION FOCUSING: plural pronouns (including indefinite)*

a. List all pronouns that refer to **requests** in sentence 2 at the top of page 50. _____

b. Which of the three pronouns that refer to **requests** are indefinite pronouns? _____

c. What is the antecedent for the indefinite pronoun **both** in sentence 5?

_____

d. What is the antecedent for the 5 plural pronouns in sentence 9? ____

e. What are the two indefinite pronouns in sentence 9? _____

CHANGING NAMES

[1]People wishing to change their names must file an application with the court specified by the law of the particular state. [2]Of the requests filed, many are not granted by the courts.

[3]Some may be denied by the court if they are opposed by other petitioners who may be badly affected by the name change. [4]In one instance cited by Alice K. Helm, in The Family Legal Advisor, an applicant's request was bitterly opposed by his wife and child. [5]The court accepted the argument that both of them were denied their connection to the applicant, who did not seem to have a very good reason for wishing to make the change. [6]In other instances, courts have refused to allow name changes because people had already changed their names once. [7]The courts' opinion was that these people had to be known by the official name they had already selected for themselves. [8]Criminals often ask for name changes. [9]Some just want to put their past behind them, but many would like their names changed in order to hide their criminal records. [10]Although courts generally decide against granting such requests, they have on occasion permitted the children of a felon to change their names, particularly if the parent was an infamous criminal.

REWRITING EXERCISE 4: indefinite plural pronouns

Copy the essay below, substituting **people** for the 7 indefinite pronouns. This change will force you to use plurals for the pronouns referring to **people**. (The change to the plural will eliminate the awkward **his or her** and **he or she**.) The two words with the **'s** become **people's**.

A P & G IN EVERY POT

[1]Last year, Proctor and Gamble spent more money advertising its products than any other company, but it was money well spent, according to an article in Fortune. [2]The article said that everybody in the United States had dozens of P & G products tucked away on his or her shelves. [3]Everyone also had dozens of P & G jingles tucked away in his or

her head. [4]If someone did not have Ivory soap in his or her bathroom, he or she surely had Crest or Gleem toothpaste in there. [5]And if he or she did not have Tide detergent in his or her clotheswasher, he or she no doubt used Cascade in his or her dishwasher. [6]Someone who might have avoided Head and Shoulders might still be fighting his or her dandruff with Prell Shampoo. [7]And could anyone have managed an entire year without Crisco in his or her frying pan or Comet for those stubborn stains in his or her sink? [8]Proctor and Gamble has probably entered everyone's awareness, if not through product, then through song. [9]But, as for profit, P & G has earned most from everybody's devotion to Pampers, its disposal diapers.

PROOFREADING STRATEGIES

1. Know what kind of error you make and proofread for that specific error.
   a. You might not have matched the plural noun with a plural pronoun.
   b. You might not have provided your pronoun with a clear antecedent.
   c. You might have an error from a HOW TO COPE segment.
2. Look for errors of the type you make. Begin by circling the pronouns that you have used in your paragraph or essay. Then look backwards for their antecedents, drawing lines to help aid in your search. Make sure each pronoun has an antecedent. Also make sure each plural pronoun agrees with a plural antecedent and each singular with a singular.
3. Correct for missing antecedents by adding them. Correct agreement errors by making antecedent and pronoun both plural or both singular.

> Choose a proofreading exercise. To demonstrate your mastery of plural pronouns, try WRITING ASSIGNMENT 2. The PROOFREADING TEST on p. 60 contains errors in articles, pronouns, and plurals.

PRACTICING PROOFREADING 1

In the paragraph at the top of page 52, locate the 6 plural pronouns and their antecedents. Replace the incorrect antecedent for 5 of the pronouns.

ADAPTED FROM HUCKLEBERRY FINN

[1]I was mighty thankful to that old doctor for doing Jim that good turn. [2]And I was glad it was according to my judgment of him, too; because I thought he had a good heart in him and was a good man the first time I saw him. [3]Then everyone agreed that Jim had acted very well and was deserving to have some notice took of it and rewarded. [4]So they promised, right out, that they wouldn't cuss him any more. [5]Then they locked him up. [6]I hoped they would take one or two of the chins off, because they were rotten heavy, or that he could have meat and greens with his bread and water; but they did not think of it.

PRACTICING PROOFREADING 2

The following paragraph has problems with 4 of its 10 pronouns, either because of a lack of agreement or because of an unclear antecedent. Make the necessary corrections.

SKUNK HOUR

[1]Last year, Onondaga County suffered greatly from skunks who were leaving their nasty odors everywhere. [2]When they appealed for help to the Department of Environmental Conservation, they were told that DET would pick up the skunks without charging them. [3]But the Department insisted that the pick-up program be used only once and that the skunks be killed. [4]When they are only trapped and released, they find their way back to populated areas. [5]The skunk smell is most severe in July, August, and September. [6]That is when the creatures forage for food in order to build up their winter fat. [7]Once they settle into winter hibernation, it will disappear—until springtime, at least.

WRITING ASSIGNMENT 2: plural pronouns

Write a long paragraph on one of the following topics, according to your instructor's suggestions regarding organization and development. Proofread specifically for errors in the use of plural pronouns.

a. Discuss the care of certain pets (such as dogs, cats, parakeets, guppies, alligators). After you mention them initially, refer to them with pronouns.

b. Compare two groups of people in various parts of the country or the world to each other; for example, compare Easterners to Westerners, English to Swiss, Mexicans to Brazilians.

c. Compare the skills and accomplishments of modern ballplayers to players of another era.

d. Consider some members of a family prominent in politics, entertainment, sports, or some other field. Is their reputation justified? Use the plural: the Cranes, the Kennedys, the Carradines, the Smiths.

e. What types of arcade games do you find most challenging, educational, or entertaining? Discuss types: pinball machines, video games, trivia quizzes.

Chapter 7

CONSISTENCY WITH PRONOUNS
(person)

ATTENTION FOCUSING: pronouns and point of view*

a. Circle all the personal pronouns.
b. Write into the boxes the numbers of the sentences containing pronouns.

Sentences containing more than one pronoun should be listed as often as necessary.

first person	second person	third person
	1,	

FROM "ESSAY SERIES #1" BY MARTIN LUTHER KING, JR.

[1]You may well ask, "Why direct action? Why sit-ins, marches, etc.? Isn't negotiation a better path?" [2]You are exactly right in your call for negotiation. [3]Indeed, this is the purpose of direct action. [4]Nonviolent direct action seeks to create such a crisis and establish such a creative tension that a community that has constantly refused to negotiate is forced to confront the issue. [5]It seeks so to dramatize the issue that it can no longer be ignored. [6]I just referred to the creation of tension as a part of the work of the nonviolent resister. [7]This may sound rather shocking. [8]But I must confess that I am not afraid of the word "tension." [9]I have earnestly worked and preached against violent tension, but there is a

type of constructive nonviolent tension that is necessary for growth. [10]Just as Socrates felt that it was necessary to create a tension in the mind so that individuals could rise from the bondage of myths and half-truths to the unfettered realm of creative analysis and objective appraisal, we must see the need of having nonviolent gadflies to create the kind of tension that will help men rise from the dark depths of prejudice and racism to the majestic heights of understanding and brotherhood. [11]So the purpose of the direct action is to create a situation so crisis-packed that it will inevitably open the door to negotiation.

REVIEW: consistency in pronouns

All writing has a point of view, indicated most clearly in the pronouns used. When you write in the **first person,** you refer to the person closest to you, yourself. Thus you use **I** and **we** in first-person writing, often to reflect your personal opinion or experience. Such writing is said to have a first-person point of view.

The **second person** refers to the second-closest person to you, someone who is present and being addressed. Therefore, when you write in the second person, you address the reading audience directly as **you.** Second-person writing is often used for process papers that explain how to do something.

The **third person** uses **he, she, it,** or **they** to discuss someone (or something) not a part of the "discussion" taking place between the writer and audience, the third-closest "person" from the writer. Writing that discusses objects or ideas may not even use pronouns and may not be about people at all, but it is still called **third person.** Academic writing is usually in the third person.

Readers or listeners identify point of view easily, even if not consciously. They are aware if writers are expressing their own views (first person), addressing them directly (second person), or discussing ideas or things (third person).

The Martin Luther King selection contains changes in pronouns because there are changes in its point of view. King begins by addressing his listeners directly (**you**—second person), shifts to a definition of nonviolent action (**it**—third person), and shifts again to a personal reference (**I**—first person).

These shifts are deliberate and necessary. King is specifically interested in the dialogue between himself (**I**) and his audience (**you**) and must also pause to explain definitions (**it**). But writers (and speakers) generally avoid changing a point of view once they have established one. Unnecessary shifts can be confusing and irritating; sometimes they can even weaken an otherwise strong piece of writing.

The most common of the unnecessary shifts is from the third person to the first person. The **I** suddenly appears in the middle of an argumentative essay otherwise written in the third person.

I believe that Destry should resign her office.

Unless the **I** is an important and needed presence, there is no reason for its use. The first person reference should be eliminated.

Destry should resign her office.

The other common shift brings the second person into writing that should be in the first or third person. The use of second person feels natural because most verbal communication is done face to face, addressing someone as **you.** As a result, writers will often find themselves unconsciously forming sentences in the second person that tell readers they do something or believe something that they don't:

Your air filter can become clogged quickly if you drive on dusty roads.

This sentence implies that all readers are drivers, but they may not all be. In all likelihood, they do not have air filters (their cars may, if they have cars). The sentence, strictly speaking, is not true. Compare the example with the rewrite that follows:

The air filter of a car driven on dusty roads can clog quickly.

No specific driver is implied, and the statement now represents a general truth.

REWRITING EXERCISE 1: consistency in pronouns*

Copy the paragraph below, making the following changes:

a. Underline all pronouns in the third person.
b. Circle all pronouns in the second person.
c. Make pronouns consistent by replacing **you** with **people** or **they.**

THE HOT DOG PERSONALITY INDEX

[1]What you put on a hot dog and how you eat it can reveal a great deal about personality. [2]At least so claims a New York City hot dog vendor. [3]Timothy Moore declares his own tastes by eating "gourmet" hot dogs on sourdough buns, topped with Poupon mustard. [4]He claims that what you prefer may be extremely revealing. [5]If you choose sauerkraut and mustard on a frankfurter, you indicate Brooklyn origins and belief in traditional values. [6]If you ask for "just mustard," you demonstrate the characteristics of a low-risk type. [7]You probably bank at just one bank

and prefer to save rather than invest. [8]If you add ketchup, you want to be noticed. [9]If you add chili, you possess a great deal of passion and want "spice" out of life. [10] If you then eat a hot dog from one end to the other, chances are that you work things through to the end, in a systematic, orderly fashion. [11]If you start at one end and switch to the other, you drive yourself intensely toward success. [12]If you begin with your toppings, saving the rest of the hot dog for later, you like to hug and kiss, often demanding instant gratification. [13]These are, of course, the results of an extremely informal study.

REWRITING EXERCISE 2: consistency in pronouns

1. Underline all third-person pronouns.
2. Circle all first-person pronouns.
3. Rewrite all sentences in the first person to the third, using **the Technology Center** or **it.**

ANNOUNCEMENT

[1]The Technology Center has received a grant to expand its current facilities to include a Materials Technology Laboratory. [2]After it is completed, the new lab will house new equipment in addition to equipment currently located in several buildings. [3]Dr. Rita Nash, Director of the Technology Center, stated that she expects work on the addition to begin in two weeks. [4]She adds that it should be completed by August.

[5]We will host a reception next Saturday to celebrate the grant. [6]We will be selling tickets at the Student Union from 9 A.M. until 4 P.M. [7]We will surely have a large turnout, so we will probably run out of tickets soon. [8]The tickets are $1 each, but they are free to our members. [9]We will stop selling tickets earlier if attendance reaches 200. [10]The festivities at our club will begin at 7 P.M.

PROOFREADING STRATEGIES

1. What to look for: inconsistency in the use of pronouns.
2. How to look for it: circle pronouns and decide on the main point of view.

   a. Justify any shift in point of view. You should have a good reason for shifting.

   b. If there is no shift, make sure that the first-, second-, or third-person point of view is appropriate.

3. How to correct it: eliminate unnecessary shifts or change pronouns.

   a. If the shift is the sudden addition of the first person, eliminate the introductory phrase that contains the pronoun:

In my opinion, no one should starve. $\longrightarrow$ No one should starve.

Johnson, I think, is wrong again. $\longrightarrow$ Johnson is wrong again.

   b. If the shift addresses the reader when the use of **you** is not appropriate, replace the second person with the third person. Because problems may arise with subject-verb agreement, consider using the word **people** and the plural third-person pronouns: **they, them, their:**

You can get anything **you** want at Alice's Restaurant.

Revised: **People** can get anything **they** want at Alice's Restaurant.

   c. Still another way of correcting the unnecessary use of the second person, particularly the possessive **your,** is to replace it with an article **(a, an, the)** or an indefinite pronoun (**any,** for example).

The technician guarantees to fix your camera in 24 hours.

Revised: The technician guarantees to fix **any** camera in 24 hours.

PRACTICING PROOFREADING

Locate the shifts in point of view. Correct the 8 pronouns that are unnecessary or inappropriate.

INTERNATIONAL SHADOW PROJECT (ADAPTED FROM JOHN COLTOUN)

[1]The International Shadow Project is a solemn memorial with a single purpose: to help people understand and imagine the disappearance of life through nuclear war. [2]The 1982 brainchild of Alan Gussow and Donna Grund Slepack now occurs, when it does, simultaneously around the world. [3]Figures are painted on walls and sidewalks, representing the effects of the atomic explosion over Hiroshima. [4]There people and animals were vaporized by the bomb, leaving behind shadows etched into stone by radiation. [5]With the Shadow Project, you can see shadows that

will fade in a few weeks. ⁶Those in Hiroshima did not. ⁷You can see odd images—a dog here, a group of people apparently crawling on the street there. ⁸The silhouettes are hauntingly lifelike, even though crude and distorted. ⁹The participants in the International Shadow Project wanted to make vivid the dangers of nuclear annihilation.

¹⁰I think they succeeded. ¹¹Viewing the shadows, you are encouraged to identify with the victims of nuclear destruction. ¹²We need to see the connection between the present arms build-up and the sort of holocaust that occurred at Nagasaki and Hiroshima. ¹³The silent, anonymous shadows that appear in cities scattered throughout the world are effective reminders of this. ¹⁴You cannot avoid making the connection when you see your shadow next to those of the Shadow Project.

WRITING ASSIGNMENT: consistency in pronouns

Write a short paragraph in the **first person,** telling how you feel about the abuse of one particular drug or substance. Rewrite the paragraph in the **second person,** advising someone you are addressing to take the same view. Rewrite the paragraph again, in the **third person,** using the drug or substance as the subject of your sentences.

MASTERY TEST FOR UNIT II: problems with nouns and pronouns

The essay below contains 20 errors in the areas discussed in this unit: 5 each in the articles **a/an** and the use of **-s** (or **-es**) to indicate plurals, and 10 in the use of pronouns (singulars and plurals).

Proofread the essay, using the proofreading strategies you have been practicing. Because the most effective proofreading searches for only one type of error at a time, it might be a good idea to reproduce this essay twice. Then, on one copy, look only for errors in **a/an,** circling, underlining, or highlighting as you wish. When you have found the 5 errors in the use of the articles, correct them on original pages and submit them. Continue by using a second copy of the essay to proofread for the 5 errors in the use of plurals, and a third copy to proofread for the 10 errors in pronouns.

THE COLUMBUS MYTHS

[1]Christopher Columbus' great error was his calculation that Asia was only 3000 mile to the west of the Canary Islands. [2]He went to his grave stubbornly believing that they had found a new route to Asia. [3]But Columbus was not the only one in error. [4]The contemporary version of his discovery of America also contains many inaccuracys. [5]Despite well documented biographies such as Samuel Eliot Morison's <u>Admiral of the Ocean Sea</u>, everyone prefers their own version of the tale.

[6]Three myths about Columbus' four voyages are the most prevalent. [7]One is the belief that Columbus lived in a age in which people thought that the earth was flat and they would fall off the edge if they persisted in a westward journey. [8]People today also accept the story that Columbus had such difficulty convincing seamen of the worthiness of his journey that they had to empty jails to find a inexperienced crew for his ships. [9]Finally, any story told about Columbus' adventures mentions the name of their ships: the <u>Nina</u>, <u>Pinta</u>, and <u>Santa Maria</u>.

[10]All of these "facts" are in error, according to William Fowler, an historian at Northeastern. [11]First, even in Columbus' time, a educated European knew that the world was round. [12]Although they expected Columbus to face many hardships, falling off the face of the earth was not one of their fear. [13]As for seamen, he had the best of his time. [14]They were

as seaworthy as the excellent ships in which they sailed. [15]The ships themselves were fine vessel̳, but they were not known by the names assigned them by popular histories. [16]Columbus' own ship was the <u>Santa Maria</u>, though her own crew called her "La Gallega," after Galicia, the province where she was built. [17]But the <u>Nina's</u> name was actually the <u>Santa Clara</u>. [18]She was called Nina because she was owned by a̅n family with that name. [19]And the <u>Pinta's</u> real name has been lost in obscurity.

[20]That the misconceptions persist is probably due to everyone's desire to create th̲e̲i̲r̲ own myths and th̲e̲i̲r̲ own heros. [21]In any case, people find repeating a story to be much easier than researching its' accuracy before passing them on.

If you were unable to locate the errors in any particular area, review the **PROOFREADING STRATEGIES** in that chapter. If you did find the errors but were unable to correct them review the **ATTENTION FOCUSING** and **REWRITING EXERCISES**.

Unit Three
PROBLEMS WITH AGREEMENT

AGREEMENT OF VERB WITH SUBJECT

You can locate the verb in a sentence more easily if you think of it as the "time word" in a sentence. It is the word that changes when the time of the action changes. The **present tense** forces another change on the verb. In addition to indicating time, it must also indicate number. This means that, if the subject is singular, the verb must be singular too. If the subject is plural, the verb must be plural too.

Singulars

Whenever the subject is a person, place, thing, or one of the singular pronouns **he, she,** or **it,** you must usually add an **s** to the verb stem in the third person.

no article	*plural noun*	*verb*		*article*	*singular noun*	*verb*
	fingers	write	⟶	a	finger	write**s**

infinitive: to write   *present stem:* write

	singular		*plural*	
	s	*v*	*s*	*v*
first person:	I	write	we	write
second person:	you	write	you	write
third person:	he (John, the poet)	write**s**	they (the Waughs)	write
	she (Jane, the novelist)	write**s**	(Evelyn and Alec)	write
	it (the pen, the finger)	write**s**		

As you can see, a present tense verb that is plural in number looks no different from its infinitive form: **to write** is the infinitive, **write** is the present stem, and **write** is the form of the verb used with plural subjects. Only in the **third person singular** does this stem change. Whenever the subject is a **plural** person, place, or thing, or the plural pronoun **they,** you simply use the verb stem.

How to Cope with the Unexpected

Verbs that end in **ch, sh, s, ss, x,** and **z** add **es,** not just **s,** to indicate that they are in the third person singular. If you say some of those words aloud—**touches, brushes, blesses**—you will find them difficult to pronounce without the **e.** Look at the words; they look strange with just an **s** ending even if you do not know the rule.

Plurals

You might remember the relationship between the plural subject and its verb by thinking of the "**s** exchange": between each subject and verb pair there is only one **s,** which they "exchange" when they go from singular to plural or plural to singular.

article	*singular noun*	*verb*		*no article*	*plural noun*	*verb*
a	finger	write**s**	$\longrightarrow$		finger**s**	write

In other words, in the present tense (also called the **habitual**), if the noun has the plural indicator **(s),** the verb should not have an ending.

Chapters 8 and 9 offer essays in which you can practice identifying verbs and their subjects and then change them in ways that will affect their **agreement.** You will practice singular agreement separately from plural agreement, but the TEST at the end of Chapter 9 will examine your skills in both.

Chapter **8**

VERB AGREEMENT WITH SINGULAR SUBJECTS

(*s* endings on verbs)

ATTENTION FOCUSING: the *s* ending on verbs*

The sentences below use only third-person singular verbs.

a. Underline all words that end with **s.**
b. Circle the verbs. (Verbs change when the time of the sentence changes.)
c. Locate the subject of each by asking **who** or **what** before the verb.
d. List each singular subject-verb pair below.

HAEMON SPEAKS (ADAPTED FROM SOPHOCLES' ANTIGONE)

1. A wise man knows when to yield.

2. Continued stubbornness indicates a shallow spirit, an empty heart.

3. He does not consider the admission of error a sign of weakness.

4. He bends like a tree to a torrent.

5. A tree straining against the flooded river snaps.

6. So too, a sailor slackens sails before a gale.

7. A wise man puts aside his anger.

8. He hears the opinions of others.

a man — knows _____ _____ _____

_____ _____ _____

WRITING ASSIGNMENT 1: the *s* (or *es*) ending on verbs

Write a short paragraph on one of the following topics. Each requires the use of the third person singular.

a. Describe how something works: a microwave, a computer, a match, a piano.
b. Describe the actions of a single actor/actress in a movie or TV show.
c. Give the job description of a worker: nurse, cook, mechanic, police officer, clerk.

> If you have made no errors in the use of *s* (or *es*) endings, try PRACTICING PROOFREADING 1 before asking your instructor to send you on to another chapter. If you did make errors, reread the discussion on singulars on p. 64 and choose a REWRITING exercise. Continue until you complete one without making any errors.

REWRITING EXERCISE 1: the *s* ending on verbs*

Make the following changes to use verbs in the third person singular:

a. Locate and circle all verbs. (Starred (*) verbs are explained after the essay.)
b. Underline each **I** that is the subject of a verb.
c. Change each **I** to **Mrs. Carton** or to **she,** writing the change in the space above each line.
d. Change each verb referring to Mrs. Carton to the third person singular. (The changes in your first line should be: **Mrs. Carton, works, gives.**)

BRUSH-OFF

¹I work as a photo retouch artist and give many people the "brush-off." ²I retouch tiny wrinkles and pimples, of course, but more often, I make full-sized adults disappear. ³I usually perform this service after divorces. ⁴People are so angry at their ex-spouses that they want to erase them from family portraits. ⁵I oblige by airbrushing ex-husbands and ex-wives from photographs.

⁶I *have the ability to remove grooms from wedding pictures and mothers from baby pictures. ⁷I obliterate former mothers- and fathers-in-law. ⁸I turn ex-wives into grass and shrubbery on their former husbands'

pictures, and I transform ex-husbands into trees on former wives' copies of the same photo.

[9]I advise folks who would like to preserve their places in family portraits not to pose at either end. [10]I *am not capable of making them disappear from the middle of a picture.

How to Cope with the Unexpected (1)

Some verbs change completely in the third-person singular. The starred (*) word **have** changes to **has** when used with **she.** Similarly, the starred (*) **am** changes to **is.** For more work with **has/have,** see Chapter 19. For more on **is/are,** see Chapter 10.

REWRITING EXERCISE 2: the *s* (or *es*) ending on verbs

Copy the essay below, making the following changes:

a. Locate and circle the 9 verbs that end in **ed.**
b. Locate and underline the subjects of those verbs.
c. Check your subject-verb selections in Appendix 3 (optional).
d. Substitute **The new Lisa Birnbach College Book** for the opening four words of the essay and change **attempted** to **attempts.**
e. Similarly, eliminate the **ed** (past tense) marker and substitute the **s** marker in the other verbs.
f. Starred (*) words are explained after the essay.

THE UNOFFICIAL COLLEGE CATALOGUE

[1]The Official Preppy Handbook attempted to prepare entering students to the unofficial aspects of college life.

[2]It provided significant information about etiquette not found in Emily Post's writings about proper behavior. [3]One entry designated where to sew a crocodile emblem on a designer sheet. [4]Another tidbit pronounced the mallard the appropriate breed of duck for decorating preppy pillows.

[5]Although not an exposé, the book also revealed information not available in college catalogues. [6]For example, it *identified college infirmaries generous about providing birth control devices. [7]It also listed the going price for "recreational substances" on various campuses. [8]Finally,

the book casually awarded "prizes" to schools with "most promiscuous," "most prudish," "best looking," and "ugliest" students.

⁹The author, seeing herself as an investigator for students, believed that her book gave her readers the "feel" of a campus.

> Proofread your rewritten essay by circling each verb ending in **s** and writing it below your essay, pairing it with its singular subject.

How to Cope with the Unexpected (2)

The base or stem of the starred (*) word **identified** is **identify.** When you add **es** (third-peson singular indicator) to **identify,** the **y** becomes an **i,** giving you **identifies.** For more work with **y** endings, see Chapter 47.

REWRITING EXERCISE 3: the *s* (or *es*) ending on verbs

Copy the essay below, making the following changes:

a. Circle the 18 verbs of the plural subjects **baseball players** or **they.**
b. Substitute for **baseball players** the singular **the average baseball player** and for each **they** the singular **he.**
c. Change the verbs to the singular to match the now-singular subjects.

BASEBALL SUPERSTITIONS

¹Baseball players possess a remarkable list of superstitions.

²Among good luck charms, they treasure hairpins. ³They believe that finding one guarantees at least one base hit for the day. ⁴They swear that placing a piece of black cloth in the opposing dugout will force good luck away from the enemy. ⁵To maintain a winning streak or a hitting streak, baseball players resort to incredible strategies. ⁶They eat the same foods daily; they take the same route to the ballpark; they wear the same clothes; they even refuse to shave or to get a haircut until the happy times end.

⁷Baseball players work just as hard at sidestepping bad luck. ⁸They try not to meet funeral processions or beer trucks on the way to the ballpark. ⁹They step over foul lines and stay away from chalk marks everywhere on the field. ¹⁰During a no-hitter, they keep silent, fearful of jinxing

the pitcher by uttering the word "no-hitter." [11]They claim that bats have only so many hits in them and will not let other players borrow them. [12]After two strikes, they stay with the bat they have, convinced that it is the wrong time to make a change.

[13]The one superstition baseball players have not recently invoked is the notion that passing a hay wagon on the way to the game brings good luck.

> For additional exercises in subject-verb agreement with singulars, see Chapter 14.

PROOFREADING STRATEGIES

1. What to look for: errors in verb endings.
   a. the omission of **s** (or **es**)
   b. misspelling of the ending
2. How to look for them: locate *all* singular subjects and their verbs.
   a. look for singular nouns (often signaled by **a/an**) and for **he/she/it**
   b. find the verbs of those subjects by looking for words that follow
   or c. find the verb and locate the subject by asking **who** or **what**
   d. look for unusual endings as noted in HOW TO COPE sections
3. How to correct them: add **s** (or **es**) endings and check dictionary or (this is more difficult because of consistency problems; see Chapter 21) make the subject plural.

Choose one of the PROOFREADING exercises. Work until you locate and correct all errors in the use of *s* (or *es*) verb endings. To demonstrate your mastery, try WRITING ASSIGNMENT 2.

PRACTICING PROOFREADING 1

Of the 10 singular verbs that require an **s** (or **es**) ending, 3 are incorrect. Locate the errors by matching each verb with its subject and then make the corrections.

THE DEAD GIVE EVIDENCE

[1]In Hong Kong, a policeman die of six gunshot wounds—behind a door locked from the inside. [2]Is it a case of suicide? [3]A young woman survives a fire in her home but suddenly die two weeks later of a liver ailment. [4]Is there a connection? [5]In North Dakota a man dies in a hotel

sauna. [6]A week later, another man dies in the same sauna. [7]Is it a coincidence or is the sauna somehow responsible? [8]William Eckert answers such questions. [9]He runs a research center called INFORM out of his house in Wichita. [10]Whenever a coroner is stumped by a death, he turns to Dr. Eckert, a crime-solving pathologist. [11]Dr. Eckert was able to prove that a person could stay alive long enough to pump six slugs into himself. [12]He found that a chemical used in firefighting cause liver problems in some instances. [13]After making inquiries in Finland, where nearly every house possesses a sauna, he was able to suggest that authorities in North Dakota should look for carbon monoxide poisoning. [14]Sure enough, a defective hot-box in the sauna's heater turned out to have been responsible for the two deaths.

PRACTICING PROOFREADING 2

Of the 23 verbs in the third person singular, 17 require an **s** ending. By matching verbs with their subjects, locate and correct the 5 errors.

MOVIE MENUS

[1]Movies do not always offer gourmet fare, but they do provide "tasty" moments for hungry viewers.

[2]A famous main dish in film history is the steak Faye Dunaway forces her adopted daughter to eat in <u>Mommy Dearest</u>. [3]Side dishes are, however, more memorable. [4]A dish of spaghetti serves as the final meal for Sterling Hayden in <u>The Godfather</u> and becomes a resting place for a drugged Malcolm McDowell in <u>A Clockwork Orange</u>. [5]Using piles of mashed potatoes, Richard Dreyfuss recreate the aliens' landing site in <u>Close Encounters of the Third Kind</u>, and Ann-Margaret wallows in baked beans in Ken Russell's <u>Tommy</u>. [6]But the hero of side dishes is Jack Nicholson, in <u>Five Easy Pieces</u>. [7]He manages to have the last word with a waitress who is giving him a hard time when he ask for a simple order of toast.

[8]As for movie desserts, who can forget the surprise Mickey Rourke puts in a box of popcorn in <u>Diner</u>? [9]In <u>Women in Love</u>, Alan Bates pro-

vides an erotic demonstration of how to eat a fig. [10]Tommy Lee Jones displays a bit more chivalry when he eat a pie Sissy Spacek had baked with salt instead of sugar in Coal Miner's Daughter. [11]In the 1980 hit, Caddyshack, Bill Murray retrieves a candy bar from a swimming pool and calmly eats it while people stare in horror. [12]Murray at least knows exactly what he is biting into. [13]Tom Cruise, in Risky Business, insists he is fully in control, but fail to realize his ice cream is melting all over his hand.

[14]Sometimes more eating seem to be taking place on screen than in theaters.

WRITING ASSIGNMENT 2: *s* (or *es*) endings on verbs

Write a long paragraph on one of the following topics, according to your instructor's specifications for organization and development. Then proofread for errors in subject-verb agreement and singular (*s* or *es*) endings, using the strategies you have been practicing.

a. Think of someone you know in a job or profession. What are some things he/she does that seem unusual or interesting?

b. Summarize the plot of a book, movie, or TV show, using the present tense throughout. Mention individual characters.

c. If you use a word processor, discuss some of the functions your particular program has. If you use a typewriter, describe any peculiarities it has.

d. Explain the rules of a game: chess, football, baseball, poker, bridge, soccer. Make clear what each player does during the game.

e. Choose a concept from one of your other courses—biology, economics, psychology, electrical technology—and explain it. (What is "fission," for example, or the "GNP," or "depression," or a "transformer"?)

Chapter 9

VERB AGREEMENT WITH PLURAL SUBJECTS

ATTENTION FOCUSING: verb agreement with plural subjects*

a. Find and circle the subject of each **verb** by asking **who** or **what** with the underlined verbs.

b. Write each **plural** subject-verb pair alongside.

SHELTER (FROM RALPH ELLISON'S INVISIBLE MAN)

1. (We) live in a home that is a hole in the ground. _____We + live_____

2. But we do not live in the cold or the dark of graves. _____

3. We live in warm holes. _____

4. Bears retire to their holes for winter. _____

5. They remain comfortable until spring. _____

6. Then they stroll out like Easter chicks, breaking from their shells. _____

7. Being invisible does not make them dead. _____

8. Living in holes does not make them dead either. _____

9. Like bears, we <u>hibernate</u> in
    a state of suspended
    animation.   _____

10. But we <u>have</u> light, giving
    us form.   _____

WRITING ASSIGNMENT 1: verb agreement with plural subjects

Write a short paragraph using one of the topics below. Make sure your present tense verbs agree with the plural subjects.

a. Describe how things work—use plurals: flush toilets, typewriters, tapes.
b. Evaluate or describe the responsibilities of public officials, discussing them as members of a group: senators, mayors, judges, board members.
c. Provide a job description of employees at your school: secretaries, deans, cafeteria workers, security personnel, lab instructors, elevator operators.

If you have made no errors in agreement using plural verbs and subjects, try PRACTICING PROOFREADING 1 before asking your instructor to let you go on to another chapter. If you did make errors, review the discussion on plurals on p. 64–65, and choose a REWRITING EXERCISE.

REWRITING EXERCISE 1: verb agreement with plural subjects*

Make the following changes to use verbs with plural subjects:

a. Write the plural forms of the nouns and pronouns that appear in **boldface** in the space above each line.
b. Make their verbs agree, writing each next to its noun or pronoun.
c. Make the starred (*) words agree with your new plural subjects.

SWORDS, CUPS, CURRENCY, AND CLOVER

[1]The four suits or pictures on cards represent various social classes of the Renaissance period when they were designed and printed.

[2]In France and Italy, **the spade** represents the nobility. [3]In Spain and Portugal, **it** stands for the military. [4]The actual item named in the spade suits of these European countries is the sword. [5]The Spanish word for sword–<u>espada</u>—gives us the English word "spade". [6]Thus, **a spade** has nothing to do with *a shovel.

[7]**A heart** symbolizes the clergy. [8]The clergy was considered a most important part of the medieval community. [9]But **a heart** transforms **itself** into *a cup in Italy, Spain, and Portugal, possibly because **it** represents faith.

[10]**The diamond** in cards evokes the *precious gem, but **it** refers instead to the diamond-shaped tiles on the floors of commodity exchanges, where merchants met with farmers and tradespeople. [11]In Italy, Portugal, and Spain, **a diamond** has been replaced by the national currency.

[12]**The club** looks less like *a club and more like clover. [13]Because the Spanish printed sticks or batons for this suit, the idea remains in the name. [14]**The club** loses out to clover, however, in the picture, thanks to the French, who printed clover—the symbol for peasants—on their cards.

REWRITING EXERCISE 2: verb agreement with plural subjects

Copy the paragraph below, making the following changes:

a. Change **the typical female** or **woman** (and any pronouns referring to her) to the plural **females** or **women** (or to plural pronouns).
b. Eliminate, where necessary, the article **a/an.**
c. Make all appropriate verbs agree with the new plural subject.

ONLY A WOMAN KNOWS FOR SURE

[1]According to a new University of Pennsylvania study, females are better than males at differentiating among odors. [2]In fact, according to the study, the typical female performs better on smell tests whether she is white or black, American, Japanese, or Korean. [3]Specifically, a Korean female has the most sensitive olfactory ability. [4]An American white female ties for second with an American black female. [5]The test itself is multiple choice. [6]A woman receives various scratch-and-sniff pads. [7]She sniffs. [8]She then chooses among answers such as, "This odor smells most like (a) chocolate, (b) banana, (c) onion, or (d) fruit punch." [9]Newspaper accounts of the study do not make clear whether a woman had determined beforehand what the odor actually was. [10]In previous tests, a woman was not used.

Proofread your rewritten essay by underlining the 9 **new** verbs agreeing with plural subjects. (One subject-verb pair is already plural.)

REWRITING EXERCISE 3: verb agreement with plural subjects

Copy the paragraph below, substituting the plural **children** for **a child.** Your new plural subject will force you to change the verbs and pronouns that refer to it. Starred words are explained after the essay.

IT'S NOT WHAT YOU EAT

[1]A child often *tries to control his or her eating habits. [2]Sometimes eating more and sometimes less, he or she operates under the belief that his or her weight depends on his or her own actions. [3]But, according to a study at the U. of Pennsylvania School of Medicine, parental advice and other environmental factors can influence only slightly what is already present. [4]What parents feed a child is less important than who the parents are, because a child inherits a tendency for body weight. [5]A child grows up thin or grows up obese regardless of his or her diet. [6]An adopted child matches the body weight of his or her biological parents rather than of his or her adoptive parents, according to researchers. [7]A thin child tends to have thin parents; an obese child probably has obese parents. [8]The study examined 540 Danish adults who had been adopted as children.

How to Cope with the Unexpected (1)

When the starred (*) word **tries** is made to agree with its plural subject **children**, it does not simply drop the **es;** it also transforms its **i** into **y** → **try.** Words ending in **y** change considerably when endings are added to them. See also Chapter 46.

PROOFREADING STRATEGIES

The errors most likely to occur in this area are failure to change inappropriate endings on verbs or incorrect matching of verb with subject.

1. What to look for: errors in verb endings.
   a. the presence of **s** (or **es**)
   b. the presence of **ed** or other indicators of the past

2. How to look for them: locate **all** plural subjects and their verbs.
   a. look for plural nouns (usually, **s** endings) and for **we/you/they**
   b. find the verbs of those subjects by looking for words that follow
or c. find the verb and, asking **who** or **what,** locate the subject, keeping in mind that intervening phrases do not contain subjects (see Chapter 11)
3. How to correct them: eliminate endings from present tense plural verbs, or (more difficult) make the subject singular.

Choose a PROOFREADING EXERCISE. If you can locate and correct all errors in the agreement of verbs with plural subjects, try WRITING ASSIGNMENT 2 to demonstrate your mastery. The PROOFREADING TEST on p. 80 contains errors in agreement with both singular and plural subjects.

PRACTICING PROOFREADING 1

Find the 12 plural subjects with their 12 verbs. Correct the 4 that do not agree.

WATER CLOCKS

[1]Working models demonstrate the ingenuity of ancient water clocks. [2]A Saxon clock from the ninth century uses a simple bowl with a hole in its bottom. [3]When set afloat in water, it sinks as it fills. [4]When it settles at the bottom, a set period of time has passed. [5]More complicated but equally accurate is a replica of the giant clock that once graced the east gate of the Great Mosque at Damascus. [6]At each "hour" of the day, two brass weights falls from the mouths of two falcons. [7]They lands in brazen cups where perforations sends the balls back to their original position. [8]Above the falcons, doors represent each hour of the day. [9]In front of each door is an unlighted lamp. [10]At each hour, the balls fall, a bell rings, and a doorway closes. [11]At night, all doors open. [12]As the balls fall, a lamp is lit. [13]By dawn, all lamps give off a red glow. [14]With the coming of daylight, lamps are extinguished, doors slides open, balls fall, and the cycle continues. [15]Of course, the replica does not require the full-time services of eleven men, as did the original.

PRACTICING PROOFREADING 2

Locate all 16 plural subjects and their verbs. Correct the 5 verbs that do not agree.

RECRUITING POINT SYSTEM

[1]Job applicants at Prudential and other insurance companies have to take a test. [2]Unless they score a minimum of 40 points, they are not even considered for a position. [3]Optimum candidates needs a score of 60 or higher. [4]The questions vary in point value.

[5]Candidates with nonworking spouses receive 10 points. [6]If they have working wives (or husbands), they are given 4 points. [7]Engaged applicants garners 2 points. [8]For work experience or college education, potential agents collect 8 points; for the two together, they accumulate a total of 10.

[9]Five points accrues to candidates over age 30, 6 for dress, and 7 for verbal skills. [10]If they possesses high motivation for money, they gain 10 points. [11]Previous track record, referrals, and scores on an aptitude test accounts for the additional 20 points.

[12]Obviously, Prudential believes that agents under a great deal of pressure work harder at selling insurance. [13]It prefers hiring an agent whose spouse does not work, providing him or her with greater financial motivation.

WRITING ASSIGNMENT 2: verb agreement with plural subjects

Write a long paragraph on one of the following topics, following your instructor's specifications for organization and development. Then proofread for errors in plural subject-verb agreement.

a. Discuss one positive or negative effect movies, books, plays, or concerts have had on you. Illustrate with specific examples.
b. Describe the function of certain pieces in games. For example: pawns, knights, bishops, rooks in chess, chips in poker, hearts in "Hearts."
c. Compare the responsibilities and pay of a specific type of blue-collar worker with those of a specific type of white-collar

worker—plumbers with lawyers, for example. Who are of greater service to society? Why?

d. Categorize certain types of people and analyze them by the label you have given them. For example: day and night people, people who tell jokes, sentimental people, athletes.

PROOFREADING TEST: agreement with singular and plural subjects

The essay below contains errors in subject-verb agreement in both singulars and plurals. Because one of the most important principles of proofreading is that you *look for only one error at a time*, proofread this essay twice, first looking for errors in the singular and second looking for errors in the plural. You may wish to review the PROOFREADING STRATEGIES for each attempt.

The essay contains five errors in subject-verb agreement. Two verbs do not agree with singular nouns and three with plural nouns.

KISSING RULES

[1]Jonathan Swift is said to have remarked, "Lord! I wonder what fool it was that first invented kissing." [2]Despite his caution, social kissing has become widespread, though the custom vary from country to country.

[3]In France, women kiss men on both cheeks, but men kiss women on their fingertips. [4]Italians kiss on the lips. [5]Russians also aim for each cheek. [6]Canadians seem to have developed kissing into an art form, conveying many subtle messages with the action. [7]Christopher Defoe, a former columnist for the <u>Vancouver Sun</u> and other newspapers, joke that certain kisses manages to convey the message, "George is leaving for Vancouver on Tuesday; drop by for tea." [8]Hostesses practice the art with particular skill. [9]They bestow very delicate kisses and expects equally light kisses in return so that their makeup remains undisturbed.

[10]A certain amount of social kissing has, of course, always existed. [11]As most children know, elderly aunts bestow kisses of a unique flavor and consistency. [12]Soccer players hug and kisses with great abandon after they have scored a goal. [13]Movie stars pucker up bravely while they hand over awards they would much rather be receiving. [14]Kissing, however, has become so common that a kissing cousin is probably a more distant relative than ever before.

Chapter **10**

PROBLEMS IN AGREEMENT WITH THE VERB *TO BE*

INTRODUCTION

As you read in Chapter 1, the verb signals the time of the action in a sentence. A change in the time of a sentence—for example, from the past to the present—will be indicated by a change in the form of the verb. Sometimes, however, the verb reacts not only to the time of the sentence, but also to the number of the subject (that is, whether the subject is plural or singular). In certain instances, when the subject changes from the singular to the plural, the verb must also change. Chapters 8 and 9 discussed this relationship between subject and verb in the present tense. This chapter will deal with the way the subject affects the forms of the verb **to be,** not only in the present, but also in the past tense.

Here is a summary of the various forms of the verb **to be:**

base or stem: **be**   present participle: **being**   past participle: **been**

	Singular	Plural
first person	present and past I am was	present and past we are were
second person	you are were	you are were
third person	he/she/it is was	they are were

Here are examples of each form in the **singular:**

	present tense	**past tense**
first person:	I **am** a U.S. citizen.	I **was** not born in the United States.
second person:	You **are** American born.	You **were** born in Iowa.
third person:	He **is** my father.	My dad **was** born in Hungary.
	She **is** my mother.	My mom **was** also born in Hungary.
	It **is** a small country.	Hungary **was** an Empire.

As you can see, the verb **to be** is affected by the change from the present to the past as well as by the change from the first person singular **I** to the second person singular **you.**

Here are examples of each form in the **plural:**

	present tense	**past tense**
first person:	We **are** speakers of English.	We **were** not fluent when we came.
second person:	You **are** native speakers.	You **were** babbling it as children.
third person:	They **are** quick learners.	They **were** surrounded by English.

The chapter continues with practice in the use of the verb **to be.** As the rules in agreement are the same as in Chapters 8 and 9, use those chapters for reference. Additional exercises using **to be** are available in the Instructor's Manual.

ATTENTION FOCUSING: agreement with forms of the verb *to be**

   a. Underline each form of the verb **to be.**
   b. Using the underlined verbs as a guide, locate and circle the subject of each form of **to be.**
   c. Indicate in the space provided if each subject-verb pair is singular or plural.

ROY'S FIRST LOSS (ADAPTED FROM BERNARD MALAMUD'S <u>THE NATURAL</u>)

   1. (Memo) was the first to roll the dice.   ————

   2. With Gus telling her to fade high, she was soon ahead $200.   ————

   3. Roy's first roll was snake eyes, and he sevened out right after.   ————

   4. There were three C notes for him to cover by the time Gus shot.   ————

   5. Gus made his point.   ————

6. He and Memo were waiting for Roy to cover the $300 dollar bill. _____

7. "Your credit is good," Gus told him. _____

8. In no time, the bookie was twelve hundred in on Roy. _____

9. Roy noticed that Gus's eyes were not working together. _____

10. While Gus's glass eye was on the dice, his good one was roaming. _____

How to Cope with the Unexpected (1)

In sentence 4, the subject of **were** is **three C notes**, located after, not before, the verb. See Chapter 12 for such "inverted" sentences.

REWRITING EXERCISE 1: agreement with *was**

Make the following changes to use **was:**

a. Asking **who?** before it, locate the subject of each **were.**
b. If the subject is **Tilley and King** (or a pronoun referring to them), make the subject singular by writing **Vesta Tilley** or one of the singular pronouns (she, her, herself) into the space above each line.
c. Change **were** to **was** and write it alongside your new singular subject.
d. Sentence 1 should read: **One of the most admired men in English theater was a woman.**
e. The second sentence contains a "subject complement." Make it singular.

VICTOR/VICTORIA

[1]Two of the most admired men in English theater were women. [2]During the Edwardian period, Vesta Tilley and Hetty King entertained millions and set the style for London's young men in the guise of male impersonators.

[3]Because their parents were connected to the stage, Tilley and King were involved in theater at an early age. [4]They appeared in male clothing, either out of curiosity or because a role called for it. [5]While they were determined to continue such roles, the men closest to them were not enthusiastic. [6]As a result, Tilley and King were forced to practice in secret.

[7]But they were so successful playing the roles of mischievous youths or brash, older men that father and husband had to accept them.

[8]During World War I, Tilley and King were in particular demand for their soldier and sailor routines. [9]They were convincing in reminding people of their sons, brother, or husbands at the front. [10]When playing roles, Tilley and King were often impish and arrogant but also quite likable. [11]The 1978 London Express thought, for example, that Tilley's exaggerations of male mannerisms were delightful.

[12]Tilley and King were celebrated to the end. [13]According to interviews, they felt it was their female perceptions which made their male impersonations successful.

REWRITING EXERCISE 2: agreement with *are/were*

Copy the essay below, substituting the plural **dwarfs** for **a dwarf** and the third person plural pronouns **they, their,** and **them** for **I** and **my.** This change means you will have to use **plural** forms of the verb **to be** with the new (plural) subjects. Underline the 7 changes to **are** and the 6 changes to **were.**

AT THE PRINCE'S COURT (ADAPTED FROM PAR LAGERKVIST'S THE DWARF)

[1]A dwarf is rarely more than 26 inches tall. [2]My hair is not black, but reddish, very stiff and thick. [3]I am beardless. [4]My eyebrows are not separated. [5]I am very strong, particularly when I am annoyed.

[6]I am not to be mocked and in return, I do not tell jokes or play tricks to make guests laugh. [7]I was not made to play with children either. [8]Rather, it was Angelica who forced herself on me. [9]I was being used by a child. [10]I was forced to go along with her. [11]Inside, I was raging with fury, but I dared not refuse. [12]I had to feed and dress her dolls and visit with her half-blind puppies and the cats in the rose garden. [13]I was so furious I hardly knew what I was doing.

[14]I am aware that sometimes I frighten people. [15]But the most frightening dwarf is the dwarf within them.

REWRITING EXERCISE 3: using *was*

Copy the paragraph below, rewriting it so that it is only about W. K. Kellogg. In 6 instances, you will have to change **were** to **was.** You will also have to change **they** to **he** where **they** refers to both Kelloggs. The starred (*) words are explained after the paragraph.

CORN FLAKE ROYALTY

[1]William Keith Kellogg and his brother, Dr. John Harvey Kellogg, were working at the Battle Creek Sanitarium in Michigan when they accidentally invented ready-to-eat cereals. [2]The Seventh Day Adventists *who ran the sanitarium were committed to a strictly vegetarian diet. [3]William and John Kellogg were always searching for ways to make the meatless food more tasty. [4]They were experimenting by baking boiled wheat and running it through a roller. [5]Expecting it to come out in sheets, they were surprised to discover individual flakes. [6]The discovery was welcomed by the patients, who continued to write for the flakes even after they were discharged. [7]W. K. Kellogg and his brother were thus able to start the Sanitas Food Company. [8]They were soon producing flakes made of rice, corn, and the original wheat. [9]The corn flakes were the least successful, until William and Harvey Kellogg made them less tough by adding malt and using only the "heart" of the grain. [10]By 1906, the Battle Creek Toasted Corn Flake Company was making thirty-three cases of dry cereal a day and competing with forty-two other cereal companies, one of them run by C. W. Post, a former patient at the clinic.

How to Cope with the Unexpected (2)

In the second sentence, words come between the verb **were** and the subject, **The Seventh Day Adventists.** See Chapter 11 for work with such intervening expressions.

PROOFREADING STRATEGIES

One common error with forms of **to be** is the incorrect matching of **is/was** with the pronoun **they.** Another is the use of **be** as a form of the verb, as in **He be here** or **They be here.** This use of **be** is a common dialectic variant but not considered standard English. In formal speech and writing, use **he was here** or **they were here.**

Proofreading for correctness in agreement with forms of **to be** is simply a matter of locating each example of the verb, asking **who** or **what** to locate its subject, and matching verb to subject. If the subject is not singular, **is/was** is being used incorrectly. If the subject is not plural, **are/were** is being used incorrectly.

To correct the error, change the verb to match the subject. You may, of course, wish to change the subject to match the verb, but changing the subject is more difficult if the sentence also contains pronouns and subject complements.

Continue with PRACTICING PROOFREADING. To demonstrate your mastery, choose a topic in the WRITING ASSIGNMENT.

PRACTICING PROOFREADING 1

Find the 18 examples of the verb **to be (is/was, are/were).** Correct the 5 errors in agreement.

HOOVER IN HOLLYWOOD

[1]FBI Director J. Edgar Hoover was influential with many entertainers. [2]Both Walt Disney and Elvis Presley were his admirers, willing to do him favors. [3]While Presley's offer to spy for the FBI was not taken seriously, Walt Disney's willingness to change the characters in two 1960s films was accepted.

[4]According to the <u>Arizona Republic</u>, Hoover was disturbed when the script of <u>Moon Pilot</u> (1962) identified two bumbling characters as FBI agents. [5]Always concerned with the image of his agents, Disney be agreeable, but in film reviews, the agents was still described as working for the FBI. [6]When Disney filmed <u>That Darn Cat</u> (1964) he agreed to portray the FBI in a "favorable light," according to a memo he sent to Hoover. [7]His task was not easy, since the film was about the need of the FBI to enlist a cat in its efforts to solve a bank robbery and were written by Mildred Gordon and her husband, Gordon Gordon, a former FBI agent.

[8]Presley was visiting President Nixon sometime in 1970, when he

entered FBI offices. [9]In an earlier letter to the FBI, he had declared that Hoover was "the greatest living American." [10]He had also suggested that the Beatles' "filthy" appearance and "suggestive" music created problems for young people. [11]While he was at the FBI, Presley explained why he was likely to make a good spy. [12]He also wanted the code name "Colonel Joe Burrows of Memphis." [13]Presley were not allowed in to meet Hoover and, of course, was never accepted as an agent.

[14]The Presley story was told by subsequent director Thomas Bishop, and the Disney details was obtained from the FBI through a Freedom of Information request.

PROOFREADING TEST: agreement with singular and plural forms of *to be*

The essay below contains errors in subject-verb agreement in both the singular and plural forms of the verb **to be.** Because one of the most important principles of proofreading is that you look for only one error at a time, proofread this essay twice, first looking for errors with the singular forms **(is/was),** and second for errors with the plural forms **(are/were).**

The essay contains 20 examples of the verb **to be;** 8 are not in agreement.

WHY YOU MUST HAVE BEEN A BEAUTIFUL BABY

[1]When people are shown pictures of baby animals, they have no difficulty deciding which creatures is "cute" and which ugly or unattractive. [2]Scientists have determined that such choices are not accidental. [3]Certain features are seen as more cute because they is more like the features of human babies.

[4]Human babies are all alike in a number of ways. [5]Their heads are large and round. [6]Their bodies are soft. [7]Their eyes is big and their noses small, at least in the sense that they do not stick out too far. [8]Finally, as they move, they is generally playful and a bit clumsy. [9]Scientists were surprised to find that animal babies who shared these characteristics were thought to be cute and in need of protection by both animal and human adults.

¹⁰A baby animal that shares these characteristics are the rabbit. ¹¹The adult rabbit's snout is long and its eyes almond shaped, but when it is born, it has a rounded head shape, a large forehead, and large, round eyes. ¹²The panda bear retains these features into adulthood. ¹³As a result, most humans is tempted to hug or "baby" even the giant panda. ¹⁴Because they wanted him to look more lovable, Disney cartoonists redesigned Mickey Mouse. ¹⁵At first, Mickey looked like a mouse. ¹⁶His forehead was low, his eyes narrow, his snout long, and his body hard. ¹⁷The cartoonists was successful in making him more lovable by making him look more like a baby. ¹⁸His head became larger, his eyes more round, and his body softer.

¹⁹"Cuteness" in infants, both human and animal, is important because it signals the parent that the creatures be in need of special care.

WRITING ASSIGNMENT: agreement with *are/were*

Write a long paragraph on one of the following topics, according to your instructor's specifications for organization and development. Proofread for errors in agreement with the forms of the verb **to be**.

a. Describe the appeal of two people who were once part of a comedy or acting team. Talk about them as both individuals and as a unit: **Laurel and Hardy were . . .** , as well as **Stan Laurel was . . .** ,

b. Write a brief statement about dancers, politicians, soldiers, farmers, writers, or immigrants of another era. Mention some specific individuals.

c. Write about the accomplishments of an ethnic group of your choice. Write about the group in the plural, as Hungarians, Mexicans, or Vietnamese, as well as about individuals: **a Hungarian was . . . .**

d. Describe how a clerk in a store, an official at school, or a civil servant in an office has treated you recently. Use **was.** Is this typical of the people in this establishment? Use **are.**

Chapter **11**

INTERVENING ELEMENTS

INTRODUCTION

As you learned in Chapter 1, you can find the verb by changing the time of a sentence. The word that changes is the verb. To find the subject, you ask **who** or **what** before the verb.

This is an effective method for locating the verb and its subject, particularly when the subject is right next to the verb. But other words often come between the subject and the verb. When the subject and verb are separated by such an **intervening element** or expression, the subject might be more difficult to locate. One of the words in the intervening phrase might appear to be the subject. When this "false" subject is singular and the verb plural or plural when the verb is singular, errors in subject-verb agreement are likely.

You need to know just one principle about subject-verb agreement when it involves an intervening phrase:

A phrase inserted between the subject and the verb does not alter the agreement of the subject and verb.

The shepherd guards his flock.

The verb: **guards**   Ask: "Who guards?"   The subject: The shepherd.

The shepherd on the hillsides guards his flock.

In the sentence above, the phrase **on the hillsides** contains a plural noun, but it is not the subject of the sentence; the one who guards the flock—the subject—is still the singular noun **shepherd.** In other words, it does not matter if the intervening element contains singular or plural words. The main verb of the sentence must still agree with the main subject, not with a word in the intervening phrase.

The adventures were exciting.

| The verb: **were** | Ask: "What were excit-ing?" | The subject: adventures |

The plural subject **adventures** agrees with the plural verb **were.** Consider the same subject and verb when they are separated by an intervening phrase:

The adventures **of the seven samurai** were exciting.

Even if you were not sure of the subject of the plural verb **were,** you would have no problem in agreement since **adventures** and **seven samurai** are both plural. An apparent problem arises when the intervening phrase is singular:

The adventures **of Mr. Sherlock Holmes** were exciting.

In this sentence, the intervening phrase **of Mr. Sherlock Holmes** is singular. However, as far as the agreement between subject and verb is concerned, there is no change; the plural subject **adventures** still agrees with the plural verb **were.**

To avoid making errors in subject-verb agreement, you must recognize the presence of intervening phrases.

TYPES OF INTERVENING EXPRESSIONS

1. The most common intervening expression is a **prepositional phrase,** easily recognizable because it begins with a **preposition** (or relation word. These prepositions are used most frequently:

about	above	around	at		before	behind	beside	between	by
during	for	from	in		inside	into	next to	of	off
on	onto	over	through		to	toward	under	without	with

2. Other intervening expressions might begin with a **relative pronoun—who, that, where, which.** These are called relative clauses. You must maintain agreement *within* these clauses between the relative pronoun and the verb, but that internal agreement does not affect the agreement of the main verb and the subject.

The Buffalo Bill **who used to ride a silver stallion** is dead.

The main verb is the third-person singular form of to be: **is.** Its subject is the singular **Buffalo Bill.** The word **stallion** is part of the relative clause and has no bearing on the agreement of **Buffalo Bill** and **is.** This agreement remains as it is even when the intervening clause contains a plural noun:

The Buffalo Bill **who used to ride silver stallions** is dead.

3. Some intervening expressions are set off by commas on either side.

Thomas More, **a man for all seasons**, was sentenced to death by Henry VIII.

The verb: **was**   The subject: **Thomas More**

PRACTICE: locating the subject in the presence of intervening phrases

Try either the singular verb **was** or the plural **were** with the expressions below and determine the subject in each, writing subject and verb in the correct column. If you seem to have an unusually long subject, try lifting a part (phrase or clause) out of it. The intervening expression gives more detail about the subject; it does not contain it.

singulars		plurals
a. *the merchant was*	the merchant of Venice	_____
b. _____	an interview with the Rolling Stones	_____
c. _____	the streets of San Francisco	*streets were*
d. _____	the decline of rhythm and blues	_____
e. _____	bombing casualties in Spain	_____
f. _____	the relationship between music and food	_____
g. _____	a walk on the wild side	_____
h. _____	the Museum of Fine Arts	_____
i. _____	a man, who is a being without feathers	_____
j. _____	the brothers who came into Egypt	_____
k. _____	a book that had no readers	_____

ATTENTION FOCUSING: intervening phrases between singulars*

a. Ask **who** or **what** before the underlined main verb in each sentence; then locate and circle the subject.
b. Cross out the phrase that comes between each subject-verb pair.
c. Indicate with **S** (for singular) or **P** (for plural) the number of each subject and verb pair.

1. (Research) by nursing professor <u>indicates</u> that pregnant women suffer fewer health problems going to work than staying home. _____

2. A job that is prestigious <u>contributes</u> to their mental health. _____

3. The professors at the University of Washington <u>think</u> working also helps pregnant women stay physically more fit. _____

4. Women who stay at home <u>do</u> have fewer leg cramps. _____

5. Fewer cases of morning sickness <u>were</u> reported by working women. _____

6. In addition, a woman in a self-fulfilling and satisfying job <u>suffers</u> fewer backaches. _____

7. Appetite loss for working women <u>occurs</u> less frequently as well. _____

8. In another health note, two health organizations, in a joint statement, <u>have</u> asked that choking victims should not be hit on the back. _____

9. Their former recommendation of four sharp blows <u>was</u> found to cause a piece of food to become more firmly lodged. _____

10. The first step in helping a choking victim <u>should</u> consist of reaching around him or her and squeezing his or her abdomen. _____

11. The action, in quick order, <u>forces</u> air through his or her windpipe, clearing the airway. _____

WRITING ASSIGNMENT 1: intervening phrases

Use the topics below to write a short paragraph that contains intervening elements (expressions that interrupt the subject and verb).

a. Describe items in your house, naming the surfaces on which one or more things rest by their location (for example, **The books on the shelf** or **The chair in the kitchen**, followed by a verb).

b. Write about what is typical or expected in TV/movies/plays, using the phrase **in the** or **of the**, as in **The hero of the <u>Rocky</u> films** or **Many characters in Westerns**.

> If you have made no agreement errors in the use of intervening phrases, try PRACTICING PROOFREADING 1 before asking your instructor to send you on to another chapter. If you did make some errors, reread the Introduction to INTERVENING ELEMENTS before moving to REWRITING.

REWRITING EXERCISE 1: intervening phrases between singulars*

a. Mark each underlined subject-verb pair as either singular **(S)** or plural **(P)**.

b. Rewrite the essay, inserting the phrases in boldface between subject and verb.

c. Mark in your rewritten essay if the subject-verb pairs are **(S)** or **(P).**

d. Starred (*) words are explained after the essay.

THE EGG, BEFORE IT IS AN OMELET

[1]Whatever its nutritional value, the egg has always been an important symbol.

[2]In pagan times it stood for fertility and the rebirth of spring. [3]**In folk medicine and witchcraft,** its wide <u>use was</u> due to the belief that it had mystic healing powers. [4]Specifically, it was thought to cure sterility. [5]**In many non-Christian societies** <u>friends give</u> it as a gift today, as a sign of good will.

[6]**Of the many tales associating the egg with Christianity,** <u>one concerns</u> Mary Magdalene. [7]According to the story, she was holding some eggs when she was told that Christ had risen from the dead. [8]If the tidings were true, she said, the eggs should turn red, representing his blood and suffering on the cross. [9]The legend states that the eggs did turn red. [10]**In Eastern Orthodox Christian communities,** <u>the Easter egg is</u> usually dyed red, as a result.

[11]*__On decorated Easter eggs,__ <u>the mark or pattern contains</u> additional symbolism. [12]**Of the earliest designs,** the most popular <u>one was</u> a dot or a circle. [13]**In the form of clusters,** <u>the markings represent</u> the tears of the Virgin Mary. [14]Other designs include nature symbols, animals, and representations of the sun and stars.

How to Cope with the Unexpected (1)

The subject in the starred (*) sentence is **the mark or pattern.** Though there seem to be two subjects, the **or** between the nouns makes the subject singular. For more work with this situation, see Chapter 13.

REWRITING EXERCISE 2: intervening phrases between plurals

Make the following changes in the essay on p. 94:

a. Underline the verb and circle the subject in each sentence.

b. Put brackets around the 10 intervening phrases.

> **c.** Change the 8 singular subjects to the plural, writing each in the space above the lines. As a result, you will have to change the verbs of these subjects. Write the new verbs next to their subjects.

SMELL AND STRESS

[1]What magical substance lowers blood pressure, increases alertness, and alleviates depression? [2]Our nose knows the answer, according to Brain Mind Bulletin. [3]The spokesman for International Flavors and Fragrances predicts that fragrances will be used to affect brain function vital to our well-being. [4]The ancient art of perfume making is being enhanced with science to create a "biology of fragrances."

[5]The intimate link between smell and the autonomic nervous system makes odor an ideal instrument for stress reduction. [6]The response of individuals to danger is always affected by the sense of smell, influencing the "flight-or-fight response."

[7]The possibility of using odors to treat schizophrenia is also being explored. [8]Receptors for smell provide direct connections with several regions of the limbic system. [9]These regions are thought to be involved in the disorder. [10]Examples of patients with olfactory hallucinations have been well documented. [11]A patient with a diagnosis of schizophrenia often complains of body odor. [12]A doctor with a sensitive nose is sometimes able to identify such patients by a characteristic odor.

[13]The person behind the research into smells hopes that new, relaxing fragrances will eventually be used on a daily basis to keep people fit emotionally and physically. [14]He considers this method of relieving anxiety to be safer than alcohol or drugs and closer to the use of music and meditation.

REWRITING EXERCISE 3: intervening phrases between singulars

Rewrite the essay, leaving out all the intervening phrases. Decide if this omission forces you to make any changes in subject-verb agreement.

LET ME COUNT THE NAMES

[1]Understanding ingredients on a label requires a knowledge of both reading and math skills. [2]Because the same ingredient can be called by different names, a shopper has to be able to figure out what the meaning of a disguised item is before adding up the totals. [3]Only then will he or she have an accurate sense of contents. [4]For example, the label on a breakfast cereal usually lists "wheat" as the first item and "sugar" as the second. [5]The shopper who pays little attention to the label thinks that the first item listed is also the largest quantity contained in the package. [6]A closer look at the boxtop informs the shopper that the third and fourth items listed are "corn syrup" and "honey." [7]Because these are also sweeteners by other names, the package may contain more sweets than any other ingredient. [8]Similarly, the typical processed food in the "deli" section is usually heavy with fat. [9]But "fat" is usually disguised under "oil." [10]In addition, "oil" is also called "hydrogenated shortening," "butter," "lard," "animal fat," and "coconut oil." [11]However, the ingredient behind the "oily" name is still "fat," a substance of very little nutritional value.

REWRITING EXERCISE 4: intervening phrases between plurals

Copy the essay below, making the following changes:

a.   Locate and circle the subject of each underlined verb.
b.   Put brackets around the 10 phrases that come between a subject and verb.
c.   Change the 9 singular subjects to the plural.
d.   Make the verbs agree with the new subjects.

STRANGE LAWS

[1]No state in the United States <u>is</u> exempt from loony legislation. [2]Even if initially well intentioned, strange laws are better off repealed or forgotten.

[3]A set of these laws <u>was</u> designed to protect animals. [4]In Lawrence, Kansas, bees in a hat <u>are</u> forbidden on the city streets. [5]A school bus in Florida <u>is</u> prohibited from transporting livestock. [6]An individual annoy-

ing squirrels in Topeka, Kansas, <u>is</u> violating the law. [7]A pigeon in flight over the rooftops of Bayonne, New Jersey, <u>has</u> to be licensed. [8]A rat in Denver <u>is</u> protected by law from mistreatment.

[9]Some ridiculous laws are intended to protect people from each other as well as themselves. [10]In Seattle, a concealed weapon of six feet or longer <u>is</u> illegal on city streets. [11]A slumlord of the meanest tenements <u>is</u> safe from bites in Rumford, Maine. [12]And in New York State there is a law available for the protection of true "deadbeats." [13]A person trying to collect a debt from a dead man <u>is</u> liable to be charged with a misdemeanor.

REWRITING EXERCISE 5: intervening phrases between plurals

Copy the entire essay, rewriting it in the present tense. Begin with **Today, foreign women traveling in Saudi Arabia have . . . ,** and continue in the *present* tense, paying careful attention to subject-verb agreement.

THE VEIL IN SAUDI ARABIA

[1]Ten years ago, foreign women in Saudi Arabia had to accommodate themselves to the strict Moslem laws of the country regarding women.

[2]They had to learn to make do without hotel staff in matters of personal needs. [3]For example, they had to pack their own manicuring and hairdressing materials because even the most lavish hotels in Riyadh, the capital, provided only barbershops. [4]Hairdressing salons were unavailable because males were not allowed to attend women, and the government forbade Saudi women from being employed in public places.

[5]In fact, the customs in the Islamic state barred a female from any "mixed" environment. [6]When she appeared at restaurants with her husband or with other women, they ate at a specially partitioned area. [7]Similarly, the coffee shops at the Al Salam Meridien in Jeddah contained a special alcove for the foreign stewardesses, and the pool saunas in many of the bustling hotels were available only to men.

[8]Female travelers in this city often filled with visitors from the West

had to modify their appearance as well. [9]Moslem women in Saudi Arabia wore the <u>abaya</u>, a neck-to-ankle-to-wrist opaque black cloak, and matching head covering. [10]Western women were also asked to dress in high neck, long sleeve, ankle-length skirts and to wear a hat. [11]Women in pants were simply not allowed in public.

PROOFREADING STRATEGIES

1. Look for intervening phrases, particularly constructions *you* use:
   a. prepositional phrases are signaled by prepositions; **one of the** is very common, as are **about, for, from, in, on, to, with**
   b. they can be shifted to another part of the sentence
   c. **who, that, which** signal relative clauses
   d. they are sometimes set off by commas on either side
2. Determine if subject-verb agreement is correct:
   a. locate the verb (singulars, in the present, end in **s** or **es**)
   b. locate the subject (ask **who** or **what** with verb)
   c. get the subject and verb next to each other by blocking out intervening phrases
3. Correct any errors in agreement:
   a. using the subject as your guide, make verbs agree with the subject (which is easier than trying to make subjects agree with verb)
   b. if you decide to leave the verb alone and make your subject agree with it, make sure that pronouns and subject complements also agree

> Choose one of the PROOFREADING exercises. Work until you complete one in which you have located and corrected all agreement errors involving intervening phrases. To demonstrate your mastery, choose a topic from WRITING ASSIGNMENT 2 at the end of the chapter.

PRACTICING PROOFREADING 1

Bracket the 8 intervening phrases, drawing a line between the subject and verb in those sentences. Correct the 3 errors in verb number.

WORLD WITHOUT SUN

[1]Geologists once believed that the bottom of the Pacific Ocean is a cold, dark, lifeless place. [2]After all, the seafloor is often miles from sunlight. [3]A lack of sunlight means extremely cold temperatures and little chance for life. [4]But a descent to the Pacific Ocean's depths have forced

scientists to revise their notions. [5]The passengers of <u>Alvin</u>, a tiny submarine designed for deep sea dives, found an oasis crowded with life at the Galapagos Rift, 8,500 feet down. [6]Warm water from vents in the ocean's floor gush upward in funnels. [7]And something in the warm torrents provide food for a large variety of strange creatures. [8]Blood-red worms of lengths up to 12 feet sway alongside creatures shaped like dandelions. [9]Clouds of black particles shoot up from the ocean floor, feeding long, pinkish whitefish. [10]There are also mussels, smooth-shelled clams, and lobsterlike clams.

PRACTICING PROOFREADING 2

Bracket the 8 intervening phrases, circling the subject and verb in sentences containing the phrase. Correct the 4 errors in verb number.

LOST WORLDS

[1]One of the world's most amazing mysteries is the lost civilization on Easter Island. [2]Dutch explorers, landing there on Easter Sunday in 1722, was amazed to discover hundreds of odd figures. [3]Some of them is small, standing only about three feet. [4]Others, with big heads and hatlike topknots, are huge. [5]According to legend, they were carved from immense blocks by people who came to settle on the island. [6]But they suddenly ceased carving in the seventeenth century. [7]Early explorers to the island were baffled to find unfinished figures and abandoned stone tools. [8]It seemed as if the carvers had simply stopped in the middle without ever resuming their work. [9]Statues of soft volcanic rock wears away. [10]Those that are carved of harder stone stares patiently inland, unmarked by time. [11]The mystery of these figures is only heightened by the presence of similar statues in the mountains of Columbia, South America.

PRACTICING PROOFREADING 3

Bracket the 10 intervening phrases, circling the subject and verb in the sentences that contain them. Correct the 4 errors in agreement.

CATACOMBS

[1]Emperor Nero's persecution of Christians forced them to gather in the catacombs of Rome for worship. [2]They felt safe from the authorities in those burial grounds. [3]In the middle of the third century, even the catacombs became unsafe, forcing Christians to dig secret entrances and tunnels. [4]When the persecution finally ceased, the catacombs came to be treated as holy shrines by pilgrims. [5]Their existence was forgotten until accidentally rediscovered in 1578.

[6]Excavations of the catacombs have provided a great deal of information about them. [7]Passages, at depths of 10 to 13 feet, usually runs straight. [8]Their width is sufficient for the passage of a bier only if it is carried by two gravediggers walking single file. [9]The stairs that lead deeper down sometimes go 40 feet underground. [10]If the passages were in a straight line, they would be longer than the Italian peninsula.

[11]Many of the catacombs have two or more levels. [12]The catacomb of San Sebastian has four. [13]The galleries at the end of passages branch off in all directions. [14]Niches for the dead was cut along the walls of these galleries. [15]The original partitions of tile or stone has fallen. [16]Present-day visitors to the typical catacomb has to walk between rows of skeletons.

WRITING ASSIGNMENT 2: intervening phrases

Write a long paragraph on one of the topics, following your instructor's specifications for organization and development. Proofread for errors in subject-verb agreement.

a. Argue how much better or worse off employees are depending on where they are employed. Identify workers by their employers: **engineers at General Electric; a waiter at the Ground Round; ushers for Cinema National.**
b. Discuss one difference in the treatment faced by veterans returning from different wars. Use the war in a prepositional phrase: **veterans from Korea; wounded men from World War II; someone returning from Vietnam.**
c. Work your way around your city, describing some streets. Identify them by their relation to other streets or by some landmark. For ex-

ample, write **the street near the streetlights** or **the house next to the car dealerships.**

d. Talk about some sports teams, identifying them by their nicknames, followed by the place where they play: **the Eagles from Boston College,** for example.

e. Compare two places where you have lived, mentioning the streets, neighbors, friends, weather conditions. Whenever you make one of these items your subject, follow it with **of the** or **in the** and the name of the place.

f. Compare the people/dishes at two meals, identifying them with an intervening phrase. **(The food at Thanksgiving; My parents during Seder.)**

g. Write how differently a person behaves alone or as part of a couple. Follow names with a **from** phrase, such as **Jack and Jill from a small town in Maine . . .** or **Bill from Arizona . . .** before continuing the sentence.

PROOFREADING TEST: intervening phrases between singulars and plurals

The essay below contains errors in subject-verb agreement in those sentences that contain intervening phrases. Because one of the most important principles of proofreading is that you *look for only one error at a time,* proofread this essay twice, first looking for errors in the singular and second looking for errors in the plural. You may wish to review the PROOFREADING STRATEGIES.

The essay contains 4 errors in subject-verb agreement. Two verbs do not agree with singular nouns and 2 with plural nouns. Proofread by looking for (and bracketing) sentences that contain intervening phrases. There are 8 such sentences.

AT THE END OF THE RAINBOW, CREDIT CARDS

[1]The color of credit cards is being used to identify users. [2]The gold of American Express, Mastercard, and Visa announce that the owner is a preferred customer. [3]A green Air Travel Card indicates that its bearer has the power to charge flights anywhere in the world, while a red card limits its owner to charging privileges within North America. [4]But one of New York's most status-conscious stores have devised a much more elaborate color scheme. [5]Bloomingdale's uses five different colored charge cards to inform its sales staff of a customer's standing.

[6]Blue is the least important color in Bloomingdale's system. [7]This is

the card color it issues to its own employees. [8]Regular customers of Bloomingdale's receives yellow cards. [9]The basic yellow is similar to cards from other department stores, allowing payment to be spread out and charging a percentage. [10]The red card in "Bloomie's" rainbow gives customers free interest for three months. [11]Its most likely owners are people with a habit of making large purchases. [12]The silver card is good for unlimited spending, but the owners of a silver card has to make all payments within 30 days. [13]The highest color in the pecking order is gold. [14]Its payment options do not differ from those of a yellow, but the gold is reserved for the use of the biggest spenders.

[15]Although this color scheme may sound confusing to most, people under the influence of status symbols have no difficulty telling them apart.

Chapter **12**

VERB BEFORE SUBJECT

INTRODUCTION

The typical sentence in English follows "normal word order." You usually name the subject (who or what does an action), before you name the verb (the action). The order makes it easy to establish agreement between subject and verb: to make sure that both subject and verb are singular or that they are both plural. Establishing agreement between subject and verb is more difficult when the sentence follows "inverted word order" and the verb appears first. You have to know the number of the subject before deciding on the number of the verb, but the verb appears first!

Here are several examples of sentences where the verb appears before the subject:

a. sentences with **here** or **there** before the verb

             (v)   (s)
singular: Here is your glass slipper.

             (v)   (s)
plural: Here are your glass slippers.

b. questions that begin with **what, where, when, which, who,** and **why**

             (v)   (s)
singular: Who was the masked man?

             (v)   (s)
plural: Who were the masked men?

c. questions that use helping verbs

singular: **am/is/was, has/had, does/did**
plural: **are/were, have/had, do/did**

            (v)   (s)
singular: Is New York still in the league?

            (v)   (s)
plural: Are the Giants still in the league?

NOTE: In questions, the different parts of the complete verb often surround the subject.

> (v)   (s)   (v)
> Does she know the way to San José?
> (v) (s)   (v)
> Do they know the way to San José?

d.   (rare) sentences that seek to emphasize the verb
>   (v)   (s)
> *singular:* Finally comes the tale of woe.
>   (v)   (s)
> *plural:* Finally come the tales of woe.

Special Note About *there is/there are*

Although you should learn to recognize all four categories of inverted sentences in which the verb comes before the subject, you should look for the most common situation first: **there** with **is/was** or **there** with **are/were.**

By the time you have completed Chapter 12, you will certainly be able to identify the verb and subject and correct any agreement errors in **there is/there are** sentences. But these sentences—even when corrected—are wordy. Because the inversion also complicates subject-verb agreement, many writers try to avoid **there is/there are** altogether, writing, for example, **Three sisters lived in the house** instead of **There were three sisters living in the house.**

In REWRITING EXERCISE 3, you will be able to practice avoiding the use of **there is/there are** altogether. You will also discover that you may also be able to correct errors in agreement better when you have rewritten the sentence.

> The chapter continues with practice in agreement when some of the sentences are inverted. The general rules of agreement were discussed in Chapter 8 (singulars) and 9 (plurals), so use them for reference. Additional exercises containing inverted sentences are available in the Instructor's Manual.

ATTENTION FOCUSING: verb before subject*

a.   Locate and circle the subject of each underlined verb.
b.   Circle the number of each inverted sentence.
c.   Indicate with **INV–S** if the subject is singular, with **INV–P** if plural.
d.   In the spaces following the sentences, write down each verb-subject pair from the inverted sentences, placing subject first.

LOGIC BEFORE DINNER (ADAPTED FROM AGATHA CHRISTIE'S MURDER ON THE ORIENT EXPRESS)

INV~S   Whose <u>is</u> the name she cannot remember?

_____ 1. There <u>are</u> great ladies who love great artists.

_____ 2. Similar <u>was</u> the love of Princess Dragomiroff for Linda Arden.

_____ 3. There <u>is</u> no likelihood that she has forgotten.

_____ 4. No doubt, the Princess <u>was lying</u>.

_____ 5. Having seen Helena, she <u>was</u> sure of her presence on the train.

_____ 6. She <u>realized</u> at once that there would be suspicion cast on her.

_____ 7. There <u>were</u> good reasons for her to lie.

_____ 8. A restaurant attendant <u>approached</u>, coughing discreetly.

_____ 9. There <u>was</u> no other sound.

singular subject + verb   *plural subject + verb*

_____

_____

_____

REWRITING EXERCISE 1: verb before singular subject*

a. Circle the numbers of the 7 sentences in which the verb precedes the subject.
b. Underline the 3 **singular** verb-subject pairs in those sentences.
c. Rewrite the 4 other inverted sentences, making the verb-subject pairs singular.

SCALPING

[1]Although Native Americans did scalp their white enemies, the practice did not originate with them. [2]There are accounts of scalping by Godwin, Earl of Essex, back in the eleventh century. [3]There were no instances of it in America until 600 years later, when the Dutch and English brought over the custom. [4]It was not used as an official means for war-

fare. [5]Rather, there was great pressure put on colonial governments by frontiersmen demanding revenge against "Indians." [6]First the Dutch, then the English began to pay for the delivery of Indian scalps. [7]There was no distinction made among the scalps of men, women, or children, or between Indian friend or foe. [8]Nor were the results what the Europeans had hoped for. [9]There was widespread retaliation by many tribes, particularly the Iroquois. [10]Eventually, they were accused of having initiated the practice. [11]Yet there are official documents from the French-Indian Wars in which General Braddock offers five English pounds for a French scalp.

REWRITING EXERCISE 2: verb before plural subject

Copy the essay below, making the following changes:

a. Circle the numbers of the 8 sentences in which verb precedes subject.
b. Make the subject plural in 5 of those sentences. Three already are.
c. Make the verbs agree with the plural subjects. The starred (*) sentence is one of 3 with a complete verb separated by a subject.

KISSING AND CALORIES

[1]*Do the "kisser" and "kissee" lose weight while kissing? [2]According to dietitians, the average kiss consumes about nine calories. [3]There are more calories used if the kiss is more intense than usual. [4]On the other hand, unlike foods, kisses do not contain nutrients. [5]Often, there is a variation in the relationship between calories and nutrients.

[6]There is, for example, an equal amount of nutrients in fresh and packaged vegetables but often more calories in the packaged because sugar is frequently added. [7]In fact, about 70 percent of the sugar in the typical American diet comes in the form of additives, hidden in processed foods. [8]Similarly, starches such as bread, pasta, and potatoes are fairly low in calories. [9]Why then does a dieter usually stay away from them?

[10]Starches keep fattening company. [11]Each tablespoon of butter adds 100 calories to the 90 contained in a baked potato. [12]Does a pat of margarine help the dieter? [13]Butter and margarine have 225 calories per ounce. [14]But there are only vegetable fats in margarine, making it cholesterol-free.

[15]Despite tales to the contrary, how a person eats has no effect on either the nutritional or the caloric content of meals. [16]Chewing food thoroughly does not absorb nutrients any better, because most digestion takes place in the stomach and small intestine. [17]But there is at least some benefit from chewing thoroughly. [18]If a person chews slowly, food takes longer to eat and he or she has no opportunity to overeat. [19]And chewing does, of course, burn up some energy.

How to Cope with the Unexpected (1)

The subject of the starred (*) verb **Do** is **the "kisser" and "kissee."** The two items together make a **compound subject,** which in this case is plural. For more work with the compound subject, see Chapter 13.

REWRITING EXERCISE 3: eliminating *there is/there are*

a. Circle the numbers of the 10 inverted sentences.
b. Rewrite them, eliminating **there is/there are**

EXAMPLE: There is a house in New Orleans called the House of the Rising Sun.

can be rewritten as

A house in New Orleans **is** called the House of the Rising Sun.

COLLEGE CONDOS

[1]Parent-owned student condos have started appearing around college campuses. [2]There are excellent reasons for buying condos during this period of climbing college enrollment and decreasing housing. [3]Students end up paying rent to their parents, who in turn receive tax benefits and the opportunity for profit when the students graduate. [4]But there are some important considerations that parents should make before buying condos.

[5]The first issue deals with the investment aspect of the deal. [6]There is no point in investing if the investment is not worthwhile. [7]Sometimes there are simply parental protective instincts at work, rather than business sense. [8]If there are no comparable rents in other condos, the deal is not a good one. [9]There is no resale likely, at least not at a reasonable profit.

[10]Another set of considerations concern convenience. [11]There is not much sense in buying a condo unless the units are located within walking distance of the campus. [12]There are not always roommates available who can provide companionship, not to say a share of the rent. [13]If there are repairs to be done, will reliable caretakers be available? [14]In fact, convenience remains a factor after graduation. [15]There are few parents who live near enough to manage the sale. [16]A good idea might be to shop for a management package along with the condo.

[17]In any case, it is a good idea to get satisfactory answers to these questions before making the investment.

PROOFREADING STRATEGIES

The most common error in inverted sentences is the use of a plural noun with a singular verb. Most people automatically begin their sentence with **There is** (or **There's**) even if the subject that follows is plural. (Using contractions complicates the search for errors. For example, **here's,** the contraction of **here is,** "hides" the verb. A good proofreading strategy is to write out your contractions, as in Chapter 29. For stylistic reasons, you should avoid using contractions in formal essays.)

1. What to look for: sentences in which the verb comes before the subject.
    a. look for sentences that begin with or contain **there** or **here,** followed immediately by a form of the verb **to be: is/was** or **are/were**
    b. look for questions that begin with a **w (why)** word or an auxiliary such as **is/does** or **are/do**
2. How to look for agreement errors: ask **who** or **what** with the verb and the signal words—**here, there, what, where, when, which, who,** and **why.** The subject and verb must agree.
3. How to correct them: change the verb. If you find a plural subject but a singular verb, change the verb to the plural: for example, **is** to **are, was** to **were, does** to **do, has** to **have.** It is easier and more reasonable to make this change than to change the subject to match the singular verb. Similarly, if you find a singular subject and a plural verb,

change the verb to match the singular subject: **are** to **is**, **were** to **was**, **do** to **does**, **have** to **has**.

NOTE: You could also rewrite the entire sentence, eliminating **there is/there are** and then determining agreement.

Continue with PRACTICING PROOFREADING. To demonstrate your mastery of the inverted sentence, try the PROOFREADING TEST and the WRITING ASSIGNMENT.

PRACTICING PROOFREADING 1

Identify the 5 inverted sentences by circling their numbers. Correct the 4 agreement errors.

[1]Here is facts not many people know. [2]According to the National Institute for Occupational Safety and Health, secretaries are among those most likely to suffer from stress-related illnesses. [3]There's only laborers in front of them on the list of the ten most stressful jobs. [4]Other jobs in the top ten include waiters and waitresses, farmers, and office managers. [5]Who's the people one would expect to be in the top ten? [6]Health professionals, to everyone's surprise, rank somewhere between tenth and twentieth. [7]Further down the list is top executives and police. [8]The chairman of the board has less stress than a small businessman. [9]Apparently there is a connection between stress and 90 percent of all diseases, according to the Center of Stress-Related Disorders at New York's Presbyterian Hospital, a fact that makes these findings very important.

PRACTICING PROOFREADING 2

Identify the 7 inverted sentences by circling their number. Correct the 2 agreement errors.

WALK, DON'T RUN

[1]That the world record for a mile has dipped under 3:50 is a continuing source of amazement to people who remember the 4:00 barrier. [2]There is, however, another world record that might be more amazing.

[3]There is race-walkers with times of 5:50 or better for the mile. [4]That is a pretty good pace even for a runner. [5]A walker does not have to be a racer to benefit from the exercise, but he or she does have to adopt the race-walking style: a faster pace, a forward lean, elbows at a 90° angle, arms pumping.

[6]Usually, there are stares at such a "hurry-up" style, but the benefits make up for the stares. [7]The striding motion forces the walker to push off and pull forward, developing both front and back thigh muscles. [8]The pumping arms tone themselves as well the chest and back. [9]There are helpful hint for sagging buttock muscles in the distinctive movements of the walker's hips. [10]Does a pitying smile matter when a person is performing exercises whose cardiovascular benefits rival those of jogging, swimming, and cycling? [11]In fact, when tested at a rate of a mile per ten minutes, race walkers were found to expend more energy than runners and burn more calories as a result.

[12]There are guidelines to follow before becoming competitive. [13]A gradual approach is best, beginning with three or four 20-minute walks per week at a rate of about fifteen minutes per mile. [14]There are special walking shoes available. [15]A good manual will offer helpful suggestions for perfecting technique.

PROOFREADING TEST

Of the 9 instances of inverted sentences, 4 have agreement errors: 3 with plurals, 1 with a singular. Try to eliminate the errors by rewriting the sentence without inverting.

FREDERICK FAUST A.K.A. MAX BRAND

[1]There are many different names on book jackets, but the man behind Max Brand, John Frederick, Evan Evans, George Challis, and twenty other pseudonyms was Frederick Faust. [2]He was a one-man book industry, writing more than two hundred books on an incredible variety of subjects. [3]There were Westerns, historical romances, sea tales, spy stories, mysteries, and science fiction. [4]There was also three television series

and a Broadway musical based on his writing. [5]He also worked on the script of more than seventy movies and created two American heroes: Destry and Dr. Kildare. [6]It would not be wrong to call his life an American adventure.

[7]As a child, Faust had tuberculosis. [8]His father was an unsuccessful lawyer so there were little money. [9]By the time he was 13, his parents were dead. [10]There followed a series of different homes with different relatives and a variety of jobs. [11]A love for books kept him going. [12]He would write stories and poems in his notebooks even while working on farms and ranches. [13]There was a lot of drinking and brawling to get out of his system before he enrolled at the University of California at Berkeley. [14]He had to work nights to pay for his tuition. [15]Though he completed all his courses, he was denied graduation due to unexcused absences. [16]Was there any alterantives other than taking on the world? [17]Faust became a reporter for the Honolulu <u>Star Bulletin</u>, enlisted in the Canadian Expeditionary Force to fight in World War I, and deserted when his departure to France was delayed.

[18]There was years as a freight handler in New York City before he sold a poem for $50. [19]Soon after, the first of his "hard-boiled" adventures was bought by <u>All-Story Magazine</u> and a movie script by Metro. [20]Many books and scripts followed, but perhaps Faust's greatest contribution was his introduction of the mysterious and mythical Western hero.

[21]Then came the adventure's end, when Faust died in Italy while serving as a war correspondent during WW II.

WRITING ASSIGNMENT 2: verb before subject

Write a long paragraph on one of the following topics, according to your instructor's specifications for organization and development. Proofread for errors in subject-verb agreement in inverted sentences. Remember that most teachers discourage the use of **there is/there are,** so you might wish to recast those sentences once you are sure they contain no agreement errors.

a. Discuss how the object, furnishing, and decorations in your room reflect your personality. Use **There is a . . .,** for singular, **There are . . .** for plurals.

b. Discuss the truth, relevance, or appropriateness of various proverbs or bits of folk wisdom, such as "A stitch in time, saves nine." When you first introduce the saying, use **There is a. . . .** You can also use an inverted sentence by asking if the saying is true or false, beginning with **Is there.**

c. Discuss two related rules, laws, or regulations that you like or dislike. Use **There are . . .** when you mention them.

d. Someone from another country wonders what a typical American student knows about his/her country. Ask these questions using **Does, Has,** or **Is,** at the beginning. For example: **Does an American student know the currency used in the Soviet Union?** Include some questions about what most Americans know, using **Do, Has,** or **Is.**

Chapter 13

SPECIAL PROBLEMS IN AGREEMENT

INTRODUCTION

Chapter 13 covers problems in agreement that occur because the number of the subject is unclear. This introductory section lists and illustrates the categories or types of special agreement situations. The REWRITING EXERCISES that follow identify the type of unusual or special situation under consideration and focus on singulars or plurals. The PROOFREADING PRACTICE and TEST contain errors in agreement in both singular and plural situations.

It is important that you learn to recognize special problems in agreement. You need not necessarily memorize all the rules regarding them right away. Rather, learn to notice their presence and pay special attention to them during proofreading, checking the rules if necessary.

a. **Compound subjects** occur when two or more individual subjects are joined by a conjunction: with **or, nor,** or **but,** they are singular if the last item mentioned is singular; with **and,** they are always plural.

singular	plural
I can never remember if Frankie <u>or</u> Johnny **is** shot and killed.	Frankie <u>and</u> Johnny **were** lovers.
<u>Neither</u> coffee <u>nor</u> tea **interests** travelers.	Love <u>and</u> marriage **go** together.
<u>Not only</u> the house <u>but also</u> the farm **is** lost.	Fishing <u>and</u> wading **are** forbidden.

b. **Indefinite pronouns** often appear as subjects.

These pronouns are singular:

anyone	anybody	everything	nobody
everyone	everybody	something	no one
someone	somebody	nothing	one

Everybody **loves** somebody sometime.   <u>Everyone</u> **comes** to Alice's Restaurant.

Both is always plural.

Others are either singular or plural, depending on the context: **all, any, many, most, none, some.**

<u>Both</u> **have** remarried, but they stay in touch.

<u>All</u> **is** fair in love and war.   <u>All</u> of the pilots **continue** to fly.
<u>Most</u> of it **is lost** in antiquity.   <u>Most</u> of the boxers **suffer** brain damage.

> **NOTE:** Sometimes, the **of** phrase (the prepositional phrase) that follows the indefinite pronoun can help clarify the number of the subject. Because **it** is singular, **most of it** is also singular. By contrast, **most of them** would be followed with the plural **are lost in antiquity.** Because **pilots** and **boxers** are plural, so are **all** and **most.**

c.   **Collective nouns** are singular in form (no **s** endings) but contain many members: for example, **committee, family, military, herd, faculty.** They can be used as either singulars or plurals depending on their context. As singular nouns, they take singular verbs. For example,

The committee **has** designed a horse. It is calling the horse a "camel."

Problems in agreement arise with the pronoun. The next sentence uses the singular pronoun **It** because it refers to the singular antecedent **committee.**

Once you have chosen to use the singular verb **is** with **committee, do not** write:

They are calling the horse a "camel."

Though a committee does have many members, the word **committee** is still singular. Similarly, you establish **company** as a singular subject if you write:

The company is laying off 400 workers.

A company may have many decisionmakers, but you would be incorrect if you followed that singular use of **committee** with:

They expect to recall 100 workers.

Rather, your sentence should read:

It expects to recall 100 workers.

The correct pronoun is the singular **It**; the correct verb, **expects**, agrees with **It**.

> NOTE: If you want to use a collective noun as a singular, you might try **a** or **an** before it. If it works with one of the indefinite articles, it is a singular noun. Thus **a couple, a pair,** and **a trio** are singular nouns and take singular verbs.

As plurals, collective nouns must agree with plural verbs and be referred to by plural pronouns. For example:

The committee have designed a horse.
They are calling the horse a "camel."

Because a committee does have many members, you can use the word **committee** as a plural as long as you remain consistent in your use of pronouns and other verbs that refer to **committee.**

Notice how Colette, in <u>Music-Hall Sidelights</u>, uses the collective noun **couple** in the plural and then makes sure both the verb and pronoun referring to it are plural.

> She picks out . . . a couple who **catch** her fancy . . . occasionally blowing **them** a kiss.

    d. **Nouns with singular meaning** have a plural form—they end with **s**—but are used as singulars, for example: **news, physics, mathematics**

singular

All the news that **is** fit to   Plastics **is** a good field.
  print.

Economics **dictates** lending money only to those who do not need it.

If you are not sure whether a particular word is singular or plural, consult a dictionary.

    e. **Titles** and **names** may have plural forms, but because they refer to a single film, book, play, song, or country, we treat them as singulars.

<u>Damaged Goods</u> **was** a Sinclair Lewis title.

"Two of Us" **appears** as the first cut on the Beatles' <u>Let It Be</u> album.

The United States **is** a permanent member of the UN Security Council.

The Union of Soviet Socialist Republics **is** another permanent member.

The United Kingdom **is** a third.

NOTE: You can recognize titles easily because, in typescript, they are either <u>underlined</u> or within "quotation marks." In print, they are usually *italicized*.

The basic rules for agreement are in Chapters 8 (singulars) and 9 (plurals). Refer to them for reference. Additional exercises for special situations are available in the Instructor's Manual.

ATTENTION FOCUSING: special situations in agreement*

a. Ask **who** or **what** before the verbs in **boldface** and locate the subject of each, circling it.

b. Identify any special situations and list them in the space provided, writing **compound subject, indefinite pronoun, collective noun,** or **title.**

c. Indicate with **S** if singular, with **P** if plural.

SUPER SLEUTH?

1. (Mathematics) **seems** not to have been Sir Arthur Conan Doyle's area of expertise.　　　　*collective noun　S*

2. His creation, the great detective Sherlock Holmes, **was** also an uninformed scientist.　　　_____

3. Doyle and Holmes **were** certainly weak in the history of science.　　　_____

4. Holmes **assigns** to Professor Moriarty the authorship of the Binomial Theorem and The Dynamics of an Asteroid.　　　_____

5. Each **indicates** Doyle's (or Holmes's) careless play with historical fact.　　　_____

6. The Binomial Theorem's author **happens** to be the Norwegian Niels Henrik Abel.

_____

7. The scientific community **have added** nothing to Abel's 1825 theorem.

_____

8. The Dynamics of an Asteroid also **contained** a tiny but real error in its very title.

_____

9. By Doyle's day, everything **was** known about asteroids.

_____

10. Professors **were** not writing about "an" asteroid but about "asteroids" in general.

_____

11. Doyle's knowledge of math as well as his familiarity with astronomy **appear** limited.

_____

12. The entire Sherlock Holmes series **demonstrates** Doyle's problems in other areas as well.

_____

13. Chemistry **is** significant in The Adventure of Shoscombe Old Place and in A Study in Scarlet.

_____

14. Both **contain** errors, particularly in describing tests that do not produce the results Holmes claims they do.

_____

15. And literature, philosophy, botany, anatomy, and geology **are** subjects that, even according to Doyle, Holmes barely knows.

_____

If you have made no errors in agreement, try PRACTICING PROOFREADING 1 before asking your instructor to let you go on to another skill. If you did make some errors, reread the chapter introduction. REWRITING EXERCISES 1 and 2 (and WRITING ASSIGNMENT a) correspond to questions 1, 3, 7, and 12, EXERCISES 3 and 4 to questions 5, 9, and 14 (and to c), EXERCISES 5 and 6 to questions 3, 8, 11, and 15 (and to b).

REWRITING EXERCISE 1: special singulars (collective nouns)*

Write all changes above the lines:

a. Replace the plural **companies** with the _singular_ **the Searle Company**.

b. Use singular verbs when referring to **the Searle Company.**

c. Also change to the singular all pronouns that refer to **the Searle Company.**

d. Write out the full form of the contraction starred (*) in the essay.

SOUR ON SWEETENERS

[1]A recent MIT study suggests that NutraSweet, the sugar substitute, should be considered "medical food." [2]Companies that manufacture the sweetener have attacked the conclusions of the study.

[3]The companies claim that the study was not conducted properly. [4]They dismiss the findings that the sweetener may lower blood pressure. [5]They *don't accept the study's claim that, just because aspartame, the generic term for NutraSweet, lowered the blood pressure of lab animals, it would do the same to human users.

[6]The companies also reject their own research, which had suggested that the sweetener can affect mood, appetite, and sleep. [7]Instead, they argue that the product is completely safe. [8]They doubt that aspartame raises brain levels of an amino acid called tyrosine. [9]Their own researchers deny that the sweetener raises people's desire for carbohydrates. [10]In their literature, the companies claim that the product can be used without hesitation.

[11]The MIT study urges additional research. [12]Its researchers are not convinced that the companies police themselves sufficiently. [13]It asks the companies to make sure that aspartame does only what it is supposed to do. [14]Should aspartame do more, companies might find themselves under the control of the Federal Drug Administration. [15]Should that ever happen, companies are likely to find themselves packaging aspartame as both a general food sweetener and as medicine.

REWRITING EXERCISE 2: special plurals (collective nouns)

Copy the paragraph on p. 118, making the following changes:

a. Replace **Washington** with the plural **the Redskins** and **New York** with the plural **the Giants.**

b. Make verbs and pronouns that refer to the **Redskins** and **Giants** agree with these new plural subjects.

A LOSING LANDMARK

[1]When Washington rolled up seventy-two points against New York on November 27, 1966, it entered the record books as having scored the most points in a professional football game. [2]Throughout the game, New York was unable to deal with blitzing by Washington. [3]Three times during the first half New York was intercepted, and three times Washington scored. [4]At the half, Washington led 34–14. [5]New York was able to score in the second half but was unable to stop Washington from scoring. [6]The score at the end was 72–41. [7]New York was inept that entire year. [8]It lost twelve games and won only once. [9]It did tie one game, but that was small consolation. [10]New York remains in the record books for the 501 points it gave up that year in a fourteen-game season.

REWRITING EXERCISE 3: special singulars (indefinite pronouns)

Write all changes in the space above each line:

a. Substitute the singular **everyone** or **everybody** for the plural **people.**
b. Make verbs (and any subject complement) that refer to **everyone** or **everybody** agree.
c. Starred (*) words are explained after the essay.

COOKING AND COUNTING

[1]People who like to cook still hate counting portions. [2]Since most recipes are designed for six, people who are cooking for just two must divide and subtract. [3]Because such calculations are troublesome, people are applauding the appearance of Cooking for Two.

[4]Cooking for Two gives people complete menus for daily situations. [5]It provides simple-to-fix suppers for people who are too busy to cook. [6]It gives people who are money-conscious ideas for low-cost meals. [7]It offers people who are overweight suggestions for low-calorie items. [8]People who

have used the book can plan ahead with selections from the "make-ahead snacks" section. [9]People are excited by more than just the recipes; they are also pleased that they are planned for two.

[10]People who like gourmet cooking also have a section. [11]The book contains recipes for unusual meals. [12]Instead of coping with mathematics, a person *can focus on taste and choose among Marengo Chicken, Beef Stroganoff, Mexican Meat Loaf, Salmon Tart, and other entrees. [13]People who are fussy eaters are offered sections on special soups, breads, vegetables, and even desserts. [14]And remember, everyone: each meal is planned just for two!

How to Cope with the Unexpected (1)

The starred (*) word **can** is called a modal auxiliary. Unlike the auxiliaries (or helping verbs) **is/was/has/does,** modals do not indicate number. You would use **can** with both a singular or a plural subject. The modals are **can, could, may, might, must, shall, should, will,** and **would.**

REWRITING EXERCISE 4: special plurals (indefinite pronouns)

Copy the essay below, making the following changes:

a. Replace the **singular** indefinite pronouns **someone/anyone/everyone/each** with one of the **plural** indefinite pronouns **all** or **some.**
b. Use plural verbs when referring to **all** or **some.**
c. Make sure pronouns and subject complements that refer to the plural indefinite pronouns are also plural.
d. The starred (*) words **an Aries** become the plural **Aries** by simply dropping the **an.** The plural form is the same as the singular.

LOVE SIGNS AND NOT SO LOVING

[1]Astrologists claim that how people behave when they are in love depends on the sign of the zodiac under which they were born.

[2]Everyone who was born under Aries tends to fall blindly in love. [3]Like the Ram that is the sign for Aries, everyone who is *an Aries jumps headlong and heart first. [4]If the romance comes to an end, Aries people tend not to give up. [5]Most of them pursue their lost loves, hoping to charm them back into the relationship. [6]Each true Aries cares little for

himself or herself while he or she is in love. [7]Whenever a romance ends, someone finds himself or herself hurt. [8]Anyone who is born *an Aries has a better-than-average chance of suffering.

[9]By contrast, someone born under the bull sign of Taurus tends to be under control. [10]He or she rarely pursues intently, preferring to be pursued instead. [11]Anyone who cares for himself or herself too much to be devastated by a love affair was most likely born between April 20 and May 21.

REWRITING EXERCISE 5: agreement with titles, compounds, indefinite pronouns

All subjects in the paragraph below are "special." Copy the entire paragraph, making the following changes:

a. Begin by substituting **This year's funniest book is** for the opening 7 words of the paragraph.
b. Change the time of the verbs in **boldface** to the present, making sure that singular verbs agree with singular subjects and plurals with plurals.

THE JOY OF CHICKENS AND THE ROMANCE OF LEPROSY

[1]One of last year's funniest books **was** a book of weird titles. [2]Bizarre Books **contained** 180 pages of authentic book titles. [3]Either Why Bring that UP: A Guide to Seasickness or Proceedings of the Second International Workshop on Nude Mice **deserved** the award for most bizarre title. [4]Russell Ash and Brian Lake **came** together to produce this grotesque list. [5]Both **seemed** inspired by a contest at the annual Frankfurt Book Fair for "a title that most outrageously exceeds all bounds of credibility." [6]Rare-book dealers and individual collectors **had taken** a second look at the titles in this book, wondering at their value. [7]Certainly New Guinea Tapeworms and Jewish Grandmothers **sounded** intriguing. [8]Jokes Cracked by Lord Aberdeen **kept** company with Fangs of Suet Pudding and I Knew 3,000 Lunatics on one list. [9]Premature Burial and How It May Be Avoided **headed** another category. [10]Some Interesting Facts about Margarine and On Sledge and Horseback to Outcast Siberian Lepers **appeared** to be the

favorites among readers writing letters to Ash and Lake. [11]<u>How to Cook Husbands</u> **remained** in strong contention, along with <u>Fish Who Answer Telephones</u> and <u>How to Boil Water in a Paper Bag</u>.

REWRITING EXERCISE 6: agreement with compounds

Copy the essay below, making the following changes:

a. Substitute **Despite** for **Before** at the beginning of the essay.
b. Change all verbs in the essay to the present tense.
c. Make sure the present tense verbs you are creating agree with their subjects.
d. Use the pronouns as clues to the number of the subjects.

BUYING AND BEING BOUGHT

[1]Before the passage of various consumer protection laws, a store and a store manager remained free to manipulate the buying public.

[2]Stores looked like mazes or animal warrens, with shrewd managers making aisles lead in all directions. [3]Both a casual and a serious shopper found such confusion difficult to penetrate. [4]As a result, they spent much more time inside the store than necessary, shopping all the time. [5]As part of the same plan, eggs, milk, and other staples waited in coolers farthest from the entrance. [6]As a result, shoppers had to walk past nearly everything else a store offered, tempting them into unnecessary purchases.

[7]The placement of items on a shelf or the placement of the shelves themselves continued to be of crucial importance in the manipulation of the consumer. [8]Chocolate, gum, and candy usually lined the shelves near the checkout counters. [9]The fruit or vegetable corner rested a bit further back but it still remained very visible, inducing the buying public to notice and purchase the high-profit items contained there. [10]Whether a product was made accessible on upper shelves or hidden out of sight on lower shelves also influenced sales considerably. [11]Most of the public preferred to exert themselves by reaching rather than bending.

[12]Sometimes a store owner or manager turned to a device called "multiplication." [13]This scheme placed many items of the same product

in a single package. [14]Either buy four or buy none was the choice shoppers faced. [15]In such a situation, most tended to buy the package of four. [16]Some stores used the packing format already available from the manufacturer. [17]Coca Cola offered a six-pack of soda as a unit but had no objections to the sale of individual cans. [18]Some stores nevertheless insisted on the purchase of the entire unit.

PROOFREADING STRATEGIES

The likely error in this area is overlooking the unusual situation. Students who make errors in these situations do not necessarily make errors in subject-verb agreement in other, more familiar instances.

1. What to look for: unusual situations.
2. How to look for them: focus on cues; analyze for number.
   a. look for the words **either-or** and **neither-nor** (singulars) or for the word **and** (plural)
   b. look for indefinite pronouns, particularly **everyone** and **everybody**
   c. look for "quotation marks" and underlining
   d. look for capital letters in the middle of the sentence: IRS, U.S. and other collective nouns, particularly as (capitalized) names
   e. look at pronouns to check up on verbs—if the verb is singular but the pronoun plural, check the subject to which they both refer
3. How to correct them: make the verb and subject agree by making the verb agree with the subject; also make sure the pronoun agrees with both its subject and verb.

> Choose one of the PROOFREADING exercises. Work until you locate and correct all errors in agreement. To demonstrate your mastery of agreement in unusual situations, take the PROOFREADING TEST and try a WRITING ASSIGNMENT that corresponds to your error.

PRACTICING PROOFREADING 1

Assume that your subject-verb agreement is correct in familiar situations. Circle the numbers heading the 4 sentences that contain unusual situations. Find and correct the 3 agreement errors in compound subjects and indefinite pronouns.

READING THE HEAVENS

[1]Either the study of astronomy or the belief in astrology are considered the reason that ancient civilizations turned their attention to the

skies. [2]The interest in astronomy was both religious and practical. [3]When to plant seed, when to expect rain, or when to harvest were known by the position of the stars. [4]The more unusual events, such as eclipses, were occasions for religious ceremonies. [5]People who study the astronomy and calendars of ancient civilizations are called "archeoastronomers." [6]Anybody who has seen the monuments, mounds, and solar circles of old civilizations have wondered about their significance. [7]Archeoastronomers decipher those mysteries. [8]Dr. Anthony F. Aveni's <u>Skywatchers of Ancient Mexico</u> is an example of their work. [9]It explains how to calculate the position of any star at any time in the history of the earth. [11]The rather simple computer program gives that star's position as observed from any geographical location at any time of the year.

PRACTICING PROOFREADING 2

Circle the number heading the 11 sentences that contain special situations. Correct the 3 errors in subject-verb agreement. Because errors in pronoun agreement tend to occur with indefinite pronouns and collective nouns, the essay also includes 2 errors in pronoun agreement **in those special situations.** There are thus 5 errors altogether.

BEATRICE

[1]Beatrice Foods is the largest conglomerate in the United States. [2]Although it has begun putting its name before the public, not many people outside the business world know it. [3]Beatrice Foods seems to prefer their anonymity. [4]As long as it is the largest conglomerate, it does not care that the Beatrice name is not very familiar.

[5]Beatrice has become a giant by buying up other companies. [6]Since 1943, it has acquired more than 400 companies. [7]Each, however, retain their own identity, despite being swallowed by Beatrice. [8]Not only the old brand name but also the old management continue. [9]Everything remains as before; only the profits end up in Chicago, where Beatrice Foods' corporate headquarters are located.

[10]Like any other conglomerate, Beatrice Foods owns companies in many fields, but food is their first interest. [11]It has bakery, confectionery,

dairy, and specialty food products. [12]For example, Beatrice owns dairies all over the country. [13]The containers of milk, cream, chese, yogurt, or ice cream in a grocery bag are from Beatrice, under different brand names. [14]Dannon, Louis Sherry, Tropicana, La Choy, and Swiss Miss is Beatrice products. [15]But Samsonite luggage, Airstream motor homes, Mac Kahn shades, Buxton wallets, and Charmglow barbecues are also controlled by Beatrice.

[16]Still, anybody who wishes to avoid the embrace of Beatrice Foods just has to say so. [17]One unusual and attractive aspect of this acquisitive conglomerate is that it has never taken over any company against the wishes of its own management.

PROOFREADING TEST: agreement with singular and plural subjects (special situations)

The essay below contains errors in subject-verb agreement in both singulars and plurals. Because one of the most important principles of proofreading is that you look for only one error at a time, proofread this essay twice, first looking for the 6 errors in the singular, and second looking for the 6 errors in the plural. You might wish to reproduce the essay to make proofreading more convenient.

AGE: THE FINAL FRONTIER OF BIAS

[1]The firm where Patricia Moore worked was unwilling to consider the elderly in their product designs. [2]They might have paid more attention if they had known how concerned Moore was. [3]Moore, at age 33, transformed herself into an old lady with the help of a gray wig, semi-opaque glasses, and elderly-style clothing. [4]Plugging her ears and putting splints on her legs was the additional methods that enabled her to travel to more than one hundred cities in fourteen states without her disguise being penetrated. [5]Not only did she discover what it feels like to be old, but she also found out how old people are treated. [6]A shopping bag lady, a middle-income woman, and a wealthy dowager was her roles. [7]Any teenager who bothers thinking about their so called "golden years" had better think again, if Moore's experiences as a "senior citizen" are typical.

[8]The elderly, Moore found, have stereotyped images. [9]Whether positive or negative, these images are applied without regard to individuals. [10]Slow, poor, cranky, crotchety, and doddering is some of the terms people who do not like the elderly say about them. [11]Most of those who do like older people say they are lovable, adorable, and bake chocolate chip cookies. [12]Both of these generalizations have to be erased before the real problems of the elderly can be examined. [13]Uninformed people can also behave badly. [14]Some merely fails to open doors or ignore old people; the more vicious beat, mug, and rob them, as they did Moore. [15]Machinery was as difficult as people. [16]They created constant problems for the elderly, with doors yielding reluctantly and trains closing their doors too quickly.

[17]Moore hopes that her experiences undercover will help dramatize the full extent of the bias against the elderly. [18]Our society needs to change their treatment of the elderly drastically. [19]After all, many people are on their way to reaching the age where a majority are abused, neglected, and cheated. [20]Instead of basing expectations on stereotypes, society needs to recognize that the abilities and interests as well as the problems and concerns of the elderly differs from those of younger people. [21]Hollywood and Madison Avenue simply creates false pictures. [22]Moore herself hopes that her own profession will become particularly sensitive. [23]Elderly need ordinary, household products and devices that are designed specifically for them and do not require the dexterity, strength or health of younger people to operate.

WRITING ASSIGNMENT: special singulars

Write a long paragraph on one of the following topics, according to your instructor's specifications for organization and development. Proofread for errors in subject-verb agreement in special situations.

a. Imagine how each below would treat a member of a minority group: (a) the military, (b) a huge corporation, (c) a major university, (d) a city in the North/South/East/West, or (e) a government agency. Use one of these as the singular subject in your sentences.

b. Discuss your preference among the choices available on TV stations or at the local "multiplex theater" on a particular evening. List the

TV shows by the hour. (For example, **Thursday at 10, either *L. A. Law* or *Knots' Landing* is available**.)

c. Discuss the special triumphs as well as the special difficulties of people your age, of people with your background, of people in your part of the country, or of people in a similar situation (married, tall, left-handed, living at home, only child), referring to all of your group with **indefinite pronouns: everybody, everyone, somebody, someone, anybody, anyone,** etc.

d. Discuss a particular band or group whose name is in the plural. A particular challenge would be a name that is plural yet singular in form, such as Motley Crue. In any case, use as your subject both the plural name and the word **band** or **group,** making sure your verb *and pronoun* references are correct.

e. Write about a local or national sports team, varying the place name and the nickname. For example, use as your subject **the Dodgers** and **Los Angeles, the Jayhawks** and **Kansas, the Oilers** and **Edmonton.** Notice that the nicknames are usually plural, requiring plural nouns, while the place names are singular, requiring singular verbs and singular pronouns.

MASTERY TEST FOR UNIT III: problems in agreement

The essay below contains 20 errors in agreement. Of these errors, 9 are in verbs with singular subjects and 9 in verbs with plural subjects. There are also 2 errors in pronoun agreement.

The agreement errors involve each of the situations discussed in this unit: when subject and verb are right next to each other (Chapters 8 and 9), when a form of the verb **to be** is used (Chapter 10), when a phrase comes between the subject and the verb (Chapter 11), when the verb comes before the subject (Chapter 12), and in special situations involving compounds, indefinite pronouns, collective nouns, and titles (Chapter 13).

Proofread the essay, using the strategies you have been practicing. As the most effective proofreading searches for only one type of error at a time, it might be a good idea to reproduce this page at least twice. Then, on one copy, look only for errors in verbs with singular subjects, and on the second copy, for errors in verbs with plural subjects.

TRACKING THE VISITORS

[1]New York State's Department of Taxation and Finance employs a group of "hunters" headed by Natalie Naba. [2]Its job is to collect taxes from a special group of non-residents. [3]Naba's unit keeps track of the million-aire athlete, the movie star, the high-priced lawyer, or some other celebrity who comes to New York City for just a few days and earns huge fees. [4]Even if one of these "high rollers" does not live here, he has to pay taxes on any money he earns in New York City. [5]The income hunters in Naba's group tracks these working visitors and makes sure that they pay this "commuter tax."

[6]As part of her work, Ms. Naba reads gossip columns, consults sports schedules, and scans the Social Register and <u>Variety</u>, the "Bible" of show business people. [7]There are outside helpers as well—Naba's parents bends down pages in newspapers and magazines that contain information about occasional but famous wage earners in New York City. [8]Using this method for tracking her prey, Naba was able to discover last year that certain sports figures were living part-time in the city. [9]Thanks to that item, she collected 1.2 million dollars in back taxes. [10]There are television sets tuned to entertainment programs at Naba's workplace also. [11]Watching daily programs was a great help to Naba's unit. [12]Commercials were particularly informative. [13]The presence of a New

York City landmark in a commercial usually signals that someone ~~were~~ *was* liable for taxation. [14]It also pays to pay attention to sports schedules. [15]They inform the unit when a millionaire athlete earns part of his salary in New York City.

[16]New York City and New York State benefits handsomely from Naba's unit. [17]For New York City, there are an income of 108 million dollars annually from the tax on non-residents. [18]For New York State, there is an average of $663 million a year. [19]Naba's group collects only a part of this total, but they earn their keep, according to department spokesperson Karl Felsen.

If you are unable to locate the errors in any particular area, review the PROOFREADING STRATEGIES for that chapter. If you located an error but found yourself unable to correct it, try a REWRITING EXERCISE in the appropriate chapter.

Unit Four

PROBLEMS WITH VERBS
(tenses)

Recommended

Assign as Needed

Chapter 14
INDICATING THE PRESENT TENSE

ATTENTION FOCUSING: the present tense*

Underline all verbs. List only the present tense verbs in the space provided.

BURIED TREASURE

1. A dog <u>buries</u> bones out of instinct.   _buries_

2. It <u>is following</u> an ancient, inbred desire for keeping its food safe.

3. The ancestors of dogs were wild animals.

4. They lived in the wilderness, hunting for their food.   _lives_   _live_

5. They hid any part of their uncompleted meal by burying it.   _hide_   _hid_

6. <u>Burying</u> the food kept it safe from scavengers.   _keeps_

7. It could also be recovered for a future meal.

8. Nowadays, domesticated dogs <u>do not need</u> to do this to survive.

9. Nevertheless, they <u>are born</u> with the instinct.

10. The manner of burial <u>remains</u> unchanged.

11. After digging the hole with its front feet, the dog <u>covers</u> the bone by pushing dirt on top of it with its nose.

WRITING ASSIGNMENT 1: the present tense

Write a short paragraph, using the present tense. Some of your sentences may be in a different tense.

a. Describe some features of your car: how it takes corners, how it builds speed, how it handles bumps. Try not to use **is** or **has.**
b. Pretend you are describing an event as it is taking place: a rodeo, a boxing match, a sports events, acts at a circus, performers in a video. Try not to use endings on your verbs.
c. Describe the appearance of a friend, mentioning his or her looks as well as items of clothing.

If you have made no errors in the use of the present tense, try PRACTICING PROOFREADING 1 before asking your instructor to send you on to another chapter. If you did make errors, read the REVIEW.

REVIEW: the present tense

Unit III dealt with **subject-verb agreement.** There you learned that the verb must often conform to its subject. In this unit, we turn to the "time" aspect of the verb—how it indicates when the action takes place. But the "agreement" aspect remains very important in the present tense. Here is a summary of how two verbs react to the **singular** subject.

	the verb *capture*	the verb *be*
the infinitive form	to capture	to be
the base form	capture	be
the present tense form in the third-person singular	capture**s**	is
the present tense form with all other subjects	capture	are (but: I am)

The verb **capture** adds an **s** (some verbs add **es**) to the base form in the third-person singular. With all other subjects in the present tense, **capture** takes the same form as its base: **capture.** Keep this aspect of agreement in mind as you continue work on the time aspect of the present tense. If you are not sure of some of the terminology or principles used in this chapter, you might wish to review Chapters 1 and 2, particularly to learn how verbs can be returned to their base or stem forms.

WHEN IS THE PRESENT TENSE USED?

If you listen to your own use of the present tense, you will notice that you tend to use it to indicate action or events that take place usually or habitually. For this reason, the present tense is often (and more precisely) called the **habitual tense.**

Right now, I **am typing.**

Notice that the sentence does not use the present tense to indicate the "nowness" of the activity. The present tense would have been: **I type.** This present tense is actually used to convey the time of a usual or habitual activity: **I type an average of four hours each day.** Sentences will frequently include words such as **always, never, nowadays, often,** or **usually** to indicate habitual activity or words such as **now, today,** or **this year** to indicate activity in the present tense. Though such words are informative, the rules of Standard English require that the verb in the sentence indicate the tense or time of the activity.

These are the most common situations in which writers use the simple present tense:

1. Summaries of content, particularly of a story, or descriptions of the act of telling that story

   Hawthorne's Goodman Brown enters the forest, though his wife urges him to remain with her.

   E. T. eventually returns to his world.

   Hemingway defines heroism as grace under pressure.

2. Statements of universal (often scientific) truths

   Water boils at 200 degrees Fahrenheit.

   Light travels at 186,000 miles per second.

   Love is blind.

3. Descriptions of habitual action

   The Chaucer class begins at 8 A.M.

   The clerk never gets there before 8:15.

4. Descriptions of a present action

   Now I understand what you mean to me.

Choose a REWRITING EXERCISE. After you complete one without having made errors, read PROOFREADING STRATEGIES and go to PRACTICING PROOFREADING.

REWRITING EXERCISE 1: the present tense*

Make all changes in the space above each line.

a. Find the subject of each verb in **boldface.** (Each is singular.)
b. Cross out each **will.**
c. Change verbs to the present, making sure each agrees with its subject.

DRIVE IN

[1]The story of Pygmalion in Greek mythology **will be** interpreted as an illustration of the power of art.

[2]Pygmalion, a sculptor, **will see** so much to blame in women that he **will resolve** never to marry. [3]Instead, he **will make** a beautiful statue of a woman out of ivory. [4]It **will seem** so lifelike that Pygmalion himself **will touch** it sometimes, as if to reassure himself it is only ivory. [5]At last, he **will fall** in love with his own creation. [6]He **will caress** it and **give** it presents. [7]He **will clothe** its limbs, **place** rings on its fingers, **hang** a necklace around its neck. [8]He **will place** her on a couch and **put** pillows under her head, calling her his wife.

[9]Pygmalion **will attend** the festivities of Venus, gooddess of love. [10]He **will stand** before the altar, **pray** for his ivory statue, and **call** her "my wife." [11]Venus **will hear** him and **grant** the sculptor his unspoken wish. [12]As a sign of her favor, she **will cause** the flame on the altar to shoot high three times.

[13]When Pygmalion **will return** home, he **will go** to see his statue. [14]Leaning over the couch, he **will kiss** it on the mouth and **be** overjoyed to discover its beginning warmth. [15]At last, a living woman **will rise** from the couch. [16]Venus herself **will bless** their marriage.

[17]George Bernard Shaw's <u>Pygmalion</u> **will use** this story as its basis, and the popular Broadway musical <u>My Fair Lady</u> **will use** the Shaw play as its model.

REWRITING EXERCISE 2: the present tense

Copy the essay on p. 135, making the following changes to indicate the present.

a. Underline each **was** and the verbs ending in **-ed;** they are in the past. (Optional: check your selections against the list in the Appendix.)

b. Return those verbs to their base or stem and change them to the present, giving the plot summary in its proper tense.

c. Make sure each verb agrees with its subject.

MOLL FLANDERS

[1]Daniel Defoe's <u>Moll Flanders</u> (1722) <u>described</u> Moll's life from her birth in prison to honest life in Virginia. [2]The first social novel and one of the earliest novels, <u>Moll Flanders</u> <u>demonstrated</u> the power of poverty to control lives.

[3]As a child, Moll was a public charge. [4]But her education and beauty convinced her not to consider her humble beginnings a handicap. [5]She desired a life of ease. [6]Though she was in love with the elder son of the house, circumstances forced her to marry the younger. [7]At his death, she was penniless and burdened with two children.

[8]Moll's subsequent life illustrated both the force of poverty and the power of men over women. [9]First, she married a gentleman draper who disappeared due to his business difficulties. [10]She then married a rich American, following him to America and bearing him three children, only to discover he was her brother. [11]She returned to England. [12]For a while she lived with a wealthy man, but after the birth of their child was alone again. [13]She moved in with a banker, then lived with an Irish highwayman, then returned to her banker. [14]His death forced her into theft. [15]She gained wealth, but her past was found out, and she was back in the prison of her birth. [16]There she encountered her Irish highwayman again. [17]Remorseful, she repented and resolved to live honestly. [18]Both escaped the hangman's noose and accepted exile to Virginia. [19]There they settled down to live a respectable and peaceful life.

> Proofread your rewritten essay for correctness in both copying and the use of present tense. Underline all examples of the present tense.

REWRITING EXERCISE 3: the present tense

Copy the paragraph on p. 136, making the following changes to indicate the present.

    a. Remove the words **observed by the Lincoln Junior High science class.**

    b. Change all verbs from the past to **the present tense** to indicate that you are now talking about the way termites habitually are.

    c. All subjects are plural, so use **are** and the base form of each verb (no **s** endings). See HOW TO COPE 1 if you are not sure how to return a verb to its base or stem.

WOOD DWELLERS

[1]Termites observed by the Lincoln Junior High science class looked like ants but were quite different from them. [2]They had thick waists, a lighter color, and evenly curved feelers or antennae. [3]They lived within wood as a colony with a king and queen. [4]They were born either soldiers or workers, and their bodies seemed well suited for their roles.

[5]The soldiers lived within the darkness of the wood. [6]They had no wings and were blind, but they defended the colony fiercely from animals and other insects. [7]The workers fed the colony. [8]They ate the wood and passed it on in digested form to the other termites. [9]Worker termites secreted a liquid in their hind intestine. [10]Thousands of single-celled animals or protozoa in this liquid were visible through a microscope. [11]These protozoa turned the cellulose in wood into sugar, providing the termites with sustenance.

How To Cope with the Unexpected (1)

To change verbs that are in another tense to the present, first return the verb to its base or stem. You might encounter some difficulty with verbs that change completely as they change tenses. Such is the case with **to be,** which changes from **were** (past) to **are** in the present. If you are not sure of the base form or stem of a verb, look for the word as it is in your dictionary. Even pocket dictionaries will list both words and explain that one is but a form of the other.

REWRITING EXERCISE 4: the present tense

Copy the paragraph on p. 137, making the following changes to indicate the present.

    a. In the first sentence, substitute the words **demonstrates daily** for **demonstrated.**

b. Change all verbs from the past to the present tense to indicate that the events at this school go on habitually. (All affected subjects are singular.)

BABY TALKS—AND READS AND COUNTS

[1]At the Better Baby Institute in Philadelphia, Glen Dorman, the "guru of early learning," demonstrated his method for teaching infants and toddlers to read and do math.

[2]He printed large red lowercase letters on white cards. [3]He began with "mommy" and "daddy." [4]Then he flashed an increasing number of white cards, decreasing the size of the letters. [5]His goal was to have the children eventually read from books. [6]One preschooler read not only in English but also in French and Japanese. [7]Dorman used flash cards in the math lessons as well. [8]He put red dots on them, from one to one hundred. [9]Just as he did not introduce the names for letters during reading, he did not teach numerals during the math. [10]He reasoned that names are merely abstractions and confusing to the children. [11]He wanted them to understand the concept of quantity first. [12]Two, in Dorman's opinion, was not too early an age for children to begin learning in this way.

PROOFREADING STRATEGIES

The errors a writer is most likely to make in the use of the present tense (other than agreement between subject and verb) generally result from choosing the wrong tense. Before looking for any errors, determine if the use of the present tense is appropriate, sentence by sentence. Some parts within a sentence could be in a different tense from that of the main verb.

1. What to look for: inappropriate choice of time words in the sentence. To determine if use of present tense is appropriate:
    a. examine the verb and other time signals
    b. examine the content
2. How to look it: change the time of the sentence—the word that changes is the verb.
    a. verbs referring to singular subjects should end in **s**
    b. verbs referring to plural subjects look like the base form
    c. the present tense of the verb **to be** is **is/are**
3. How to correct it: if present tense is appropriate, verbs should not have **ed** endings—return verbs to base form and add **s** (or **es**).

> After you correct all errors in a PRACTICING PROOFREADING exercise, demonstrate your mastery with WRITING ASSIGNMENT 2.

PRACTICING PROOFREADING 1

Locating all verbs, determine which require present tense. Correct the 3 errors. (All present tense verbs should refer to plural subjects.)

BARBER POLES

[1]The red and white stripes on a barber's pole symbolize tasks barbers used to perform a long time ago. [2]Barbers once combined haircutting with minor surgery, such as treating wounds and bloodletting. [3]"Bloodletting" was a procedure thought to cure illness by allowing "bad blood" to drain from the patient. [4]To indicate their profession, barbers hung bandages and a bowl on a red pole in front of their place of business. [5]What we today called a barber pole replaced the old sign of the surgeon-barber. [6]The red stripes represented blood, and the white stripes stood for bandages. [7]Because even barbers themselves no longer know the origin of the pole, people sometimes refer to it as a candy-cane pole.

PRACTICING PROOFREADING 2

Correct the 3 errors. Underline all verbs and determine if the content requires present tense. All subjects are plural.

MARBLES

[1]Many of us played with marbles when we were children. [2]They are called "marbles" because once they really are made out of stones such as marble or agate. [3]Today, most marbles are made of glass. [4]Marbles are made by forming molten glass into balls. [5]To add the bright swirls and stripes, colored strips of hot glass are twisted into a rod and covered with a layer of clear glass. [6]With the glass still hot and soft, "marble scissors" snipped off chunks the size of marbles. [7]Once they are pressed into round shapes inside metal molds, they hardened quickly.

WRITING ASSIGNMENT 2: indicating the present tense

Write a long paragraph on one of the following topics, according to your instructor's specifications for organization and development. Make sure that your use of the present tense is appropriate. Proofread for errors in subject-verb agreement as well.

a. Explain the ideas behind a song or poem. What is the singer or poet trying to say? What is he or she trying to make you feel?

b. Do people wear clothes to make statements about themselves? Talk about what a particular style or fashion "says" about its wearer.

c. Describe a typical weekend in your life.

d. Retell a fairy tale, legend, or folktale, using the present tense.

e. Think of something that represents a nation or an ethnic group—a flag, an emblem, an animal, a song—and explain what the relationship is between this representation and the group. (For example, what do the fifty stars in the American flag represent?)

Chapter 15

INDICATING THE PAST TENSE OF REGULAR VERBS

ATTENTION FOCUSING: *ed endings**

Circle all indicators of the past tense, writing them in the spaces below.

AMY (ADAPTED FROM ROSS MACDONALD'S MEET ME AT THE MORGUE)

1. Amy Miner (turned.) *turns*
2. Her thin torso leaned tensely forward from the hips. *leans*
3. She batted her eyes and sprinted for the door and the sunlight. *bats* *sprints*
4. The man in the doorway grabbed her around the waist, immobilized her flailing arms, and passed her to the police guard. *grabs* *immobilizes*
5. The guard pushed her toward the black car that waited at the end of the drive. *pushes* *pushes* *waits*
6. Her angular shadow merged with the shadow of the car. *merges*

turned _____ _____ _____ _____

WRITING ASSIGNMENT 1: *ed endings*

Write a short paragraph in the past tense, using one of the topics below. You may use the regular verbs listed with the topic or your own.

a. Describe what happened at an event in your family's history: birth, graduation, wedding, funeral. (graduate, marry, decide, dress, consider)

b. Discuss how your favorite team perform**ed** in the World Series, Super Bowl, Stanley Cup, or NCAA Championship. (score, bat, pitch, kick, pop, leap)

c. What frighten**ed** you when you were a child? (yell, scare, grab, jump, turn)

d. Describe last night's scene at the dinner table. (pass, hand, cook, turn)

e. How did you acquire some valuable possession? (purchase, discover, save)

If you have made no errors in using *ed* endings, try PRACTICING PROOF-READING 1 before asking your instructor to send you on to another chapter. If you did make errors, read the following REVIEW.

REVIEW: the past tense

Many English sentences in which an action or event took place in the past contain words that say so: **yesterday, in the past, back then, last year,** and others. But those words, although informative, do not by themselves meet the requirements of Standard English. Standard English requires that information about the time of the action be carried by the verb. When the time of the action changes, so does the form of the verb (or verbs) in a sentence. Of course, you can always add words such as **yesterday** or **last year** to your sentence to help remind yourself that the action is taking place in the past. But whether you add these words or not, your verb must always indicate the time of the action in a sentence.

HOW TO INDICATE THE PAST TENSE

a. Regular verbs add **ed** to their base forms.

present tense

The U.S. Government **places** a federal income tax on all Americans.

past tense

The Ottoman Empire **placed** a special tax on all Christian families.

The present tense verb **places** returns to the base form—**place**—then adds the past tense indicator **ed→placed.** (Notice that the "silent **e**" drops—Chapter 48 offers additional practice with the "silent **e**" ending.) The **ed** at the end of a regular verb signals that the action has already taken place, that it is in the past, that it has ended.

b. Other verbs **(irregular verbs)** indicate the past tense by changing, rather than by adding a past tense indicator in the final position.

present tense

In the United States, people   **pay**   their taxes with cash or checks.

past tense

In ancient China, people   **paid**   their taxes with large sheets of tea.
In ancient Greece, citizens   **paid**   their taxes with personal service.

Chapter 16 will offer practice with the past tense of iregular verbs. If you are unsure about the past tense form of a verb, consult your dictionary. When no past tense is indicated next to a verb, it is a regular verb and takes **ed** to indicate its past. Any verb that has an irregular past tense form will have that form listed. Similarly, dictionaries indicate if there are any other changes in the verb as a result of adding **ed.**

c. The verb **to be** also changes its form in the past tense. Unlike other verbs, the verb **to be** has different forms for singulars and for plurals.

singular	present tense	past tense	plural	present tense	past tense
I	am	was	we	are	were
you	are	were	you	are	were
he/she/it	is	was	they	are	were

How to Cope with the Unexpected (1)

As you look for words that indicate time, do not be confused by verbs preceded by **to.** Though they appear to show action—**stop, be, lack**—they are actually infinitives. Leave them as they are. The change in time from present to past does not affect them.

They like **to ski.** (present tense)   They liked **to ski.** (past tense)

The infinitive **to ski** is unchanged even though the time of the sentence changes. (See also Chapter 1: Locating the Verb.)

Continue by choosing a REWRITING EXERCISE. After completing one without making any errors, read PROOFREADING STRATEGIES and choose from PRACTICING PROOFREADING.

REWRITING EXERCISE 1: *ed* endings*

Make all changes in the space above each line.

a. Locate and circle each verb (there are 22).
b. Check your choices against the list in the Appendix.

c. Write above each regular verb its past tense **(ed)** form. Do this by adding **ed** to its base form. For example, return the first verb **looks** to its base **look** and then add **ed.**

d. Note: starred (*) verbs and other verbs whose base form ends in **e** drop the **e** before adding the **ed** ending.

MR. TAFT'S HIGH TECH TUMMY

[1]Ted Taft looks like all the other elderly tourists in Las Vegas. [2]He walks around the city's Strip wearing garish jewelry. [3]But when Taft waits at the Marina Casino's blackjack table, the crowd watches his rising pile of chips, not his appearance. [4]Despite stupid mistakes, his winnings *continue to mount. [5]But his success depends on electronics, not luck. [6]A styrofoam belt surrounds his waist. [7]Within that belt rests the most modern cheating equipment in Vegas.

[8]A television camera *snuggles inside Taft's belt buckle. [9]The styrofoam also conceals an ingenious arrangement of prisms, cathode ray tube, and radio/transmitter. [10]Beneath this layer rests a baseball catcher's athletic supporter. [11]The radio receiver utilizes two wires running from inside the metal cup of the athletic supporter. [12]Each time the dealer offers a card, Taft's belt-buckle-camera photographs the card's face, sending it to a receiver inside his accomplice's camper truck.

[13]Taft's partner, Rodney Weatherford, operates an electronic command post inside this truck. [14]His videotape recorders register the identity of each "hole" card. [15]A computer analyzes the information and calculates the composition of the remaining cards in the deck. [16]An electronic shock notifies Taft. [17]Taft places his bets according to those messages inside his socks or athletic supporter. [18]Their total "earnings" amount to $30,000, though they switch casinos after winning $1,000 on any night.

REWRITING EXERCISE 2: *ed* endings

a. Circle the ten verbs that are not in the past.

b. Check your choices against the list in Appendix 3.

c. Begin the first sentence with: **Back in 1901** and write the past tense **(ed)** form above each regular verb.

d. The verb **jam** becomes **jammed** in the past. The starred (*) word is explained after the paragraph.

THE STAMP THAT LAUNCHED A THOUSAND WORDS

[1]Senator Mark Hanna prefers a canal running through the isthmus of Panama, rather than through Nicaragua. [2]To turn sentiment toward his position, his lobbyists plant a news report of a volcanic eruption at Mount Momotombo. [3]The *concocted report fails to mention Momotombo's 100-mile distance from the proposed route. [4]It also neglects to note the absence of any eruptions in Nicaragua since 1835. [5]The Nicaraguan government of course denies the possibility of volcanic activity. [6]Undaunted, Sentator Hanna's friends search stamp dealers in Washington. [7]They locate a Nicaraguan 1-peso stamp of Momotombo in the midst of an eruption. [8]They jam copies of the stamp in envelopes and mail them to each of the ninety senators in an attempt to convince them of the potential danger to a canal in Nicaragua. [9]The Senate selects the site in Panama.

How To Cope with the Unexpected (2)

A few words in the essay above already end with **ed.** They are not verbs even though they appear to be. The easy way to determine whether they are verbs or not is to see if they change when the time changes. You will see that they do not. For example, the starred (*) sentence above contains the phrase:

The concocted report fails to mention . . . (present tense)

When you change the time of the phrase, **concocted** remains unaffected. It is thus not a verb or time word.

The concocted report fail**ed** to mention . . . . (past tense)

For more work with **ed** endings that are not verbs, see Chapter 35.

REWRITING EXERCISE 3: *ed* endings

Using your own paper, rewrite the entire essay, making the following changes:

a. Locate and circle the 10 verbs.

b. Replace the first 5 words of the essay with **The Pentagon recently replaced.**

c. As you rewrite the entire essay, add **ed** to the verbs.

d. The starred (*) word **tops** becomes **topped.** See explanation after essay.

A HANDGUN FOR NATO

[1]The Pentagon is considering replacing the legendary Colt .45 with the Baretta, a handgun of Italian design.

[2]The Baretta offers many advantages to soldiers in the field. [3]In ease-of-handling tests, it tops the Colt and all its seven other competitors. [4]Its smaller size helps its accuracy, making it more reliable. [5]The Colt .45, by contrast, receives a great deal of criticism for its weight and large size. [6]In addition, its heavy recoil causes vibrations all the way to the shoulders. [7]Though sufficiently powerful to stop a horse with a single bullet, the 2.8-pound Colt tends to be unwieldy. [8]It also seems to lack the glamor of the sleek Beretta, James Bond's favorite gun in the Ian Fleming novels.

[9]America's European allies favor the 9 mm. Beretta, and the Pentagon inclines toward going along in an attempt to standardize NATO logistics.

> Proofread your rewritten essay for correctness in both copying and rewriting. Underline each verb ending in **ed.**

How to Cope with the Unexpected (3)

Some verbs of one syllable double the final consonant before adding **ed** or other suffixes. This is the case with **top.** The base of the present tense verb **tops** is **top.** When you add the **ed** to indicate the past, you must double the **p: top**p**ed.** Dictionaries indicate this. See also Chapter 47: Proofreading Doubled Consonants.

PROOFREADING STRATEGIES

The error writers are most likely to make in the use of the regular past tense is choosing the wrong tense or omitting the **ed** ending to indicate the past. Remember to make sure that you really need to use the past tense. Even if most of the essay is in the past, individual sentences may need the present tense. Even if a main verb is in the past, a verb within a clause may remain in the present.

1. What to look for: errors in regular verbs
2. How to look for them: change the time of the action in the sentence and circle the verb.
3. How to correct them: if the content and presence of other time words indicate that the use of the past tense is appropriate, add the **ed**; if the verb is irregular, see Chapter 16 and Appendix 2 for its correct form in the past.

> After you locate and correct all errors in a PROOFREADING EXERCISE, demonstrate your mastery with WRITING ASSIGNMENT 2. The PROOFREADING TEST after Chapter 16 contains past tense errors in both regular and irregular verbs.

PRACTICING PROOFREADING 1

The paragraph below has 9 verbs. Of the 7 regular verbs, find and correct the 4 that need **ed** endings.

¹The 1950s and 1960s generated new musicals. ²The themes of these new shows had genuine substance. ³They range from politics (Fiorello), to big business (How to Succeed in Business Without Really Trying). ⁴Other topics include gang rivalry (West Side Story), the underworld (Pal Joey), and tradition (Fiddler on the Roof). ⁵These shows influenced musicals of the 1970s. ⁶Stephen Sondheim returned to earlier themes in Company and A Little Night Music. ⁷Of course, he also provide musical breakthroughs with those works. ⁸His innovations continue into the 1980s as well. ⁹His Sunday in the Park with George was a critical as well as financial success.

PRACTICING PROOFREADING 2

The essay below has 28 verbs. Of the 21 regular verbs, 11 need **ed** endings. Circle all verbs and correct the 11 errors.

PRESIDENTS AND SPORTS

¹President Garfield used to write with both hands at the same time. ²To amuse himself, he wrote Greek with one hand and Latin with the other. ³Other presidents participated in sports for diversion.

[4]Early presidents share an interest in horses. [5]According to newspaper accounts, President Washington often attend horse races. [6]Like most people in 1771, he also rode horses. [7]President Jackson raise horses and race them as well. [8]He won a famous race in 1806, aboard Truxton, his bay stallion. [9]U. S. Grant gained fame for his feats on horseback, and people call Teddy Roosevelt "cowboy" for his riding skills.

[10]Twentieth-century presidents preferred football. [11]While he was an undergraduate at Stanford, Herbert Hoover managed the school's football team. [12]Dwight D. Eisenhower injured his knee while playing halfback for West Point. [13]He was tackling the great Jim Thorpe when the injury happen. [14]John Kennedy's painful back end his football career at Harvard, but he continued to play touch football. [15]President Nixon warm the bench for Whittier College, but his successor in the White House, Gerald Ford, played better football than perhaps any other president. [16]He played in the College All-Star Game and actually receive an offer to play pro football.

[17]President Lincoln had an unusual pastime. [18]He wrestled when he was a clerk in Illinois. [19]Spectators who place their bets against the tall, thin young man usually end up losing their money.

WRITING ASSIGNMENT 2: *ed* endings

Write a long paragraph on one of the following topics, according to your instructor's specifications for organization and development. Proofread for errors in the use of **ed** endings.

a. Write a letter to a store complaining about or complimenting a salesperson on how he or she serv**ed** you.

b. Write a letter to a company describing how an appliance operat**ed** before it ceased functioning (Use the words **work, buzz, plug, play, roll**).

c. Write the obituary of a famous person (Use the words **live, work, raise, marry, learn**).

d. Describe the events that preced**ed** an important decision you once made.

e. Describe the best or worst bit of advice you have ever receiv**ed.**

f. Write about what inspir**ed** or discourag**ed** you about a figure from history (Use the words **live, marry, invent, work, establish**).

Chapter 16

INDICATING THE PAST TENSE OF IRREGULAR VERBS

ATTENTION FOCUSING: the past tense of irregular verbs*

a. Underline all verbs that are in the past tense.
b. Write in the space provided all irregular verbs, including forms of **to be.**

THE BRASSY LADY (ADAPTED FROM JOHN D. MACDONALD'S THE BRASS CUPCAKE)

1. Halfway up the stairs, I <u>saw</u> movement out of the corner of my eye.   *saw*

2. I turned and saw her, coming out from her hiding spot behind my car.

3. She wore a sun suit in aqua.

4. In her hand, she held a Colt .45 automatic.

5. It pointed right at me.

6. The moment froze forever in memory.

7. Every cinder in the small parking area stood out.

8. I felt the grain of the gray wooden railing under my hand.

9. She looked up at me, her blonde hair ratty and her face puffy.

10. "Stand still for it," she said.

WRITING ASSIGNMENT 1: the past tense of irregular verbs

Write a short paragraph on one of the following topics. If you reuse a topic from Chapter 15, make sure that most of the verbs are irregular.

a. Describe what happened at an event in your family's history: birth, graduation, wedding, funeral. (lead, cost, put, grow, throw, become)
b. Describe an eating scene. (put, drink, fit, sit, cut)
c. How did you acquire some valuable possession? (buy, sell, take, make)

> If you have made no errors in using *ed* endings, try PRACTICING PROOF-READING 1 before asking your instructor to send you on to another chapter. If you did make some errors, read the following REVIEW.

REVIEW: the past tense of irregular verbs

Irregular verbs indicate the past tense by changing rather than by adding a past tense indicator in the final position.

present tense

In the United States, people   **pay**   their taxes with cash or checks.

past tense

In ancient China, people   **paid**   their taxes with sheets of tea.
In ancient Greece, citizens   **paid**   their taxes with personal service.

Check your dictionary for the past tense form of an irregular verb. When no past tense form is indicated, the verb is regular and takes **ed.**

> After you complete a REWRITING EXERCISE without making any errors, read PROOFREADING STRATEGIES and choose a PROOFREADING EXER-CISE.

REWRITING EXERCISE 1: the irregular past tense*

a. Circle all verbs, checking your choices in Appendix 2.
b. In the space above each line, write the past tense form of each circled verb.
c. The starred (*) verb **set** remains the same in both past and present. Other starred (*) words are explained after the essay.

CORVETTE MAGIC

[1]The 1986 Corvette is absolutely wonderful, whether on the move or standing still, according to car enthusiasts.

[2]First, it is filled with technical innovations. [3]Two computers keep the power train operating at its optimum. [4]They make the mechanical goings-on interesting by reporting on them through color graphics in its "Star Wars" dashboard. [5]The bargraph speedometer and tachometer and a panel in the middle of the dash keep the driver informed about action under the hood. [6]An outside thermometer lets the driver know about external road conditions. [7]The Corvette also has forced aluminum steering knuckles, magnesium valve covers, and plastic leaf springs front and rear. [8]But, while the leather bucket seats are tempting to thieves, a new innovation with the key is likely to stymie them. [9]The carmaker *set a microchip in the key, making it impossible to operate the car without it. [10]Neither the electrical nor the fuel systems become operable without the microchip's permission.

[11]But what is even more exciting, the 1986 Corvette is a machine **that flies on the road. [12]The four-speed transmission draws top mileage from an overdrive, averaging over 17 miles per gallon, even with occasional surges at 120 miles per hour. [13]The smooth handling and braking make the driver want to push out the frontiers of driving. [14]The car sticks to the road, thanks to outstanding suspension and tires. [15]An anti-lock braking system is both silent and effective, preventing skids almost completely.

[16]Marshall Schuon, a test driver, says that if he simply *thinks about setting it in motion, the sensitive Corvette almost *drives by itself.

How To Cope with the Unexpected (1)

Because the verb **flies** is a part of clause beginning with **that** (**), it is not the main verb in the sentence. Change it to the past in this instance, but remember that the verb tense in such situations could differ from the main verb tense. In sentence 16, the starred (*) **thinks** and **drives** remain in the present even after the other verb is changed to the past.

REWRITING EXERCISE 2: the irregular past tense

Begin with **By the end of this year,** and copy the essay, making the following changes:

a. Circle **will** + each verb accompanying it, checking your choices in Appendix 2

b. Eliminate each **will** and change each verb to its past tense form.

HOLLYWOOD I—X

[1]Hollywood will again set before the American public nine samples of its most durable product—the sequel. [2]Rather than work with new scripts, studios will take the concepts of past box office hits and make new films out of them.

[3]Ghostbusters II will come to the screens in time for Christmas, along with the third installment in the Indiana Jones series, starring Harrison Ford. [4]Karate Kid will become Karate Kid II, Gremlins II will break into theaters, and Star Trek will go from III to IV. [5]Romancing the Stone will find its sequel named Jewel of the Nile, but, as with Star Trek, the name Police Academy will sell more tickets with a new number after it, rather than with a new title. [6]The fifth movie in Clint Eastwood's Dirty Harry series, however, will find itself with a new name change. [7]The presence of the familiar star in it will make sure that moviegoers are presented with a familiar commodity.

[8]One of the few previous hits that will leave lovers of sequels unsatisfied is 1983 Academy Award winner Terms of Endearment, which ended with the death of a major character. [9]As for the sequels that Hollywood will send into release, their goal is the success achieved by the Rocky remakes, in which the third in the series outgrossed the original.

REWRITING EXERCISE 3: the irregular past tense

Rewrite the headlines in the spaces provided, changing the verb in each headline to its past tense form. (The past tense of the starred [*] word **can** is **could.** See explanation after the exercise.)

1. Congress cuts the budget.   _____

2. Reagan does a double take.   _____

3. Terror spreads after Tylenol kill-ing. _____

4. Tapes tell of torture and death. _____

5. IBM withdraws support for Sys-tem/34. _____

6. Sicily's Mafia goes on trial. _____

7. Haiti hits Baby Doc's troops. _____

8. The Fed makes money out of thin air. _____

9. Jury throws flag on U. of Georgia sports. _____

10. <u>Today Show</u> rises to top. _____

11. Fitness craze brings back bare midriffs. _____

12. Western Airlines *can fly over Salt Lake. _____

How to Cope with the Unexpected (2)

Can (present tense) and **could** (past) are called **modals.** They are widely used as helping verbs (or auxiliaries). Here are the others (with present tense forms in parentheses): **had (has, have), did (does, do), could (can), should (shall), would (will).**

PROOFREADING STRATEGIES

The errors writers are most likely to make in the use of the irregular past tense include incorrect choice of tense and incorrect use of the **ed** ending to indicate the past. Remember to make sure that you really need to use the past tense. Even if most of the essay is in the past, individual sentences may need the present tense. Even if a main verb is in the past, a verb within a clause may remain in the present.

1. What to look for: errors in verbs
   a. verbs without endings
   b. verbs that already end in **ed**
2. How to look for them: change the time of the action in the sentence and circle the verb.
3. How to correct them: if the content and presence of other time words indicate that the use of the past tense is appropriate, change the ir-regular verb to its correct form in the past tense or substitute a reg-ular verb.

> After you locate and correct all past tense errors in a PROOFREADING
> EXERCISE, you can demonstrate your mastery with WRITING ASSIGN-
> MENT 2. The PROOFREADING TEST on p. 155–156 contains past tense errors
> in both regular and irregular verbs.

PRACTICING PROOFREADING 1

Assume that the use of **ed** is correct and look only for the 4 incorrect
forms of irregular verbs.

STRIKES AND SPARES

[1]Implements found in the grave of an Egyptian child suggest that a
game much like bowling was played more than 7,000 years ago. [2]There
might even have been a game during the Stone Age in which large peb-
bles or rocks were rolled at a group of pointed stones. [3]Written records
indicate that bowling was used as part of a religious ritual in European
monasteries about 700 years ago. [4]Peasants would carry clubs for protection, even to church. [5]To help dramatize a point, priests tell the people
to stand their clubs in the corner and to pretend they stood for the devil.
[6]The peasants then throw a large stone at the club. [7]If they hit it, they
were praised; if they missed, they were urged to lead a more virtuous
life. [8]Eventually the priests themselves begin to play the game, and soon
the nobility and landed gentry took it up. [9]It then spread to Germany
and from there to England and elsewhere. [10]Dutch settlers bring a version called ninepins to America and played it on Bowling Green in New
York.

PRACTICING PROOFREADING 2

Of the 20 irregular past tense verbs (including forms of the verb **to
be**), 5 are wrong.

THE PERFECT MATCH

[1]The cast of many famous films and TV shows seems so perfect that
people cannot imagine other performers in the roles. [2]Yet, in many cases,

the choices became perfect after the fact; the casting was often purely accidental.

[3]For Casablanca, that very popular film, the original choices for the lead roles were Ronald Reagan and Ann Sheridan. [4]The second choice for Rick, the cabaret owner, was George Raft, and for his lost love, Hedy Lamarr. [5]The two who get the roles—Humphrey Bogart and Ingrid Bergman—were not even third choices. [6]Similarly, in retrospect, July Garland made an ideal Dorothy in The Wizard of Oz, but Shirley Temple had the first refusal for the role. [7]Charlton Heston let slip by the opportunity to star in High Noon, Robert Redford lead Dustin Hoffman in the fight for the role of Benjamin in The Graduate, and Sylvester Stallone stood first in the hearts of studio executives for the Eddie Murphy role in Beverly Hills Cop.

[8]TV also has a list of accidental stars. [9]Bing Crosby could have been Columbo instead of Peter Falk. [10]Tom Selleck's other commitments saved him from a bomb called A Man Called Sloane, made him available for Magnum, and then costed him the Harrison Ford role in Indiana Jones. [11]The entertainment head of NBC, Brandon Tartikoff shaked his head "no" to both Michael J. Fox as Alex Keaton in Family Ties and Don Johnson as Sonny in Miami Vice. [12]The producers of the two shows fight bitterly to keep the actors they thought perfect for the roles. [13]In these instances, the producers were certainly right.

[14]When it came to casting these shows, luck (fortunately) took a greater hand than either art or science.

WRITING ASSIGNMENT 2: the irregular past tense

Write a long paragraph on one of the following topics, according to your instructor's specifications for organization and development. Proofread for errors in the past tense of irregular verbs. Some of the topics are the same as for Chapter 15. If you use any of the sentences here, make sure they contain irregular verbs.

a. Discuss what you liked about the service at a fast-food store (take, send, sell, think, lead, leave, give).
b. Write a letter to a company describing the fate of an appliance that has ceased functioning (break, sit, fit, fly, fall, drive, catch, hang, go).

c. Discuss the positive accomplishments of a relative who is no longer alive (sew, bear, think, meet, say, make, sell, drive, ride, take, build, catch).

d. Describe that part of your past schooling that contributed most to your presence in college today.

e. Describe the best or worst trip you have ever taken (get, swim, go, take, ride, tell, fall, draw, fly, swear, slide, glide, bend, eat, drink, see, hear).

f. Explain why the losing team failed to win the World Series, Super Bowl, Stanley Cup, or NCAA Championship (lose, throw, run, shoot, fly).

PROOFREADING TEST: past tense of both regular and irregular verbs

The essay below contains 6 errors in the past tense: 4 with regular verbs, 2 with irregular verbs. Because one of the most important principles of proofreading is that you *look for only one error at a time,* proofread this essay twice, first looking for errors in the past tense of regular verbs (**ed** endings) and second looking for errors in the past tense of irregular verbs. You may wish to review the PROOFREADING STRATEGIES for each attempt.

TOP HAT AND TAILS

¹In 1961, in a <u>Life</u> interview, Roseanne Ellis admit that, although she conformed to many chimney sweep traditions, she had never hesitated to use modern equipment.

²She dressed in the accepted uniform of top hat and tails. ³She liked the top hat because it kept soot out of her eyes and because it provided people with the opportunity to touch it for good luck. ⁴The tails added elegance to a grimy job and also remind her of another chimney sweeper maxim not to mess up customers' houses. ⁵She demonstrated old-fashioned grit in pursuing her demanding profession. ⁶In the tradition of chimney sweeps, she worked alone.

⁷But Roseanne Ellis displayed her modern side as well. ⁸She used a specialized chimney vacuum and work out of a yellow truck filled with up-to-date equipment. ⁹The truck served her as both transportation and workshop during the extremely busy fall season. ¹⁰She charged $40 dollars per chimney—usually an hour's work. ¹¹When she advised people to

rid their chimneys of "soot and wax build-up" and to reduce the chances for "spontaneous combustion," she comes on like a professional trained in fire prevention.

[12]Owning her own business permit Ellis to work at her own pace, but she often felt exhaustion and fear. [13]Nevertheless, she said that she would not trade places with anyone.

Chapter 17

INDICATING THE FUTURE TENSE

ATTENTION FOCUSING: the future tense*

a. Locate and underline the word **will.**
b. List **will** plus the verb when it is being used to indicate the future.
c. In the spaces provided below, list other words that indicate the future.

PLANT GENETICS

1. <u>Will</u> there <u>be</u> square vegetables some day?   *will be*

2. Where there is a will, there is a way.   _____

3. There already is a way to make square tomatoes.   _____

4. They will be meatier, tastier, and redder than today's tomatoes.   _____

5. Their cubed shape will make them easier to package.   _____

6. Easier packaging will decrease their price.   _____

7. Many familiar foods might change due to plant genetics.   _____

8. For example, there will be corn plants with three ears.   _____

9. Instead of six, they will only be four feet high.   _____

10. As a result, they are going to need less fertilizer.   _____

11. A decreased need for fertilizer is going to mean lower prices.   _____

_____ _____ _____

WRITING ASSIGNMENT 1: the future tense

Choose one of the following topics and write a short paragraph using **will.**

a. Predict the future for some famous person.
b. Imagine a typical day in your own life ten years from now.
c. Predict the fate of some current songs or videos.
d. Predict the results in an upcoming election.
e. Make a series of resolutions for the new year.

If you have made no errors in the future tense, try PRACTICING PROOF-READING 1 before asking your instructor to send you on to another chapter. If you did make some errors, read the REVIEW.

REVIEW: the future tense

The future tense is used to indicate a coming event. It requires only the word **will** (or **shall**) and the verb in its base form. There is no difference between singulars and plurals in this tense.

According to Samuel Delany's science fiction novel <u>Triton</u>, people from earth **will settle** Mars and the moons of Jupiter.

Everyone **will go** on welfare at one time or another.

If you need to change any tense into the future, simply return the verb to its base form and use **will.**

past	**future**
Citizens **received** 22-digit ID numbers. ⟶	Citizens **will receive** 22-digit ID numbers.

present	**future**
Bureaucracy **controls** life on Triton. ⟶	Bureaucracy **will control** life on Triton.

The verb **to be** appears as **be** in the future tense.

present—with the verb to be	**future**
Triton **is** the center of civilization. ⟶	Triton **will be** the center of civilization.

The future tense also contains a progressive tense that will be discussed in greater detail in Chapter 18.

<table>
<tr><td align="center">**present progressive**</td><td align="center">**future progressive**</td></tr>
</table>

The government **is taping** all citi-——→The government **will be taping** all
zens.   citizens.

Many speakers indicate future action with words other than **will.**
Those alternatives are grammatically correct but not always accepted in
formal writing.

going to	People on Triton are **going to** decorate their bodies.
about to	Fashion is **about to** end.
is coming	The day **is coming** when men and women have sim- ilar names.
the future holds	**The future holds** much confusion for Triton.
from now on	**From now on** Tritons cannot be trusted.

Similarly, when the modals (**can/could, may/might, must,
shall/should, will/would**) express possibilities or conditions, they indicate the future.

The citizens of Triton **might enjoy** destroying the planet that colo-
nized them.

Continue with a REWRITING EXERCISE until you complete one without
making any errors. Then read PROOFREADING STRATEGIES and go to
PRACTICING PROOFREADING.

REWRITING EXERCISE 1: the future tense*

Write all changes in the space above each line.

a. In the first sentence, change **says** to **predicts.**
b. Locate and circle each verb.
c. Change each verb to the future tense by using **will** and, when neces-
    sary, returning the verb to its stem or base form.

HAIR WAVE

[1]Johnny Hawkins, a hairstylist for Soul Scissors, a chain of hair salons specializing in cuts for black women, says that black women reject
both straightened hair and huge Afros. [2]Black women are relaxing their
hair. [3]Even those who want to straighten their hair do not use the old-
fashioned way, preferring blow dryers instead. [4]The most popular style
is the bob. [5]It has a very carefree look. [6]Women just have to shake their

head. [7]It is cut with one side longer than the other, very short in the back, or even shoulder length. [8]The length and style depends on the woman; whatever the length, however, the bob is maintenance-free. [9]Other "in" styles for black hair are the basic pageboy and the feathered snatch-back.

REWRITING EXERCISE 2: the future tense

The words in **boldface** convey the future without using **will.** Copy the paragraph and make the following changes to indicate the future tense:

a. Circle each group of words in boldface.
b. Change them or make substitutions so that **will** (or **will be**) is the only indicator of the future tense.

MINORITIES AND TELEVISION

[1]In the 1965–1966 television season, Bill Cosby was the only minority performer in a starring role, sharing top billing with Robert Culp in I Spy. [2]By contrast, of the seventy-one shows in the 1985–1986 line-up, fourteen starred or co-starred minority performers, and nearly all the others featured them in smaller roles. [3]There **are likely to** be more. [4]Certainly changes are necessary before television **can** reflect a fair picture of America's racial and ethnic composition. [5]Despite the appearance of some Asians in supporting roles, the number of their starring roles **is going to** have to increase. [6]Roles for Latino performers **are expected to** rise also. [7]In addition to roles in regular series, openings **are coming** in TV movies. [8]There **are going to** be more than the three last season (out of more than 100) in which minority characters played principal roles! [9]The future **has to** contain more films like The Defiant Ones, in which a black convict and a white convict escape while chained together.

Proofread your rewritten paragraph for correctness in both copying and use of the future tense. Underline each **will** and its verb.

REWRITING EXERCISE 3: the future tense

As you copy the paragraph on p. 161, change each verb to the future tense by using **will** and, when necessary, returning the verb to its stem or base form. This paragraph contains many examples of the verb **to be.** Do not change sentence 11.

A MOTHER'S LIFE

[1]The baby is teething. [2]The children are fighting. [3]My husband calls and tells me to eat dinner alone. [4]I straighten the children's bedrooms, placing toys neatly on the shelves and clothes neatly in the closet. [5]I prepare a perfect dinner and find the salad picked clean of olives and a cake with finger traces in the icing. [6]The tablecloth is stained with spaghetti sauce. [7]My lipstick has no point. [8]I have PTA meetings and silly school plays to attend. [9]I have to carpool and to listen to blaring stereos. [10]I get wet oatmeal kisses and sticky fingers to clean. [11]"Grow up!" I yell. [12]Next thing I know, they are grown up.

> Proofread your rewritten essay for correctness in both copying and use of the future tense. Underline each **will** and its verb.

PROOFREADING STRATEGIES

The error writers are most likely to make in using the future tense is the use of **gonna,** the incorrect substitution for **going to,** which is itself an informal substitute for **will.** Another common error involves the contraction **will not—won't.**

1. What to look for: errors in the use of future tense.
2. How to look for them: circle key words.
   a. **gonna**
   b. **won't**
   c. **will** followed by a verb that is not in its base form
3. How to correct them:
   a. write out **going to** and **will not**
   b. return verbs to base form

> After you have located and corrected all future tense errors in a PROOF-READING exercise, demonstrate your mastery in WRITING ASSIGNMENT 2.

PRACTICING PROOFREADING 1

The 4 errors in the paragraph on p. 162 are in sentences that contain more than 1 verb. Find those sentences and correct the errors.

MOOD SHOES

[1]People's shoes will often reveal their mood as well as their self-image. [2]A woman feeling sexy and alluring in the morning will put on boots or high heels. [3]If she feels drab and dull, she is goin to choose sensible shoes. [4]If her plan is to avoid calling attention to gender, she will wears loafers or sneakers. [5]Men will also communicate their sense of themselves through their footwear. [6]They wo'nt wear the same things if they are macho, neuter, or sensuous types. [7]If podiatrists have their way, however, people will wear whatever is most comfortable. [8]From their point of view, whatever will suits the mood will not necessarily serve the feet. [9]A woman choosing high heels will be uncomfortable and off balance all day. [10]The lack of balance and discomfort, after an extended interval, will lead to hammertoes, bunions, and other toenail problems.

PRACTICING PROOFREADING 2

Locate and correct the 4 future-tense errors.

SUN SIGNS

[1]Linda Goodman, an astrologer and author of many books, thinks that people who know their birth chart we'll be able to make predictions about their lives. [2]The position of heavenly bodies at the time of birth will exert an influence on an individual's entire life. [3]The sun's influence will be the most powerful, but power will also be exerted by the position of the moon and the planets. [4]People born on June 9, for example, wont have all their qualities determined by the Gemini Sun. [5]All people born on June 9 will shared basic qualities, but differences among them will exist due to the positions of the other heavenly bodies. [6]For example, in matters of speech, the position of Mars is important. [7]If Mars is in Taurus, then that person's speech patterns are gonna be closer to a Taurean's. [8]In other matters, Gemini characteristics will dominate.

WRITING ASSIGNMENT 2: the future tense

Write a long paragraph on one of the following topics, according to your instructor's specifications for organization and development. Proofread for errors in the use of the future tense indicator.

a. How would the acquisition of some household item affect your daily life?

b. In ten years, will the responsibilities of married people undergo change?

c. What effect on behavior will some current fads, styles, or heroes have?

d. What kind of a parent will you be? (If you are already a parent, what would you do differently with another child?)

e. Imagine that you received a financial windfall. What will you do with your riches?

Chapter 18

INDICATING THE PROGRESSIVE TENSES

ATTENTION FOCUSING: progressive tenses*

a. Underline verbs in the progressive tenses.

b. Indicate in the space provided if verbs are in the present or past progressive. (NOTE: In some of these sentences, two concurrent events are taking place.)

FROM HAWTHORNE'S NOTE-BOOKS

1. Two people <u>are expecting</u> an event to take place.   *present prog.*

2. They are waiting for the principal actors in the event.   _____

3. Even as they wait, the event takes place.   _____

4. They realize that they are themselves the chief actors in the event.   _____

5. Another person was writing a story.   _____

6. He found that the story was being shaped against his intentions.   _____

7. The characters seemed to act according to their own will, not his.   _____

8. Unforeseen events began, occurring without his consent.   _____

9. He could not avert the catastrophe that came about.   _____

10. He realized that, as he wrote, he was struggling
with his own fate. _____

WRITING ASSIGNMENT 1: progressive tenses

Choose one topic and write a short paragraph. The progressive tenses require the use of the verb **to be,** so pay attention to subject-verb
agreement.

a. What were you doing at the moment when you heard the news about
the death of some well-known public figure(s)? (use **was**)
b. Imagine what the rest of the household is doing while you are asleep.
c. While the star of a concert, show, or movie is performing, what are
some of the other people on stage or screen doing?

> If you have made no progressive tense errors, try PRACTICING PROOF-
> READING 1 before asking your instructor to send you to another chapter.
> If you did make some errors, read the REVIEW.

REVIEW: the progressive tenses

The **progressive** tenses are used to indicate ongoing or continuous
action—action still in progress. They are indicated with a form of the
verb **to be—am, is,** and **are** in the present, **was** and **were** in the past,
and **will be** in the future—plus the **present participle** of the verb, which
is the base + **ing.** A word ending in **ing** without **am/is/was/are/were** does
not indicate tense.

verb: **look**   infinitive: **to look**   base form: **look**

present participle: **looking**

present progressive	The evil stepmother **is looking** into her magic mirror.
past progressive	Snow White **was looking** for shelter in the dwarfs' home.
future progressive	The hunter **will be looking** to explain himself to the queen.

The verb *to be*

When the verb in a sentence is a form of the verb **to be—am, is,
are, was,** or **were**—the progressive is formed with **being.** The present
participle of the verb **to be** is **being.**

present	present progressive

Snow White **is** disobedient ⟶ Snow White **is being** disobedient.

The form of the verb **to be** used in the present and past progressive is determined by the subject. Singular subjects take **is** or **was;** plural subjects take **are** or **were.** We discussed the agreement of subjects with **is/ was** and **are/were** in Chapter 10. Here is an illustration of the progressive tenses with **plural forms:**

verb: **move**   infinitive: **to move**   base form: **move**

present participle: **moving**

present progressive	California and Mexico **are moving** closer to each other daily.
past progressive	Scientists **were moving** heaven and earth for an answer.
future progressive	Though the two terrains **will be moving** closer, they **will be doing** it at the rate of only four inches per year.

NOTE: The complete verb in the progressive—a form of the verb **to be** plus the participle (**ing** form) of the verb—can be interrupted with **not, also,** and other words. **Evacuations are not being considered.**

NOTE: The progressive forms in the perfect tense (with **has, have, had**), will be discussed in Chapter 19: Indicating the Perfect Tenses.

WHEN SHOULD YOU USE THE PROGRESSIVE TENSES?

The progressive tenses are used to indicate ongoing or continous action—action in progress. The present (or habitual) tense often conveys the same general sense of time as the present progressive, but the progressive usually refers to a more clearly defined period of time than the simple present. Compare **(Presently) I am driving a '78 Buick** and **(Habitually) I drive a '78 Buick.** The progressive is therefore useful in sentences that describe events occurring at the same time. For example:

While I was waiting for prices to go down, I saved up enough money for the expensive car.

Keep in mind that, in any sentence with more than one subject-verb pair (that is, with more than one clause), verbs are not always in the same tense (time). They do, however, maintain a logical connection. In the example above, it would be incorrect to use the present tense in the second clause and write:

While I was waiting for prices to go down, I save up enough money for the expensive car.

Continue with a REWRITING EXERCISE. When you have completed one without making any errors, read PROOFREADING STRATEGIES before doing PROOFREADING PRACTICE.

REWRITING EXERCISE 1: the past progressive*

Write all changes in the space above each line.

a. Locate verbs in those sentences that **do not** contain an **ing** word.
b. After returning them to their base form, add **ing.**
c. Use **were** to indicate past progressive (plural).
d. When you attach the **ing** to the starred (*) word **use** drop the silent **e** at the end of the word: **use + ing → using.**

SOAP

[1]When ancient people washed themselves, they did not* use soap. [2]They kept the harsh soap from their skin, washing their clothes with it instead. [3]The Greeks and Romans, who loved cleanliness, removed their dirt and sweat by beating their bodies with twigs or with a kind of scraper called a strigil.

[4]While civilized people beat and scraped themselves, so-called barbarians made progress. [5]The Gauls made real soap from goat's tallow and beech tree ashes. [6]They used this soap to give their fair hair extra sheen. [7]Considering the Gauls uncouth, Europeans ignored their invention for almost a thousand years.

[8]By the end of the Middle Ages, while European countries imported soap in great quantities, the Spanish made excellent soap, especially in the province of Castile. [9]In many languages, "Castile" is still being associated with fine soap. [10]Still most people did not make everyday use of soap. [11]Most avoided bathing more than once a month anyway. [12]The English Puritans did bathe more often, but distrusted soap, taxing it heavily.

REWRITING EXERCISE 2: the past progressive

Copy the paragraph below, changing verbs to the past progressive. (After returning verbs to their base form, add **ing** and use a form of **to be.**) The use of the starred (*) word **got** is discussed after the essay.

FRIARS TOP PANTHERS

[1]The favored Pitt Panthers expected an easy victory, but, with less than seven minutes left in the game, the Providence Friars led by a point.

[2]Over the next few minutes, the Panthers found out about the tough level of play in the Big East. [3]At that seven-minute mark, the Friars just *got started. [4]As Billy Donovan, the junior guard, scored six straight points, the Friars moved decisively past one of the pre-season favorites in the league. [5]While Joey David scored a game high 18 points for Pitt, Providence's Billy Donovan and Alan Roth combined for 31 to win the game. [6]The Pitt Panthers continue to disappoint their fans, falling to 5–8 in the conference.

How To Cope with the Unexpected (1)

The present participle of the starred (*) word **got** is **getting.** Some writers use **getting** instead of **being**; for example, they write: **He is getting paid too much money.** Most writers, particularly in formal situations, would write: **He is being paid too much money.** Although **getting** will be understood, it does not always replace **being,** so limit its use to casual situations.

REWRITING EXERCISE 3: the present progressive

If you were actually announcing the game in EXERCISE 2, you might have used the **present** progressive. Rewrite "Friars Top Panthers," substituting **are** for **were** and **is** for **was** to indicate the present progressive.

REWRITING EXERCISE 4: the present progressive

As you copy the essay below, substitute for the first sentence: **The only place where lefties are receiving help is in Ms. Morlock's store for lefties in St. Louis Park, Minnesota.** Continue by changing all verbs in the past progressive to the present.

LEFTIES IN THE RIGHT

[1]For a long while, the only place where lefties were receiving help was in Ms. Morlock's store for lefties in St. Louis Park, Minnesota.

[2]Lefties have long been in need of simple tools and utensils. [3]Scissors, teapots, and drinking mugs were not being designed for lefties. [4]When cutting, drinking, or pouring, lefties often feel clumsy and inefficient. [5]The store for lefties was helping by providing items such as lefty

soup ladles and lefty can openers. ⁶All items were selling briskly but none at the rate of a lefty watch, with its winding stem on the left instead of the right side. ⁷Fishing rods, power saws, and sports equipment were also being made available to lefties.

⁸Lefty students were receiving particular aid. ⁹A special ruler, with numbers running from right to left, was one item being offered. ¹⁰A notebook opening from front to back was another popular item being sold in the store. ¹¹Notebooks for righties do not work for lefties because they make their arms rest uncomfortably on the spiral binding. ¹²Quick-drying ballpoint pens were also being made available. ¹³When lefties write, they smear regular ink as their hands move across the lettering.

¹⁴A cheerful sign hanging in the store was reassuring for lefties to read. ¹⁵"If the right side of the brain controls the left side of the body, then only left-handed people are in their right minds."

> Proofread your rewritten essay for corrections in both copying and use of the progressive. Underline each progressive form and the verb to which it attaches.

PROOFREADING STRATEGIES

The errors writers are most likely to commit in the use of the progressive tenses is faulty agreement of verb and subject. Another common error is inconsistency in tense (discussed in greater detail in Chapter 20). You might switch from simple present to simple past, for example, but forget to make the corresponding shift in the progressive, or you might create confusion between two verbs in the same sentence. (If you forget to drop the silent **e** when adding **ing** to the base form of the verb, see Chapter 48 for practice.)

1. What to look for: the **ing** word.
2. How to look for the error:
    a. circle any **ing** words
    b. find if it is paired with **am/is/was/are/were**
    c. note tense of other verbs
3. How to correct the error:
    a. if in the past, use **was/were**
    b. if in the present, use **am/is/are**
    c. eliminate vowel in front of **ing**

> After you locate and correct all progressive tense errors in a PROOF-READING EXERCISE, demonstrate your mastery with WRITING ASSIGN-MENT 2.

PRACTICING PROOFREADING 1

Locate and correct the 2 errors in the use of the present progressive tense.

SEEING THE EYE

[1]Make-up experts are urge women to evaluate themselves honestly before choosing cosmetics. [2]They are not doing themselves any favors by selecting the color that happens to be popular at the moment. [3]If they are being honest enough with themselves to admit that they have puffy eyelids, for example, they will help themselves most with a brown shade. [4]Brown is being used by many women to help make puffy eyelids seem less swollen. [5]It can also make a jutting eyebrow seem less prominent. [6]Women are not being sufficiently careful about the amount of make-up they were applying. [7]Using the brush delicately is essential. [8]Laying on crayon or powders heavily will not keep make-up on for the rest of the day. [9]But light make-up, if refreshed during the day, will have staying power.

PRACTICING PROOFREADING 2

Locate and correct the 5 errors in the use of the progressive.

HANDWRITING ANALYSIS

[1]People are slowly accepting graphology—the study of how hand-writing reveals personality—as a trustworthy means of studying their nature and character. [2]Europeans are studying it more seriously than Americans, with Universities at Basel and Bern establishing departments devoted to the subject. [3]Still, at least one college in the United States—the New School of Social Research in New York City—is offering courses

in graphology. [4]The three basic notions in this field are the stroke, the openings, and the shapes of letters

[5]A person who writes with heavy pressure and dark strokes was revealing a robust, sensual nature. [6]One who writes using very light pressure is probably a sensitive but impractical idealist. [7]Even pressure is a sign of average feelings, neither shallow nor long lasting.

[8]Certain letters are bein studied more intensely than others as a clue to character. [9]An opening at the top of the oval letters, **a, d, g,** and **o,** indicates a truthful person. [10]Ovals left wide open point to a talkative person who is having trouble keeping secrets. [11]The person who closes ovals completely is good at hiding inside information, and one who locks ovals with double loops were hiding a good memory with lies.

[12]As for shape, rounded letters are used by people who are relaxed and receptive. [13]Pointed letters are found in the writings of people who are competitive and take themselves and others quite seriously.

[14]The significance of slant, capitalization, and end strokes is just getting developed by students of graphology.

WRITING ASSIGNMENT 2: the progressive tenses

Write a long paragraph on one of the following topics, according to your instructor's specifications for organization and development. Proofread for errors in the use of progressives.

a. Describe the behavior of two people you are watching at a party. (Use **am** for yourself and **is** for each of the two people you are watching.)
b. What were the fans in the stands doing during a sporting event you attended or watched on television? (Use **were.**)
c. Think of someone who is very different from you, someone with whom you grew up or someone who was at camp, in school, or at work with you. What was this individual doing while you were going about your business (or play)? (Use **were.**)
d. While you are attending school, what is a close friend or family member doing with his or her life? (Use **is.**)
e. Associate yourself with another person, a group, a political movement, or a club. Describe your goals and the process you are using to achieve those goals. (Use **are,** as in **We are hoping to raise enough money for a new gym.**)

Chapter 19

INDICATING THE PERFECT TENSES

ATTENTION FOCUSING: the perfect tenses*

a.   Circle the numbers of sentences using one of the perfect tenses.
b.   List the present perfect verbs (verbs with **has/have**) in the space provided alongside.
c.   List the past perfect verbs (verbs with **had**) in the space provided below.

FROM LAWRENCE BLOCK'S <u>EIGHT MILLION WAYS TO DIE</u>

1.   Kim and her faceless friend have done it.   *have done*

2.   Since they swore eternal love, they have spent their time behind closed doors.   _____

3.   At first, they probably went out together.   _____

4.   He had probably shown her off in some circle or another.   _____

5.   Maybe he talked to somebody who has since talked to someone else.   _____

6.   I had a strong feeling about this but no answers yet.   _____

7.   By the time I left the meeting, the rain had quit.   _____

8.   Even the wind had died down somewhat.   _____

9.   I had to get out of my hotel room, take a few taxis, spend some money.   _____

10. I have not been doing much of that lately.   _____

_____   _____   _____

WRITING ASSIGNMENT 1: the perfect tenses

Write a short paragraph on one of the topics below. The present perfect involves subject-verb agreement, so proofread carefully.

a.   Mention some roles a favorite actor or actress has played, beginning with the very first and working your way forward. (Use **has.**)

b.   Do (a), but begin with the most recent role the actor/actress played and move further and further back. You will have to use **had.**

c.   Consider photographs of yourself that cover about a five-year period. Describe some gradual changes that have taken place. Begin with your appearance now and work your way backward. (After the first sentence, use **had.**)

d.   Do (c), but begin with your appearance in the earliest picture and move forward. (Use **have,** as in **I have changed my hairstyle.**)

If you have made no errors in the use of perfect tenses, try PRACTICING PROOFREADING 1 before asking your instructor to send you on to another chapter. If you did make errors, read the REVIEW.

REVIEW: the perfect tenses

When it is used to signify tense, the word **perfect** means "whole" or "complete."

The present perfect

The **present perfect** tense is used to indicate an action or event that began in the past and continued into the present where it is essentially complete or "perfect." By contrast, actions indicated with the **simple past** took place at a definite time in the past and were completed at that time.

The **present perfect** is formed with **has** (for singulars) or **have** (for plurals) and the **past participle** of the verb. The past participle of a regular verb usually has the same form as the past tense. The past participle of irregular verbs usually ends with **n** or **en,** as in **thrown** or **eaten.** There are, however, many exceptions and variations, making a dictionary indispensable. Consult one whenever you are are unsure what form of the verb you should use with **has/have/had.** APPENDIX 2 in this book provides a list of the principal form of irregular verbs.

singular	**present tense**	
Denmark	**uses**	the cross on its flag.

singular	**present perfect**	
Denmark	**has used**	the cross on its flag since the Crusades.

NOTE: The past participle form of the regular verb **use** is **used.**

plural   **present tense**
The flags of Norway, Sweden, and Finland also **retain** the Crusaders' cross.

plural   **present perfect**
The flags of Norway, Sweden, and Finland **have also retained** the Crusaders' cross.

Notice that the past participle forms of the regular verbs **use** and **retain** are the same as their simple past forms. But, although the past tense of the irregular verb **fly** (below) is **flew,** its past particple is **flown.**

    past tense   **present perfect**
Banners **flew** high in victory.   Banners **have flown** high in victory.

Present perfect of the verb *to be*

Forms of the verb **to be** become **been** in the perfect tenses.

present tense form of **to be:**   The waving flag **is** a rallying point.
       present perfect form: The waving flag **has been** a rallying point.

Again, past participle forms vary often enough to make it necessary to learn them individually or to make it a habit to consult a dictionary when you are unsure.

The past perfect

The **past perfect** indicates an action that already ended (became complete or "perfect") in the past. It is used most often to distinguish between two events in the past, one of which took place before the other. The **past perfect** is formed with **had** and the **past participle** of the verb.

                      simple past
Banners with streamers **replaced** animal figures as rallying points.

Using the **past perfect,** the next sentence moves further back in the past:

Before banners with streamers replaced animal figures as rallying points, the Romans **had used** a staff with an eagle.

Events presented in chronological order do not require the perfect tense:

The Romans **used** a staff with an eagle. Then banners with streamers **replaced** animal figures as rallying points during battle.

NOTE: Both the present and past perfect combine with the **progressive:**

The Greek flag **has been carrying** the cross emblem nearly as long as the Swedish flag.

Although the Saracens **had been carrying** flags, they had not invented them.

Continue with a REWRITING EXERCISE. After you complete one without making any errors, read PROOFREADING STRATEGIES and go on to PRACTICING PROOFREADING.

REWRITING EXERCISE 1: the present perfect*

Write all changes in the space above each line.

a. Circle all verbs; underline their subjects.
b. Change the verb in the first sentence to **has been considering** and continue to change other verbs into their **past participle** form.
c. Write out the subject and present perfect with **has** or **have.**
d. Change sentences already in the present perfect to the past perfect **(had).**
e. The starred (*) word **could've** is a contraction of **could have.** When **have** disappears into the contraction, it is often erroneously written as **of.**

EDISON, WHERE ARE YOU?

[1]The U. S. Patent Office received the patent applications of a new batch of madcap inventors.

[2]One inventory applied for a patent on extremely long elastic suspenders to be used as a fire escape. [3]He has not, however, worked out all the kinks. [4]He lands safely each time he leaps from a hotel room, but the suspenders yank him right back in. [5]Another such "Gyro Gearloose" developed an alarm clock for heavy sleepers. [6]His idea is to hang it on the wall and to have it drop a hammer to wake the sleeper below it. [7]The "knock-clock" is not catching on.

[8]Some other inventions have already been rejected by the Patent Office. [9]One invention has tried to bilk naive buyers by promising to make dollar bills. [10]Another *could've earned its inventor a fortune if it had

managed to turn tap water into gasoline with the help of a magic pill. [11]A third, claiming the ability to diagnose illnesses, has been given a drop of rooster blood. [12]Its analysis declared it to be the blood of an alcoholic.

REWRITING EXERCISE 2: the present perfect

Copy the essay below, but begin by substituting for the first sentence **New research has reopened the study of Paul Revere's ride.**

a. Continue by changing other verbs into their **past participle** form and use them with **has,** forming the present perfect.
b. Change sentences already in the present perfect to the past perfect **(had).**

REVELATIONS REGARDING REVERE'S RIDE

[1]A report on the research into the famous story of Paul Revere's ride found many errors. [2]It revealed that Revere had not been the only horseman riding to warn the Patriots about the movement of British troops. [3]The research showed that William Davis had also been riding to Lexington, having been dispatched there by Dr. Joseph Warren, president of the Provincial Congress in Massachusetts [4]Work by other students of the period has shown some errors in the story of the famous lanterns. [5]There has been no question of the message, "One if by land and two if by sea." [6]Rather, doubt existed as to the identity of the recipients of the message. [7]Research in Revere's own accounts of the night indicates that Revere had already known that the British were coming by sea. [8]It had been another group of patriots, waiting on the Charlestown shore, who had needed the information. [9]Finally, despite legend having him arrive in Concord, research in British documents shows Revere intercepted, questioned, and released by British scouts well short of Concord.

Proofread your rewritten essay for correctness in both copying and the use of perfect tenses. Underline each **has** and its subject.

REWRITING EXERCISE 3: the past perfect

Begin to rewrite the paragraph by opening it with **Before technology eliminated the instruments responsible . . .,** and continue to change other verbs into the past perfect. The starred (*) verb is in the progressive tense. To combine it with the perfect tense, retain the **ing** and add **had been.** There are 3 other examples of the progressive in the selection.

NAMING THE HURTS

[1]The American Medical Association *was having a hard time keeping up with exotic injuries. [2]The difficulty lay not so much in treating them as in giving them names. [3]Still, the AMA managed to come up with intriguing names for damages to the finger. [4]Apparently beer drinkers, chicken neck wringers, and garage mechanics hurt their fingers in previously unnamed ways. [5]The rings of pop-top beer cans were giving beer drinkers swollen and discolored fingers. [6]People employed as chicken neck wringers were developing dislocated fingers. [7]Garage mechanics, using high-pressure nozzles, were perforating their fingers. [8]The AMA, as a result, officially named these injuries "Beer Drinkers' Finger," "Chicken Neck Wringers' Finger," and "Grease Gun Finger."[9] The AMA also threw in "Scandinavian Blubber Finger," an injury common among Norwegian seal hunters and "Money Counters' Cramp," experienced by many bank tellers.

> Proofread your rewritten essay for correctness in both copying and the use of perfect tenses. Underline each verb in the perfect tense.

PROOFREADING STRATEGIES

Writers seem to make two types of errors most often when using the perfect tenses. Some allow the auxiliaries—**has, have, had**—to disappear, sometimes altogether, sometimes into contractions. Others use the incorrect form of the past participle, particularly of irregular verbs.

1. What to look for: errors in the use the perfect tenses.
2. How to look for them: determine if the use of a perfect tense is appropriate (you will find yourself using **have/has**), and circle or underline the following:
   a. contractions
   b. complete verbs with **has/have/had,** paying special attention to endings.
3. How to correct them:
   a. write out all contractions
   b. check past participle form in dictionary

> After you correct all errors in a PRACTICING PROOFREADING exercise, demonstrate your mastery with WRITING ASSIGNMENT 2.

PRACTICING PROOFREADING

Locate and circle the 10 instances of **had** plus the verb. Correct the 4 errors in the form of the past participle.

O'HIGGINS'S ARMY

[1]The patriot-general of Chile's war for independence from Spain had the improbable name of Bernardo O'Higgins. [2]He had received his name from his Irish father, an adventurer who had came to South America and had married a Chilean woman. [3]Bernardo was not a patriot while he lived at home. [4]It was after he left the country to receive an education that he had been converted to the cause of national independence. [5]By October of 1814, his small, underequipped army had been fighting for four years. [6]The end seemed near on October 2, as his army lay outside the city of Santiago, surrounded by a superior Spanish army. [7]During fighting the previous day, O'Higgins's army had lost many men, and he had been wounded himself. [8]Desperate, he thought of a plan. [9]Because he had setted up camp near a farming village, he knew there would be many animals around. [10]He had his soldiers empty barns, stables, and pastures of all livestock. [11]Behind the protection of mules, cows, sheep, and dogs, his army charged through the Spanish lines. [12]He later discovered that the Spanish regulars had actually broke rank and had ran from his ragtag bunch.

PRACTICING PROOFREADING 2

Locate and circle the 12 examples of the perfect tenses. Correct the 4 errors. Pay special attention to **of.**

THE TWO-DOLLAR BILL

[1]The U.S. Treasury has ceased its production of the two-dollar bill. [2]With this action, it has concede that it had made a serious error in reis-

suing it in 1976. [3]At the time, James A. Conlon, the director of the Federal Bureau of Printing and Engraving, had expected the bill to replace half of all one-dollar bills in circulation. [4]He had foresaw a savings of $7 million in printing costs. [5]But these expectations have remained unfulfilled. [6]The two-dollar bill has turned out to be quite impractical.

[7]The Bureau claims that no one could of known that retailers would find the bill impractical. [8]Yet anyone familiar with cash registers knows that they have no extra slots available for a new denomination. [9]The bureaucrats should of also known that habit is very powerful. [10]Because the Treasury had kept the bill out of circulation for ten years before reissuing it in 1976, people had become used to putting dollar bills in particular slots, to giving change of $5 with five singles, and to dividing by one. [11]They did not want to get used to a new denomination, and they were afraid of confusing it with the one-dollar bill.

[12]Even collectors lost interest. [13]The Bureau had printed just too many of the bills.

WRITING ASSIGNMENT 2: the perfect tenses

Write a long paragraph on one of the following topics, according to your instructor's specifications for organization and development. Proofread for errors in the use of the perfect tenses.

a. Who or what has influenced you most since you left high school? (Use **have been** as in **I have been influenced by my father** or use **has** as in **My father has influenced me.**)

b. Identify a goal you once achieved. Then move back in time and describe how you **had come** to set the goal and what steps you **had taken** toward achieving it. (Use **had.**)

c. Using **have been** plus the progressive, discuss what you have been doing to establish connections with other people.

d. Think of someone you have known for a while. Mention some qualities this person had when you first met. Since then, what new skills, abilities, or characteristics has he or she developed?

e. Write a character sketch of a well-known individual in politics, entertainment, academia, sports, or some other field. (Use **has** and **has been.**)

f. Rewrite assignment (*e*). in the past perfect **(had),** after establishing in your first sentence that the individual has changed in some way.

Chapter **20**

CONSISTENCY OF TENSE

ATTENTION FOCUSING: shifts in tense*

a. Circle all verbs in the passage.
b. In the boxes below the passage, record the numbers of those sentences that contain the tenses indicated.

NOTE: Sentences 6, 7, 10, and 11 use more than one tense.

KING ON SCREEN

[1]The history of the screen adaptations of Stephen King's works (is) a short but busy one. [2]In 1976, Carrie, his first novel to be turned into a movie, was an immediate success. [3]In 1978, Stanley Kubrick announced that he planned to direct The Shining; after its release, it was criticized by some as taking too many liberties with the plot. [4]The next November, Salem's Lot came to television.

[5]However, it was in the 1980s that King's name started to become commonplace on the screen. [6]Creepshow, The Dead Zone, and Christine came out in rapid succession, reflecting how quickly Hollywood always capitalizes on a craze. [7]These shows were followed by the movie Stephen King calls his favorite screen adaptation of one of his works, Cujo. [8]Other adaptations followed—Firestarter, Children of the Corn, Cat's Eye, and Silver Bullet. [9]In July 1985, filming began on Maximum Overdrive, a project that King, the director, described as a "moron movie." [10]1986 saw

the release of the very successful <u>Stand by Me</u>, an adaptation of King's story "The Body," which appears in the book <u>Different Seasons</u>. [11]This is undoubtedly not the last movie the viewing public will see with King's name attached. [12]Today, several of his works still await their screen adaptations.

Past Tense	Present Tense	Future Tense
	1	

REVIEW: consistency of tenses

You studied the tenses in Unit IV separately, to make their identification, use, and proofreading easier. But in an essay or paragraph, a writer may sometimes have to use more than one tense in a single sentence, shifting from a tense already established to another in order to show a change in time.

Shifting is, of course, not necessary unless there is a change in time. Sentence 3 of "King on Screen" does not require a shift because the time of the events remains in the past:

> In 1978, Stanley Kubrick **announced** that he **planned** to direct the The Shining; after its release, it **was criticized** by some as taking too many liberties with the plot.

The verbs in boldface let the reader know that the events being discussed took place in the past. The writer should therefore maintain the same tense unless there is a reason for shifting. In sentence 5, no reason for shifting exists:

> However, it **was** in the 1980s that King's name **started** to become commonplace on screen.

The date in this sentence **(in the 1980s)** signals the need to remain in the past tense, as did the date in the previous sentence **(In 1978).** In sentence 6, **always** signals the need to shift to the present (habitual) tense by using the present verb **capitalizes** to indicate the new time frame.

> Creepshow, <u>The Dead Zone</u>, and <u>Christine</u> came out in rapid succession, reflecting how quickly Hollywood always **capitalizes** on a craze.

More often, however, the writer must decide when to shift tenses without the help of indicators such as dates or content words like **always, now,** or **then.** In such cases, the writer must select verb tenses on the basis of content. Consider the following:

Tomatoes **are** a garden favorite in the United States. They **grow** in almost all climates, **produce** an abundant harvest, and **process** easily for storage. They **were** considered poisonous. . . .

The first verbs words in the passage relate facts about tomatoes that are true at present. Because tomatoes are no longer considered poisonous, however, the writer had to shift to the past tense **were** in the last sentence. It would have been inaccurate to retain the present tense.

EXERCISE 1: tense shifts

Consider the essay topics that follow. Indicate in the space provided if each requires mostly the present, the past, or the future tense.

1. Describe what factors a college takes into consideration before accepting or rejecting an applicant. _____

2. Discuss the factors you took into consideration before deciding to attend college. _____

3. To what extent is the car you drive similar to the car you consider ideal? _____

4. How is the common cold spread from person to person? _____

5. Analyze the lyrics of a song you like. _____

6. Tell of your experience the last time you ate out. _____

7. Imagine a day in your life ten years from today. _____

PROOFREADING STRATEGIES

A sentence that contains an unnecessary shift in tense may sound fine out of context. Each sentence must, however, be considered in relation to other sentences in a paragraph. You need to be aware of the overall sense of time in each paragraph and watch for any unneeded shift.

1. What to look for: unneeded tense shifts.
2. How to look for them: determine the overall sense of time in the paragraph (or essay) by considering the topic and reading the first few sentences. Time may be signaled by content words: **then, now, before, later.** More often, you will have to determine time on the basis of content.
    a. Underline all verbs that are not in the basic tense of the paragraph.
    b. Decide if each underlined verb was shifted unnecessarily.
3. How to correct them: change verbs to a tense consistent with the overall sense of time or the context of the particular sentence. If you

must make changes, be sure that any affected subjects and verbs remain in agreement.

PRACTICING PROOFREADING 1

Locate and correct the 5 errors in tense consistency.

THE FIFTH STRING

[1]The American banjo underwent many changes before settling into its present form. [2]The three-stringed rebec, an ancestor of the banjo, originated in Arabia about 1,000 years ago. [3]It spread with the spread of Islam, and it was eventually brought to the United States by slaves. [4]Thomas Jefferson refers to the slaves' instrument as the "banjar," an instrument with four strings. [5]Although some variants of the banjar had five strings, the distinction of adding the odd-looking fifth string, which goes only halfway up the neck of the five-string banjo, belongs to Joel Walker Sweeney, who adds the string in that configuration in 1831. [6]During his lifetime, Sweeney made a command appearance for Queen Victoria and is a hit on the New York stage. [7]His company was the first of a long line of minstrel shows that enjoy popularity into the 1890's. [8]At the time of his invention, no other instrument was strung the same way. [9]The addition of the high-pitched fifth string brightened the sound of the banjo and gives it its characteristic sound. [10]Not long ago, some said that the addition of the fifth string to the banjo ranks as America's greatest contribution to the world of musical instruments; it was certainly one of the most distinctive.

PRACTICING PROOFREADING 2

Locate and correct the 5 errors in tense consistency. (Determine if the tense is appropriate to the content of each sentence.)

[1]Chocolate comes from cacao beans. [2]They grow inside pods on cacao trees. [3]The beans are roasted, shelled, and ground, releasing the cocoa butter inside the beans. [4]Cookbooks call the mixture of this cocoa butter with finely ground pieces of the bean "chocolate liquor."

[5]Chocolate liquor is the base for all chocolate products. [6]By the time the early Spanish explorers reach Mexico, the Aztecs are drinking chocolate. [7]The explorers take some cocoa beans back to Spain in 1528. [8]Over the next 200 years, all of Europe develops a great liking for chocolate, though for a long while people drink it unsweetened.

MASTERY TEST FOR UNIT IV: the tenses

The essay below, adapted from Stephen Crane's <u>The Red Badge of Courage</u>, contains 7 errors in the use of tenses, including lack of consistency. Because one of the most important principles of proofreading is that you look for only one error at a time, proofread this essay as many times as there are types of errors for which you are proofreading.

RETURNING

[1]The youth went slowly toward the fire his friend indicate. [2]As he reeled, he thought of his comrades' welcome. [3]He had a conviction that he would soon feel in his sore heart the barbed missiles of ridicule. [4]He could of invented a tale but he had no strength for it; he would be a soft target.

[5]He had make vague plans to go off into the deeper darkness and hide, but they were all destroyed by the voices of exhaustion and pain from his body. [6]His ailments were force him to seek the place of food and rest, at whatever cost.

[7]He swing unsteadily toward the fire. [8]He saw the forms of men throwing black shadows in the red light, and as he went nearer he could somehow sensed that the ground was strewn with sleeping men.

[9]Of a sudden he was confronted by a black and monstrous figure. [10]A rifle barrel catches some glinting beams. [11]"Halt! Halt!" [12]He was dismayed for a moment, but he presently thought that he recognized the nervous voice. [13]As he stood tottering before the rifle barrel, he called out, "Why, hello, Wilson, you—you here?"

Unit Five

PROBLEMS WITH SENTENCE BOUNDARIES
(fragments and run-ons)

INTRODUCTION TO SENTENCE BOUNDARIES

In Unit V, you will be working to identify and correct any problems you might have with sentence boundaries. The "boundaries" of a sentence are marked by a capital letter at its beginning and a period, question mark, or exclamation point at its end. When less than a sentence or more than a sentence is placed within those markers, two distinct (though often related) problems result. If there is less than a sentence between the markers, the result is called a **sentence fragment,** or simply a **fragment.** Unit V provides exercises for the elimination of five different types of fragments: dependent-word (21), added-detail (22), missing-subject (23), **ing** (24), and **to** (25) fragments. If you have a problem with fragments, you probably make them in only one or two habitual patterns and should focus on only those, though doing the other chapters may help to reinforce your sense of completeness in writing sentences.

If two or more sentences are placed within the boundary markers, the result is called a **run-on sentence** or simply a **run-on.** Unit V provides work in two different types of run-ons: the comma splice (26) and the fused sentence (27). Again, your difficulties may lie more with one than the other.

Sentence Fragments

As its name implies, a sentence fragment is a piece of a sentence—some people call it a "broken" sentence. In order to be whole or complete, a sentence must possess a **subject,** a **verb,** and a complete idea. Many people do not realize they have created a fragment because, as they proofread their paragraph, they unconsciously use sentences that come before and after the fragment to complete it. The many deliberate examples of fragments in advertisements, on product labels, in television program descriptions, and in instructions also contribute to the difficulties writers have in avoiding fragments. Often these commonly seen fragments are used to save space, to call attention to themselves, to portray conversational, informal English, and perhaps even to mislead consumers. At other times they are used unintentionally; there are just plain errors. See if you can figure out the purpose of the fragments (in **boldface**) in the examples taken from a placemat in a restaurant:

Faraway in a magic, make-believe ice cream land called Friendlyville™ lives a wonderful wizard.

He's called The Friendly Ice Cream Wizard™ because he can make all your ice cream dreams come true.

All you have to do to go to Friendlyville™ is be a friend to anyone. **And then pretend.** Pretend you see The Wizard's ice cream castle. **And Fribbles 10 feet tall. Super sundaes bigger than you are. Ice cream cones as tall as trees. And sprinkles raining down.** The Friendly Wizard will whisk you off to Friendlyville™ whenever you're ready to make believe in make-believe. **Like right now.**

Run-ons

Writers should avoid run-on sentences for basically the same reasons they avoid sentence fragments: they can be confusing to the reader, and they can be very annoying. If readers cannot sort out the writer's meaning, they have no access to the writer's ideas. At other times, readers might actually make out the intended meaning but find annoying the writer's inability or unwillingness to punctuate according to accepted rules or conventions. In such a situation, the writer's ideas may never penetrate the readers' irritation or overcome the readers' belief that the writer does not know the rules of grammar. Just one example should illustrate how a run-on can interfere with the communications process:

Charles skis well Britt skis better.

What you have just read is either a comma splice or a fused sentence, depending on which of two meanings the writer intended to convey:

Charles skiis well. Britt skiis better.

or   Charles skiis. Well, Britt skiis better.

To tell what the writer really meant, a reader would have to be a psychic. The potential for uncertainty increases with the length of the sentence.

Rest assured, however, that your sentence boundary problem is not likely to be very serious. If you did not already possess an internal sense of completeness, most of your sentences would be fragments or run-ons. But, in fact, you are likely to make boundary errors in only a small percentage of your sentences. Eliminating boundary errors thus often requires no more than the ability to notice which of your sentences are different from others. Once you learn to set a few aside and examine them individually, you should be able to locate your error.

Chapter 21

DEPENDENT-
WORD FRAGMENTS

In this chapter, we call both **relative pronouns** and **subordinating conjunctions** "dependent words." When one of these words begins a part of a sentence that contains a subject and a verb, that segment is called a **clause.** More specifically, relative pronouns begin **relative clauses,** and subordinating conjunctions begin **subordinate clauses.** But both are **dependent** because they depend on another part of the sentence for completeness. In the REVIEW following ATTENTION FOCUSING, we will discuss these clauses in greater detail.

subordinating conjunctions

after	as	once	unless	wherever
although	as if	since	until	while
anyhow	because	so that	when	why
anytime	before	though	whenever	
anywhere	if	till	where	

relative pronouns

that	whom
what	whatever
which	whoever
who	whose

ATTENTION FOCUSING: dependent words*

   a. Locate and circle the dependent words in the sentences on p. 191.
   b. Write each dependent word in the space next to its sentence.
   c. Underline the part of the sentence headed by each dependent word.
   d. Write the remaining part of each sentence in the space provided below it. Notice that it is capable of standing by itself. The rest of the sentence depends on it for completeness.

1. (While) Colonel Lee was Superintendent at West   *while*
   Point, one of the cadets under his charge was
   James McNeill Whistler.

   One of the cadets under his charge was J. M. Whistler.

2. Lee supervised Whistler before the painter be- _____
   came famous.

3. Before he discharged Whistler, Lee offered him _____
   the opportunity to avoid disgrace by resigning.

4. Lee later recalled that Whistler declined. _____

5. The discharge was apparently necessary be- _____
   cause Cadet Whistler had a poor attitude.

6. When he was asked to produce diagrams of a _____
   water crossing, Whistler added to it two boys
   sitting on a bridge.

7. He was informed that the additions were un- _____
   necessary.

8. The painter drew the children on the shore once _____
   he erased them from the bridge.

9. After he was told to eliminate them completely, _____
   Whistler complied.

10. In the distance there appeared two little graves, _____
    as if the boys had died.

NOTE: When a sentence begins with a dependent word, a comma is
placed at the end of the clause. (The preceding sentence illustrates
this point, as does Sentence 1 in ATTENTION FOCUSING.)

> If you have made no errors in ATTENTION FOCUSING, try PRACTICING
> PROOFREADING 1 before asking your instructor to let you go on to an-
> other chapter. If you did make errors, read the REVIEW.

REVIEW: dependent words

A dependent clause contains a subject and a verb, and yet it cannot stand by itself because of the dependent word. When you add one of the words listed at the beginning of this chapter to a complete sentence, you reduce its completeness; you make it dependent on a part of a sentence that can stand on its own—an independent clause.

Here is a complete sentence: **The Braves left the ballpark.**

Add a dependent word to it: <u>when</u> **the Braves left the ballpark**

Despite the presence of a subject **(Braves)** and a verb **(left),** you now have a partial or broken sentence that depends on some other information to make it complete. What else was happening when the Braves left the ballpark? Did the fans cheer? Did lightning strike home plate? Until you complete that sentence, your reader will simply not know. Without additional information, the idea expressed in the partial sentence is incomplete. More precisely, the idea is now **subordinate,** or lower in importance, than another, complete idea that you will have to add to it.

The words called **relative pronouns** similarly make clauses depend on another part of the sentence for completeness.

Here is a relative clause with **that: that I found under the car.**

The word **that** clearly refers to something outside the clause in which it appears.

Here it is in a sentence: **He lost the ball that I found under the car.**

In the complete sentence, the word **that** "relates back" to the noun—**ball**—and must thus be attached to the independent clause. The relative pronouns (**that, who,** and **which** are the most common) in a sense add details to the sentence. Chapter 22 provides a more detailed discussion of how they create fragments.

For suggestions on how to make **dependent-word fragments** convey a complete idea, see the section on PROOFREADING STRATEGIES. For now, learn to recognize the dependent words that appear most often in **your** writing. Some of them might have more than one meaning and use, but, if you get used to noticing them, you are well on your way to the first step toward effective proofreading: knowing how to look for dependent-word fragments.

REWRITING EXERCISE 1: using dependent clauses*

a. Circle the dependent word (subordinate conjunction) of each fragment.
b. Invent a complete sentence for each fragment, and make the fragment part of that sentence.
c. If you place the subordinate clause at the beginning of your sentence,

mark its end with a comma. If it comes at the end of your sentence, it usually needs no comma.

d. The word **as** is the dependent word in item 2 even though it is the second word. Such words as **even, not, just,** and **only** sometimes precede the dependent word.

1. if the shoe fits _____ *If the shoe fits, you should wear it.*
You should be satisfied if the shoe fits. _____

2. just as Sheila came onto the boat _____

_____

3 if she looked over the boat's rail _____

_____

4. whenever Sheila rides a boat _____

_____

5. although there is no possible connection _____

_____

6. because she feels sick after boat rides _____

_____

REWRITING EXERCISE 2: combining sentences with dependent words

Copy the passage that follows, making the following changes:

a. Choosing among the dependent words **although, if, because,** or **when,** combine sentences 1 and 2, 4 and 5, 6 and 7, and 9 and 10.
b. Pay attention to punctuation, especially the placement of the comma.

SMART SHOPPING

[1]You want to become a better shopper. [2]You should remember that the store has been arranged to part you from your money. [3]The store makes high-profit items easily visible. [4]You see things near the checkout or the door. [5]You can be sure they have a high markup. [6]Some items are placed at eye level. [7]This is done to make it more likely you will buy them. [8]Of course, the placement of items is not the only trick. [9]You may need only one can of tuna. [10]You may be tempted to buy three priced "3 for $1.79." [11]Being aware of the tricks stores use can make you a better shopper.

How To Cope with the Unexpected (1)

In sentence 11 above, there is a relative pronoun, even though you cannot see it! The word **that** has been left out, as it often is in English:

Being aware of the tricks ~~that~~ stores use can make you a better shopper.

Although fragments rarely result from this "implied" **that,** knowing about it can help you better understand how clauses are joined; this in turn decreases your chances of writing a fragment.

REWRITING EXERCISE 3: combining sentences with dependent words

Copy the essay below, making the following changes:

a. Combine at least 4 pairs of sentences using dependent words.
b. Pay attention to the punctuation of the sentences you create.
c. Using dependent words as your guideline, underline all clauses that would be fragments if they were not attached to sentences.

ADAPTED FROM THE STAR ROVER BY JACK LONDON

[1]It is a funny thing, this hanging of a man. [2]I have never seen a hanging. [3]I have been told by eyewitnesses the details of a dozen hangings. [4]I know what will happen to me. [5]I will stand on the trap, leg-manacled and arm-manacled. [6]The knot will be tightened against the neck. [7]The black cap will be drawn. [8]They will drop me down until the momentum of my descending weight is fetched up abruptly short by the tautening of the rope. [9]The doctors will group around me. [10]One will relieve another in successive turns in standing on a stool. [11]His arms will be passed around me to keep me from swinging. [12]His ear will press close to my chest. [13]He will count my fading heartbeats. [14]Sometimes twenty minutes elapse after the trap is sprung. [15]The heart stops beating. [16]They make most scientifically sure. [17]A man is dead once they get him on a rope.

PROOFREADING STRATEGIES

1. What to look for: dependent-word fragments.
2. How to look for them: beginning with the last sentence, circle each dependent word at or near the beginning of a sentence. Look for the dependent words you use most often.

a. When you have found a dependent word, see if the sentence contains any subject-verb pair other than the pair in the dependent clause.

b. If there is another subject-verb pair, forming an independent clause, you have a correct sentence because the dependent clause is attached. If there is no other subject-verb pair, you have a fragment.

3. How to correct them: either join the fragment to a nearby sentence (as in REWRITING 1) or drop the dependent word, enabling the clause to stand by itself. For example:

The crowd went wild. **When the Braves left the ballpark.** No one on the team was smiling.

The fragment in boldface can be attached to the sentence on either side:

The crowd went wild **when the Braves left the ballpark.**
or **When the Braves left the ballpark,** no one on the team was smiling.

The fragment can also stand by itself if the dependent word **When** is dropped:

The Braves left the ballpark.

NOTE: This last method will provide correct sentences but may also create short, choppy sentences that seem to lack cohesion (which is why the correct sentences in REWRITING 2 and 3 are combined.)

PRACTICING PROOFREADING

Of the 14 dependent words, 4 begin fragments. Correct them.

CAT MYTHS

[1]Even though cats were domesticated several centuries ago, several myths about them exist to this day. [2]Perhaps the most common is that cats will always land on their feet. [3]Although this may be true most of the time. [4]Even the most agile cats can misjudge heights or get clumsy. [5]A modern ailment for cats is high-rise syndrome, called so because the source of many cats' injuries is their jumping from windows in high-rise apartments. [6]Another myth is that cats cannot be trained. [7]Cats will come when called, walk on a leash, and even give up bad habits such as clawing and spraying. [8]After they have been trained patiently. [9]Some

people believe that cats have ESP, but, in truth, they just have senses that are more acute than ours. [10]Their hearing and vision surpass ours, and they have a special smelling organ in the roof of their mouths. [11]Which is why a cat sometimes smells things with his mouth open. [12]Finally, cats and dogs are not necessarily enemies. [13]Friendship between the two is most easily established if a young animal is introduced to the home of an older one. [14]The young cat or dog learns to accept the other species while it is growing up. [15]The two animals will play together, near each other, and even defend each other. [16]Although it is best to feed them in separate locations. [17]Most myths about these mysterious animals have some basis in fact, but few are absolutely true.

PRACTICING PROOFREADING 2

Circle all dependent words. Correct the 5 dependent-word fragments.

FLOPPY DISKETTES

[1]The floppy diskettes used in microcomputers can reliably store a great deal of information. [2]Like any tool, they do best if they are well cared for. [3]They should never be bent or flexed. [4]Even though they are called floppy diskettes. [5]The exposed surfaces of the magnetic media should not be touched or allowed to come into contact with any hard surface. [6]When they are not being used, they should be stored in protective sleeves in a vertical position. [7]Although particles of dust might seem negligible to you. [8]To the magnetic head of a disk drive, they seem like boulders. [9]Even an invisible smoke particle can create problems. [10]The diskettes should not be exposed to extremes of temperature. [11]Even if they are in their protective sleeves. [12]Also, magnetic fields can cause the erasure of the records the diskettes hold. [13]Because diskettes can also be ruined by liquids like soda. [14]It is best to store them in a safe place where nothing can accidentally spill on them. [15]Finally, there are the heads in the disk drives. [16]That read the data stored on the diskettes. [17]These heads should be cleaned.

WRITING ASSIGNMENT: using dependent clauses

Write a long paragraph, following your instructor's specifications for organization and development. Then proofread for dependent-word fragments, using the strategies you have learned.

a. Look at the world through the eyes of a small child. Write about the problems you face, using your own dependent clauses or some of the following clauses:

just because I am small   which I really hate
whenever I am near big people   although I look tough
as if I didn't even matter   ever since I can remember
until I grow up   when I get older

b. Describe two people playing tennis, dancing, or grocery shopping together. Using dependent words, show how one person reacts to the actions of the other. **(George removed the live lobster that Judy put in the cart.)**

c. Describe your expectations for your future. Use subordinating conjunctions to relate these expectations in time **(After I graduate, . . .).** You might also want to use some conditional sentences **(If. . . . then. . . .).**

Chapter **22**

ADDED-DETAIL FRAGMENTS

ATTENTION FOCUSING: added details*

a. In the paragraph below, circle the nouns in **boldface.**

b. Some of these nouns are followed by a group of words that add details to them. Underline the phrases or clauses that add detail to the noun that precedes them.

JAPANESE FOODS

[1]To Americans, Japanese **foods** may seem strange and exotic. [2]Some grocery stores now carry a wide variety of Japanese **foods** and ingredients. [3]For example, there is (daikon,) a white radish that can grow a few feet in length. [4]The produce section might also carry **bean sprouts,** which are tiny green mung beans that have sprouted in darkness. [5]Also available is **tofu,** which is a protein-rich food made of soybean curd. [6]Roasted or canned **tofu** is called yake tofu. [7]**Shiratake** is usually sold canned. [8]Made from yams, shiratake is a springy **noodle** that is used in suki-yaki. [9]Also used in suki-yaki are **chrysanthemum leaves,** a delicacy difficult to find in the United States. [10]Spinach leaves are often used as a **substitute.** [11]The Japanese also provide us with several varieties of odd-looking but tasty **mushrooms,** mushrooms that are canned or dried. [12]Another widely used ingredient is **kelp,** and edible seaweed used in sushi, soups, and rice crackers. [13]For those looking for something less exotic, there are several kinds of rice and the **mutsu apple,** an apple first grown in Japan.

If you complete the ATTENTION FOCUSING without any added-detail fragments, do PROOFREADING 1 before asking your instructor to let you go to another chapter. If you did make errors, read the REVIEW.

REVIEW: adding details

Fragments sometimes occur when writers wish to add some information to a sentence, particularly to a noun or a noun phrase at the end of a sentence. Instead of simply continuing the sentence, they begin a new sentence. Their new "sentence," however, is actually a fragment because the subject and verb remain in the previous sentence.

An example of such a phrase or clause (also called a **postmodifier**) that follows a noun and modifies it would be the words in **boldface:**

The shoes come in two colors, **red and blue.**

By themselves, those words would constitute a fragment because they lack both subject and verb.

Another example of an added-detail fragment would be the words in **boldface** in the next sentence. Notice that they "echo" or repeat the noun.

Mary spent most of her time looking for a good man, **a man who would return her love.**

Again, if those words in boldface were not attached to the rest of the sentence, they would constitute a fragment.

As writers add details in the form of examples or a partial list of items, they sometimes feel the sentence is becoming too long and cut it off with a period. The new "sentence" they create seems complete to them because they are keeping in mind the subject and verb established at the very beginning. But the "sentence" is instead a fragment, lacking the subject and verb necessary for completeness. The words in **boldface** constitute an added-detail fragment:

The Flexible-Neck Fire Starter is a small torch for lighting charcoal grills, pilot lights, fireplace logs. **And matches that won't light.**

To complete the fragment and enable it to stand by itself, you would have to add a subject and a verb:

And it can light matches that won't light.

NOTE: The pronoun **it** is a perfectly good subject. Although it is true that you need to know from the previous sentence what **it** stands for, the pronoun is a subject and completes the sentence.

By far the most common type of added-detail fragment begins with one of these words: **which, who, that, where,** and **how.** Each of these words usually begins a clause that provides additional information to a noun that has already appeared before it. The entire phrase is thus no more than a kind of description or elaboration of a subject. Because it does not contain the subject, it must remain attached to the part of the sentence that does have a subject and a verb.

I bought a ticket from my cousin Charles, **who works in the local Ticketron office.**

By itself, **who works in the local Ticketron office** would be a fragment, an incomplete sentence, unable to stand on its own. It must remain connected to the part of the sentence that contains a subject (**I**) and a verb **(bought).**

The situation is similar in the following sentence:

He liked musical groups from the 1960s and 1970s **that included the Beatles, Led Zeppelin, and Procol Harum.**

By itself, **that included the Beatles, Led Zeppelin, and Procol Harum** would be an added-detail fragment, unable to stand on its own. The clause beginning with **that** provides additional information about the noun **groups.** The subject for the entire sentence is **He,** and the verb is **liked.**

If you wanted to separate the clause beginning with **that** from the first half of the sentence, you would have to replace the relative pronoun **that** with a subject that can stand on its own.

He liked musical groups from the 1960s and 1970s.
The groups included the Beatles, Led Zeppelin, and Procol Harum.

REWRITING EXERCISE 1: combining sentences to add details in the same sentence*

Rewrite the paragraph, using the relative pronouns **who** (with people), and **that** and **which** (with objects, events) to combine sentences 3 and 4, 5 and 6, 8 and 9, 11 and 12, and 14 and 15. Example:

The passage details nuclear winter. Nuclear winter is considered to be one possible result of nuclear warfare.

The above sentence can be combined by using **which:**

The passage details nuclear winter, **which** is considered to be one possible result of nuclear warfare.

ADAPTED FROM <u>THE COLD AND THE DARK</u> BY ERLICH AND SAGAN

[1]Within a week after nuclear war, the amount of sunlight at ground level would be reduced to a few percent of normal. [2]The hardships that

would result include extreme cold, water shortages, and lack of food and fuel. [3]Particularly hard hit would be urban survivors. [4]They would probably attempt to leave their cities. [5]All survivors would be desperate for food. [6]The food would be difficult to find. [7]Even in a summer war, subfreezing temperatures would damage or kill crops, and most farm animals and wildlife would be weakened or killed by radiation. [8]The freeze would also affect most sources of water. [9]Water would be needed for survival. [10]Ruptured chemical tanks would spill into streams and rivers. [11]Even the ocean would be affected by low light levels. [12]They would hinder photosynthesis, the key to life. [13]Plankton would die off rapidly, and links in the food chains would be disrupted. [14]The disruptions would include human beings. [15]They will be unable to get food from the ocean because of several factors, including pollution and inaccessibility due to violent coastal storms.

REWRITING EXERCISE 2: adding details

Rewrite the passage, making new sentences of each clause that begins with an "echo" word in boldface. Your new **second** sentence would be **They arrive in a definite order.** You can also write **Smells arrive in a definite order.**

THE SMELLS OF SPRING

[1]The first signs of spring for me are smells, **smells** that arrive in a definite order. [2]First and most pleasant is the odor that makes itself known at night. [3]I will leave work one damp night and know that nearby is a skunk, **a skunk that has recently awakened from its winter sleep.** [4]The next smell I enjoy happens only once a year. [5]After the snow has melted, but before the grass has begun to turn green, there is a smell that comes from the earth, **earth that has been frozen and hidden all winter.** [6]The first whiff is fresh and clean, unlike the muddy smell the spring rains will give it. [7]Those rains produce the next odor, **an odor** to be repeated many times during the year. [8]Still, its first occurrence is pleasant just because it is a sign of spring. [9]Finally, there is the odor of growth that begins shortly after the rains and continues for weeks as the grass

shoots up; buds form on trees and shrubs; and crocuses, dandelions, and other spring flowers come into bloom. [10]I enjoy all these smells, **smells** that let me know the long winter has ended.

REWRITING EXERCISE 3: combining sentences to add more than one detail in the same sentence

Until now, you have been adding (or detaching) one detail at a time. But you can add more than one detail to the same sentence:

He looked to the horizon, **the distant horizon, blue with haze.**

Notice that a comma separates the two phrases that add detail or modify the noun **horizon.**

Combine the two sentences that follow each numbered sentence, attaching them both to the first sentence. Underline the added details or **postmodifiers** you have created. Notice that once you make postmodifiers out of the sentences, they can no longer stand on their own.

SNAP-ON ROOFS, TOO?

[1]Your next house may be built of styrofoam. It is a combination of expanded polystyrene. It is the newest concept in building material. [2]The igloo-shaped dwelling could be built on site. It would be cottage-sized. It would be completed in just a few hours. [3]The styrofoam system is cheaper than conventional housing. It is a better insulator. It is more fire retardant. [4]The producer of this plastic construction material is Dynatherm Systems. It is a recent entrant in the American market. It is a member of the National Association of Home Builders.

_____
_____
_____
_____
_____
_____
_____
_____
_____
_____
_____
_____
_____
_____

PROOFREADING STRATEGIES

1. What to look for: added-detail fragments.
2. How to look for them: begin reading your essay in reverse order. This process will be particularly productive in looking for added detail fragments, which will have nothing to modify if read out of order.
   a. Look for relative pronouns (**who, which, that**) by themselves or in combination with indefinte pronouns (**some of which, those that, one who**) at the beginning of sentences.
   b. Look for any repetition or restatement in the sentence of a noun at the end of the previous sentence.
   If the sentence lacks a subject or a verb or a sense of completeness when considered by itself, you have a fragment.
3. How to correct added-detail fragments: Add the fragment to the sentence just before it. After all, it is simply adding detail to a noun in that sentence. If the detail is important enough to deserve its own sentence, add to the fragment the subject (usually a noun or a pronoun) or the verb it needs. You can correct the common fragment that begins with **For example** by adding both a subject and a verb: **One example of this is. . . .**

PRACTICING PROOFREADING 1

Locate and correct the 4 added-detail fragments, paying careful attention to punctuation and capitalization.

MYSTERY DISEASE IN OLD CATS (ADAPTED FROM <u>SCIENCE NEWS</u>, 3/15/86)

[1]Around 1980, veterinarians began noticing that some older cats were displaying symptoms similar to humans with hyperactive thyroid glands. [2]The problem is of near-epidemic proportions in some areas, according to Leslie Bullock. [3]Who is a veterinarian studying the disease. [4]One percent of cats over eight years old may have the disease in two highly affected cities. [5]Boston and New York. [6]Untreated cats with the disease would likely die, but there are effective treatments, including radiation therapy, removal of the glands, and control of gland activity with a daily pill. [7]No relationship between the disease and diet, general health, environment, or time spent outdoors has been found. [8]Yet vets are concerned that the illness might be a response to an environmental factor. [9]Possibly exposure to a pollutant. [10]If so, they say these older cats

may be a forewarning of what is in store for other species. [11]Species that include humans.

PRACTICING PROOFREADING 2

Correct the 4 added-detail fragments.

ADAPTED FROM ENIGMA OF THE MIND BY ROBERT CAMPBELL

[1]The real-life heroine of The Three Faces of Eve, the famous film about a multiple personality, was Chris Sizemore. [2]A woman who was not one but three people, each with dissimilar characteristics.

[3]The story began for Chris at the age of five, when her grandmother died and her mother made her kiss the corpse. [4]A psychiatrist later concluded that the experience had triggered the problem. [5]Which was a psychological breakup in the girl. After that Chris was different people in turn. [6]One of them, whom her psychiatrist called Eve White, was demure, retiring, almost saintly. [7]Another, Eve Black, was a vain, rowdy, irresponsible woman. [8]Who once tried to strangle her child. [9]A third was Jane, a subtle mix of Eve White and Eve Black. [10]The film was made about these three personalities. [11]Chris was then 25 years old.

[12]By her doctor's account, she later went on to assume eighteen other personalities. [13]One was the Spoon Lady. [14]Who collected spoons, and the Blue Lady, who wore only that color. [15]Some could sew or drive a car; others lacked those skills. [16]At last, in 1975, Chris was declared fully recovered, and she revealed that she was the subject of the movie.

WRITING ASSIGNMENT: adding details

Write a long paragraph on one of the following topics according to your instructor's specifications for organization and development. Proofread for errors in added-detail fragments.

a.   Make a list of some daily activities: brushing teeth, eating breakfast, meeting friends, going to school, going to work, etc. Divide the activities into categories of "things I enjoy doing," "things I don't mind doing," and "things I hate doing." Then write a paragraph that explains these categories or groupings and gives some examples of each.

b. Consider some teachers you have had over the years, both ones you disliked and ones you liked or respected. Discuss some, placing their names or the names of the classes they taught at the end of the clauses with which you introduce them. Then add some detail about the nouns at the end of the sentences. For example: **My favorite art teacher was Mr. Mack, who not only made me enjoy art but also entertained the class with his bushy eyebrows.**

Chapter 23

MISSING-SUBJECT FRAGMENTS

ATTENTION FOCUSING: adding subjects*

Some of the sentences below contain a single subject but two verbs, each with a phrase that modifies it. The verbs are in boldface.

a. Locate the subject by asking **who** or **what** before the verb(s) in **boldface.**
b. Circle the numbers of those sentences that contain a single subject and two verbs.
c. Underline the group of words that contains a verb but not the subject.
d. Split the **verb phrase** off and make it a new sentence, supplying an appropriate subject.

COOTIES

1. We **have** no supervised Cootie leagues, but more people in the United States **have played** Cooties than baseball, basketball, and football combined.

_____

_____

2. It **began** to be popular sometime after World War I and today **is** America's unofficial game.

   And today it is America's unofficial game.

_____

3. Cooties **are** "imaginary germs" or "contaminated bugs" and **can crop up** anywhere, at any time.

_____

_____

206

MISSING-SUBJECT FRAGMENTS **207**

4. To start a game, a child **touches** someone, and then he or she **says,**
   "You've got cooties!"

   _____

   _____

5. The child **may specify** the source of the infection by saying, "You've
   got Larry's cooties!" and **may add,** "No tag backs."

   _____

   _____

6. Children **mimic** immunization shots with ballpoint pens or just
   mark a magic X on their hands with an appropriately named Magic
   Marker.

   _____

   _____

7. They **write** "CP" on their tennis shoes for "Cootie Protection" and
   play the game in class as well as on the playground.

   _____

   _____

8. A child **goes** to sharpen his pencil, and he or she **passes** on Larry's
   cooties.

   _____

   _____

9. A smart alec **will** even **give** the teacher those cooties and **watch** in
   anticipation with the rest of the class.

   _____

   _____

10. The next person that he or she touches **gets** them, and everyone in
    the room **is** aware of it except him or her.

    _____

    _____

If you have successfully completed the ATTENTION FOCUSING segment,
go on to a PROOFREADING EXERCISE. If you can locate and correct the
missing-subject errors, you are ready for a different chapter. Otherwise,
continue with the REVIEW that follows.

REVIEW: subjects in complete sentences

Every sentence must have a subject, a verb, and a complete idea. Of these three requirements, the need for a subject is probably the most obvious. A sentence has to be about something! Nevertheless, many would-be sentences fail to make the grade because they lack subjects.

Often a piece of writing will contain several sentences in a row about the same subject. For example, if you were to try to describe this page in detail, giving its dimensions, texture, color, smell, degree of shine, and weight, you would probably need to write more than one sentence. Although you might use **the page** or some other words referring to it as the subject of more than one of them, you might also drop the subject in some. After all, there is a sort of understanding between speaker and listener as to the subject being discussed. Such understood material is often avoided in conversation, as in the following example:

Joe: Where are you going?
Pat: ~~I'm going~~ to the library.

Sue: What are you doing?
Roger: ~~I'm~~ fixing my brace.

The crossed-out words are not spoken because they are understood by both parties. After you have written a few sentences about **the page,** you know that your reader is aware of the subject at hand, and you might drop that subject in much the same way that you would in a conversation. Take a look at one possible result:

The page crinkles softly if I crumple it, and it does not lie flat afterward. Except for the lines I just made in it, the page has a bright newness, a crispness that makes me think that it just came off the press. **Smells like it has, too.**

The boldfaced words are a sentence fragment; there is no subject for the verb **smells.** This kind of fragment is called a **missing-subject fragment** because it does not contain a subject. It does not matter that you can "figure out" what its subject might be. To be complete, a sentence must generally have a subject somewhere between the capital letter at its beginning and its end punctuation. (We deal with a common exception—the implied subject—in the HOW TO COPE section that follows.) Although the few sentences just given as an example do not allow much room for confusion, consider the following example:

David Zukerman works nearly 18 hours a day at the company founded by his father, Louis Zukerman, who is still a workaholic. And runs the whole company by himself, even though he could well afford to leave it in someone else's hands.

The second unit punctuated as a sentence is a missing-subject fragment, and even though you might think you know who is running the company, you do not. If you think you know, you have made an assumption about which person the writer intended as the subject of that missing-subject fragment. You don't really know whether it's David or Louis. To clear up the ambiguity here, the writer would need to supply a subject.

How To Cope with the Unexpected (1)

Sometimes the verb in a perfectly good sentence will have an **implied subject** rather than an explicit one. When you are giving instructions, commands, directions, or advice, you use what is called the **imperative mode.** In this mode, the subject **you** is understood, and there is no need to repeat it. The persons receiving the instruction or command understand that they are being addressed. If someone asks you how to get to the library, you can say, in the normal **(indicative)** mode:

You go to the end of the block and turn left. Then you walk two blocks. The library is the second building from the corner.

However, you would probably give the same instructions in the **imperative** mode:

Go to the end of the block and turn left. Then walk two blocks. The library is the second building from the corner.

Either mode is correct. Even though the imperative mode produces sentences that might look like missing-subject fragments, they are perfectly acceptable.

REWRITING EXERCISE 1: adding subjects*

In the space above each line, rewrite the sentences that need to be changed.

a. In each sentence, verbs are in boldface and their subjects are underlined.
b. Notice that some of the sentences contain at least one verb that has no subject within the sentence. Those "sentences" are actually missing-subject fragments.
c. Rewrite the reviews, correcting the missing-subject fragments by supplying appropriate subjects.
d. The missing subject of **Examines** in Book Review 2 must be a singular noun. When you provide a subject, make sure it agrees with its verb.

BOOK REVIEW 1

[1]The <u>Penguin</u> <u>Dictionary</u> <u>of</u> <u>Psychology</u>—Arthur S. Reber. [2]**Defines** approximately 17,000 terms from psychology, psychiatry, and related

fields. [3]Also **points out** how each <u>term</u> **is** actually **employed** and how <u>it</u> **has been used** and sometimes **abused** in the past. [4]Viking/Penguin, 1985, 848p., $25, paper, $7.95.

BOOK REVIEW 2

[1]<u>To Do No Harm</u>: <u>DES and the Dilemmas of Modern Medicine</u>— Roberta J. Apfel and Susan M. Fisher. [2]Two <u>psychiatrists</u> **use** the story of DES, formerly prescribed to women with difficult pregnancies, to illustrate the complexity of modern medicine. [3]**Examines** the pressure to experiment with new techniques and drugs, doctors' risk-taking and responses to errors. [4]**Suggests** how the <u>trust</u> essential to a good patient-physician relationship **can be destroyed** when <u>things</u> go wrong. [5]**Traces** the history of DES and its uses and **tells** of the overwhelming impact of the DES tragedy on mothers and daughters. [6]**Was** originally **published** in hardback in 1984. Yale U Pr, 1986, 199p., $8.95.

REWRITING EXERCISE 2: adding subjects to avoid missing-subject fragments

Each of the sentences on p. 211 contains an independent clause with one subject and two verbs in phrases joined by a coordinating conjunction (**and, or, but**).

a. Underline the coordinator and the verb phrase that follows it in each sentence.

b. Notice that the verb phrase you have underlined cannot stand by itself as a sentence.

c. Separate the verb phrase you have underlined from the first part of the sentence, supplying an appropriate subject to make it into a complete sentence.

EXAMPLE: From gorilla suits to hobo outfits, costumes are an integral part of Halloween <u>and let us suspend our self-image for a short period of time.</u>

becomes

From gorilla suits to hobo outfits, costumes are an integral part of Halloween. Costumes let us suspend our self-image for a short period of time.

1. The blocks of the great pyramid at Giza number about 2.3 million and weigh about 2½ tons each.

    _____

    _____

2. The sides of the pyramid face the points of the compass and are all within a few inches of 755 feet long.

    _____

    _____

3. Such precision is indeed remarkable after centuries of exposure to settling but creates questions about the pyramid's building process.

    _____

    _____

4. The builders no doubt employed sophisticated mathematics and must also have had a large workforce at their disposal.

    _____

    _____

5. Even today, the pyramid's base is a large structure and could hold the base of almost any of the Earth's largest buildings.

    _____

    _____

6. A person must marvel at such an enduring structure and must wonder about the staying power of today's buildings.

    _____

    _____

REWRITING EXERCISE 3: eliminating intentional fragments

The box in this exercise is a partial reproduction of the label of an institutional floor-cleaning product, Buckeye Blue™. Probably because label space is always at a premium, product descriptions often contain sentence fragments of one sort or another, and this label is no exception. It contains 6 intentional missing subject fragments for you to correct.

a. All verbs are in boldface.
b. Try to find the subject within the sentence or fragment in which each verb occurs.
c. If you find no subject, the unit marked as a sentence is actually a missing-subject sentence fragment. Underline it.

d. Rewrite the label as a paragraph describing the product. Add a subject (either **Buckeye Blue** or **It**) to each fragment to make it a complete sentence or join the fragment to the sentence before it, making a sentence with one subject and two verb phrases.

---

¹BUCKEYE BLUE **keeps** your floor finish "New Looking" months longer. ²And **needs** no added rinsing.

³BUCKEYE BLUE **is** unsurpassed in restroom sanitation. ⁴**Cleans** ceramic tile floor, partitions, walls, restrooms. ⁵**Contains** no harsh abrasives.

⁶BUCKEYE BLUE **is** an excellent choice for automatic scrubbers. ⁷**Saves** buying duplicate products.

⁸BUCKEYE BLUE **handles** transportation vehicle cleaning with ease. ⁹**Cleans** vinyl seats, painted bulkheads, mats, etc.

¹⁰BUCKEYE BLUE **specializes** in maintaining light industrial and manufacturing facilities. ¹¹**Cleans** floors, walls, skylights, and nonelectric equipment fast and efficiently.

PROOFREADING STRATEGIES

In any proofreading task, it is important to know the error for which you are looking. If you make many missing-subject fragments, copy a few of them onto one sheet of paper to get an idea of what they look like out of context. You might find some pattern you can use to help in your proofreading task. For example, certain verbs might recur in your fragments, or many of them might express the final action in a series of actions.

1.   What to look for: the missing-subject fragment.
2.   How to look for it: as with any fragment error, reading your sentences in reverse order helps to break up the flow they normally have and increases your chances of noticing the fragment.
   a.   Underline the verbs in the sentence unit.
   b.   Locate the subject of each verb. If you cannot find the subject, make sure that the sentence is not a command or other instruction in the imperative mode (**you** is the understood subject) and that it is not a sentence in which the subject follows the verb **(there is . . . subject).**
   c.   If you have found the verb in a sentence and can find no subject, you have a missing-subject fragment.
3.   How to correct it:
   a.   Add a subject, changing the verb if necessary.
                              or
   b.   Attach the fragment to the preceding sentence if it has the same subject.

PRACTICING PROOFREADING 1

Correct the 5 missing-subject fragments in the selection that follows.

HIGHLIGHTS

[1]There are many advantages to BASIC Primer. [2]Since BASIC statements and commands are derived from English words, students will find it easy to learn and use. [3]Teaches lessons easily. [4]Even young students can follow BASIC Primer's clearly written lessons. [5]And realize it is not just a tool for BASIC. [6]Lets the student write sample programs and sharpen his or her computing skills.

[7]The program reviews the student's progress. [8]Makes use of frequent recaps in lessons to aid comprehension. [9]Gives on-screen words of encouragement.

PRACTICING PROOFREADING 2

Correct the 4 missing-subject fragments in the following selection.

PUBLIC TIME (ADAPTED FROM <u>LISTENING TO AMERICA</u>)

[1]Until the nineteenth century, only the wealthy owned their own clocks. [2]Most people depended on sun and stomach to tell the time. [3]Or told time from sundials or simple sun marks on windows and used sandglasses to time sermons, classes, and cooking. [4]Also, a man might step into an inn or tavern. [5]And check the time, as these establishments usually had a prominent clock. [6]It was often a large "Parliament clock," the name harking back to the days when the British Parliament taxed clocks heavily. [7]Boston was talking about its new "public clock" in 1660. [8]However, the term "town clock" was not in general use until the 1770s. [9]Then, usually found on the city hall or other public building, became the local pride and the time standard of cities and towns all over America. [10]Now the town clock may be doomed. [11]Digital clocks have become less expensive. [12]And have worked their way inextricably into most Americans' lives.

WRITING ASSIGNMENT: adding subjects to fragments

a. Write a short review of a textbook or any nonfiction book you have read recently. Include the title, author(s), and a description of what the book does. Here are some verbs you may wish to use: **teaches, explains, shows, tells, defines, explores.** Once you have written the review, proofread it for missing-subject fragments.

b. Think of one item that you use nearly every day such as a comb or a pencil. Write a product description of it that tells what the item does. Include at least five things that the product does well and three things that it does not do well. Some description of the product should cover what it looks like, but the main purpose of the writing is to evaluate how well it works. Example:

	positive	negative
My phone	is activated by my voice	rings too loudly
	has a redial button	picks up radio signals
	remembers numbers	breaks easily
	matches the room decor	
	lights up in the dark	

Write a paragraph, making complete sentences out of the fragments contained in your outline or catalogue. Each of the items in the example lacks a subject, though you know it is the phone.

c. It's baseball time, and the pathetic Bridgeport Bengals are the team you own. You watched them lose yesterday, and now you are writing a letter to the manager telling how sad they really looked. Begin by writing one sentence for each position (pitcher, catcher, first base, second base, third base, shortstop, left field, center field, and right field) that gives one criticism of the player (e.g., **The catcher drooled while he chewed his gum**). Then add a second, more absurd criticism of each position (e.g., **He also managed to get the gum wrapped around his glove**). Proofread for missing-subject fragments.

Chapter 24
ING FRAGMENTS

An **ing** fragment is a sentence fragment composed of an **ing** word introducing a phrase that cannot stand by itself. It is known as a **participial phrase,** named after the form of the verb, as discussed in Chapter 1: the base + **ing.** Examples are **smiling** (smile + **ing**), **crying** (cry + ing), **frowning** (frown + **ing**).

ATTENTION FOCUSING: *ing* fragments*

a. Underline each word ending in **ing.** (There are 12.)
b. Circle any **ing** word that is not part of a subject-verb pair and follows a comma. (There are 6.)
c. Write in the space provided any phrase begun by such an **ing.** Because each of these phrases is a fragment, do not punctuate it as a sentence.

1. The electronics explosion of the last few decades has been changing the way we do everything. _____

2. It has made life easier as well as more entertaining and secure.

    _____

3. The first thing on the market was the inexpensive quartz watch, (appearing) out of nowhere in the late 1960s. _____
    appearing out of nowhere in the late 1960s.

4. The pocket calculator was next, capping the evolution from huge calculating machines of the 1800s to electric desktop models to the credit-card sized electronic devices. _____

    _____

5. The home computer appeared in the mid 1970s, heralding a multi-billion dollar industry. _____

6. Video games have come, changing from the simple PONG to the complex arcade simulators. _____

7. The VCR arrived for Christmas 1985, making the cover of <u>Time</u>.

_____

8. Prices were coming down for all these items, enabling people to indulge themselves in many electronic devices. _____

_____

> If you completed ATTENTION FOCUSING without making any errors, try PRACTICING PROOFREADING 1 before asking your instructor to send you on to another chapter. If you did make errors, read the REVIEW.

REVIEW: *ing* words and phrases

A word ending in **ing** can appear anywhere in a sentence. For instance, it can be the subject, verb, or adjective.

subject	**Talking** in your sleep can be dangerous.
verb	Secrets **are churning** inside all of us.
adjective	You might want to mention certain **interesting** people.

In addition, an **ing** word can begin a participial phrase that is separated from the main part of the sentence and adds details to it. This occurs when the **ing** (set off by a separating comma or commas if the phrase occurs in mid-sentence), is used to combine ideas in a sentence, particularly when events occur at the same time.

a. My teacher walked into the classroom.
b. My teacher stumbled on an eraser.
c. He fell flat on his face.

The subject of each sentence is **My teacher,** even though in sentence *c* it has been replaced by the pronoun **He.** The subject, then, has been repeated three times. You can avoid this repetition as well as indicate that the set of actions occurs at essentially the same time by creating a series of **ing** phrases that share the same subject:

My teacher walked into the classroom, **stumbling on an eraser** and **falling flat on his face.**

You can also place these **ing** phrases at the beginning of the sentence:

Stumbling on an eraser and **falling flat on his face**, my teacher walked into the room.

Or you can place them in the middle of the sentence:

My teacher entered the room and, **stumbling on an eraser,** fell flat on his face.

The fragment problem arises when a writer attempts to use just the **ing** phrase as a sentence. By themselves, such participial phrases lack subject and verb. They must remain attached to the part of the sentence that does contain a subject and a verb. When they are punctuated on their own, with a capital letter at their beginning and a period at their end, they would be incomplete sentences or fragments.

My teacher walked into the classroom, stumbling on an eraser.

WRONG: Falling flat on his face.

WRONG: Stumbling on an eraser, falling flat on his face.
My teacher walked into the classroom.

Of course, as you read the sentences, they sound perfectly fine. But the incorrect punctuation has created a fragment. Whenever we used such an **ing** phrase in ATTENTION FOCUSING, we always attached it to a complete sentence. The **ing** phrase in each of those was set off by a comma because it came after the main part of the sentence—the independent clause containing a subject and verb. But, as the examples earlier have illustrated, when the **ing** phrase begins a sentence, it is followed by a comma, and when it occurs midsentence, it is set off by commas both before and after.

In general, if you have trouble with **ing** fragments, look for sentences that begin with an **ing** word and check to make sure it is attached to an independent subject-verb pair. (**Being** is the most commonly misused **ing** word.)

REWRITING EXERCISE 1: using *ing* phrases

Attach the **ing** fragments to complete sentences you invent. Place them in any position that makes sense, but do not change any words. Although a noun, **Lincoln,** comes before **being** in 3, it is not the subject of the sentence, and **being** is still a participle, not a verb. (It means that Lincoln was president at the time the events of the sentence took place.)

1. making me incredibly angry _____

   _____

2. looking for all the world like a wet rat _____

   _____

3. Lincoln being president at the time _____

   _____

4. not wanting to take the the risk _____

_____

5. acting more like a model _____

_____

REWRITING EXERCISE 2: forming and combining *ing* phrases

Copy the essay below, making the following changes:

a. Cross out the subjects (including *a* and *the*) in sentences 2, 4, 6, 10, and 13.
b. Make the verb in those sentences into a present participle by adding **ing** to its base form.
c. Using a comma, connect this newly formed phrase to the sentence before it.
d. Underline each new phrase you have created. Note that it cannot stand by itself.

> EXAMPLE: The state fair is a boon to the city. It sometimes draws a 100,000 people in one day. ⟶ The state fair is a boon to the city, sometimes **drawing** 100,000 people in one day.

TRADING COMMODITIES

[1]Commodity trading is an exciting activity. [2]It makes fortunes for some while it ruins others. [3]The reason for the great degree of risk involved is "leverage." [4]Leverage uses a small number of dollars to control a large number. [5]For example, a contract for frozen pork bellies (the stuff from which bacon is made) controls 40,000 pounds of the product. [6]A contract requires good faith money from the purchasers or sellers of the contract or a "margin" of about $1,200. [7]A rise or fall of 1/10 of a cent per pound seems negligible. [8]Such a change translates into $40,000. [9]However, a change of 10 cents per pound can occur each week. [10]The result translates into $4,000. [11]If buyers make $4,000 on their initial $1,200, they have increased their money by over 300 percent. [12]Things do not work out as well on the other side of the trade, the sellers of the contract having run up $2,800 of debt over and above their initial $1,200. [13]The sellers lose 300 percent of their "investment."

REWRITING EXERCISE 3: making sentences out of *ing* phrases

Copy the paragraph, making the following changes:

a. Circle each **ing** word that is being used to continue sentences.
b. Underline the phrase that each of these **ing** words begins.
c. Rewrite the **ing** phrase, changing it into an independent sentence. You can do this by adding a subject, returning the **ing** word to its base form, and making it agree with the subject.

THE DODO

[1]The last dodo was probably killed on the island of Mauritius in 1681 by Dutch settlers. [2]The dodo was one of the queerest creatures known to man, looking as if it had been designed by a prankster to play a joke on naturalists. [3]The short, fat bird stood on tiny yellow legs, having a small tail that stood up like a feather duster. [4]It weighed about 50 pounds and could not fly, possessing wings too small to carry its weight. [5]Its large hooked bill was nine inches long, giving the dodo bird's face a comical look.

[6]Unfortunately for the dodo, it was an excellent source of meat, even though it was rather stringy. [7]The dodo was suddenly being hunted down, after centuries on an island free of enemy animals. [8]One stuffed specimen ended up in a museum in Oxford, but, during a spring cleaning, it was thrown out and burned, the reason being that it was rather "ratty-looking." [9]Today, the only specimens are ones built by taxidermists from recovered bones. [10]The disappearance of the dodo was so dramatic that it has become the ultimate example of extinction, giving us the expression "as dead as a dodo." [11]Perhaps its Latin name gives us a clue to its failure to adapt—<u>Didus ineptus</u>.

PROOFREADING STRATEGIES

As in other proofreading situations involving sentence boundaries, to correct **ing** fragments, read your essay from back to front, sentence by sentence. Incomplete or broken sentences will show up more easily when your eyes treat each sentence individually. The word **Being** at the beginning of a sentence often signals a fragment.

1. What to look for: **ing** fragments.
2. How to look for them: watch for **ing** words (participles) at or near the beginning of your sentences, the most likely place for them to occur in a fragment. When you find one, decide if it is being used correctly or not.
   a. An **ing** word rarely causes fragments when it is in a segment of the sentence containing a subject-verb pair that can stand on its own (an independent clause). When it is part of the verb, one of the helping verbs (**am, is, was, were, can,** etc.) should accompany it.
   b. If the **ing** word and the phrase it begins are not in an independent clause, it must be attached to an independent clause with a comma. If it is standing by itself, punctuated as a sentence, it is a fragment.
3. How to correct an **ing** fragment: either attach it to the sentence on either side where the connection makes sense (as in REWRITING EXERCISE 1) or make a complete sentence out of it by adding a subject and changing the participle (**ing** form) to a form of the verb that agrees with the subject (as in REWRITING EXERCISE 3). In either case, punctuate carefully.

After you correct all errors in a PRACTICING PROOFREADING exercise, demonstrate your mastery with WRITING ASSIGNMENT 2.

PRACTICING PROOFREADING 1

The following paragraph has 14 **ing** words, of which 5 are beginning fragments. Correct the fragments using one of the methods discussed in PROOFREADING STRATEGIES.

POLISHING OFF YOUR CAR

[1]Waxing a car is far from a cool job. [2]Requiring some physical effort for satisfactory results. [3]However, it can be highly rewarding, making an old auto look years newer. [4]You should start with a quality car wax, suited to your car's finish. [5]Using paints different from domestic autos, some foreign cars require a special wax. [6]Of course, the car should be clean. [7]The reason being you do not want to trap any dirt in the wax. [8]It should also be cool and dry, in a shaded spot or even in a garage. [9]You should work on a small area at a time. [10]Using a circular motion with the applicator. [11]Move on to another area. [12]Letting your first section dry to a haze before buffing vigorously. [13]Buffing is also done with a circular

motion. [14]Using a soft, clean cloth, you should be sure to change cloths when the one you are working with loads up. [15]Slowing you down, making your work even harder.

PRACTICING PROOFREADING 2

The following paragraph has 15 **ing** word, 5 of which begin fragments. Correct the fragments using one of the methods discussed in PROOFREADING STRATEGIES.

ADAPTED FROM THE CHRYSANTHEMUM AND THE BAT: BASEBALL SAMURAI STYLE

[1]Japan may be the only country in the world where a losing team feels obliged to offer its followers an apology. [2]But that is what one would expect from a country where the Tomiuri Giants sent out thousands of cards in 1975. [3]Apologizing for finishing in the cellar that season. [4]Such behavior reflects the deep sense of responsibility Japanese teams feel toward their paying customers. [5]This attitude is prevalent throughout the country. [6]Elevating the team/fan relationship to an almost personal level. [7]No one seems immune from the attitude. [8]Players even apologizing for getting hurt. [9]Batters apologizing for batting slumps. [10]Winning pitchers apologize for not pitching a shutout. [11]Veteran players will often apologize for playing too long. [12]The reason being they are not giving younger players a chance to play ball. [13]On the other hand, retiring players apologize for retiring too soon.

WRITING ASSIGNMENT: using *ing* phrases

Write a long paragraph on one of the following topics according to your instructor's specifications for organization and development. Proofread for errors in **ing** fragments.

a. Think of a comedy routine or something funny that you have seen someone do. Describe the funny person's actions in a series of simple sentences, each describing only one action. Write ten or more short sentences. Using **ing** phrases, add at least one detail to each sentence that clarifies the action or tells what the comic does that is special or different.

b. Look at some busy scene. It could be students changing classes, a puddle full of insects, a family gathering, or any scene with lots of activity. Describe what each participant is doing, and give at least one detail about *how* it is being done in an **ing** phrase. Use at least seven **ing** phrases.

c. Imagine a foreign land or a scene on an imaginary planet. Using plenty of **ing** phrases (at least seven), describe the details of what you see. Hint: Although **ing** phrases are very useful for showing motion, they can also be used to show a lack of it.

Chapter **25**

TO **FRAGMENTS**

A **to** fragment is any phrase that begins with **to** and is not attached to (or part of) an independent subject-verb pair. It thus cannot stand by itself. In the REVIEW, we discuss this kind of fragment and offer ways to correct it.

ATTENTION FOCUSING: *to* fragments*

a. Underline each **to** and the phrase it begins. (Go to the end of the sentence if you are not sure where the phrase ends.)
b. Write the underlined phrases in the space after the essay. Because each is a fragment, do not punctuate it as a sentence.

THE RELUCTANT BATTER

[1]Taking the bat from the batboy, Strawberry started to walk toward the plate. [2]He paused and looked at the bat, and then he hefted it, bringing it up to the level of his eyes. [3]He turned toward the sunlight to his left to sight along the bat better. [4]He confused the few watching people by tossing it from hand to hand. [5]Something apparently did not fit right. [6]He walked back and returned the bat to the batboy. [7]He selected another bat only to repeat the process twice more. [8]Finally, he seemed to find a satisfying piece of hardwood. [9]It also seemed to please in him that odd sense batters have about their bats. [10]Luckily, only batting practice was being held up. [11]If Strawberry had done the same thing in a game, someone might have thought he was trying to delay the game.

_____

_____

_____

_____

_____

If you completed ATTENTION FOCUSING without making any errors, try PRACTICING PROOFREADING 1 before asking your instructor to send you on to another chapter. If you did make errors, read the REVIEW.

REVIEW: *to* phrases

The word **to** has two different functions. It forms the **infinitive**, which, as we explained in Chapter 1, consists of the word **to** and the base or stem of a verb. Some examples are **to run, to go, to occupy, to be.**

The word **to** is also a preposition. As we discussed earlier, prepositions show the relationship between a noun and another word. Some examples are **in, on, under, between, over, through,** and, of course, **to.**

The fact that thousands of people lose the lottery every day is a benefit **to the person who wins it.**

The **to** phrase in this sentence adds details to the rest of the sentence (as we discussed in Chapter 22).

When a **to** phrase of any kind appears somewhere in the middle or near the end of one of your sentences, it is unlikely to be part of a fragment. A **to** phrase is more likely to be part of a fragment when it appears at or near the beginning of your sentence.

The fact that thousands of people lose the lottery every day is a benefit. **To the person who wins it.**

Punctuating the **to** phrase as a sentence does not make it one. It needs to be attached to one of the sentences on either side of it, depending on the context.

Of course, a **to** phrase at the beginning of a sentence does not automatically mean a fragment. As long as the **to** phrase is attached to (or part of) an independent subject-verb pair, it is not a fragment. The sentences that follow begin with **to** but are attached to (or part of) an independent subject-verb pairs and are thus complete sentences. (The **to** phrases are in boldface.)

To lose weight, Joe went on a diet.

To the right, we saw a deer.

To win was his only goal.

In the first two sentences, the words after the **to** phrase constitute an independent clause, containing the subject and verb that enable them to stand by themselves. The **to** phrases could not stand by themselves and must be attached to these clauses. In the third sentence, the phrase **to win** is actually the subject of the sentence. Together with the verb **was,** it makes a complete sentence. Notice that in none of the sentences can the **to** phrase stand on its own. The **to** phrases that follow are all fragments.

to prove herself and be part of the crowd

to annoy the children she played with

to stop her from stealing her friends' toys

just to see if she could get away with it

In each case, the **to** phrase does not form a complete idea on its own. It needs to be part of a sentence, acting either as a noun or as a modifier to provide added details.

REWRITING EXERCISE 1: using *to* phrases*

Rewrite the paragraph below, moving the **to** phrases in sentences 1, 3, 5, and 7 to the beginning of each sentence. Remember to use capitals at the beginning of the sentences and to place a comma at the end of each **to** phrase that you have moved.

WHAT LIZA DID

[1]Liza often took dares to prove herself. [2]When Ralph dared her to "borrow" an item from a friend's house every day for three months, Liza accepted the dare. [3]She stole something each day from her friends' rooms to see if she could get away with it. [4]Her friends noticed but did not know how to deal with it. [5]Liza continued stealing to annoy them. [6]Eventually her parents found out. [7]They grounded her to keep her from stealing her friends' toys. [8]Her friends never quite understood why she stole.

REWRITING EXERCISE 2: creating *to* phrases

An **ing** phrase can sometimes be turned into an infinitive phrase (**to** + the base form of the verb) without altering its meaning. Certainly, the change from **ing** to **to** does not alter the completeness of the idea expressed—both phrases, by themselves, are fragments, unable to stand on their own.

  a. Underline each **ing** phrase that follows a comma.
  b. Rewrite the paragraph, changing each **ing** you have underlined to an infinitive phrase (**to** + the base form of the verb). For example, change **gathering his thoughts** to **to gather his thoughts.**

[1]When winter sets in and the snow lies deep on the driveway, some people like settling into their homes for the long haul. [2]The wood is stacked next to the fireplace, and a fire burns, giving the place a cozy atmosphere. [3]Other, more adventuresome souls, may like skiing on a weekend like this. [4]It is a thrill, racing downhill or meandering over cross-country trails. [5]Snowmobilers, too, like taking to the trails. [6]When conditions are right and the ice thick enough, ice fishers often stake out a spot on the ice, augering holes for their tip-ups and lines. [7]Sail-sledders may whiz by them. [8]The wind fills the triangular sails, pushing the sleds at speeds of over 30 miles per hour. [9]However, when the day is over, these hearty souls' thoughts will turn homeward, imagining the warmth of the fireplace that others have never left.

REWRITING EXERCISE 3: using *to* phrases

Rewrite the paragraph, bringing a **to** phrase to the beginning of each sentence that contains one. Because you are making introductory phrases out of them, follow each with a comma before continuing the sentence. Underline each **to** phrase in your rewritten essay. Note that not all **to** phrases can be moved.

SHARES OF STOCK

[1]The idea of a share of stock is poorly understood and therefore threatening to some people. [2]Only a few concepts, however, need to be explained. [3]"Shares" are issued to show ownership of a portion of a company. [4]If there are 100,000 shares in a company, each share represents 1/100,000th of the company. [5]Shares are usually traded in "blocks" of one hundred to make bookkeeping easier. [6]However, single shares can also be purchased. [7]A stockbroker is employed to make trades for shareholders.

[8]A "trade" is simply the sale and purchase of shares of stock. [9]"Dividends" are paid by many companies to allow shareholders a share in the profits of a company. [10]Some companies do not pay dividends so they can have that money available to help themselves grow or develop new products. [11]Some companies that do well will "split" the shares of their stock to keep the share prices affordable for most investors. [12]When this happens, one share might become three, with each new share worth one-third of an old share.

PROOFREADING STRATEGIES

Whenever you are proofreading for sentence boundaries, read your essay from end to beginning, sentence by sentence, so that you can treat each sentence individually. This technique will help you recognize more easily any sentence that fails to express a complete idea. Another way to isolate sentences is to cover up sentences on either side of the one you are considering.

1. What to look for: **to** fragments.
2. How to look for them:
   a. circle any **to** within four words of the beginning of your sentences, to account for introductory words such as **just, in order, not.**
   b. reading out loud, decide if the **to** phrase is attached to (or part of) an independent subject-verb pair,
3. How to correct a **to** fragment error:
   a. attach it to a nearby sentence (usually the previous one), to which it is simply adding some details or
   b. construct a complete sentence around the **to** phrase, making out of it a noun, verb, or other appropriate part of the sentence: I woke up at 10 o'clock. **To find that Josh had left an hour before.**

The fragment in **boldface** can be corrected by attaching it to the sentence before it: I woke up at 10 o'clock **to find that Josh had left an hour before.**

Or the fragment can be corrected by adding a subject and changing the verb form: **I found that Josh had left an hour before.** If you are changing the **to** + **verb** (the infinitive) to a verb, remember to use the correct verb form.

PRACTICING PROOFREADING

Locate and correct the 5 **to** fragments on p. 228.

VOICES FROM THE GRAVE?

[1]In April 1982, George Meek startled those attending a press conference at the National Press Club by announcing that he had succeeded in recording the voice of a dead person. [2]An electronics engineer and the holder of several electronic patents, Meek had been working since his retirement in 1970 to achieve his dream. [3]To establish two-way communication with the dead.[4] He presented taped evidence at the conference of conversations between William O'Neill, a medium from Pennsylvania, and George Mueller, an electrical engineer who had been dead for several years. [5]Mueller's voice sounded tinny and robotic and was imposed on a noisy blend of thirteen notes Mueller himself had given to the medium. [6]Only to improve the quality of the communication. [7]On the tapes, Mueller presented facts about himself that included his social security number, details about his education and career, and information about where his death certificate could be found. [8]The Spiricom, the device used to record the conversations, also recorded Mueller's suggestion to O'Neill. [9]To have his friend Meek check the facts. [10]To check the facts, Meek traveled the country. [11]Much of Mueller's information was confirmed, but one remained a problem. [12]Meek could not find a copy of a book Mueller claimed to have written in the 1940s. [13]To instruct Army recruits in electronics. [14]Finally, the book was found in the Army archives in Wyoming, and Meek felt encouraged. [15]Enough to bring his invention to the public in the hope that others would pursue similar experiments.

WRITING ASSIGNMENT: using *to* phrases

Write a long paragraph on one of the following topics, according to your instructor's specifications for organization and development. Proofread for errors in **to** fragments.

a. Give rules and guidelines by which a person can live. Use **to** phrases to describe the purpose of these rules, placing them at both the beginning and end of sentences: **To keep out of arguments, never discuss politics. Never discussing politics is a good way to avoid arguments.**

  b. Write an imaginary will in which you leave different personality traits and possessions to different people. Use **to** phrases to show the purpose—**To show him how much I love him, I leave Bill my attack fleas**—as well as the person to whom you are leaving things: **To my brother Bill, I leave my attack fleas.**
  c. Describe how you get somewhere from your home: **To get to Florida . . . .**

Chapter 26

PROBLEMS WITH COMMA SPLICES

**ATTENTION FOCUSING: commas
with coordinating conjunctions***

Some of the sentences consist of two simple sentences that have been joined together with a comma plus a special joining word such as **and, but, or,** or **yet.**

a. Circle the number of each sentence constructed in this manner.
b. In the space provided alongside, write the "joining" comma plus the "joining" word that follows it (the coordinating conjunction).
c. In the space provided below, rewrite the joined sentence as two independent sentences, making sure to use correct punctuation and capitalization.

GREAT GRAPES (ADAPTED FROM <u>GARDEN WAY BULLETIN A-53</u>)

_____ **1.** Classic European wine grapes are grown in chalky, sandy, or shale soils where nothing else will thrive.

_____

_____

_____*, and*_____ **2.** Such soils are very poor, and they encourage the plants to put their energy into the fruit rather than the leaves.

Such soils are very poor. They encourage the plants to put their energy into the fruit rather than the leaves.

_____ **3.** These famous "noble" soils are poor in some nutrients, but they are rich in the mineral elements that contribute to the final flavor and aroma of the great wines.

_____

_____

_____ 4. Fortunately for grape lovers everywhere, the vine will grow in many different soil types.

_____

_____

_____ 5. Well-drained, deep, fertile loams are excellent, yet grapes will thrive on soils containing clay, slate, gravel, shale, and sand.

_____

_____

_____ 6. Gravelly, stony soils generally drain well, and they absorb and reflect the sun's warmth to give the vine bottom heat.

_____

_____

_____ 7. A soil that drains poorly is quite unsuitable, and shallow soils underlaid by hardpan, gravel, or sand are also bad.

_____

_____

_____ 8. Soils with high levels of organic material tend to make vines with excessive foliage, and grapes grown in such soil will often bear a heavy crop of late-ripening, low-sugar fruit.

_____

_____

_____ 9. They give modest crops of fruit that mature earlier and have considerable sugar in the berry. Leaner soils are more desirable.

_____

_____

_____10. Grape vines will tolerate a variety of soil types, but the soils should be tested for nutrients.

_____

_____

WRITING ASSIGNMENT 1: joining sentences

a. Make a list of ten items that you would take with you to a deserted island. They need not be the only things you would take, just things that you would like to have for some reason.

b. For each item, write two simple sentences. In one sentence, identify the item and give a short description, if appropriate. In the second sentence, give your reason for taking it along, but do not name the item.

EXAMPLE: One item I would take with me is my radio with the detachable speakers. I love music.

c. Write a paragraph in which you combine each pair of sentences, using a comma and a coordinating conjunction (see also Chapter 34).

EXAMPLE: I love music, **so** one item I would take with me is my radio with the detachable speakers.

Feel free to add any other sentences to your paragraph that you think would improve it, such as an explanation of why you are going to the island.

d. Proofread your paragraph for comma splice errors and correct any that you find.

> If you have successfully completed the ATTENTION FOCUSING exercise and written a paragraph in which you have combined at least ten pairs of simple sentences without making comma splice errors, try PRACTICING PROOFREADING 1 before asking your instructor to send you on to another chapter. If you did make errors, read the REVIEW that follows.

REVIEW: the comma splice error

Comma usage is largely a matter of conventions that writers follow to make reading easier. Knowing when to use a comma is important, of course, but so is knowing when not to use one. One misuse of the comma is so frequent and so serious that it merits its own name: the **comma splice.** Writers make this error when they attempt to join two sentences end to end with a comma, to **splice** them the way one would tape together two pieces of recording tape.

It is often extremely confusing to use a comma alone for joining sentences. Pretend for a moment that you are reading an article about a school function. You read this sentence:

The "Un-Clambake" will be held next Sunday, Monday and Tuesday ticket sales were brisk, so be sure to get your tickets soon.

You have no way to know which of the following combinations the writer intended:

1. The "Un-Clambake" will be held next Sunday, Monday, and Tuesday. Ticket sales were brisk, so you had better get your tickets soon. (You think a comma was left out after Monday.)
2. The "Un-Clambake" will be held next Sunday. Monday and Tuesday ticket sales were brisk, so you had better get your tickets soon. (You assume the first comma should have been a period.)

Of course, the writer understands the sentence, but you do not have a clue. You might assume that there is going to be a three-day event or a one-day event; the writer will not be there to explain.

What should the writer of this comma splice have done? The sentence could be split in two, but that would not show the relationship between the two ideas. As a result, simply separating spliced clauses is rarely the best solution. The writer of a comma splice usually has a valid reason for attempting to join two clauses but has merely gone about it in the wrong way.

In the REWRITING EXERCISES, we will offer practice in correctly joining sentences end to end at the spot where the comma incorrectly "splices" independent clauses. Additional exercises in such "end-to-end" joining appear in Chapter 34.

REWRITING EXERCISE 1: combining independent clauses with coordinating conjunctions*

Copy the essay below, making the following changes:

a. Join sentences 1 and 2, 5 and 6, 9 and 10, and 14 and 15 with a comma plus **and.**
b. Join sentences 3 and 4 and 12 and 13 with a comma plus **but.**

THE HANDSHAKES PUZZLE

[1]My wife and I attended a dinner party. [2]Eight other couples were present: the Ailsas, the Blacklers, the Carsons, and the Duncans. [3]After introductions, a certain number of handshakes took place. [4]No one shook hands with himself or herself, nor with his or her spouse, nor more than once with anyone else. [5]At the end of the evening, I asked each person how many hands he or she had shaken. [6]I was surprised to find that all the answers I received were different. [7]Also, the total number of hand-

shakes made by the other four men was the same as the total made by all five women.

[8]The only woman I had shaken hands with was my dear friend Mrs. Ailsa. [9]We had a long talk. [10]Then I took her to one side. [11]My curiosity piqued, I asked her how many hands she had shaken. [12]Mrs. Ailsa was unable to tell. [13]I was able to work it out from the earlier information I had gathered.

[14]How many hands did Mrs. Ailsa shake? [15]How many hands did my wife shake?

REWRITING EXERCISE 2: combining independent clauses with semicolons

Often the semicolon (;) is the only punctuation needed to connect two independent clauses. Although it should not be overused, it is an effective way of joining two sentences that can stand on their own but that contain closely related ideas.

Copy the passage below and use a semicolon to combine sentences 1 and 2, 4 and 5, 6 and 7, 8 and 9, 11 and 12, and 13 and 14.

WHAT'S YOUR POISON

[1]Most people think of spiders and snakes when they think of poisonous animals. [2]They should, however, also consider the creatures of the sea. [3]Some of the deadliest creatures live there. [4]One of the most terrifying is the blue-ringed octopus of the Pacific. [5]Its venom, injected through its horny beak, can kill a person in two hours. [6]The poison has done its job before that. [7]Antidotes, as a result, are nearly useless. [8]Even faster is the sting of the sea wasp, a type of jellyfish. [9]Within minutes a victim can break into a fierce sweat, go blind, gasp for breath, and die. [10]In a twenty-five year period, sixty people died from sea wasp stings while bathing off beaches in Queensland, Australia. [11]The Indo-European stonefish injects poison through the spines in its back. [12]Excruciating pain, delirium, and even death can result. [13]In the same waters lives the venomous cone shell. [14]This is thus not a great place to swim. [15]Several people have died from the paralyzing fluid the coneshell injects with a needlelike tooth.

REWRITING EXERCISE 3: separating joined sentences

Copy the essay, making the following changes:

a. Underline each conjunction: **and, but, or, nor, so, for,** and **yet.**
b. Underline any commas that appear before one of these conjunctions.
c. Circle the commas and conjunctions that connect two independent clauses.
d. Rewrite the connected sentences into two separate sentences.

THE WHALE

[1]The whale is a warm-blooded, air-breathing mammal, and, like all mammals, it originated on land. [2]There are many signs of this. [3]Its front flippers, used for steering and stability, are vestiges of feet, and there are similar traces of hind feet inside the body. [4]It is unknown how such a mammal can store enough oxygen to stay underwater for an hour, but a specialized system of blood vessels may be involved. [5]How whales withstand the great pressures underwater remains a mystery, yet whales are known to dive to 3,200 feet, where the pressure is 1,400 pounds to the square inch. [6]Some whales have a "cask" of oil in their heads, and this may automatically adjust the internal pressure of their bodies. [7]For all the studies of whales that have been done, some mysteries remain, but more and more answers about these distant relatives are being found every day.

PROOFREADING STRATEGIES

If you make comma splice errors, begin a collection of them. Copy your errors together, one under the other, and look at them. You will probably find that they have something in common, especially if you look at the clause that follows the comma. The goal here is to learn the particular way in which you make this error, because you will most likely make it only in certain situations. If you can see a pattern, it will help you find your errors. But even if you do not see the pattern, you can still proofread for comma splices effectively.

1. What to look for: the comma splice error.
2. How to look for it: first look for any sentence that has a comma in it. Without a comma, there cannot be a comma splice.
  a. Account for the comma if you can. You will recognize immediately that some of your commas separate items in a series, set off

an introductory phrase or clause, or perform some other legitimate function (see Chapter 34 for review). Circle those commas whose function you cannot explain.

  b. If there is a comma that you cannot account for, check the material on either side of it. If there are independent clauses on either side, the comma cannot join them by itself.

  c. Check for a coordinating conjunction separating the independent clauses. If there is none, you probably have a comma splice.

3. How to correct it: make sure that you want to join the two clauses. If you do, add a coordinating conjunction after the comma (REWRITING EXERCISE 1) or substitute a semicolon (REWRITING EXERCISE 2). If you do not want to join the two clauses, separate them into two sentences (as in ATTENTION FOCUSING and in REWRITING EXERCISE 3). In Chapter 21, we discuss joining clauses with dependent words when you want to emphasize the logical relationship between them.

PRACTICING PROOFREADING 1

Circle each comma and determine if it is being used correctly. Correct the 3 comma splices.

CANDY

[1]Most people cannot believe that I have a spider monkey for a pet. [2]When I first got Candy, I was a little apprehensive about how she would act. [3]I had no reason to worry, monkeys make great pets. [4]She is fun to watch and to play with, and she is relatively easy to care for. [5]At times she acts strangely, she starts crying for what seems to be no good reason. [6]Actually, she just wants attention. [7]If I give her some attention, she stops her crying and settles down. [8]The only problem I have shows up when it comes time to give her her bath, she splashes.

PRACTICING PROOFREADING 2

Circle each comma and determine if it is being used correctly. Correct the 5 comma splices.

LIVEBEARERS

[1]Guppies belong to a group of fish called livebearers. [2]They give birth to live young, they don't lay eggs. [3]The eggs are retained in the

female's body where they are fertilized. [4]They mature there, they hatch inside the mother's body. [5]At maturity, the babies' eyes can be seen near the vent, looking like pairs of dark spots. [6]When born, the babies can swim freely, often they sink instead. [7]They come to rest on the bottom, hiding on the bottom or in plants. [8]The parents may eat them, other fish may eat them. [9]The baby guppies make quick, short darts, followed by periods of rest. [10]At first, they eat only small bits of food. [11]Later, they will attack pieces of food, the pieces can be larger than they are. [12]The baby guppies grow quickly, and it doesn't take them long to mature. [13]They can reproduce after a few weeks, but they may not reach full size for several months.

PRACTICING PROOFREADING 3

Circle each comma and determine if it is being used correctly. Correct the 4 comma splices.

COMPUTERS AND STATIC ELECTRICITY

[1]If you ever use a computer, there are a few things you should know about static electricity. [2]Anytime a static impulse is introduced into the computer's system, it can cause a specific function to be performed. [3]You do not want static around a computer, it can cause the computer to do something you do not want it to. [4]Experts say that up to 92 percent of daily systems interruptions are caused by static electricity, I do not doubt it one bit. [5]Engineers estimate that static causes up to 60 percent of all equipment service calls. [6]It can result in damage to vital computer components. [7]Static is caused by two materials coming in contact then they separate. [8]In other words, static is generated as people and materials move throughout your computer's environment. [9]Static charges of 10,000 volts are developed every day in a computer environment, charges of only a few hundred volts can cause your computer to malfunction. [10]Remember, most computer signals are only a few volts, there is not much room for error.

WRITING ASSIGNMENT 2: commas and independent clauses

Write a long paragraph on one of the following topics according to your instructor's specifications for organization and development. Make sure you are not using commas by themselves to join two independent clauses.

a. Make a list of ten foods that you either like very much or do not care for at all. For each food, write one sentence that tells what the food is and your opinion of it. Then write a sentence in which you tell why you feel that way about the food. Two of your sentences might be:

I find that lima beans are the food I like the least. They do not have much flavor, and they are gritty.

Then combine the pairs of sentences using any of the methods that were shown in the REWRITING EXERCISES. The example might become:

I find that lima beans are the food I like the least; they do not have much flavor, and they are gritty.

b. You have been given an assignment to design a calendar that will present one picture for each month. Each month's picture is to represent something associated with that month. Compose a list of the months and what you want pictured with each. Try to have a consistent theme or tone—kooky, traditional, inspirational, nature-oriented—for the whole year. For each month, write a sentence of at least two clauses that tells what the month is, what its picture will be, and why you chose it.

c. Look at a magazine composed of sections of regular features; a weekly news magazine is organized in this way, but so are many other magazines. Describe the sections of the magazine, using a sentence of more than one independent clause for each section. You are to tell someone who has never seen the magazine what each section is called, what its purpose is, and perhaps what a representative article would be about.

EXAMPLE: The "Features" section highlights some aspect of computer use, and it often presents a program related to that aspect; the longest and most probing articles are usually found here.

Chapter 27
PROBLEMS WITH FUSED SENTENCES

ATTENTION FOCUSING: joined sentences*

Each of the paired sentences below contains two independent parts. In one, the two parts (or **clauses**) are joined with a comma plus a special word (**and, but**) or with a semicolon (**;**). In the other, the two parts are fused—that is, they are joined without correct punctuation.

a. Underline each sentence that contains no special kind of joining.
b. Rewrite it in the space provided, using the same method of joining that is used by its correct, pair sentence.
c. Underline the subject and verb that follow the point where you joined the sentences.

THE FLIES ON THE WALL

1. The union called a strike it had no choice. The city administration was unhappy, but it had no satisfactory contract to offer.

   _____

   _____

2. Odors soon became a most noticeable problem, and no corner of the city was spared. Trash piles lined the street some were as high as twenty feet.

   _____

   _____

3. The strike went on for eight weeks; each smelled worse than the last. A state of emergency was declared by the mayor she had to do it.

   _____

   _____

239

4. A settlement was finally reached but the memories remained. Many house flies did not leave the garbage, but only because they were too full to move.

_____

_____

5. Because the sewer workers' negotiations are not going well, worse may be yet to come. Many flies are around a health hazard remains even with a quick end to the strike.

_____

_____

> If you have made errors in ATTENTION FOCUSING, read the REVIEW before working on REWRITING EXERCISES. If you have made no errors, go to PRACTICING PROOFREADING 1.

REVIEW: fused sentences and sentence boundaries

When you are listening to someone, you know that a sentence has come to an end when you hear the speaker's voice drop off slightly or pause briefly. This holds true whether the sentence contains one independent clause or many. When you are reading, you look for periods to indicate the ends of sentences and for commas and conjunctions (**and, but, or, yet**) or semicolons to indicate that independent clauses are being joined.

A fused sentence runs two or more sentences together by omitting periods that would separate them or punctuation that would join them properly.

A fused sentence not only violates agreed-on conventions for joining sentences but also often confuses the reader. Unlike the comma splice error in which the comma at least indicates where the writer intends to join the second independent clause to the first, the fused sentence contains no clues. Read the fused—and thus incorrect—sentence that follows.

We were eating the driver instead was pointing out the sights.

Because readers are unacquainted with the intentions of the writer, they might, at first glance, read **We were eating the driver.**

Only by rereading will the reader understand that the writer meant **We were eating. The driver instead was pointing out the sights.**

Students sometimes argue that a careful reading will always make a writer's intention clear. Although that may be true, the writer—not the reader—is responsible for making the meaning of the text clear and for following the rules of punctuation. Personnel managers looking at letters of application are not likely to think, "Let me see if I can understand what this really means." Rather, they are likely to go on to the next letter and the next applicant.

eliminating fused sentences

To help clarify the meaning of fused sentences, you can often simply separate them with a period. But because writers of a fused sentence often have a valid reason for joining the two parts, they should know how to combine two independent clauses without fusing them. These methods are the same as those discussed in Chapter 25: Problems with Comma Splices. They include:

1. Joining the independent clauses with a coordinating conjunction **(and, but, or, yet)** preceded by a comma.

    We were eating; the driver was instead pointing out the sights.

2. Joining independent clauses with a **semicolon.**

    We were eating; the driver was instead pointing out the sights.

3. Transforming the second independent clause into a dependent clause by substituting a **relative pronoun (who, which, that)** for its subject or object and joining it to the first independent clause.

    My father bought us a pizza. We ate it in the living room.

    The second sentence (independent clause) can be transformed into a dependent clause by substituting the relative pronoun **which** for the relative pronoun **it,** then joining this new relative clause to the first independent clause.

    My father bought us a pizza, **which** we ate in the living room.

4. Transforming one independent clause into a dependent clause by adding to it a subordinator such as **while, since, because, although,** or **when** (see Chapter 21), and joining it to the other independent clause.

    While we were eating, the driver instead was pointing out the sights.

    or We were eating **while** the driver instead was pointing out the sights.

    Notice that when the subordinator begins the sentence, the clause is followed by a comma. This is not necessary when the newly created dependent clause ends the sentence, as with the second example.

REWRITING EXERCISE 1: joining sentences*

a. Each numbered sentence is followed by another that comments or elaborates on it. Join each pair of sentences, using the various methods of combination that we discussed in the REVIEW, and rewrite the paragraph in the space provided.

b. On the rewritten paragraph, mark with a slash (/) the place where you joined the paired sentences. Notice that without the conjunction and/or punctuation you use to connect them, they would be fused sentences.

JEEPS FOR $49.95?

[1]The Defense Reutilization and Marketing Service of the Defense Logistics Agency of the Department of Defense offers a wide selection of military materials for sale. Not many people know about this agency or its surplus goods. [2]The items for sale are no longer needed by the U.S. Armed Forces. They are sold at regional and national auctions. [3]The goods are sold at a fraction of their actual worth. They are of little use in everyday life. [4]The DRMS hopes Americans will buy them anyway. They would be sold for scrap otherwise. [5]For sale are clothing, furniture, office equipment, paint, and electronic equipment. This includes old TV sets. [6]Also available is a landing craft that once transported ebony in Africa. This was a rarely used item. [7]If you are interested, contact the nearest DRMA office. It will be listed in your phone book under "U.S. Government."

_____

_____

_____

_____

_____

_____

_____

_____

REWRITING EXERCISE 2: joining sentences

Copy the selection, making the following changes:

a. Join sentences 2 and 3, 5 and 6, 9 and 10, 13 and 14, 16 and 17, using some of the methods of combination discussed in the REVIEW.
b. Circle the punctuation and/or conjunctions you use.
c. Mark a slash where you joined the sentences. Read aloud and listen for the drop that your voice makes at the slash mark.

ADAPTED FROM <u>WALDEN</u> BY HENRY DAVID THOREAU

[1]However mean your life is, meet it and live it; do not shun it and call it hard names. [2]It is not so bad as you are. [3]It looks poorest when you are richest. [4]The faultfinder will find faults even in paradise. [5]Love your life, poor as it is. [6]You may perhaps have some pleasant, thrilling, glorious hours, even in a poor-house. [7]The setting sun is reflected from the windows of the almshouse as brightly as from the rich man's abode; the snow melts before its door as early in the spring. [8]I do not see but a quiet mind may live as contentedly there, and have as cheering thoughts, as in a palace. [9]The town's poor seem to me often to live the most independent lives of any. [10]Maybe they are simply great enough to receive without misgiving. [11]Most think that they are above being supported by the town; but it oftener happens that they are not above supporting themselves by dishonest means, which should be more disreputable. [12]Cultivate poverty like a garden herb, like sage. [13]Do not trouble yourself much to get new things, whether clothes or friends. [14]Turn the old; return new.

[15]Things do not change; we change. [16]Sell your clothes and keep your thoughts. [17]God will see that you do not want society. [18]If I were confined to a corner of a garret all my days, like a spider, the world would be just as large to me while I had my thoughts about me.

REWRITING EXERCISE 3: separating joined sentences

Rewrite the sentences in ATTENTION FOCUSING, "The Flies on the Wall," separating each sentence into two complete sentences. Use the paragraph form.

PROOFREADING STRATEGIES

When you are trying to locate **fused sentences** in your writing, you will need a few invaluable skills. Because you are looking for two independent clauses that have been joined improperly, it is important that you be able to identify subjects and verbs. You should also be able to understand how a clause is joined to another—and if it is. Finally, you need to be able to hear when a sentence that you read aloud comes to an appropriate close.

1. What to look for: the fused-sentence error.
2. How to look for it: first, gather in one place any fused-sentence errors you have made and look for any patterns, especially at the beginning of the second clause. Do most of them tend to begin with a particular pronoun or phrase? If so, add those words to the list of key words below.
   a. Identify all the subjects and verbs that go together in a sentence. If there is more than one pair in a sentence, go to the next step. Otherwise, go to the next sentence.
   b. Notice how the clauses are being joined, whether with semicolons, coordinating conjunctions, or dependent words.
   c. If you cannot explain how the clauses are joined, check to see if they are being joined by an understood but not stated **that,** or **which,** or **who,** as in: **He is a man** ~~that~~ **I do not understand.**
   d. Mark any spot that has a key word or a joining that you cannot explain. Use a slash (/) to do this.
   e. Read the material that follows the slash out loud. Does it sound like a sentence? If so, you have probably found a fused-sentence error, but read the material before the slash as well to make sure. In a fused sentence, the material on either side of the slash can stand alone.
3. How to correct the fused-sentence error: use one of the methods of sentence combination reviewed in this chapter.

PRACTICING PROOFREADING 1

Correct the 4 fused sentences. In each, a subject pronoun is at the beginning of the second fused clause.

SWORD OF HONOR

[1]The material symbol of the martial spirit of the times was the warrior's principal weapon, his sword. [2]In later years the privilege of carrying this deadly, razor-sharp blade came to be reserved for the knightly samurai, but during the Kamakura period some men of lower birth also had swords they used them to carve their way to glory. [3]A sword was not,

however, a weapon only it was the central object of an elaborate cult of honor, especially for the samurai. ⁴For a samurai to be parted from his sword was to lose his honor.

⁵Swords were thought to have miraculous powers and lives of their own. ⁶Soldiers defeated in battle prayed at the shrines of the war-god Hachiman they asked him why their swords had lost their spirit. ⁷Many stories have come down about the spiritual powers of notable blades; one tells about two famed swordsmiths, named Muramasa and Masamune, who were almost equal in their skill. ⁸When a sword made by Muramasa was held upright in a running stream, every dead leaf that drifted against the edge was cut neatly in two. ⁹This was a good performance, but not the best. ¹⁰When a Masamune sword was put to the same test, the floating leaves avoided its edge and passed unhurt on either side it therefore was believed to possess spiritual power over the leaves and was superior to its rival.

PROOFREADING EXERCISE 2

This exercise contains 5 fused-sentence errors.

THE MEANING AND IMPORTANCE OF FAIRY TALES

¹There is a right time for certain growth experiences childhood is the time to learn, bridging the immense gap between inner experiences and the real world. ²To the child, and to the adult who knows that there is still a child in the wisest of us, fairy tales reveal truths about mankind and oneself.

³In "Little Red Riding Hood" the kindly grandmother undergoes a sudden replacement by the wolf, which threatens to destroy the child. ⁴How silly a transformation when viewed objectively, and how frightening; we might think the transformation unnecessarily scary, contrary to all possible reality. ⁵But when viewed in terms of a child's ways of experiencing, is it really any more scary than the sudden transformation of his own kindly grandma into a figure who threatens his very sense of self when she humiliates him for a pants-wetting accident? ⁶To the child,

Grandma is no longer the same person she has become an ogre. [7]How can someone who was so very kind, who brought presents and was more understanding and uncritical than even his own mommy, suddenly act in such a radically different fashion?

[8]The child is unable to see any congruence between the different manifestations he truly experiences Grandma as two separate entities, the loving and the threatening. [9]She is indeed Grandma and the wolf. [10]By dividing her up, so to speak, the child can preserve his image of the good grandmother. [11]If she changes into a wolf, well, that's certainly scary he need not compromise his vision of Grandma's benevolence. [12]And in any case, as the story tells him, the wolf is a passing manifestation she will return triumphant.

WRITING ASSIGNMENT

Make a list of ten television shows that you either like very much or do not care for at all. For each television show, write one sentence that tells what the show is and your opinion of it. Then write a sentence in which you tell why you feel that way about the show. Two of your sentences might be:

The Jeffersons reruns are my favorite television show **because it** is the only one that ever makes me laugh out loud.

Then combine the pairs of sentences by any method that you feel is appropriate. The example might become:

The Jeffersons reruns are my favorite television show **because it** is the only one that ever makes me laugh out loud.

Chapter **28**

CONSISTENCY IN PHRASING
(PARALLELISM)

ATTENTION FOCUSING*

For each boldfaced conjunction in the paragraph below, write in the corresponding space after the paragraph the words, phrases, or clauses that are parallel.

SOMETHING FOR NOTHING?

[1]This morning I received a phone call. [2]A robot-like voice told me my family had been selected to receive "an $800 shopping spree" **and** instructed me to call a number to get details from a human. [3]Having doubts **yet** not wanting to pass up a legitimate prize, I called the number. [4]A young woman verified my phone number **and** told me that I had won a contest sponsored by a local radio station. [5]For a small, one-time-only processing fee, I would receive a coupon book with coupons good for free services, free merchandise, **and** deep discounts. [6]There were many "prizes" for my car: $200 worth of free service, three free tuneups, a free vehicle inspection, **and** twelve free oil changes. [7]There were eighty-three restaurants offering a free meal of equal or lesser value than one purchased. [8]She informed me that some restaurants had time restrictions **and** that other restaurants had date restrictions. [9]Health spas, golf clubs, **and** bowling alleys all had offers: free games, membership discounts, **or**

two-for-one offers. [10]If I registered immediately, I would receive **not only** the coupon book, **but also** a free 35 mm. camera **and** coupons good for 100 free rolls of film and development. [11]All merchants had signed contracts with the promoter, **and** the promoter offered a money-back guarantee. [12]I asked how much the processing fee was. [13]When she told me $100, I hung up the phone and called the Better Business Bureau.

2. _A robot-like voice told me_____

   and _instructed me_____

3. _____ yet _____

4. _____

   and _____

5. _____ , _____ , and _____

6. _____ , _____ , _____ ,

   and _____

7. _____ or _____

8. _____

   and _____

9. _____ , _____ , and _____

   _____ , _____ or _____

10. not only _____ , but also _____

    _____ and _____

    _____ and _____

11. _____

    and _____

13. _____ and _____

Writers must often present a series or list in a sentence. They might have to give examples to support some point they are making, give the categories of a classification, or show a set of related actions. To make the items in a series or list easier for a reader to comprehend, most writers follow a sensible convention known as **parallelism.**

Lists are composed of like things. After all, there would be little point in making a list of a category, an action, a reason, and a thing. If you start to read a list of things, say a shopping list, you expect the things on that list to be similar. For example, a shopping list to be used in a grocery store would probably contain foods and other items available in the store in the grammatical form of nouns and noun phrases: **carrots,** fish, peanut butter, bread, **don't forget Brenda**, milk. . . . Wait! What is that **don't forget Brenda** doing on the list?

To the writer of the list, **don't forget Brenda** probably makes sense, but to someone finding and reading the list, it would not. Clearly, Brenda is not for sale in the store, but beyond that, the reader is lost. Is a gift for a girl named Brenda called for? Is Brenda a pet hamster in need of feed? Is Brenda a wife to be picked up from work after the shopping is done? Placing **don't forget Brenda** in a grammatical form like the other items on the list would make things clearer for the reader. **Brenda Lee album** is a noun phrase that would fit into the list with the nouns given.

Parallelism is thus simply making sure the items in a list or series (even a short list of two things joined by a conjunction) are in the same grammatical form so they make sense to the reader. After all, a series sets up expectations in the reader that you as a writer must fulfill. Look at this beginning of a sentence as a reader would:

> There were many "prizes" for my car: $200 worth of free service, three free tuneups, a free vehicle inspection, **and** _____.

What do you expect to go into the blank? Certainly, you have no way of guessing the next item, but you should expect it to be a noun phrase. The first three noun phrases lead to that expectation. Effective writing calls for that expectation to be fulfilled.

Besides making sure that items in your list are parallel grammatically, logic demands that your categories be of the same class:

> Near the U.N., he saw three Israelis, a Nigerian, two Canadians and _____.

The blank logically needs to be filled with a phrase that gives both an indication of number and a nationality. Both of the following would be incorrect:

> Near the U.N., he saw three Israelis, a Nigerian, two Canadians and Spaniards.

> Near the U.N., he saw three Israelis, a Nigerian, two Canadians and a Moslem.

Several Spaniards would fit, but **a Moslem** cannot be made to fit; the list calls for nationalities, not religious persuasion. Some Israelis, Nigerians, and Canadians are also Moslems.

REWRITING EXERCISE 1

   a. Rewrite the ATTENTION FOCUSING EXERCISE, adding several expensive items in sentences 5, 6, 9, 10, and 11 to make the prize more attractive, even outrageous if you wish.

   b. Make sure the things you add are in the same grammatical form and of the same logical class as the other items on the list.

REWRITING EXERCISE 2

Complete the following sentences by filling in the blank with a word, phrase, or clause that is parallel to the words, phrases, or clause before the boldfaced conjunction or comparative word.

1. I enjoy watching movies, going to concerts, **and** _____.

2. I like to watch movies, go to concerts, **and** _____.

3. Her mother will not let her voice an opinion, make any decisions, **or** _____.

4. I would rather fight **than** _____.

5. On Mondays he is busy, **but** _____.

6. Gregor wants to live in a quiet place, to raise a quiet family, **and** _____.

7. We traveled over the river, through the woods, onto the plains, **and** _____.

PROOFREADING STRATEGIES: parallel construction

Conjunctions signal the need for parallel construction. In a list or series, the last two items are usually joined by a conjunction.

Constructions such as **not only** _____ **but also** _____ or **either** _____ **or** _____ also call for the items that would fill in the blanks to be grammatically equal. The following are not parallel:

She not only **wants to be an astronaut** but also **a marine biologist.** (a verb phrase is needed)

Either **get out of here** or **I will go crazy.** (This should be: **Either you will get out of here or I will go crazy.**)

Finally, comparisons call for parallelism. One common error is to omit the second item of the comparison (advertisers do this intentionally):

I get **more** pleasure from playing the guitar. (more than what?)

A less frequent but more awkward error is failure to parallel the elements being compared:

His views are opposed to **his wife.** (This should be **his wife's views**)

1. What to look for: errors in phrase consistency (parallelism)
2. How to correct them:
   a. Locate all the coordinating conjunctions in the passage you are proofreading.

b. Determine grammatical form of the first item in the list or series. For example, it might be a phrase starting with an infinitive, a relative clause starting with **that,** or a noun.

c. If it is a noun or noun phrase, determine its logical category. For example, it might be a country or the model of a car.

d. Check to make sure the other items in the list are in the same grammatical form and logical category.

3. How to correct them:

a. If you find an item in the wrong form, either change it to the correct form or eliminate it.

b. If you find an item in the wrong logical category, think of another item that fits. This may involve changing the form of the word that does not fit. For example, if you are making a list of beliefs, you could change **patriot** to **patriotism.**

PRACTICING PROOFREADING

Correct the 5 errors in parallelism.

a. Proofread the following essay for faulty parallelism, using the techniques outlined in PROOFREADING STRATEGIES.

b. Identify the correct parallel structures in the essay.

c. Rewrite the essay, correcting the errors you find.

THE AIRLINE PYRAMID

[1]A new con scheme has surfaced in the area recently; like many other schemes, this one targets the greedy and those who are gullible. [2]It is a classical pyramid scheme, relying for its success on bringing more and more people into the game. [3]A person starting a game is called a pilot. [4]The pilot then gets a "crew," consisting of two navigators, four flight attendants (sometimes called "stews"), and eight passenger seats. [5]First, two navigators are brought in, each contributing $2,200 to buy a navigator's "seat." [6]Each navigator then finds two stews to buy seats, also at $2,200. [7]The four flight attendants must each find two passengers willing to buy seats, again for $2,200. [8]The attraction is that, once a full crew is assembled, the pilot takes the money and moves on, allowing each crew member to move up a seat and a chance at making more money. [9]Each navigator then becomes a pilot, taking the two stews as the new navigators. [10]The stews' passengers move up to become stews; each must find two new passengers. [11]Thus each member of the crew theoretically has the chance to turn $2,200 into $17,600 if the airline keeps flying.

[12]Unfortunately, by the time the first passengers move up and become pilots, sixty-four new passengers are needed. [13]When those 64 become pilots, 512 new passengers must be found, then 4,096, then 32,768, then 262, 144. [14]The number needed soon outstrips the population available in any location and eventually growing greater than the population of the country and of the Earth. [15]Because passengers have no idea of how long the airline has been flying, they have no way of judging their chances of becoming pilots before the airline falls apart, as it must. [16]The airline pyramid is illegal and immoral. [17]It hurts not only those who are greedy but also those who are gullible and some cannot afford to buy a seat.

MASTERY TEST FOR UNIT V: sentence boundaries

The passage below contains errors of every type covered in the chapters on run-on sentences and sentence fragments. Proofread separately for each type of error and then rewrite the passage, correcting all the errors. The passage contains 14 errors.

[1]Every day, money is spent on "new and improved" specialized cleaning products that arrive on the store shelves in convenient, read-to-use packages. [2]Although these products generally perform as advertised, I wonder if all those specialized products are needed. [3]To do each and every cleaning chore. [4]Household bleach used to be a standby for many purposes. [5]Such as disinfecting bathrooms and whitening fabrics. [6]Now there is a whole array of products for each of these jobs. [7]Do they work any better? [8]After all, bleach can be used to purify drinking water it certainly must kill bacteria. [9]The next time I go grocery shopping, I will try to keep that in mind. [10]At least while I am in the cleaning products aisle. [11]Trying to choose between bathroom cleansers. [12]There are just too many products available, I get confused. [13]And grab the one closest to me.

[14]I know bleach can present problems and has to be treated with respect. [15]For example, it can bleach the clothes I am wearing. [16]If I happen to spill some on me, [17]It also gives off poisonous gases if I mix it with ammonia. [18]Another old all-purpose cleaner. [19]As long as I do not use them near each other or pour them down the same drain, there is no danger. [20]Ammonia cuts through grease and oils well, and it can strip old wax off floors. [21]Or clean glass and porcelain, as well as most hard surfaces. [22]With ammonia, I have only one problem. [23]To get by the smell. [24]Mixed it with water and a little vinegar, it makes a satisfactory window cleaner. [25]Reason being the vinegar eliminates most of the odor problem. [26]Remembering the ammonia at the store will be harder than remembering the bleach it comes in a smaller bottle that is easier to overlook.

[27]In a way, things have come full circle with the specialized products, at least one advertises that it cleans glass, "plus a whole lot more."

Unit Six

PROBLEMS WITH MARKERS

Chapter 29
ELIMINATING CONTRACTIONS

This chapter shows how to eliminate contractions rather than how to use them. Except in direct quotations, contractions are too casual for use in formal writing; they are more appropriate in speech than in essays. In addition, contractions often create errors and complicate proofreading. For example, some writers place the apostrophe between the wrong letters. Others, used to the *sound* of a contraction, write it incorrectly—using **would of** instead of **would've**—or they confuse **their** and **they're**. Finally, because the apostrophe (') is such an important marker in indicating possession—as **'s**—the presence of apostrophes in contractions creates confusion and difficulty during proofreading.

ATTENTION FOCUSING: eliminating contractions*

a. Circle all words that have apostrophes.
b. Write out each contraction in the space provided.

ADAPTED FROM PETER LOVESEY'S <u>THE FALSE INSPECTOR DEW</u>

1. "(Let's) all sit down," suggested the captain. _Let us_

2. "I'm not one to beat about the bush," he continued. _I am_

3. "I haven't asked you here for cocktails." _have not_

4. He wanted to know if they'd heard about the drowning of the woman. _they had_

5. "It's being investigated by the master-at-arms." _It is_

6. He explained that he has full confidence in someone who's used to dealing with stowaways and smugglers. _who is_

7. "Still, I'm confiding in you, Mr. Dew." _____

8. Walter could've looked puzzled because the captain stared at him. _____

9. "You are Dew, aren't you?" _____

10. "What's this all about?" Walter asked. _____

11. "You're the one who arrested Dr. Crippen, are you not?" _____

12. When Dew nodded, Captain Rostron leaned back. "That's a relief." _____

> If you have made no errors in ATTENTION FOCUSING, try PRACTICING PROOFREADING 1 before asking your instructor to send you on to another chapter. If you did make errors, read the REVIEW.

REVIEW: contractions

When you combine two words to make one, you have formed a **contraction.** You use an apostrophe (') to indicate that a letter or letters are missing. Thus the apostrophe in **can't** indicates the missing **no** (cannot); in **could've** it indicates the missing **ha** (could **have**).

When the contraction contains **'s,** you cannot always tell what letter or letters are missing unless you read some other words around the contraction: **John's** may be either a possessive, as in **John's alligator,** or a contraction, as in **John is bringing his pet alligator.** The exercises that follow contain contractions within sentences so that you can see them in context.

REWRITING EXERCISE 1: eliminating contractions*

a. Circle the 21 apostrophes (') in the selection.
b. Put an X through the 12 contractions.
c. In the space above each line, write out the contractions and the sentences in which they occur.

I SEE YOU NEVER

[1]In <u>The World's Best Short Short Stories</u>, there's a Ray Bradbury story about Mrs. O'Brian's best tenant, a Mr. Ramirez. [2]"I See You Never" recounts their last meeting in the doorway to Mrs. O'Brian's kitchen. [3]She opens the door to his soft knocking and finds he's accom-

panied by two policemen. [4]They're taking him back to Mexico because his residency permit's expired. [5]Mrs. O'Brian's five children are in the midst of dinner and they're impatient to continue. [6]It's not as if Mr. Ramirez is part of the family! [7]Mrs. O'Brian doesn't have much to say to Mr. Ramirez, other than that he's been a good tenant. [8]She's sorry but there's nothing she can do. [9]His final words to her are "Oh, goodbye, Mrs. O'Brian, I see you never!" [10]While her children resume their meal, she lays down her own knife and fork. [11]"What's wrong, Ma?" asks one of her sons. [12]"I just realized," she answers, "I'll never see Mr. Ramirez again."

REWRITING EXERCISE 1: eliminating contractions*

   a. Circle the 21 apostrophes (') in the selection.
   b. Put an X through the 17 contractions.
   c. Rewrite the entire essay, writing out all contractions.

THE WOLF, THE LAMB, AND THE GOAT

[1]One of Aesop's fables concerns a lamb being mothered by a goat. [2]A wolf notices and says to the lamb, "Child, you're making a mistake. [3]That's not your mother. [4]Look among the sheep." [5]He pointed off in the distance. [6]"They're there, and your mother's among them."

[7]"Maybe you're right," answered the lamb, "but I'm not leaving. [8]This goat's been a mother to me all these years. [9]She's even denied her own kids so that I shouldn't go hungry. [10]I've had all the food and kindness I could've received. [11]I would've been long dead if it hadn't been for her. [12]As far as I'm concerned, she's my real mother."

[13]Aesop's moral might be that neglectful parents don't deserve consideration, but, if strangers offer kindness, they're deserving of credit.

REWRITING EXERCISE 3: eliminating contractions

   a. Circle the 18 apostrophes (') in the selection.
   b. Put an X through the 15 contractions.
   c. Rewrite the entire story, writing out all contractions.

THE LION, THE FOX, AND THE WOLF

[1]Another of Aesop's fables tells the story of a scheming wolf. [2]It seems that the lion, the king of beasts, had grown old and ill. [3]All the beasts of the forest came to see him except the fox. [4]The sly wolf didn't miss this chance to play a trick on his old enemy, the fox. [5]He went to the lion and said, "Your Majesty, the fox should've been here to see how you're faring in your illness, but he's so filled with insolence that he's absented himself from your presence."

[6]Fortunately for the fox, he wasn't that far away. [7]At once he hurried to the lion and bowed to him. [8]"Sir," he said, "I think I'm as loyal a subject as any who've been to see you. [9]After all, who's taken the trouble that I've certainly taken to help you? [10]I've searched far and wide for a cure for your illness, and I've found one."

[11]"Tell me at once what it is," cried the lion.

[12]"It's very simple," replied the fox. [13]"All you'd have to do to be cured is skin a live wolf and wrap yourself in that wolf's warm skin."

[14]Although the wolf's skin was spared, he learned that his unkind action could've come back upon himself.

PROOFREADING STRATEGIES

One of the common errors resulting from the use of contractions is the confusion of **'ve** or **have** with **of.** Another is incorrect placement of the apostrophe. This rarely happens in typed manuscripts because the apostrophe must be hit in sequence. When they are writing by hand, however, most people tend to write all the letters and then move back to place the apostrophe—sometimes between the wrong letters. The other (and most frequent) error is the use of contractions for other words that sound the same but mean something else. These are the most common:

it's (it is)	for	its
they're (they are)	for	their
you're (you are)	for	your
who's (who is)	for	whose

If you cannot tell these words apart, see UNIT VII, which contains a chapter on each of the above as well as a number of other commonly confused terms. If you do know the difference between these various "sound-alikes," but, precisely because they sound alike, do not notice that you have used them incorrectly in your writing, PROOFREADING STRATEGIES will help you eliminate contractions by writing out their complete forms. This technique will automatically enable you to notice that you have used the wrong word. When you write out the complete form of a contraction, it no longer sounds like the term with which you might confuse it.

> A PROOFREADING PRINCIPLE: Eliminate all contractions by writing them out.

As you will see during the PROOFREADING EXERCISES, you may discover errors while writing out the complete forms of contractions that you might not otherwise have caught. This is particularly true, if, in addition to the contractions listed on the previous page, you use contractions with nouns, such as the contraction of **waiter is** in **The waiter's coming with our order.** These kinds of contractions unnecessarily (yet significantly) complicate any attempt to master the use of apostrophes to indicate possession.

1. What to look for: errors in the use of contractions.
   a. apostrophe in the wrong place
   b. contraction incorrectly substituted for another word
2. How to look for the error:
   a. circle all words with apostrophes
   b. mark all contractions
   c. write out the complete form of all contractions
   d. read the <u>entire</u> sentence (Does it make sense with the contraction written out? If it does, leave it. If it does not, correct it.)
3. How to correct the error: see the previous page for the word you have confused with the contraction and substitute it.

After you correct all errors in a PRACTICING PROOFREADING exercise, demonstrate your mastery with a WRITING ASSIGNMENT.

PRACTICING PROOFREADING 1

Circle the 20 words with apostrophes; 17 are contractions. Write out the contractions and correct the 5 errors.

HOW TO RECOGNIZE AN ARIES

[1]If you've recently met an unusually friendly person with a forceful manner, an instant smile, and a firm handshake, chances are you've run into an Aries. [2]Be prepared for quite an experience, because it's tough to keep up with an Aries. [3]Both a male and a female Aries fight for what

they think is right. [4]They're not bashful about voicing they're opinions and they're likely to state those opinions to representatives of the law or to outlaws. [5]They'll regret it later, but they wo'nt think of regrets in the heat of the moment. [6]Such action is not surprising, considering the zodiac's sign they're born under. [7]After all, it's both the ram and the first sign. [8]Who's a ram conscious of but itself? [9]Who's concerns are more important to an infant than it's own? [10]Like infants, people born under Aries are concerned with the world only as it's related to themselves. [11]On the other hand, it's pretty hard to resist babies, and like babies, people born under Aries innocently give their smiles and their favors to anyone who satisfies their demands. [12]As for an Aries' physical appearance, it's very much like that of the ram.

[13]The way an Aries' brows join the bridge of the nose is similar to the face of the ram with it's triangle of horns.

PRACTICING PROOFREADING 2

Circle the 28 words with apostrophes. Write out the complete forms of the 23 contractions and correct the 12 that are incorrect.

CLOCKS FOR THE BODY, CLOCKS FOR THE MIND

[1]It's a mystery to many people why they're work is more efficient at a particular time of day than at another. [2]Scientists suggest that a person's efficiency depends on internal time. [3]People are controlled by they're own biological clocks. [4]Scientists deliberately use the plural "clocks" rather than the singular "clock." [5]It's they're feeling that one clock may control task performance while another clock controls sleeping and waking. [6]They think that there's a clock in charge of people's core body temperature and it's this same clock that affects their performance of tasks. [7]New research suggests that the rhythm of thinking, on the other hand, is on the same clock as the rhythm of sleeping and waking.

[8]Timothy Monk of New York Hospital's Cornell Medical Center, conducted an experiment on a young man who's internal clocks he threw out of cycle. [9]It's been calculated that the natural cycle of the temperature

clock is 24.8 hours. [10]Monk stretched the subject's day into 25.8 hours during the research by putting him into a room that had no outside light. [11]Over a forty-day period, he discovered that the subject's ability to perform tasks depended on his peaks of temperature. [12]His ability to think or reason, however, wasn't up to par except right after he woke up. [13]Monk concluded that thinking has it's own internal clock that's reset while a person's asleep. [14]But the inner clock for temperature (and performance) isn't subject to the same kind of interference.

[15]This experiment has it's practical applications. [16]It's results suggest that rotating workers on shifts can affect they're performance. [17]They're temperature clocks are too difficult to adjust. [18]If they're asked to work during hours when they're core temperature is low, they're production level and quality will be low. [19]At the least, they should be given time for adjustment if they're shifted from day to night work or the other way around. [20]Jobs requiring careful work with the hands should not be given to workers who's hours have just been shifted.

WRITING ASSIGNMENT: contractions

Write a long paragraph on one of the following topics, according to your instructor's specifications for organization and development. Use contractions freely. They will be perfectly appropriate for the informal topics below. When you are satisfied with organization, development, and content, review your essay and replace all contractions with their complete forms.

a. In a letter to a friend, ask some questions, using **who's** and **what's.**
b. Pretend you are a broadcaster and report on a few minutes of action in some sports event. Write as you would speak—using contractions.
c. Write down a joke that you like to tell, making sure your language is informal enough to use contractions.
d. Mention some favorite sayings of people whom you know. Identify each with the name + **'s** (as in **Mom's favorite saying**), and repeat the words. Comment on some of the sayings, using **it's** (as in **It's a funny line**).

Chapter 30

INDICATING POSSESSION WITH 's

To show possession or ownership, add 's to the owner or possessor, and make sure there is something that is owned or possessed. The only rule you will have to remember to indicate possession correctly is **add 's.** In the course of this chapter, you will learn some refinements to the rule, but the rule itself will not change. The 's indicates possession.

ATTENTION FOCUSING 1: indicating possession with 's

a. If the owner or possessor is singular, write **one**; if plural, write **many.**
b. List what is owned or possessed. (This consists of more than one word.)

		possessor + 's	possessed
1. Gulliver's travels to Lilliput	(one)	Gulliver + 's	travels
2. the Americans's ordeal in Iran		+	
3. the Grimm Brothers's fairy tales		+	
4. Nevada's Senator Laxalt		+	
5. straight from the horse's mouth		+	
6. my brother's keeper		+	
7. the Democrats's convention		+	

8. television's newest
   star

9. <u>Uncle Tom's Cabin</u>

10. the girls's gym

11. Mother's Day

c.   List the four plural owners or possessors:

_____   _____   _____   _____

Notice that we first indicate whether an owner or possessor is singular or plural: its **number.** Second, we indicate ownership or possession with **'s.** To indicate plural possession, we must then eliminate or blacken out the second **s,** leaving the familiar sight of a word ending in an apostrophe. However, to ensure that you are putting the apostrophe in the right place, always put **'s** at the end of the word you wish to make possessive. Then eliminate the second **s.** You will thus never have to ask "Where do I put the apostrophe?"

_____   _____   _____   _____

To indicate possession for owners or possessors ending in **s,** add **'s** and then eliminate the second **s.** Chaucer's <u>The Canterbury Tales</u> contains a story entitled "The Prioress's Tale." Notice that the (singular) word **Prioress** receives **'s** to indicate possession. Recently, common usage has been removing the second **s,** leaving "The Prioress' Tale." Traditionally, however, the **'s** is eliminated only with Moses, Jesus, and Greek names ending in an "eez" sound. You might thus check with your instructor to see if he or she would find removing the second **s** acceptable.

Moses's anger (Moses' anger)

Androcles's lion (Androcles' lion)

and in many newspapers and magazines:

Sayres's novels (Sayres' novels)

If you go through the process of adding **'s** and then eliminating the second **s,** you will not make the error of placing the apostrophe into the wrong spot.

If you have made no errors in the use of the **'s,** try PRACTICING PROOF-READING 1 before asking your instructor to send you on to another chapter. If you did make errors, work on the next ATTENTION FOCUSING before doing a REWRITING EXERCISE.

ATTENTION FOCUSING 2: indicating possession with 's*

    a. Circle the 8 words that use **'s** and write them below.
    b. Write **one** for singulars, **many** for plurals.
    d. List alongside each what it owns or possesses.

BLUEBEARD

[1]All versions of the legend contain a number of beautiful women who are killed after they disobey their husband's order not to enter a forbidden room. [2]But there is some disagreement as to the number of Bluebeard's victims. [3]The version by Perreault contains seven victims. [4]A Middle European version records eleven, with the twelfth saved by a gooseherd. [5]The Grimm Brothers's version tells of three sisters, the third of whom rescues the other two. [6]In this version, all potential victims's lives are eventually saved by their brother. [7]The tale's moral lesson (directed at women) seems to be that curiosity and trespassing are dangerous. [8]The legend's historical foundations have never been established. [9]In his introduction to an edition of Perreault's *Tales*, the Scottish journalist and historian Andrew Lang mentions two historical counterparts for Bluebeard (or Barbe-Bleu). [10]He has been identified as a mythical, sixth-century Breton prince named Cormorus or Comorre and as a fifteenth-century marshal of France, the Baron Gilles de Rais. [11]But the tale's essential elements are also found in countries that have never heard of Comorre or de Rais.

possessor + *'s*	*possessed*	*possessor* + *'s*	*possessed*
(one) husband's	order	_____	_____
_____	_____	_____	_____
_____	_____	_____	_____
_____	_____	_____	_____

Blacken out the second **s** in the two plural possessors.

REWRITING EXERCISE 1: indicating possession with 's*

    a. Circle the possessive pronouns that refer to the nouns in **boldface.**
    b. Underline what the possessive pronouns own or possess.

c. Substitute the singular **the tree's** or the plural **trees'** where appropriate.
d. Write **all** possessives and what they possess in the space above each line.

LIGHTING UP CHRISTMAS

[1]On December 22, the time of the winter solstice, nature seems dead. [2]Primitive human beings, wanting to make sure that vegetation would return, used **the evergreen tree** in magical rites. [3]Its green branches reminded them of living nature. [4]They also decorated its branches with lit candles, another sign of life. [5]To the Norse, its greenness symbolized not just the return of spring but also everlasting life. [6]The Romans cut its branches and placed them in their homes and temples during their season of merrymaking and good will at the end of the year.

[7]**The Christmas tree's** present use originated in Germany. [8]Queen Victoria's German husband (called the Prince Consort) brought the idea to England in 1841. [9]He wanted to surprise his young son and provide himself with a reminder of home, so he had **Christmas trees** brought into Windsor Castle. [10]Their lights became a visible sign of Christmas. [11]Soon most British homes were using their lights as holiday symbols.

REWRITING EXERCISE 2: indicating possession with 's

Copy the essay below, making the following changes:

a. Make each phrase in **boldface** possessive by adding **'s** to the last word in the phrase and placing the word first: **the hat of Jim** becomes **Jim's hat.**
b. If, after adding **'s** to a possessor, you see an **s's,** blacken out the second **s.**

MARY HAD A LITTLE LAMB

[1]The famous nursery rhyme "Mary Had a Little Lamb" was written in 1829 by Sarah Joseph Hale. [2]Mrs. Hale was editor of **Magazine of Ladies** at the time. [3]Lowell Mason, who composed occasionally, asked Mrs. Hale for lyrics to a **song of children.**

[4]Fifty years later, a campaign was launched to save the Old South Church of Boston, the building where the rally that led to the Boston tea party had been held. [5]One of the **saviors of the building** turned out to be a Mary E. Tyler. [6]She took stockings that she claimed had been knitted from "Mary's Lamb," unraveled them, and made little bundles with ribbons. [7]Tying them to cards, she sold them for 10 cents apiece, contributing to the **fund of the building.** [8]**The story of Mrs. Tyler** was that she really did have a pet lamb that walked her to her schoolhouse at Redstone Hill when she was 11. [9]It was also **the claim of Mrs. Tyler** that the rhymes about the little lamb were **the creation of John Roulstone,** who happened to be standing there.

[10]The authorship was hotly debated. [11]**A letter of Mrs. Hale,** dated December 29, 1975, claimed she had written "Mary's Lamb" back in 1829. [12]But, when the Redstone Hill schoolhouse became a landmark, the **memorial plaque of the building** named Roulstone as the author of the **first twelve lines of the verse** and Sarah Hale of the last twelve.

REWRITING EXERCISE 3: indicating possession with 's

The short essay below about a Mark Twain exhibit uses the pronoun **his** on 8 occasions to indicate that something "belongs" to Twain. Rewrite the essay, substituting Twain's real name, **Clemens, + 's** for **his.**

THE TWAIN ANNIVERSARIES

[1]Samuel Clemens (better known as Mark Twain) once said that, for the person who invented anniversary celebrations, "mere killing would be too light" a punishment. [2]His explanation was that such commemorations paid attention to something lost rather than to something gained. [3]The National Geographic Society's Executive Board, however, rejected his counsel completely.

[4]In March of 1985, the Society opened an exhibit in New York City that marked the one hundred-fiftieth anniversary of the author's birth. [5]The exhibit also noted that 1985 was the one hundredth anniversary of his publication of The Adventures of Huckleberry Finn, as well as the seventy-fifth anniversary of his death.

[6]The items at the Society's exhibit included three pages from <u>Huck Finn</u> written in his own hand, his writing table, and a jacket from one of his white suits. [7]There was even a fragment from a motion picture that showed his appearance late in life.

REWRITING EXERCISE 4: indicating possession with 's

a. Change each noun using the possessive **s** to the plural. (You might add a word such as **two** or **the** to family names to emphasize plurals.)

b. Rewrite the headlines using these plurals. (Dictionaries indicate if a noun forms its plural with anything other than **s**.)

c. Make sure you return the **'s** to the now-plural words and cross out the second **s** when any **s's** occurs.

1. THE COOPERATIVE'S EARNINGS DOUBLED THIS FISCAL YEAR

   the plural of **COOPERATIVE:** _____

   _____

2. SMITH'S GROCERY EXPANDS TO COMPETE WITH GIANT P & C

   the plural of **SMITH:** _____

   _____

3. YOUR DOLLAR'S WORTH ON DECREASE

   the plural of **DOLLAR:** _____

   _____

4. JACOBS' CAVERN AT LEAST 1,900 YEARS OLD

   the plural of **JACOBS:** _____

   _____

5. THE WHISPERER'S LEGACY NOT AS DEADLY AS FEARED

   the plural of **WHISPERER:** _____

   _____

6. PUBLISHER'S DISCOUNT AVAILABLE

   the plural of **PUBLISHER:** _____

   _____

7. WHALE'S SPOUTS SIGHTED IN N.Y. HARBOR

    the plural of **WHALE:** _____

    _____

8. NORTHERN CITY'S POPULATION DIMINISHING

    the plural of **CITY:** _____

    _____

9. CHILD'S PARENTS BANNED FROM MEETING

    the plural of **CHILD:** _____

    _____

10. SANTOS'S LUGGAGE RECOVERED

    the plural of **SANTOS:** _____

    _____

How to Cope with the Unexpected (1)

In REWRITING EXERCISE 4, each **'s** word is followed by a word (or words) that is possessed or owned. Occasionally, the thing possessed is omitted, as in the names of restaurants or theaters: **Mario's, Loew's, Garfield's.** Nevertheless, in your own writing, make sure that you follow every **'s** word by the thing it possesses. This will help you locate such errors as the omission of the apostrophe or the use of unnecessary apostrophes. (See the PROOFREADING section that follows.)

PROOFREADING STRATEGIES

Before trying these strategies for identifying, locating, and correcting errors in the use of the possessive, **eliminate all contractions** by writing out their correct forms. You can then deal more easily with any problems in the use of the apostrophe.

There are four basic errors in the use of the possessive **'s:**

1. omission of the apostrophe
2. incorrect placement of the apostrophe
3. unnecessary use of the apostrophe
4. omission of both the **s** and the apostrophe

Each of these errors appears separately in the passages that follow, along with strategies for locating it. A discussion of ADDITIONAL STRATEGIES FOR DEALING WITH THE **'s** follows PRACTICING PROOFREADING. The WRITING ASSIGNMENT is followed by a test that contains errors of all four types discussed here.

TYPE 1: the omitted apostrophe in possessives

1. What to look for: nouns ending in **s** that require the apostrophe.
   a. underline all words ending with **s**
   b. underline the next word (or two)
2. How to look for them:
   a. eliminate (as possible places for the apostrophe) all **s** words followed by a comma
   b. eliminate all **s** words followed by verbs, conjunctions, or prepositions
   c. consider carefully only those **s** words that are followed by nouns
3. How to correct them: determine if the second noun "belongs to" or is "possessed by" the **s** word. Then,
   a. if the word is singular, insert the apostrophe between the end of the word and the **s**
   b. if the word is plural or already ends in an **s**, also add **'s**, but eliminate the second **s** when an **s's** combination occurs.

PRACTICING PROOFREADING 1

The paragraph below contains 31 words ending in **s**. Locate and correct the 2 with missing apostrophes.

OWED TO ADAM

[1]The story of Adam and Eve has given rise to a number of terms in the English language. [2]For example, the thyroid cartilage of the larynx is called the "Adam's apple." [3]Because this cartilage is more noticeable in men than in women, it was said to have originated in the story of humankind's first sin. [4]When Adam took a bite of the apple offered him by Eve, the piece stuck in his throat. [5]Water is also jokingly called "Adam's ale" ("Adams wine" in Scotland), as it was the only beverage available in the Garden of Eden. [6]"Adam's needle" is a common name for a species of yucca, a member of the lily family. [7]The connection to Adam may stem from the lines in Genesis that tell how Adam and Eve sewed leaves together to make aprons or coverings for themselves. [8]The yucca plant's fibers and sharp spines could have been used in this enterprise. [9]And, of course, the term "Adam's rib" derives from the story that Eve, the first woman, was fashioned from the first mans rib.

PRACTICING PROOFREADING 2

The paragraph below contains 22 words ending in **s.** Locate and correct the 5 with missing apostrophes.

THE WAR OVER AN EAR

[1]A 1739 war between England and Spain was, according to historians of the period, the result of an outrage against Robert Jenkins, a British captain. [2]The Spanish were limiting England's trade with South America by guarding its coast. [3]When a Spanish ship stopped the Rebecca, a Scottish merchant ship, it found no illegal cargo. [4]But the Rebecca's captain, Robert Jenkins, later reported that the Spanish had torn off one of his ears and told him to carry it back to his king. [5]The king was to understand that, if he had been in Jenkins' shoes, he would have shared Jenkins' fate. [6]Seven years after the event, Jenkins' testimony in the House of Commons helped move England closer to the war with Spain. [7]Later historians viewed Jenkins tale with skepticism. [8]Lord Mahon's History of England (1858) acknowledged that Jenkins' head carried only one ear but found no proof that it had been lost due to a Spanish officer's interference.

PRACTICING PROOFREADING 3

The paragraph below contains 28 words ending in **s.** Locate and correct the 3 with missing apostrophes.

ST. ELMO AND FIRE

[1]The sailors patron saint is St. Elmo. [2]He was a martyred bishop from Italy's Campania province, where the port city of Naples is located. [3]During storms, as sailors clung to the ship's rigging for safety, they would take courage from eerie lights that flickered at the tips of masts. [4]These blue or bluish-white lights were discharges of electricity, but, to the sailors, they were proof of the saint's watchful care. [5]They began to

call the sparks "St. Elmos fire." [6]When Portuguese sailors in the thirteenth century adopted the Blessed Peter Gonzalez as their guardian, they called the flashes "St. Peter's lights." [7]But St. Elmos fire has remained in general use, even when the electricity is seen dancing on church steeples or other tall spires.

TYPE 2: the misplaced apostrophe in possessives

1. What to look for: misplaced apostrophes.
2. How to look for them: circle all words containing the apostrophe (').
3. How to correct them: determine if the word to which the **s** is attached is singular or plural (look for clues in articles and pronouns).
   a. if it is singular, the apostrophe belongs before the **s**
   b. if it is plural, also add **'s**, but eliminate the second **s** if the word now ends in **s's**

PRACTICING PROOFREADING 4

Of the 7 words with **'s,** the apostrophe is misplaced in 3.

CAT IN THE DARK

[1]A cat's eyes contain a special reflecting membrane called the <u>tapetum.</u> [2]This lining acts like a mirror, collecting light rays and reflecting them to the cells of the cat's own eyes. [3]In the process, the membrane also reflects light outward. [4]A cat's eyes thus glow in the dark. [5]A cat's vision is also helped by the ability of its pupils to make great adjustments. [6]In dim light, they widen and became great circles, allowing more light to enter. [7]Cats can thus see even when there is very little light available. [8]On the other hand, cats (as well as dogs, deer, and most other wild animals) are color blind. [9]Because they are active mostly at night, cats never needed to develop color perception. [10]Cat's eyes probably see only black, white, and shades of gray. [11]A monkey's eyes, however, see all the same colors that a human beings' eyes do.

PRACTICING PROOFREADING 5

Of the 9 words with **'s,** the apostrophe is misplaced in 6 (p. 274).

THE REBELLION OF DANIEL SHAYS

[1]In 1786, after only three year's peace with England, a former captain in the Revolutionary War led debt-ridden farmers and other poor people in a rebellion against the taxation and financial policies of the Commonwealth of Massachusetts. [2]Business at this time was poor. [3]Taxes were too high, and the country's currency—the Continental—was not worth the paper it was printed on. [4]Massachusett's farmers were particularly hard hit, burdened with high mortgages and afraid of foreclosure and eviction. [5]They hoped that their livestock would be used for money, but the state's legislature refused. [6]Under Shay's leadership, the angry farmers armed themselves, marched on the State Supreme Court at Springfield, and seized the town of Worcester. [7]A small group of militia failed to put down Shay's rebels. [8]Finally, a militia of 4,400, led by General Benjamin Lincoln, defeated Shay's men at Springfield. [9]Lincoln's troops followed the remnants of Shay's army into New Hampshire, where 150 men, including Shays, were captured. [10]Shays was tried and sentenced to death but pardoned after John Hancock's election as governor.

TYPE 3: the unnecessary apostrophe

1. What to look for: unnecessary apostrophes.
2. How to look for them: circle all words with **'s** and make sure
    a. each is a noun
    b. each is followed soon after by a noun that belongs to it
3. How to correct them: if the word with the apostrophe does not meet the above requirements, eliminate the apostrophe.

PRACTICING PROOFREADING 6

The apostrophe is unnecessary in 4 of the 10 words that use it.

THE DAY FOR LOVERS

[1]The linking of lover's with St. Valentine's feast day is a curious combination of Christian and pagan custom. [2]In ancient Rome, on February 15, boys would draw from an urn the name's of girls who would

then be their sweethearts for the year. [3]After Christianity was established, saints' names would be substituted in the urn. [4]The saint drawn would be considered that person's patron for the following year. [5]Because in 269 A.D., during Claudius' reign, two saints named Valentine were both beheaded on February 14, the day of drawing was merged with the feast day honoring the two martyrs'. [6]By Chaucer's time, legend claimed that birds began to mate on Saint Valentine's Day. [7]The connection with lovers was re-established fully in England and Scotland, where young men and women chose their valentines by lots and exchanged gifts in a kind of betrothal. [8]Later, the writing of fancy message's substituted for the exchange of gifts.

PRACTICING PROOFREADING 7

The apostrophe is unnecessary in 4 of the 9 words that use it.

A BICYCLE BUILT FOR ONE

[1]Unlike that of a boy's bicycle, the top bar in the frame of a girl's bicycle curve's downward. [2]The bicycle for girls' was initially designed to be ridden side-saddle. [3]It was, however, too difficult to balance. [4]But the long skirts' worn by women made it equally difficult for them to ride the standard bicycle. [5]Finally, in 1884, the dropped frame was invented, providing clearance for women's skirts and enabling them to ride easily. [6]The distinction between a boy's bicycle and a girl's bicycle somehow still remain's, even though the need to accommodate long, flowing skirts has disappeared.

TYPE 4: the missing **'s**

1. What to look for: instances where the use of the possessive **'s** is necessary.
2. How to look for it:
    a. look for the presence of possessive pronouns (**his, her, their**) to signal the existence of possessive situations
    b. look for nouns followed by nouns and ask if the first "owns" the second
    c. look for living beings (**John**'s hat, **Mary**'s coat, the **lion**'s den), living "concepts" (**America**'s destiny, **freedom**'s call), and a few

objects or places we think of as being "alive" (the **ship**'s captain, the **theatre's** lobby). Other objects do not use the **'s** to indicate possession (the roof of the house, **not** the house's roof)

3. How to correct it: if you must indicate the possessive, add **'s.** If you now have an **s's** ending, you can eliminate the second **s.**

PRACTICING PROOFREADING 8

Five possessives are missing the **'s.**

APRIL FOOL

[1]The custom of setting aside a day for practical jokes may go back to ancient India or Rome, but its most likely origin is sixteenth-century Europe. [2]At that time, New Year Day was celebrated on April 1. [3]In 1564, Europe Catholic countries replaced the Julian Calendar with the Gregorian Calendar. [4]The new calendar moved New Year Day to January 1. [5]Eventually, Europe Protestant countries also adopted the new calendar, but many people either resisted the change or did not know about it. [6]These people—often from the countryside—became the butt of jokes and pranks. [7]They were considered fools, specifically April Fools, and the day became known as April Fools Day.

PRACTICING PROOFREADING 9

Four possessives are missing the **'s.**

WHY GEORGE WASHINGTON NEVER SMILED

[1]Although the stories that George Washington had teeth made out of wood are untrue, he did have difficulties with false teeth. [2]Washington problems with gum disease were such that he lost all but one tooth to it by the time he became president. [3]He was thus forced to chew with false teeth made out of a variety of materials, including ivory and both human and animal teeth. [4]Most of Washington suffering was caused, however, by the bases on which these false teeth were mounted. [5]Made of ivory, gold, and lead (one of them possibly Paul Revere handiwork), these bases

could not follow the shape of the gums and caused their wearer endless irritation and infection. [6]The awkwardness of these dentures are probably responsible for Washington unsmiling, closed lips in all portraits, including the one on the one-dollar bill.

ADDITIONAL STRATEGIES FOR DEALING WITH THE POSSESSIVE 'S

If you still find yourself making errors with the possessive 's, you might consider avoiding it altogether. The English language provides a number of ways to indicate that something belongs to someone or something.

1. You can use a possessive pronoun—if first you have established the noun to which it refers. These pronouns are listed on p. 27 and p. 45. (Remember **not** to use the apostrophe when you use the pronouns.)

how to avoid using 's.

using the 's

The theater's insides were torn out.

using the possessive pronoun

The theater was closed. Its insides were torn out.

2. You might use **of the** to show possession.

using the 's

✓ The theater's insides were torn out.

using *of the*

The insides of the theater were torn out.

3. You might turn the owner or possessor into an adjective.

using the 's

Europe's breadbasket
the president's papers
America's self-image

using the adjective

the European breadbasket
the presidential papers
the American self-image

Using these alternatives is, however, often more difficult than learning to use the 's correctly. Because you must rethink and rewrite your sentences, you might complicate their grammar. Still, if you can use the methods suggested above to avoid or correct errors in the use of the 's, go ahead!

In any case, limit your use of the apostrophe to the possessives. This is not a grammatical rule but a suggestion. The apostrophe just does not appear that often in the typical formal essay. If you do not use contractions and try to avoid the use of the apostrophe to indicate plurals, as in the infrequent cases below, you will find that you can isolate the 's problem and deal with it more easily.

Instead of writing **the 1920's,** you can write either **the Twenties** or **the 1920s.** In fact, simply adding an **s** to indicate the plural is becoming more and more acceptable as it is consistent with the general rule for forming plurals: add **s.** In the sentence **I received four A's last semester,** you can write: **four A grades** or **four "A"s** or **four *A*s** or **four As.** You can even rewrite the sentence: **I received an A in all four courses last semester.**

WRITING ASSIGNMENT: indicating possession with the 's

Write a long paragraph on one of the following topics according to your instructor's specifications for organization and development. Proof-read for **your** specific type of **'s** error.

a. Recommend a film, book, video, or concert, stressing the skills of the person in charge. Talk about the **director's, author's,** or **stage manager's** work.
b. Describe a family member, attributing his or her physical appearance and character to various older members. Use the **'s** as in **Laura has Uncle Henry's skill with machines.**
c. Name some outstanding individuals in a category of your choice (say, people who have overcome handicaps) and enumerate their accomplishments, using the **'s,** as in **Helen Keller's writings. . . .**
d. Using the plural **neighbors,** tell about how well or badly you get along with them, using the **'s** to describe their home, appearance, or behavior, as in **My neighbors' dogs help guard my house.**

PROOFREADING TEST: four types of 's errors

Locate and correct the 10 errors in the use of the possessive **'s.** The essay contains at least 2 errors of each type.

FORD'S THEATER

[1]Although most people know that it was in Ford's Theater where President Lincoln was assassinated on Friday night, April 14, 1865, not everyone know's the other interesting facts related to that evening and and to the theater afterward.

[2]The playhouse itself, on 10th Street, N.W., Washington, D.C., was owned by John T. Ford. [3]The offering that night was the comedy <u>Our American Cousin</u>, starring Laura Keene. [4]Box Sevens' occupants, in addition to Mr. and Mrs. Lincoln, were Major Henry R. Rathbone, and Major Rathbone's fiancée, Clara Harris, New York Senator Ira Harri's daughter. [5]The Civil War's end on April 9 allowed the President his first

opportunity for relaxation in four years. [6]After President Lincoln's body-guard, John J. Parker, inspected the box and settled everyone in, he went next door to Taltavul's Tavern for a drink. [7]John Wilkes Booth, the more famous actor Edwin Booths brother, saw Parker's arrival to Taltavuls Tavern and moved quickly. [8]The sequence that followed is well known: the single shot, Booth 14-foot leap to the stage, his shout "<u>Sic semper tyrannis.</u>" [9]Less familiar is the subsequent history of Ford's Theater.

[10]Following the tragedy, the government confiscated it. [11]Ford reclaimed it and even scheduled a play in it, but the public's outrage forced him to close down. [12]Eventually the theaters insides were torn out, and the building was refurbished. [13]Later, it served as an Army medical museum, as an office, and as a storage place. [14]In 1893, the third floor's collapse resulted in the death of twenty-two workers. [15]In 1932, under the control of the Park Service, it became a Lincoln Museum.

[16]In 1967, it was decided to restore the theater. [17]Alexander Gardner and Matthew Brady's* photographs, taken shortly after the assassination, were used as model's for the interior. [18]The restoration, completed in 1968, was a faithful recreation of Ford's original playhouse, with some slight differences. [19]The theaters seating capacity was reduced to 600 from the original 1,700, and electricity replaced the gas lights. [20]In this new theater, only the first floor is used for performances. [21]The second is set aside for special programs, and the third houses a 2,500 volume Lincoln library, including some of the Presidents' books.

[22]The opening performance on Jaunary 21, 1968, was Stephen Vincent Benêt's <u>John Brown's Body</u>, an anti-slavery play.

How To Cope with the Unexpected (2)

In the starred (*) sentence, two people, Gardner and Brady, are the owners of the photographs. Notice, however, that the possessive **'s** is attached only to the owner closest to the noun being possessed or owned. You have the option of attaching the **'s** to both names in case of such joint ownership. However, if ownership is individual, you must indicate possession for each noun: **NBC's reporters and ABC's reporters** would be written as **NBC's and ABC's reporters.** If the two networks shared reporters, you may use just one possessive: **NBC and ABC's reporters.**

Chapter **31**

USING
CAPITAL LETTERS

Capital letters are used less frequently than lower-case letters. Thus words that begin with capitals are more noticeable. Some people try to draw attention to words by capitalizing the first letter. Advertisements frequently use this method of making certain words significant, as do playbills for films and plays, where the most important performers' names may be entirely in capitals.

Although this method of emphasis may work on billboards and playbills, its use in formal essays is not accepted. Capitalization follows certain established guidelines. In general, the first letter of a word must be capitalized if it falls into one of the categories set out in the following list. There is no need to capitalize a letter unless it falls into one of these categories.

1. Capitalize the first letter of a sentence, including a quoted sentence (even when it appears within another sentence).
2. Capitalize the first letter of the first word in the title of a work and the first letter of all other words in a title except "function" words such as articles **(a/an/the)**, conjunctions **(and/but/or** and others), prepositions **(of, on,** etc.), and the infinitive **to.**
3. Capitalize the first letter(s) of proper names—the actual names of particular people (including their titles), things, areas, organizations: **John, Chevrolet, Michigan, American Federation of Teachers.**
4. Capitalize the first letter of words derived from proper names: **American, Mexican, Catholic.**
5. Capitalize the word **I.**
6. Capitalize the first letter of days of the week, months, holidays: **Sunday, July, Easter.**

How to Cope with the Unexpected (1)

As you write, you will have to decide how to capitalize in so many special situations that it would be more helpful to keep a recent college dictionary handy than attempt to memorize all the rules of capitalization. You will find, for example, that the word **God** is usually capitalized, as, of course, are all other names for the supreme being (such as **Jehovah** or **Allah**). Some writers will also capitalize pronouns that refer to the deity. Words *referring* to God—such as **the deity** or **the supreme being**—are rarely capitalized. The starred [*] acronym **NIH** in an exercise that follows consists of the initial letters in **National Institute of Health.** Such shortened forms of capitalized word groups are always capitalized. Other examples: **IRS** (Internal Revenue Service), **CBS** (Columbia Broadcasting System), **OPEC** (Organization of Petroleum Exporting Countries). Sometimes even lowercase word groups become capitalized abbreviations: **ante meridiem** and **post meridiem** are best known as A.M. and P.M., and **AM** and **FM** on your radio dials stand for **amplitude modulation** and **frequency modulation.**

ATTENTION FOCUSING: capital letters*

a. Circle each capital letter.
b. For each capital letter in **boldface,** choose one of the numbered categories mentioned earlier to explain its presence. Enter the number in the space provided.

1. One famous scientific hoax is the "discovery" at **P**iltdown.   3 _____

2. In 1908, a British lawyer and archeologist named **C**harles **D**awson, found a bone fragment near Piltdown in southeastern England.   _____

3. **T**hree years later, he found another piece of skull in the gravel pit.   _____

4. He took the bones to **S**ir Arthur Smith Woodward.   _____

5. The geologist at the **B**ritish **M**useum thought the bones belonged to a peculiar human fossil.   _____

6. After their discovery of an ape-like lower jaw, Woodward announced the findings, naming the fossil after **D**awson.   _____

7. **A**nthropology books subsequently noted the names of the two, even if they disagreed that the skull and jaw were from the same creature.   _____

8. In 1953, the **B**ritish archeologist Kenneth Oakley and his associates used chemical analysis in an attempt to date the fossils.   _____

9. **T**hey discovered that the jaw was not a fossil at all, but a bone from a modern ape, treated to make it look ancient.   _____

10. Martin Gardner, in his book <u>F</u>ads and <u>F</u>allacies in the <u>N</u>ame of Science, lists five criteria for recognizing fake scientists. _____

11. One indication is, "**H**e considers himself a genius." _____

> If you have made no errors in capitalization, try PRACTICING PROOF-READING 1 before asking your instructor to send you on to another chapter. If you did make errors, reread the discussion and work on the appropriate REWRITING EXERCISE. Sentences 3, 7, 9, and 11 in ATTENTION FOCUSING correspond to REWRITING EXERCISE 1. Work for errors made in all other sentences can be found in EXERCISES 2 and 3.

REWRITING EXERCISE 1: capital letters at the beginning of sentences*

Write all changes in the space above each line.

a. Spell out each number, paying attention to capitalization. (**9 → nine**)
b. The starred (*) words **God** and **NIH** were explained in HOW TO COPE 1.

1 PAPER TOO MANY

[1]John Darsee's career at Harvard University's Brigham and Women's Hospital advanced rapidly. [2]100 of his publications found their way into various journals by the time he was just 33 years old. [3]7 years after he received his medical degree at Emory University, he was already being considered for an assistant professorship and a lab of his own at Harvard. [4]Then his troubles began.

[5]1 week's worth of data was discovered by Darsee's co-workers to have been only a few minutes of cardiac recordings. [6]Challenged, Darsee confessed to the falsification, but hoped that God* and his colleagues would forgive him and not let 1 isolated incident ruin his career. [7]2 of his fellowships were terminated, but he was allowed to complete 1 project he had under contract to the National Institute of Health. [8]A further look, however, raised additional questions.

[9]1 year's investigation by a panel of 5 cardiologists appointed by the *NIH discovered that Darsee had falsified nearly all his data at Harvard.

[10]1 committee at Emory University then uncovered discrepancies in Darsee's early work there. [11]2 papers he had written and published during his 4 years of undergraduate work at Notre Dame might also have contained fraudulent data.

[12]Eventually, the NIH asked Brigham and Women's Hospital to repay more than ½ the money of the contract it had awarded Darsee. [13]It also declared, "10 years must go by before Darsee may receive federal research funds."

[14]The hospital plans to repay the money. [15]Darsee did not appeal.

REWRITING EXERCISE 2: capital letters within sentences

Rewrite the essay below, substituting an actual proper name for each segment in **boldface.** Capitalize when necessary. Invent a name if you do not know an actual one. Starred (*) words are explained after the essay.

A NOSE THAT KNOWS MONEY

[1]According to **a science magazine (sixth month,** 1983), many over-the-counter remedies contain at least one ingredient of dubious effectiveness. [2]The article quotes *Doctor Steven Jones, employed by **a consumer group,** who says that buying these medicines is a waste of money and selling them a violation of federal law.

[3]Products most often cited by **the consumer group** are headache and cold remedies. [4]**A liquid cold medicine,** for example, contains ephedrine sulfate, a useful treatment for stuffy noses. [5]But **the federal agency that deals with matters relating to drugs** has declared that ephedrine sulfate is effective only when it is applied topically. [6]In other words, explains **the doctor, the liquid cold medicine** will unstuff noses only if it is squirted right into the nostrils! [7]Drinking **the liquid cold medicine** will relieve only the fullness of your wallet, not your nose.

[8]Another product making unprovable claims is **a headache remedy,** advertised as containing "the pain reliever doctors recommend most." [9]The pain reliever is, of course, aspirin, cheapest when bought in its ge-

neric form. [10]But each pill of **this headache remedy** also contains 32 milligrams of caffeine. [11]Despite claims by the manufacturer of **this headache remedy,** the evidence that caffeine enhances aspirin is not conclusive, according to **a government panel.** [12]Excedrin, the main competitor to **this headache remedy,** also contains caffeine, but accompanying it as an active ingredient is acetaminophen, an effective non-aspirin pain reliever.

[13]Other over-the-counter drugs cited by **the government agency** include **a familiar hemorrhoidal relief preparation** and **a famous mouthwash** accused of "mediciny" taste. [14]The cream in a tube of **the hemorrhoidal preparation** does contain shark liver oil and a live yeast derivative, but, according to the Federal Drug Administration, its concentrations are too low to be effective. [15]As for the active ingredients in **the mouthwash**—thymol, eucalyptol, methyl salicate, and menthol—they may fight against bad breath, but they lose the struggle because they are ineffective.

[16]To help consumers, The Health Research Group has in **eighth month** published the book <u>Over-the-Counter Drugs</u>.

How To Cope with the Unexpected (2)

The starred [*] **Doctor** is capitalized because it is the individual's title. The word **doctor,** by itself, would not be capitalized. The rules of capitalization for such titles present much difficulty—words that by themselves would be lowercase become capitalized when they are combined with other proper names. You must write **a president** but **President Kennedy, east** and **street** but **East Genesee Street, high school** but **George Washington Carver High School,** somebody's **grandma** but **Grandma Moses.**

REWRITING EXERCISE 3: using capital letters in names and titles

Rewrite the playbill in the spaces provided, leaving capital letters only where they are required by the rules of capitalization.

a.   PLYMOUTH THEATRE   _____

b.   EMANUEL AZENBERG, THE SHUBERT ORGANIZATION,   _____

c.   ICARUS PRODUCTIONS, BYRON GOLDMAN, IVAN BLOCH,   _____

d.   ROGER BERLIND, AND MICHAEL CODRON   _____

e.   PRESENT   _____

f.   JEREMY IRONS   AND   LAILA ROBBINS   _____

g.   IN   _____

h.   THE REAL THING   _____

i.   BY   _____

j.   TOM STOPPARD   _____

k.   ALSO STARRING   _____

l.   LESLIE LYLES   SIMON JONES   _____

m.   ANNE MARIE BOBBY   PETER GALLAGHER   _____
        CAMBELL SCOTT   _____

n.   SCENERY BY COSTUMES BY LIGHTING BY   _____
o.   TONY WALTON   ANTHEA SYLBERT   _____
      THARON MUSSER

p.   SOUND BY   PRODUCTION SUPERVISOR   _____

q.   OTTS MUNDERLOH   MARTIN HERZER   _____

r.   DIRECTED BY   _____

s.   MIKE   _____
t.   NICHOLS   _____

u.   <u>THE REAL THING</u> WAS ORIGINALLY PRO-   _____
v.   DUCED IN LONDON BY MICHAEL CODRON.   _____

w.   THE ORIGINAL BROADWAY CAST ALBUM IS   _____
x.   AVAILABLE ON NONESUCH RECORD AND   _____
    CASSETTES.   _____

y.   THE PRODUCERS AND MANAGEMENT ARE   _____
z.   MEMBERS OF THE LEAGUE OF NEW YORK   _____
    THEATRES AND PRODUCERS.   _____

PROOFREADING STRATEGIES

When writers make errors with capital letters, they either use them unnecessarily or forget to use them when their presence is required. The selections in PRACTICING PROOFREADING contain errors of either one type or the other. The instructions will identify the type of error you should look for. The MASTERY TEST at the end of the unit contains errors in both.

PROOFREADING FOR UNNECESSARY CAPITAL LETTERS

1. What to look for: unnecessary use of capital letters, focusing on
   a. words for people that are not their names—mother, friend
   b. words that strike you as needing emphasis—you might have tried to stress them by capitalizing
   c. specific errors *you* make—in titles, for example.

2. How to look for it: circle or underline all capital letters and attempt to justify the use of each.
3. How to correct it: if you cannot justify the use of the capital letter by referring to one of the categories at the beginning of this section, change it to a lowercase letter.

After you correct all errors in a PRACTICING PROOFREADING exercise, demonstrate your mastery with the WRITING ASSIGNMENT.

PRACTICING PROOFREADING 1

The prose version of this anonymous ballad contains 58 capital letters (including those in the title). Locate and correct the 14 that are unnecessary.

The House Of The Rising Sun

[1]There is a house in New Orleans They call the Rising Sun. [2]It has been the ruin of many a poor girl, And I, oh Lord, was one. [3]If I had listened to what mama said, I'd be home today. [4]But being so young and foolish, poor girl, Let a gambler lead me astray.

[5]My mother is a Tailor. [6]She sews those new Blue Jeans. [7]My Sweetheart is a drunkard, Lord, down in New Orleans. [8]The only thing a drunkard needs is a suitcase and a trunk. [9]The only time he's satisfied is when he's on a drunk. [10]He'll fill his glasses to the brim; he passes them around. [11]And the only pleasure He gets out of life is bumming from town to town.

[12]Go tell my Baby Sister never to do as I have done. [13]Shun that House in New Orleans they call the Rising Sun. [14]It's one foot on the platform and the other one on the train. [15]I'm going back to New Orleans to wear the ball and chain. [16]I'm going back to New Orleans. [17]My race is almost run. [18]I'm going to spend my life Beneath that Rising Sun.

PROOFREADING FOR MISSING CAPITALS LETTERS

1. How to look for the error:
    a. look in *your* area of weakness—titles or quotations, for example.
    b. look near words already capitalized; some of the words before or after may also need capital letters.

   c. look near punctuation marks, particularly periods, which must be followed by a capital letter.

   d. look for any unusual situations—names of battles, for example, or words you do not recognize immediately.

2. How to correct the error: if the word fits into one of the categories for capitals listed at the beginning of the section, capitalize it, reminding yourself to check the word in a dictionary.

PRACTICING PROOFREADING 2

Correct the 8 missing capital letters.

THE DANCE OF SALOME

[1]According to the story in Mark 6:17–28, a dance using seven veils was performed by Salome, daughter of Herodias, before king Herod, who rewarded her with the head of John the baptist. [2]John had denounced the marriage of Herodias to Herod, earning himself her hatred. [3]But because king Herod considered John a righteous man, he protected him from his wife.

[4]On Herod's birthday, during a banquet, princess Salome danced for the king. [5]he was so pleased, that he swore to grant any wish she had. [6]Prompted by her mother, Salome asked for the head of John the baptist. [7]Forced to honor his promise, Herod ordered the execution. [8]A guard brought Salome the head on a platter.

[9]Oscar Wilde, in his 1893 play <u>Salome</u>, fashions a different story. [10]In his version, Salome is in love with the man who had baptized Christ, but John rejects her and rebukes her for her relationship with her stepfather. [11]she demands John's head on a platter as her own revenge, not her mother's.

PROOFREADING TEST: missing and extra capitals

Review the PROOFREADING STRATEGIES before testing your skills. Locate and correct the 20 errors in capitalization (9 instances of unnecessary capital letters and 11 cases of missing capitals) in the passage on p. 288. Consider the title of the essay as well.

The "ten Most Wanted" List

[1]Back in the 1940s, newspapers would distribute stories about major criminals wanted by the FBI. [2]The Associated press, the United press, and the International News Service chose which criminals they considered most wanted. [3]In 1950, the Bureau decided to work with the newspapers. [4]It then selected and publicized a list of ten particular Criminals.

[5]For a Criminal to be placed on the list, he or she had to have a lengthy record of serious crimes and/or had to be considered extremely dangerous to Society. [6]but only those Criminals were put on the list whose apprehension was likely as a result of Nationwide publicity.

[7]Here is the average profile of someone on the "ten most wanted" list, as compiled by the FBI: 5 feet, 9 inches tall; 167 pounds; 36 years old at time of capture; 157 days on the List; 969 miles distance between scene of crime and place of apprehension. [8]of the nearly 400 who have made this "Ten Most Wanted" list, only six have been women. [9]More than 350 of these Criminals have been apprehended, about a third thanks to information from Citizens. [10]Six men have made the list more than once and One, Charles Lee Herron, has been on it for fourteen years, the longest evasion of the federal bureau of investigation.

WRITING ASSIGNMENT: capital letters

Write a long paragraph on one of the following topics according to your instructor's specifications for organization and development. Proofread for errors in the use of capital letters.

a. List some of the films, TV shows, or other appearances of a favorite performer. Include the names of characters that the performer has played.

b. Discuss some of the people who have influenced you greatly over the years, both positively and negatively. Give their names (or make up names for them), any titles or official positions they might have held, organizations to which they might have belonged, or other kinds of identification using proper names.

c. Write a letter of support or complaint to an administrator at your school, local government agency, company representative, or other official. Make sure your letter contains both your and the individual's title and address. Use the names of your courses, the names of departments, or the names of products.

Chapter 32

USING QUOTATION MARKS

Whenever you use someone else's words or ideas, you should make your source clear. Whether you **quote** (reproduce someone's exact words), **summarize** (give a short version of someone's main ideas), or **paraphrase** (use your own language to convey another's ideas), you must identify the source for the words or ideas.

Why would you wish to use the exact words you have heard or read? Perhaps the words are extremely vivid or interesting and thus worth preserving in their original form. More likely, the precise words are important so that readers may study them as they were originally offered rather than read them as interpreted by you. Quotation marks in such situations inform your reader that the material within is reproduced exactly as it appeared in the original document.

If the original material contains an error, reproduce the error, but add [sic] immediately after the error. This Latin word for "thus" informs readers that the error belongs to the quoted text, not to you.

FROM <u>ROBINSON CRUSOE</u> BY DANIEL DEFOE

I understood him in many things and let him know I was well pleased with him; in a little time I began to speak to him and teach him to speak to me; and first, I made him know his name should be Friday, which was the day I saved his life. I called him so for the memory of the time.

quoting a sentence: Crusoe writes in his diary, "I made him know his name should be Friday."

quoting one word: Crusoe names the man Friday for the "memory" of the day.

289

<table>
<tr><td>missing words in quotation:</td><td>Crusoe writes, "I . . . let him know I was . . . pleased with him."</td></tr>
<tr><td>paraphrasing:</td><td>Crusoe named him Friday to commemorate the day he found him.</td></tr>
</table>

In addition to their use with citations, quotation marks have two other functions: to indicate the titles of short works such as articles, chapters, stories, poems, songs, and TV and radio programs, and to indicate that a word is being used in a special sense.

ATTENTION FOCUSING: quotation marks*

Circle the quotation marks and indicate their purpose in the space provided; write **quotation, title,** or **special sense.**

1. Blake's "The Tyger" contains a number of references to the Fall.   _title_

2. Once he mentions the time when stars "watered heaven with their tears."   _quotation_

3. All creation groaned aloud when Adam and Eve "fell."   _special sense_

4. Blake also asks, "What hand dare seize the fire?"   _quotation_

5. Though he does not name Lucifer, he is referring to that defiant angel who was, in Milton's words, "headlong hurled" to hell.   _quotation_

6. Blake describes the tiger's symmetry as "fearful."   _quotation_

7. This poem is often contrasted with "The Lamb."   _title_

8. David R. Pichaske, in <u>Beowulf to Beatles</u>, lists Blake's poems as well as songs by Judy Collins and Phil Ochs under "Symbol."   _title_

9. How schools use songs is discussed by D. E. DeMorse, in "Avant-Rock in the Classroom," <u>English Journal</u>, 58 (February, 1969).   _title_

10. Leonard Cohen's famous "Suzanne" is part of a longer poem.   _title_

How to Cope with the Unexpected (1)

Throughout the exercise, whenever a comma (,) or a period (.) follows a quoted passage, it goes *within* the quotation. Although there are some exceptions to this rule (see Chapter 34), in nearly all instances, a comma or a period is placed *within* the quotation marks. Practice writing these punctuation marks with the following words, taken from the sentences in ATTENTION FOCUSING. Add to each word the comma or period and the quotation mark(s) as they appear in ATTENTION FOCUSING.

Sentence 2: <u>tears</u>   Sentence 4: <u>fire</u>   Sentence 7: <u>Lamb</u>
Sentence 3: <u>fell</u>   Sentence 5: <u>fearful</u>   Sentence 8: <u>Symbol</u>

WRITING ASSIGNMENT 1: quotation marks

Choose one of the topics and write a paragraph or a series of sentences that requires the use of quotation marks.

a. Write down a joke in which two people are talking to each other.
b. Pretend you are writing the story of your life; supply ten chapter titles.
c. In different sentences, state the motto, song, and nickname of your school, state, club, group, or team. (Use quotation marks around each.)

If you have made no errors in the use of quotation marks, try PRACTICING PROOFREADING 1 before asking your instructor to send you to another chapter. If you did make errors, read the REVIEW.

REVIEW: quotation marks

Quotation marks (" ") are used in three different situations:

1. They indicate the beginning and end of a speaker or writer's *exact* words. Note the quotation marks in the following references to Daniel Defoe's novel, <u>Robinson Crusoe</u>. (A reproduction of a section of text and the references to it are placed side by side.)

reproduction	**quotations**
I understood him in many things and let him know I was very well pleased with him; in a little time I began to speak to him and teach him to speak to me; and first, I made him know his name should be Friday, which was the day I saved his life. I called him so for the memory of time.	Defoe has Crusoe write in his diary, "I made him know his name should be Friday."
	(Use quotation marks even around a partial sentence or one word.)
	Crusoe names the man "Friday."

2. They indicate the titles of short works: articles, chapters, stories, poems, songs, and TV and radio programs.

The chapter in which Robinson Crusoe finds his companion is "I Hear the First Sound of a Man's Voice."

James Moffatt discusses Defoe's <u>Robinson Crusoe</u> in "The Religion of Robinson Crusoe," a 1919 article in the journal <u>Contemporary Review.</u>

Curtis Mayfield's song "Isle of Sirens" has a 1961 copyright.

One of PBS's 1986 <u>Great Performances</u> featured the ballet "Boxes."

3. They indicate that a word is being used in a special sense. In the examples that follow, the writers use quotation marks to suggest that a word or words have more than one meaning or do not literally mean what they seem to say.

Suzanne, in Leonard Cohen's poems by that name, is described as wearing rags and feathers and living by the river, but she may be a "tramp" in other ways as well.

Parents think of a future son-in-law as someone who is going to take their "little girl" away.

In punctuating a quotation, you might need to use more than just quotation marks. If you quote an entire sentence, you must follow the speaker's name or any other introductory phrase with a comma and capitalize the first word in the quoted sentence. We will call your attention to other kinds of punctuation involving quotation marks in the REWRITING EXERCISES.

Continue by choosing a REWRITING EXERCISE. It will provide practice in the use of quotation marks. Work until you complete one without making any errors. Then go to the section on PROOFREADING.

REWRITING EXERCISE 1: quotation marks*

Rewrite each line of dialogue, using quotation marks. Introduce each quotation with the speaker and the word **said** or **asked.**

1. EMPLOYER: How long did you work at your last job?

     _____

2. APPLICANT: 65 years.

     _____

3. EMPLOYER: And how old are you?

     _____

4. APPLICANT: 45.

_____

5. EMPLOYER: How could you work for 65 years if you're only 45 years old?

_____

6. APPLICANT: I put in a lot of overtime.

_____

How to Cope with the Unexpected (2)

In each instance, the question mark goes _within_ the quotes.

REWRITING EXERCISE 2: quotation marks

Copy the entire essay, using both upper- and lowercase letters for the words in CAPITALS. Because these are either titles or quotations, use quotation marks where appropriate. The (" ") in the starred (*) sentence become ('). See the explanation after the essay.

WE SING YOU A MERRY CHRISTMAS

[1]The worst song Johnny Marks ever wrote began with the words, I WISH MY MOM WOULD MARRY SANTA CLAUS. [2]But he can afford to admit mistakes because in 1949 he wrote RUDOLPH THE RED-NOSED REINDEER, which has sold more than 130 million records. [3]It has been recorded by about 500 artists, the first of whom was Gene Autry, the SINGING COWBOY, and the most recent, Paul McCartney, with RUDOLPH THE RED-NOSED REGGAE.

[4]The odds against a Christmas hit are tremendous. [5]*DURING A THREE WEEK PERIOD, YOU'RE COMPETING WITH 500 OTHER SONGS, INCLUDING PERENNIAL FAVORITES LIKE "WHITE CHRISTMAS" AND "RUDOLPH," explains Marks. [6]Still, in addition to RUDOLPH, Marks has written three other yuletide superhits, including I HEARD THE BELLS ON CHRISTMAS DAY, first sung by Bing Crosby. [7]One he did not write sold 4 million records during its first year. [8]It was called IF IT DOESN'T SNOW ON CHRISTMAS DAY. [9]Never heard of it? [10]Perhaps you have heard of the song on the B side of that record. [11]It was a little song called RUDOLPH THE RED-NOSED REINDEER, a THROWAWAY in the view of the record company.

How to Cope with the Unexpected (3)

When you place quotation marks around a sentence that already contains them, change the quotation marks within to **single quotes** or (').

When Steve Lawrence sang "Go Away Little Girl" on a telethon, the poster child facing him became alarmed.	<u>Variety</u> reports, "When Steve Lawrence sang 'Go Away Little Girl' on a telethon, the poster child facing him was alarmed."

How to Cope with the Unexpected (4)

A quotation needs an introductory phrase, which can appear at the beginning, middle, and end of the quotation.

beginning: **Dr. Brothers said,** "Try to put yourself in their position."

end: "Try to put yourself in their position," **Dr. Brothers said.**

middle: "Try," **Dr. Brothers said,** "to put yourself in their position."

REWRITING EXERCISE 3: quotations and quotation marks

a.   In a complete sentence, state the title of the article.
b.   In other sentences, using the names of the authors (B. D. and Dr. Brothers) with **said** or **wrote,** quote the words in **boldface.**

MEETING IN-LAWS BY DR. JOYCE BROTHERS

DEAR DR. BROTHERS: [1]I am very serious about a young woman and eventually hope to marry her, but **I still freeze** when I have to visit her parents.   -B.D.

B.D. said, "I still freeze."

DEAR B.D.: [2]Listen, I am sure you are not the only one who tenses up at such meetings. [3]One of the reasons for this discomfort is **because everyone has different**

expectations and everyone feels vulnerable. [4]If your friend's family members know that you are as serious as you are, they are looking at you as a potential son-in-law. [5]**They may also look at you as someone who is going to take "their little girl" away.** [6]While some fathers are pleased by their daughters' **romantic attachments,** more often they are apt to be critical and possessive.

        [7]*It will help if you try to put yourself in their position. [8]Imagine you were the father and this was your daughter. [9]**Wouldn't you tend to be super-critical and cautious, too?**

_____
_____
_____
_____
_____
_____
_____
_____
_____

_____
_____
_____
_____
_____

ADDITIONAL INFORMATION ABOUT PUNCTUATING QUOTATIONS

        The placement of the question mark (**?**), exclamation point (**!**), dash (**—**), colon (**:**), and semicolon (**;**) in relation to quotation marks is a bit confusing. The question mark, dash, and exclamation point can go either before or after the closing quotation marks depending on context. If the the question mark, dash, or exclamation point refers to the quoted material, it goes **before** the endquote.

        Marks asked, "Do you know how many songs compete with each other?"

        If, however, the question mark, dash, or exclamation point refers to the sentence as a whole, it goes **outside** the endquote.

        Did you know that Marks wrote "Rudolph the Red-Nosed Reindeer"?

        The colon and the semicolon are always placed **outside** the quotation marks.

The company demanded "old songs"; the advertising agency offered a group of fifteen from the 1960s similar to "Devil in a Blue Dress": "Born to Be Wild," "Help," "Heat Wave," and others.

PROOFREADING STRATEGIES

1. What to look for: errors in the use of quotation marks
   a. missing, misplaced, or excessive quotation marks
   b. incorrect placement of punctuation around quotation marks
2. How to look for errors in the use of quotation marks:
   a. look near capitalized words (they may be titles)
   b. look near clue words such as **she said**
   c. if there are quotation marks, pay special attention to the punc-
   c. tuation around them
3. How to correct them: follow the correct forms on pages 291–292.

PRACTICING PROOFREADING 1

Correct the 7 missing quotation marks.

POETS ON BANKERS

[1]Many famous literary figures have offered negative opinions about the world of finance. [2]Robert Frost said, "A bank is a place where they lend you an umbrella in fair weather and ask for it back when it begins to rain. [3]Ogden Nash seemed to agree with Frost's description of banks as "fair weather friends." [4]He once said, The one rule banks have is never to lend money to people unless they do not need it. [5]Mark Twain's wit was directed at the stock market. [6]"October, he said, is one of the dangerous months in which to speculate in stocks." [7]Then he went on to list the rest of the dangerous months: the other eleven in the year. [8]Ludwig von Mises mocked the "ability" of his country to print money. [9]"Government is the only agency that can take a useful commodity like paper, slap some ink on it, and make it totally worthless," he said. [10]G. B. Shaw complained about economists, not institutions. [11]He joked, If they were all laid end to end, they still would not reach a conclusion.

PRACTICING PROOFREADING 2

In the selection at the top of p. 297, locate and correct the 5 instances where the position or use of quotation marks is incorrect.

HISTORICAL VALUE

[1]Letitia Harris of Syracuse collects material of historical importance to black Americans, but she believes that even her own grandmother "would probably spin in her grave" if she saw her namesake's "Our Hidden Past" collection. [2]Although Harris does own such black Americana as slave freedom documents, illustrations of black pioneers, and Booker T. Washington half dollars, she also owns many knicknacks considered derogatory to blacks: "Mammy" cookie jars, trading cards that call blacks "chocolates" and "licorice sticks", signs that say "Colored Seated in Rear", and belittling caricatures on boxes of chocolates, on tobacco cans, and on cereal boxes. [3]To people who object to her collection, Mrs. Harris says, "It's part of our history", and she won't hide any of the items. [4]Charles L. Blockson, the curator of Temple University's Afro-American collection, agrees, explaining, "If you're going to make an accurate study of history, you must take the good with the bad". [5]Randolph Hawkins, a Syracuse University professor of Afro-American Studies, in "Making Sure Our History is Accurate" (Syracuse <u>Herald Journal</u>, June 2, 1986, D1), approves the preservation but would like to retain the 'taboo" on the buying and selling.

PROOFREADING TEST

Locate and correct the 12 errors in the position or use of quotation marks.

A SONG OR THOUSAND WORDS?

[1]People can always tell who the target of an advertiser's pitch might be by identifying the date of the song used in the jingle.

[2]Because consumers between ages 30 and 45 have the greatest disposable income, many songs from the 1960s—when the musical tastes of these people were formed—are used by advertisers. [3]Lincoln-Mercury, for example, has used "Born to Be Wild", "Heat Wave", the Beatles' song "Help", and more than a dozen other songs from the 1960s. [4]Makers of California Coolers have used "Green Onions", "Tutti-Frutti", and "Louie,

Louie", among others. [5]One cereal maker sells the fiber in its product to the strains of "This Is Dedicated to the One I Love", a Shirrelles hit from the 1960s. [6]Products such as soft drinks are meant to appeal to younger consumers, which explains Pepsi-Cola's use of Michael Jackson's "Billie Jean" and Glenn Frey's "Better in the USA". [7]That Scott towels appeals to youth is less apparent, but the company has been using Dr. John singing the words Let the Scott Towels Roll, to the tune of "Let the Good Times Roll." [8]The musical clue is particularly helpful in a Citizen Watch ad. [9]As TV viewers watch a model dressing for an evening out, the Al Jolson classic "About a Quarter to Nine" informs them that this company does not sell the youthful digital watches.

[10]The songs, of course, are not always as aptly selected as the choice of Who Wears Short Shorts by Neet, a product for removing hair from legs.

WRITING ASSIGNMENT 2: quotation marks

Write briefly on one of the following topics according to your instructor's specifications. When you are satisfied with organization, development, and content, proofread for errors in the use of quotation mark, using the strategies you have been practicing.

a. Quote some speaker. Explain what you think the person really wanted to say.
b. Quote and explain words or phrases you used when you were a child.
c. Name a favorite song or poem. Quote some lines, identifying the poet or songwriter and explaining why you like the lines or what they mean for you.
d. Summarize a section in one of your texts, quoting lines you consider important.
e. React to some famous statements or mottos—by Nathan Hale, Patrick Henry, the United States Treasury. Write them down, interrupting the quotation to identify the speaker. For example: **"I regret," said Nathan Hale, "that I have but one life to give for my country."**

Chapter **33**
USING UNDERLINING

Typewritten and handwritten papers use underlining in place of the italics used in most printed matter. (Newspapers tend to use quotation marks and boldface instead of italics, so do not use them as models.)

Unless you find it unavoidable, do not use underlining to emphasize words. Use underlining for the titles of books, films, and TV series; for the names of newspapers, magazines, ships, airplanes, and rockets; and for foreign words and expressions.

Reviewing John Updike's novel Roger's Version in Newsweek, David Lehman wrote that it reminded him of Hawthorne's The Scarlet Letter.

     books: Roger's Version, The Scarlet Letter
magazine: Newsweek

"The Bulls Are Back" was the title of the first episode in the HBO series, Training Camp. The Herald Journal reminded its readers that the series was formerly called First and Ten.

  TV series: Training Camp, First and Ten
newspaper: Herald Journal

The Right Stuff, directed by Phil Kaufman, was based on Wolfe's book. It was particularly humorous in depicting Alan Shepard's predicament while waiting for Mercury I to take off.

movie: The Right Stuff
rocket: Mercury I

James Strachey, in his introduction to Freud's Jokes and Their Relation to the Unconscious, speaks about the difficulty of translating into English the German witzig.

foreign word: witzig
     book: Jokes and Their Relation to the Unconscious

ATTENTION FOCUSING: underlining*

Circle the number of sentences with underlined words. In the space provided, write the reason for the underlining: **title, special name, foreign word.**

title _____ 1. The <u>Times</u> recently reported the existence of the Vampire Research Center in New York.

_____ 2. Founded in 1972 by Dr. Stephen Kaplan, it is only one of thirteen other vampire organizations and fan clubs worldwide.

_____ 3. The Center publishes a bibliography—<u>Vampires Unearthed</u>—listing 1,116 entries.

_____ 4. These listings include vampire novels, short stories, poetry, movies, recordings, and comic books.

_____ 5. Works on Vlad Tepes, the historical Dracula from Transylvania, are also listed, along with (perhaps <u>ad nauseum</u>) material on human blood drinking.

_____ 6. Although Bram Stoker's <u>Dracula</u> is the prototype for fictional vampires, it was preceded by <u>Varney the Vampire</u>, published in England <u>fifty</u> years earlier.

_____ 7. The bibliography demonstrates the interest of both scholars and the general public.

_____ 8. Alongside mass market books for the <u>hoi polloi</u> are university press books and articles in such magazines as <u>Commonweal</u>.

WRITING ASSIGNMENT 1: underlining

Write a short paragraph on one of the following topics. Make sure you use the correct indications for titles.

a. Using a newspaper or entertainment guide, describe the offerings for a typical night of television. In each sentence, mention only the program, not the title of the particular episode.
b. Make up a conversation that includes words from another language.

If you have made no errors in underlining, try PRACTICING PROOFREADING 1 before asking your instructor to send you on to another chapter. If you did make errors, review the earlier discussion and go to REWRITING.

REWRITING EXERCISE 1: underlining*

    a. Circle the words in CAPITALS. They are either quotations or titles.
    b. Rewrite them, using capitals only where they are necessary.
    c. Underline the film titles; place quotation marks around quotations.
    d. Capitalization is discussed in Chapter 31, quotation marks in 32.

THE UNSPOKEN WORDS

[1]Many lines quoted from old movies were never spoken in the films at all. [2]Perhaps the most often quoted line is thought to have been spoken by Humphrey Bogart in the film CASABLANCA (1943). [3]But Bogey never says PLAY IT AGAIN, SAM. [4]He does tell his friend Sam to play the piano a number of times, but never with those words. [5]The famous exchange between Johnny Weissmuller's Tarzan and Maureen O'Sullivan's Jane never took place either. [6]Instead of saying, ME TARZAN, YOU JANE, Weissmuller, in the classic TARZAN, THE APE MAN (1932), points at himself and says TARZAN three times. [7]Then he points at Miss O'Sullivan and says JANE three times. [8]Nor did W. C. Fields ever say, ANY MAN WHO HATES DOGS AND BABIES CAN'T BE ALL BAD, at least not in MY LITTLE CHICKADEE, THE BANK DICK, or any other of his well-known films. [9]The line was made up by a journalist. [10]However, Bela Lugosi did say I NEVER DRINK WINE, with a hesitation before WINE, in his film DRACULA (1932).

REWRITING EXERCISE 2: underlining

    Rewrite the entries from the newspaper into the column on the right, using underlining for titles instead of quotation marks and boldface.

(MAX) **Movie** ★★
"Lone Wolf McQuade"
(1983) Chuck Norris,
David Carradine.
_____
_____
_____

Movie   ★★½
"Chained" (1934) Joan
Crawford, Clark Ga-
ble.
_____
_____
_____

(HBO) **Movie** ★★½
"Sweet Liberty" (1986)
Alan Alda, Michael
Caine.

(TMC) **Movie** ★★½
"Making Love" (1982)
Kate Jackson, Michael
Ontkean.

Sol Madrid, David
McCallum, Stella Ste-
vens.

Paradise Alley,
Sylvester Stallone, Ar-
mand Assante.

Mr. Lucky, Cary
Grant, Laraine Day.

REWRITING EXERCISE 3: underlining

Write a sentence with 5 of the foreign words that follow, explaining definitions or providing some other information. Include the foreign word in your sentence. For example: **The word apropos is from the French.**

apropos   (adjective) appropriate, referring to, per-
taining to (French, "to
the purpose")

bella   (adjective) beautiful
(Italian)

ciudad   (noun) city (Spanish)

dinar   (noun) the basic mone-
tary unit of Iraq, Jor-
dan, and Kuwait (Ara-
bic, from late Greek
Denarion)

jefa   (noun, feminine) chief
(Spanish)

protégé   (noun) a favored
charge; one whose
training is promoted
by an influential per-
son (French, "pro-
tected")

sang-froid   (noun) composure,
equanimity (French,
"cold-blood")

tête-à-tête   (noun) a private conversation between two
people (French, "head
to head")

vamos   (verb) let's go (Spanish, from Latin "to go")

PROOFREADING STRATEGIES

Chances are that you have already capitalized any titles you are using, forgetting only to use the appropriate underlining for the book,
movie, or TV title. Look for capitalized letters in the middle of sentences;
these might need underlining. If you are copying titles out of books or

newspapers, do not be confused by their use of italics, boldface, or quotation marks. Also, read the text carefully to see if the title under discussion is a book, film, magazine, or other. Many writers will mention that a particular work is a "novel" or an "article."

After you correct all errors in a PRACTICING PROOFREADING exercise, demonstrate your mastery with WRITING ASSIGNMENT 2.

PRACTICING PROOFREADING 1

Locate and correct the 4 errors in underlining.

FREUD AND WIT

[1]Freud had an early interest in jokes. [2]In a letter to Wilhelm Fliess (June 12, 1897), Freud quoted a joke about two "schnorrer" (German for "beggars") and wrote, "I have been putting together a collection of Jewish anecdotes of deep significance." [3]A number of those stories appeared in <u>The Interpretation of Dreams</u>. [4]Theodor Lipps (1851–1914), a Munich professor, was another influence on Freud's interest in jokes. [5]Letters to Fliess reveal that Freud had read an early book by Lipps, "The Basic Facts of Mental Life" (1883). [6]Then Freud discusses a paper that Lipps delivered on the unconscious at a psychological conference in 1897. [7]Freud devotes a long section to it in the final chapter of <u>The Interpretation of Dreams</u>. [8]But, in 1898, Lipps, who is credited with having introduced the term Einfuhlung (German for "empathy"), published yet another book, "Komik and Humor." [9]This work, Freud states in <u>Jokes and Their Relation to the Unconscious</u>, encouraged him to embark on his study of jokes.

PRACTICING PROOFREADING 2

Locate and correct the 9 instances of failure to underline.

CATALOGUE 23

[1]George Houle's bookstore, Fine Books and Autographs, located in Los Angeles, offers the following first editions for sale: Lewis Carroll's

Alice in Wonderland 1866; Charles Dickens's Bleak House, David Copperfield, and Pickwick Papers; D. H. Lawrence's Lady Chatterley's Lover, a signed copy, and Pansies, one of fifty signed copies; Gertrude Stein's Before the Flowers of Friendship Fade . . .; and Mark Twain's Adventures of Huckleberry Finn. [2]Among his autographs, letters, and manuscripts, Houle offers: J. P. Donlevy's working script for the stage production of Ginger Man, as well as material from Jack London, Napoleon, Cole Porter, Upton Sinclair, and John Steinbeck.

WRITING ASSIGNMENT 2: underlining

Write on one of the following topics, according to your instructor's specifications for organization and development. Proofread for errors in underlining.

a. Write down the title of a favorite film, book, or record album. How does the title add or detract from its effects? Make up some alternative titles.

b. Using the information provided in a dictionary, discuss the meaning and origin of the following. Remember to underline those items that are italicized in the dictionary: Madonna lily, Mafia, Magen David, Magi, maharani, and mañana.

c. Discuss the development of a favorite actor or actress through a number of films and TV series, mentioning, if possible, the titles of individual episodes.

d. If you were telling the story of your family's history, what would be the titles of books or films? What would be some chapter headings? If you know your family's ethnic origins, try to include some foreign words and expressions that would be appropriate mottos for your family.

Chapter 34
USING COMMAS

Although many people think of commas as corresponding to actual pauses in speech, they often follow the rules of grammar rather than rhythms in speech. In fact, they connect as often as they separate. Think of them as conventions—rules that have been agreed upon—that you need to learn. If you wish to think of commas as road signs, think of them as speed limit indicators that sometimes slow you down and at other times speed you up but never bring you to an actual halt. It is the period that corresponds to pauses and paragraphing that indicates a full stop.

Of course, a comma often seems logical, enabling the reader to understand a sentence that might otherwise be confusing. For example, consider the following entry from a restaurant's menu:

Mussels with garlic bread and salad

Depending on where you place a comma, the restaurant is offering either:

Mussels with garlic, bread and salad.

or Mussels with garlic bread, and salad.

Without the comma, you cannot tell if you will get a dish of garlic mussels and plain bread or plain mussels and garlic bread.

In many other situations, however, comma placement is determined by rules as much as by logic. The sentence might be perfectly clear to you without a comma, but the rules might still require it.

Here is a summary of the uses of commas. A detailed discussion follows the WRITING ASSIGNMENT.

1. Commas separate
   a. items in a series from one another
   b. items in dates and addresses from one another
   c. introductory material from the rest of the sentence
   d. direct quotations from the rest of the sentence
   e. parenthetical expressions from the rest of the sentence

2. Commas connect
   a. complete sentences when used with **and** or other coordinators
   b. clauses to sentences when used with **although** or other subordinators
   c. phrases to sentences when used with **ing** words

This chapter will discuss the two most common uses of the comma: as separators and as connectors. If you feel that you are well versed in the intricacies of commas, try the ATTENTION FOCUSING exercise and WRITING ASSIGNMENT that follow. If you make errors, carefully read the discussion on commas before attempting a REWRITING EXERCISE.

ATTENTION FOCUSING: commas*

After circling all commas, consult the summary and write the purpose of the commas in the space provided below each sentence.

ADAPTED FROM THE SHIPMAN'S TALE BY CHAUCER

1. Once upon a time, a merchant lived at St. Denis.
   separates introductory material

2. Because he was rich, people considered him exceedingly wise.
   _____

3. He had an exceedingly beautiful, sociable, and adventurous wife.
   _____

4. The poor husband, as husbands always must, had to pay and pay.
   _____

5. For the sake of his own honor, he clothed her and dressed her richly.
   _____

6. He kept a fine house, and he always had a large number of visitors.
   _____

7. Among all his guests, high and low, there was a handsome man.
   _____

8. This bold man, a monk, rose early one morning.
   _____

9. He walked back and forth in the garden, saying his devotions.
   _____

10. The merchant's wife greeted him, "Why did you rise so early?"

_____

11. "Five hours' sleep ought to be enough for anyone," he answered.

_____

If you have made no comma errors, try PRACTICING PROOFREADING 3 before asking your instructor to send you on to another chapter. If you did make errors, read the REVIEW. Then choose a REWRITING EXERCISE that corresponds to your particular area of need.

REVIEW: the use of commas

1. Commas separate.
   a. Commas separate items in a series—single words or groups of words that are "parallel" or used similarly.

   Students in an experiment were told that they had to record **the stock name, volume, and closing time** for all stocks that day.

   Punishment for failure was not **mentioned, threatened, or meted out.**

   b. Commas separate specific items such as city from state, state from country, day from calendar date, calendar date from year, and street address from city.

   The article describing this experiment was reprinted in **Syracuse, New York,** on **Monday, June 2, 1986.**

   c. Commas separate introductory material from the rest of the sentence.

   At the end of the sessions, all subjects filled out a questionnaire.

   d. Commas separate direct quotations (especially when complete sentences) from the rest of the sentence.

   The groups that observed a co-worker receiving a cut in pay **"produced significantly more,"** the study said.

   e. Commas separate parenthetical expressions—phrases that interrupt a continuous idea—from the rest of the sentence.

   Myron Lubbel, **a reporter for Knight Ridder Newspapers,** began his article on the use of punishment with a mention of the cruel Captain Bligh.

The students, **recruited through a university placement office,** were divided into five groups.

They did not know, **of course,** that they were part of a study sponsored by a psychology journal.

2. Commas connect *when used with certain other words.*
    a. Commas connect two complete sentences when used with **and, or,** or **but.**

Punishment may reduce the onlooking workers' morale, **and** it may signal that the punishing supervisor is being unfair.

We can separate the sentence into two different sentences, each capable of standing on its own if we eliminate the comma and the coordinator **and**.

Punishment may reduce the onlooking workers' morale. It may signal that the punishing supervisor is being unfair.

Similarly, the following two sentences can be joined with a comma + **or.**

You might remember Captain Bligh in the film. You might have read about him in Nordoff and Hall's <u>Mutiny on the Bounty</u>.

You might remember Captain Bligh in the film, **or** you might have read about him in Nordoff and Hall's <u>Mutiny on the Bounty</u>.

    b. Commas connect complete sentences to clauses that cannot stand by themselves (dependent clauses), particularly when preceded by **although, since, when,** or other **dependent words** *at the beginning of the sentence.*

When workers observed a co-worker threatened with a pay cut, they worked harder. **Although** they seemed concerned, they did not report lower morale.

The part of the sentence beginning with **Although—Although they seemed concerned**—cannot stand by itself. The comma connects it to **they did not report lower morale,** which is a complete sentence.

    c. Commas connect participial phrases (**ing** phrases) acting as modifiers to complete sentences. Until connected to the complete sentence, **ing** phrases are fragments, unable to stand by themselves.

Bligh's use of punishment was less successful, **triggering** a mutiny aboard his ship.

REWRITING EXERCISE 1: using commas to *separate* items in a series*

Rewrite the paragraph below, inserting the word(s) in the margin before the **and** in each line. Use the appropriate punctuation.

GARLIC POWER

[1]According to legend, garlic has magical pow- ers. [2]People claim it can cure the common cold and *add strength* ward off evil spirits. [3]According to recent experi- ments, some of these beliefs may be supported by science. [4]Studies in India and West Germany indi- *Japan* cate that garlic helps break up cholesterol in blood vessels, decreasing the chances for heart disease. [5]Other experiments in Russia show that cloves of fresh garlic help eliminate toxic metals from the body. [6]They collect lead and mercury, enabling the *cadmium* body to remove them during bowel movements. [7]Still other research suggests that garlic can help in the treatment of diseases such as anemia and arthri- *diabetes* tis. [8]Paava Airola, the author of The Miracle of Garlic, recommends two small and fresh cloves of *fragrant* garlic each day.

REWRITING EXERCISE 2: using commas to *separate* parenthetical expressions from the rest of the sentence

Rewrite the paragraph below, inserting the phrases in the margin after each name. Use the appropriate punctuation.

WHAT'S IN A NAME?

[1]Many trademarks and names are chosen acci- dentally. [2]"Avon Cosmetics" came about by way of *the well-known brand* its founder's personal whim. [3]D. H. McConnell *a door-to-door salesman* would hand out free samples of perfumes to house-

wives as he would begin his sales pitch. ⁴Because the perfume seemed to keep doors from slamming in his face, McConnell decided to start a company and sell perfume instead. ⁵As his firm became a success, McConnell renamed the company after the birthplace of Shakespeare. ⁶Richard Joshua Reynolds selected the camel as both name and symbol for his cigarettes because he considered the animal as exotic as his tobacco. ⁷Hearing that Barnum and Bailey had arrived in town, he sent someone to photograph Old Joe. ⁸Old Joe was particularly irritated that day and provided the indignant pose that still appears on the Camel package.

abandoning his books

Stratford-on-Avon

R. J. Reynolds's founder

the world famous circus

one of the camels always ornery

REWRITING EXERCISE 3: using commas to *separate* direct quotations from the rest of the sentence

Rewrite the sentences in **boldface** by introducing them with the words **According to Klapisch** or **Klapisch says,** and providing commas and quotation marks where appropriate.

FISHER FARMED; DRABEK RECALLED (BY BOB KLAPISCH)

¹No more middle-of-the-plate fastballs from Brian Fisher. ²No more lazy sliders. ³**The Yankees ran out of patience with their troubled righthander yesterday.** ⁴He was optioned to Columbus. ⁵**Righthander Doug Drabek was recalled to take Fisher's place in the bullpen.**

⁶Surprised? ⁷Don't be. ⁸**Lou Pinella's face was tight with anger Sunday.** ⁹The Yankees lost an

_____
_____
_____
_____
_____
_____
_____
_____
_____
_____
_____
_____

8–7 game to the Angels and Fisher
allowed two, two-run doubles and
blew his fifth save in eight
chances this year.

_____

_____

_____

_____

> For more exercises with commas that *separate* see Chapters 24 and 32.

REWRITING EXERCISE 4: using a comma (and a word) to connect

Rewrite the essay, placing the dependent words at the beginning of your new sentences and making the appropriate changes in capitalization.

a. Connect sentences 1 and 2, 6 and 7, and 20 and 21, using **although.**
b. Connect sentences 3 and 4, 12 and 13, and 17 and 18, using **when.**
c. Connect sentences 8 and 9 and 22 and 23 with **because.**

STAGE SUPERSTITIONS

[1]People in show business are exciting and glamorous. [2]They are also extremely superstitious.

[3]For example, eager friends come to wish performers well. [4]They have to be careful with their language. [5]"Good luck" are words that may not be uttered. [6]"Break a leg" is not used frequently. [7]It is preferable to "Good luck." [8]Actors believe that <u>Macbeth</u> is bad luck. [9]They never quote lines from it while they are inside a theater. [10]Many actors avoid mentioning the play altogether, referring to it only as "that play."

[11]There are many other taboos. [12]Performers visit each other backstage. [13]They avoid wearing green, a color considered an ill omen. [14]They also avoid whistling in the dressing room. [15]People guilty of whistling must leave the dressing room immediately. [16]They can return only if they knock on the door three times. [17]A play sometimes folds. [18]People in the cast immediately perform certain rituals to ward off more bad luck. [19]They burn all telegrams they had received congratulating them on opening night and scrape their dressing rooms clean of the tiniest bit of soap.

[20]Some performers believe that certain Broadway theaters are haunted. [21]They are still willing to work there. [22]One famous actor is convinced that actresses carry with them either good or bad luck. [23]He refuses to work with those he believes to be bearers of bad luck.

How To Cope with the Unexpected

The comma in each new sentence is necessary only because your **when, because,** or **although** clause begins it. If these **dependent clauses** would come at the end of the sentence, you would generally not need a comma. Sentences 1 and 2, for example, could be combined with **although** in the middle of the sentence: **"Break a leg" is not used frequently although it is preferable to "Good luck."**

For more work with commas and such words as **although, when,** and other **subordinators,** see REWRITING EXERCISES in Chapter 22.

REWRITING EXERCISE 5: using commas to *connect* certain participial *(ing)* phrases to sentences

Rewrite the essay below, making the following changes:

a. Change the *second* word in sentences 2, 4, 6, 8, 12, and 16, into its **ing** form.
b. Using a comma, connect each of the sentences to the previous sentence.
c. Make sure you eliminate the first word in sentences 2, 4, 6, 8, 12, and 16. It has now become unnecessary.

THE 1,000-POINT MAN

[1]During the 1921–1922 season, a fellow by the name of Bobby Thompson scored 1,000 points in high school. [2]He played basketball for Passaic High School.

[3]Back then, there was a center jump after each basket. [4]This made the average high school game a very low-scoring affair. [5]But from 1919 to 1925, the Passaic teams outscored their opponents by a margin of three to one. [6]They often ran up tallies of 100 points. [7]In Bobby Thompson's senior year, Passaic scored 2,293 points in thirty-three games to only 612 for its opponents. [8]It averaged sixty-nine points a game. [9]Bobby Thomp-

son had more than 1,000 points that year, although record keepers at Passaic have not been able to provide an exact point total.

[10]A rule that helped Thompson score so many points was the one that allowed players other than the one fouled to shoot foul shots. [11]Bobby was an excellent foul shooter. [12]He got the opportunity to take all those foul shots earned by other players. [13]But Thompson did earn his totals. [14]His shooting prowess was legendary. [15]One alumnus remembers that Thompson put on an exhibition once from the sidelines. [16]He shot twenty-three straight baskets. [17]At that point he was asked to stop so that the game could be played.

[18]Although Thompson enrolled at Syracuse University in the fall of 1922 and played freshman basketball, he developed rheumatic fever at the end of the year and never played again.

For more work with commas and **ing** words *(participles)*, see REWRITING EXERCISES in Chapter 24.

REWRITING EXERCISE 6: using commas (and another word) to *connect* sentences

Rewrite the essay below, making the following changes:

a. Connect sentences 2 and 3, 9 and 10, and 15 and 16, using **and.**
b. Connect sentences 4 and 5, 6 and 7, and 12 and 13, using **but.**
c. Pay attention to the comma and capitalization.
d. Starred (*) words are explained after the essay.

LEMMINGS

[1]Lemmings are mouselike creatures that live in northern Scandinavia. [2]They are about six inches long. [3]They have small eyes and ears, short legs, and very stumpy tails. [4]Their fur is grayish black. [5]Some varieties change their pelts to white in the winter. [6]They usually eat green vegetation like reindeer moss. [7]When that is scarce, they will eat almost anything. [8]While their food is plentiful, a single female will produce from thirty to fifty offspring a year. [9]When their numbers increase, their food

supply decreases. [10]Then lemmings migrate by the millions, eating anything they can on their way. [11]These rodents, *which normally fear water and avoid it, cut right across streams and lakes during their march toward the sea.

[12]When they finally reach the sea after weeks of running, the lemmings cast themselves into the water, row upon row. [13]For a short time they remain afloat. [14]Soon the frantic creatures tire, sinking to their doom. [14]A Norwegian steamer captain once reported steering through lemming corpses for more than an hour. [15]No one seems to know why thousands commit suicide in this manner. [16]As a result, their name has come to mean mindless self-destruction.

ADDITIONAL INFORMATION ABOUT COMMAS: restrictive and nonrestrictive clauses

In the essay "Lemmings," the words **which normally fear water and avoid it** (sentence 11) are set off by commas on either side. As with other **parenthetical expressions,** you can lift the clause right out of the sentence without changing its meaning. Because the clause does not in any way limit the meaning of the main sentence, it is called a **nonrestrictive** clause. When a clause does limit or restrict the main part of the sentence, it is called a **restrictive** clause and is not set off by commas.

The boy who cried "wolf" too often was eventually ignored.

If you lift the clause **who cried "wolf"** from the sentence, you would get **The boy was often ignored.** But that is not what you meant at all. In this sentence, therefore, **who cried "wolf"** is **restrictive.** It is not a mere parenthetical expression to be set off by commas on either side.

> For more work with commas and such words as **and, but, or,** and other coordinators, see REWRITING EXERCISES in Chapter 26.

PROOFREADING STRATEGIES

As always, you must know your particular error. You need to know more than the simple fact that you have difficulties with commas. You need to know specifically which comma situation is most troublesome for you. Most beginning writers use the comma effectively when it separates: in a series, before a direct quotation, after an introductory phrase, and with parenthetical expressions. They find it more difficult to use the comma correctly in connecting situations, where the use of the comma follows rules rather than "pauses." Sometimes, after receiving a lesson in the use of commas, students begin to use too many. When that occurs, the grade-school admonition—*when in doubt, leave it out*—applies. Begin your proofreading, therefore, by knowing the comma situations that present problems for you.

1. What to look for: a missing comma where one is needed as a connector.
2. How to look for it: circle the words that accompany or signal connecting commas—coordinators **(and, or, but)**, subordinators **(although, when, because, since)**, and **ing** words.
3. How to correct it: if the signal words are being used with clauses that need to be attached to a complete sentence, add the comma.

If you tend to use too many commas, circle all commas and try to justify their presence. If you cannot give a good reason why you are using a comma, do not use it.

> Choose a PROOFREADING EXERCISE that deals with your specific problem. PRACTICING PROOFREADING 3 contains comma errors in all situations.

PRACTICING PROOFREADING 1

Correct the 4 errors in the use of commas as connectors; one of those errors is an unnecessary comma.

ON YOUR TOES

[1]Ballet dancers did not always dance on their toes. [2]For hundreds of years, classical ballet was based on five positions of the feet as established in the fifteenth- and sixteenth-century Italian and Spanish courts where the dance originated. [3]Louis XIV, the Sun King, derived his name from a ballet written for him in which he appeared as the sun. [4]Female ballet dancers, burdened by floor-length dresses, were of secondary importance on the stage. [5]In the mid-eighteenth century, Marie Ann de Cupis de Camargo startled audiences by showing her ankles but that was nothing compared to the innovation introduced by Marie Taglioni.

[6]This young Italian dancer was very frail, appearing to float rather than dance across the stage. [7]Her excellent, dancing technique overcame her slight figure, which differed so greatly from the typical ballet dancers

of the nineteenth century. [8]Because she wanted to emphasize her other-wordly quality, Taglioni danced on the tips of her toes. [9]Audiences went wild over this new style acclaiming her for twenty years. [10]Naturally, other dancers began to imitate her, but they were hampered by the lack of support in their ballet shoes. [11]Only late in the nineteenth century were the first blocked shoes made. [12]Men initially resisted dancing on their toes, considering it effeminate. [13]Partially as a result, the role of the female dancer increased and male dancers became mere support to the airborne females.

PRACTICING PROOFREADING 2

Correct the 3 errors in the use of commas as separators.

[1]A motorist who was driving through a flooded area asked a farmer if it was possible for a car to get through. [2]The farmer nodded "I reckon so."

[3]Full of confidence, the motorist drove forward. [4]In no time at all, his car was under water. [5]After struggling clear, the motorist returned to the farmer and angrily shouted "What made you think a car could drive through here?"

[6]The farmer shrugged and motioned with his hand "The water only came up till *here* on the ducks."

PRACTICING PROOFREADING 3

Correct the comma errors—2 commas used as connectors, 4 used as separators, and one used unnecessarily.

PASTRY SHOPS

[1]Ferenc Molnar the Hungarian playwright used to say "Five o'clock tea in Budapest means chestnut pureé with whipped cream." [2]The Hungarians certainly have a sweet-tooth and it is indulged by countless pastry shops and cafes in the capital. [3]Along with a love for pastries, Hungarians are fond of strong, black coffee. [4]This remnant of the long years

of Turkish occupation is so strong th[...]
adrenalin pump through the veins. [5]Th[...]
ian *cukràszda*), thus also serves "simple" [...]
[6]But between coffee at five and cognac at si[...]
rich but light pastries. [7]The flour and butter[...]
compositions of walnut, hazelnut, poppy-seed,[...]
gredients. [8]Ah yes, chestnuts, in all forms are alw[...]
winter, they roast on street corners in charcoal bra[...]
available all year round in pastry shops as mousse, flav[...]
or liquors and topped with piles of sweet whipped cream.[...]

WRITING ASSIGNMENT 2: commas

Try a longer paragraph from WRITING ASSIGNMENT 1, or see pp.
204, 221, and 228, for WRITING ASSIGNMENTS with commas as **separators** and pp. 197, 238, and 246, for WRITING ASSIGNMENTS with
commas as **connectors**.

Chapter 35
USING
OTHER MARKERS

ATTENTION FOCUSING: suffixes*

In the following passage, underline all those words that end with **ed, er, est, ing,** or **ly.** There are 25 such words in the passage.

[1]One of the silliest looking creatures on earth is the <u>duck-billed</u> platypus. [2]Sleek-furred and small, the platypus is a true mammal with milk glands for suckling its young. [3]However, it is easily one of the oddest mammals, laying one to three eggs at a time instead of giving birth to live young, as do most mammals. [4]It incubates the eggs in its nest for about ten days, and the young leave the nest about seventeen weeks after hatching. [5]Once heavily hunted for its fur, the animal is now a relatively common sight in slowly moving streams in Eastern Australia and Tasmania. [6]It has a leathery bill like a duck's, and the larger male has poison spurs on its hind legs. [7]The feet are webbed and well adapted for swimming. [8]On land it moves with a waddle some say is funnier than that of a goose. [9]For years after it was discovered in 1797, it was considered a hoax, but in 1922 the first living specimen ever seen outside Australia was exhibited by the New York Zoological Park. [10]The case of the platypus remains one in which the truth is stranger than many hoaxes.

REVIEW: markers

You have already seen how some markers work. For example, the **es** and **s** endings are used to mark both plural nouns (see Chapter 5) and third-person singular, present-tense verbs (see Chapter 14). The **ed** ending is used to mark past tense in regular verbs (see Chapter 15). This chapter deals with some other common endings that mark a special meaning, and some other meanings marked by endings you have already seen in use.

There are two reasons for reviewing these markers. First, some writers become confused about when to use them, and, second, some writers drop them, as people often do in conversation. It is therefore often necessary to proofread for their presence.

The Comparatives: *er* and *est*

When comparing two items or qualities, **er** is often added to an adjective or an adverb to make the comparison. The adjective **easy** in **The town doctor led an easy life** receives an **er** ending to indicate the comparative: **Once antibiotics were invented, the town doctor led an easier life than before.**

When three or more things are compared, the **est** ending, or **superlative,** is used: **Among the judge, the lawyer, and the doctor, the doctor led the easiest life.**

With many other words, however, **more** indicates the comparative and **most** the superlative, while with still others, the entire word changes: **good** → **better** → **best, bad** → **worse** → **worst.** There are some general patterns for when to use **er** and **est** as opposed to **more** and **most,** but there are exceptions. You will probably have to get used to the endings of particular words as you encounter them. Thus the adverbs **fast** and **strongly** in the sentences that follow indicate comparatives differently.

Bannister ran fast. ⟶ Bannister ran the mile **faster** than anyone had before.

Spitz finished strongly. ⟶ Spitz finished **more strongly** than the other swimmers.

In any case, when you use comparitives or superlatives, use the correct form. Dropping the **er/est** ending or using such an ending in addition to **more** or **most** are errors you should avoid.

The Adverb Marker: *ly*

Most adjectives can be made into adverbs by adding **ly** to the end of the adjective. Thus the adjective form, **He had quick hands,** can be made into an adverb by adding **ly: His hands moved quickly.** The spelling pattern here is simple: the **ly** is added with no change. Exceptions: an adjective ending in a consonant plus **y** will change the **y** to an **i** (**easy** + **ly** = **easily**), and **due** and **true** drop their silent **e**'s (**duly** and **truly**). Because many adjectives end in **al,** many adverbs end in **ally.** A common spelling error is to use only one **l** in such a case.

The Adjective Endings: *ed* and *ing*

You may think of **ed** and **ing** as verb endings, and, indeed, they are. These endings form the past and present participles, from which adjectives are made. The adjective form depends on the verb form, as illustrated below:

Verb Form	Adjective Form
The committee **is planning** the party. (present progressive tense)	The **planning** committee will meet three more times.
The party **was planned** for next Tuesday. (past tense, passive voice)	The **planned** party is sure to be success because of the efforts the committee members.

Those who are learning English as a new language will sometimes have difficulty determining which form is needed, but native speakers more commonly drop an ending, especially the **ed** ending. This may occur because the **d** sound at the end of the word tends to blend into the next sound if it is a **d** or **t** sound. Try to hear the sound made by the **ed** endings in the following phrases:

the interested dean the planned decline
three overplayed tunes the talented team

In practice, there is little difference between the sound of "the planned decline" and "the plan decline." Often it is necessary to think about how the words are being used to determine if an **ed** ending is called for. However, substituting a different noun that does not start with one of the sounds similar to a **d** sound will make the decision clear. If "decline" were changed to "failing" in our example, the distinction in sound between "planned" and "plan" would be clear. So strong, however, is the blend of the two sounds, that in many informal (and sometimes formal) writing situations the **ed** has actually disappeared. The drink is an **iced** tea, while the frozen dessert was once actually written as **iced** cream.

This blending of sounds is responsible for a very common error in the use of **ed** endings when they indicate the past tense. The correct forms are:

suppos**ed** to used to determin**ed** to

The presence of **to** should warn your eyes to search for the **ed** endings even if your ears cannot hear them.

The following exercises focus on one of the marker types discussed. If you know you are having problems with only one type of marker, go to the exercise on that particular marker. A general PROOFREADING exercise that includes errors with all the markers discussed can be found at the end of the chapter.

REWRITING EXERCISE 1: the comparative and superlative forms*

The following passages contain comparison using **more** or **most** plus an adverb or adjective. Another adverb or adjective appears in parentheses. Rewrite the sentences in the spaces above the lines, changing each word in parentheses to the correct form.

EXAMPLE: Judy is <u>more mysterious</u> (strange) than I thought.

becomes

Judy is <u>stranger</u> than I thought.

LEONARDO

[1]Leonardo Da Vinci (1452–1519) remains the *most outstanding* (good) example of the Renaissance Man. [2]Though he is *more easily* (soon) recognized as the painter of the <u>Mona Lisa</u> and <u>The Last Supper</u>, he was also a *more energetic* (busy) sculptor, mathematician, geologist, engineer, and architect than people think. [3]A 1987 exhibition at the Montreal Museum of Fine Arts showed the *most extensive* (large) collection of these "other" works by Da Vinci. [4]It was the public's *most attractive* (great) opportunity to view Da Vinci drawings, manuscripts, notebooks, full-scale machines, and architectural models. [5]The space needed to show his accomplishments as engineer and architect required *more spacious* (roomy) exhibit halls than expected—a full two floors.

REWRITING EXERCISE 2: the adjective forms—*ed* and *ing*

In the sentences below, fill in the blanks with **ing** or **ed**, whichever is appropriate to the meaning of the sentence. Then write a sentence that uses the other ending on the same base word to form an adjective.

EXAMPLE: The annoy<u>ed</u> policeman scowled at the jaywalker.
The jogger swatted at the annoy<u>ing</u> fly.

1. The team pleased the excit____ fans.

_____

2. The hate____ dog barked at all who passed by.

_____

3. All in all, it was a bor____ lecture that put me to sleep.

_____

4. The fascinat_____ tourist watched as the snake danced.

_____

5. The interest_____ dean listened attentively to the students.

_____

6. It was an absorb_____ play that held the audience's attention.

_____

7. The observ_____ delay is not as long as it seems.

_____

REWRITING EXERCISE 3: adverbs ending in *ly*

Rewrite the following sentences, making the underlined adjective into an adverb ending in **ly**. Begin rewriting with the pronoun after "when" or "as."

EXAMPLE: She was <u>angry</u> when she threw up her hands.

becomes

She threw up her hands angri<u>ly</u>.

1. He made it look <u>easy</u> when he broke the track record.

_____

2. The disc jockey's voice was <u>hurried</u> when he spoke.

_____

3. He was <u>loving</u> when he spoke about his wife.

_____

4. The magician was <u>agile</u> when she used her hands.

_____

5. The union members were <u>tentative</u> when they accepted the agreement.

_____

6. The wolf made a <u>fierce</u> sound as it howled.

_____

7. The mother was <u>strict</u> as she raised her children.

_____

PROOFREADING STRATEGIES

This chapter covers a mixture of problems that are only loosely related. They all deal with markers used at the ends of words to change their meanings or usage, but the chances are that, if you have a problem with any of these, it will be with one only. Also, the problem will probably be either one of incorrect usage or of dropped endings, not both. The first thing you should do is identify the problem you are having (with the help of your instructor) and focus on that. The strategies given here are necessarily general; if you identify your problem, you can make the corrections specific to that problem.

1. What to look for: dropped markers and incorrect usage of comparative / superlative forms or adjective / adverb forms.
2. How to look for them: first identify your problems. If you are having more than one problem in the areas covered, check for each with a separate proofreading. For either type of problem, you will need to be aware of usage.
   a. Check your writing for the specific type of word that gives you a problem. For example, if dropped adjective endings are a problem, identify all the adjectives in your writing. If you tend to use **more** with an **er** ending in making comparisons, underline any words ending in **er** and underline **more** wherever you see it.
   b. Check to see if you have made the particular error you are proofreading for. If you drop **ed** markers before words beginning with **d** or **t**, try substituting another word that does not begin with those letters—the word **blank** may work well, or you may need to find a word with a similar meaning. If you use the comparative (two-item) form when you need the superlative (three-or-more-item) form, check to see how many items are involved.
   c. Proofread again for another problem if you have more than one.
3. How to correct them: add the appropriate ending or change the words to reflect the proper usage.

PRACTICING PROOFREADING 1

Locate and correct the 9 dropped endings.

[1]Autumn blew in like a buzzard on bust wings, tumbling hot and cold before it landed in earnest after Indian Summer. [2]By then, the cough had settled in again and Mama rubbed hot mustard plaster soft on my naked chest. [3]The cloth settled in, clinging to my ribs as she buttoned my pajama top. [4]The cough was heavy this year than last; I was old enough now to remember. [5]I would wheeze in a deep breath, and it would come out all at once, burning more than the foul smell plaster. [6]Danny use to come by with school work and read some of it to me. [7]He was the young of my three friends and the only one who bother to come by anymore. [8]Billy and Ray had given me up for dead, the way they always would

when we played cowboys down in the gully. [9]Once in a while, Danny would mark his place on the fade page and look over to me sadly. [10]That is how I remember him the best, with that trouble, dense look on his young face. [11]By December the buzzard turned its eye to Danny, and he was gone.

[12]I think of him still, whenever I cough.

PRACTICING PROOFREADING 2

Locate and correct the 7 errors in usage.

[1]The salmon run is on, and you are all invited for the fishing derby this weekend. [2]Chinook are most plentiful than last year, and the Coho are more larger. [3]Some records are suppose to be broken this year, with a purse of $25,000 to be divided among any record breakers. [4]Other prizes are available for the heavier catch of each day for each species. [5]Every hour, a ticket stub will be drawn for cash awards and prizes of tackle supplied by local sporting goods stores. [6]Someone can become rich quick if a Coho tag in August by the D.E.C. is caught during the derby. [7]A local bank has put up $100,000 for this prize, and a blank check awaits some lucky fisherman or fisherwoman. [8]If money is not your desiring goal, how about a brand-new 26-foot fishing boat, complete with trailer? [9]A Chinook salmon will be caught and tagged this week somewhere along the Black River, so it is sure to be in the waters covered by the derby. [10]Come out and try your luck!

MASTERY TEST FOR UNIT VI: problems with markers

The essay below contains 18 errors in the use of markers. The errors involve at least 2 in each of the situations discussed in this unit: contractions (Chapter 29), apostrophes (Chapter 30), capitals (Chapter 31), quotations (Chapter 32), underlining (Chapter 33), commas (Chapter 34), and endings on adjectives and adverbs (Chapter 35). Proofread this essay, using the strategies you have been practicing. As the most effective proofreading searches for only one type of error at a time, you might wish to reproduce this page a few times so that the various circlings and underlinings do not make the page too confusing.

THE PERSISTENCE OF VISION

[1]Although the name "movies" comes from "Moving Pictures", movies do not really move at all. [2]Our eyes inform our brains that movement is taking place, operating under a principle in optics known as "the persistence of vision". [3]The phrase was first used by Peter Mark Roget, compiler of the famous thesaurus, in an 1828 Scientific Paper. [4]During the 47 years that Roget labored on his book, he found time for other interests. [5]Roget's paper described a toy that is still available today. [6]It consists of a stiff paper disk which would rotate really quick when strings attached to opposite sides were pulled tight apart. [7]On one side of the disk theres a picture of a horse, and on the other side theres a picture of a jockey. [8]When the disk spins, the jockey appears to be sitting on the horse's back because a viewers brain continues to see the first side of the card by the time the other side comes into view.

[9]Although a number of other investigators, many of them Roget's contemporaries were working on the same idea, no practical use for this "persistence of vision" was developed. [10]Then, in the 1870s, Leland Stanford, the Governor of California, wanted to prove that all four feet of a galloping horse were in the air at the same time. [11]To prove his point and collect a $25,000 bet at the same time, he hired an English photographer named Eadweard [sic] Muybridge. [12]Muybridge, the photographer in Philip Glass 1983 album "The photographer," took twelve pictures of a horse running on a track spacing the shots very closely. [13]When the pictures were put in order and flipped through rapidly, the horse seemed to

be running. [14]It appeared to be running to the viewer's eyes because under the principle of the persistence of vision the brain retained the one image of the horse when the next one, in a different position, appeared. [15]Muybridges photographs, employing Roget's principle, essentially established the basis for the motion picture.

[16]In a reel of movie film there are thousands of little frames, each frame is complete in itself. [17]When considered one at a time, one sees only still photographs. [18]But if the frames are run through a projector at the rate of twenty-four per second, the eyes perceive moving pictures.

If you are unable to locate the errors in any particular area, review the PROOFREADING STRATEGIES for that chapter. If you located an error but found yourself unable to correct it, try a REWRITING EXERCISE in the appropriate chapter.

Unit Seven

PROOFREADING FOR CONFUSING TERMS

Recommended

INTRODUCTION

Assign as Needed

This unit offers exercises in proofreading for commonly confused terms. Such confusion is usually the result of a similarity of sound. When two words sound alike, they are often mistaken for each other, despite their considerable differences in spelling and meaning.

Although you have probably had many of these confused terms explained to you before, your ability to understand the explanations does not guarantee your ability to locate and correct any errors in their use. Take this opportunity to practice your proofreading skills, using the strategies provided here in PROOFREADING STRATEGIES.

The basic proofreading strategy here is the same as it has been throughout:

a. Know what your error is.
b. Look only for that error during a reading.
c. Correct that error.

If you know what error you make, and if you look specifically for that error, you will find it without any difficulty. Once found, an error is easy enough to correct—particularly if you have a strategy for correcting it.

In addition, remember the basic rule of proofreading first mentioned in Chapter 29: **Eliminate all contractions by writing them out.**

As you will see, many of the commonly confused terms are, in fact, contractions. When a contraction is spoken (or "heard" during proofreading), it often sounds like another, different word. If you avoid writing contractions or eliminate them during proofreading, you will go a long way toward correcting the misuse of some of these terms.

In this chapter, we offer proofreading practice for the following commonly confused terms:

Terms that Sound Alike

its	(to be distinguished from **it's**)
there	(to be distinguished from **their** and from **they're**)
your	(to be distinguished from **you're**)
whose	(to be distinguished from **who's**)
than	(to be distinguished from **then**)
too	(to be distinguished from **to**)
were	(to be distinguished from **where**)

A Mispronounced Term

lose   (to be distinguished from **loose**)

In addition, we provide brief proofreading strategies in Chapter 44 for many other terms that writers often confuse.

As a first step to learning how to use these terms correctly, you might begin by not thinking of the confused terms as pairs. Instead, associate each term with a word that is similar to it in function. In other words, pair the term with a word that you can substitute for it in a sentence. Substituting a word that has the same function will, of course, change the meaning of the sentence, but it will not alter its grammar. Thus, as the individual chapters will demonstrate, a sentence that uses **were** should still make grammatical sense with **are,** even though you have changed its time from the past to the present.

Here are some words with which to associate the confused terms. When you substitute an associated word, the sentence should still make sense, indicating that you used the original word correctly. If the substituted word makes no sense, the word it replaces was incorrect as well.

its—his, her	your—our	were—are
there—here, where	then—when	lose—drop
who's—who is	too—also or very	their—your

Chapter **36**

PROOFREADING
ITS AND IT'S

If you confuse the two terms,.writing **it's** all the time, go to p. 332. If, instead, you write **its**, continue here.

---

its

The word **its** is a possessive pronoun. It replaces the possessive form of a singular noun. You would not write: The hurricane lost **the hurricane's** power. Instead, you would use the possessive pronoun: The hurricane lost **its** power.

Writers usually confuse the word when they write **it is** as the contraction **it's.** Some also think that, because **its** indicates possession or ownership, it must take an apostrophe.

TESTING THE CORRECTNESS OF *ITS*

a. Locate and circle all examples of **its.**
b. Substitute **her** or **his.**
c. If your sentence makes sense, you used **its** correctly; if the sentence no longer makes sense, you should be using **it is.**
d. Also, you might look at the word right after **its.** Usually, it will be a noun that "belongs" to it or is "possessed" by it. The presence of such a word right after **its** signals that **its** is correct.

NOTE: The words **its, her,** and **his** can be substituted for each other only to test their grammatical similarity—they are all possessive pronouns (singular). However, their meanings differ, so do not use them interchangeably.

ATTENTION FOCUSING 1*

The word **its** is used correctly in "Circles." Circle the 2 instances of the word.

CIRCLES

[1]The doctor picked up his stethoscope and placed its flat circle against the patient's chest. [2]"It's surprising to see you so soon. [3]Have you been following my instructions? [4]It's very important that you do, you know."

[5]The patient fidgeted on the chair, rubbing its curving arms. [6]"It has been difficult, doctor, but I have tried to follow all your instructions exactly."

[7]"Have you taken the long walk every morning as I suggested? [8]It's as important as the diet I gave you."

[9]"I tried, doctor, but it's making me dizzy."

[10]"What do you mean?"

[11]"Well, it's like this, doctor," the man explained. [12]"I forgot to tell you that I am a lighthouse keeper."

REWRITING EXERCISE 1: substituting for *its*

From the essay "Circles," rewrite the 2 sentences containing **its,** substituting **her** or **his.** The sentence should make sense, indicating that you have used **its** correctly.

a. _____

b. _____

REWRITING EXERCISE 2: using *her* or *his*

To continue testing the effectiveness of substituting **her** or **his** for **its,** choose a sentence that contains **it's** and write it below, substituting **her** or **his** for **it's.** Read the sentence out loud. It should make no sense at all. Put an X through the incorrect form.

_____

Practice your proofreading skills on pp. 334–336.

it's

The word **it's** is simply the contraction of **it is.**

It's raining. It's snowing. ⟶ It is raining. It is snowing.

TESTING THE CORRECTNESS OF *IT'S*

    a. Circle all examples of **it's.**

    b. Rewrite the sentence, writing out the contraction as **it is.**

    c. If your sentence makes sense, you used **it's** correctly; if the sentence no longer makes sense, you should be using **its,** the possessive pronoun.

ATTENTION FOCUSING 2*

    The word **it's** is used correctly in "Circles." Circle the 5 instances of the word.

CIRCLES

[1]The doctor picked up his stethoscope and placed its flat circle against the patient's chest. [2]"It's surprising to see you so soon. [3]Have you been following my instructions? [4]It's very important that you do, you know."

[5]The patient fidgeted on the chair, rubbing its curving arms. [6]"It has been difficult, doctor, but I have tried to follow all your instructions exactly."

[7]"Have you taken the long walk every morning as I suggested? [8]It's as important as the diet I gave you."

[9]"I tried, doctor, but it's making me dizzy."

[10]"What do you mean?"

[11]"Well, it's like this, doctor," the man explained. [12]"I forgot to tell you that I am a lighthouse keeper."

REWRITING EXERCISE 3: substituting for *it's*

    From the essay "Circles," rewrite 3 sentences containing **it's,** eliminating the contraction by writing it out as **it is.** The sentences should make sense, indicating that you have used **it's** correctly.

    a. _____

    b. _____

    c. _____

REWRITING EXERCISE 4: using *it is*

To continue testing the effectiveness of writing out the full form of a contraction as a way of testing its correctness, try to "write out" the word **its.** Choose a sentence containing **its** from the essay "Circles" and rewrite it below, making **it is** out of **its.** The sentence should make no sense at all. Put an X through the incorrect form.

PRACTICING PROOFREADING 1

The essay "Fasteners" contains 11 instances of **its** and **it's.** Circle all instances of these "sound alikes" and correct the 6 errors.

FASTENERS

[1]The people who invented the modern fasteners—the safety pin and the zipper—did not make any profit from their inventions.

[2]The safety pin, in it's early form, was in use in Europe as early as 4,000 years ago. [3]The trouble with it was its safety. [4]Its sharp tips poked out, scratching the skin. [5]In 1849, however, a New Yorker named Walter Hunt designed a pin with a clasp enclosing it's point. [6]Hunt came up with the idea because he owed fifteen dollars and his creditor offered to cancel the debt if Hunt could come up with a useful device made out an old piece of wire. [7]Its out of three hours of twisting that the safety pin was born. [8]The creditor cancelled the debt, paid Hunt an additional $400 for the rights to the pin, and went on to make a fortune.

[9]Its a similar story as far as the inventor of the zipper is concerned. [10]Whitcomb Judson, dissatisfied with the laces, hooks, and eyes people of his time used to fasten their clothes, invented a "clasp locker or unlocker for shoes." [11]Its' only shortcoming was that it came undone too easily. [12]People had no confidence in it and its lack of sales nearly bankrupted Judson. [13]Twenty years later, in 1913, a Swedish engineer patented a fastener. [14]Its success was assured when the Navy bought it for flying suits and B. F. Goodrich for its rubber boots. [15]Unfortunately for Judson, Gideon Sundback's version was the one that captured the market and earned its' inventor a fortune.

PRACTICING PROOFREADING 2

The essay "The Edsel" contains 13 instances of **its** and **it's**. Circle all instances of these "sound alikes" and correct the 6 errors.

THE EDSEL

[1]The name "Edsel" to this day brings back memories of one of the great fiascoes in name giving. [2]It's the name that was given to the new car Ford Motor Company unveiled in 1957 and discontinued making in 1959, after losses of 350 million dollars. [3]Its not due entirely to its name that the Edsel was such a disaster. [4]The recession of 1958, the crowded market, and its unattractive grill that appeared to be sucking a lemon, all combined to make it fail. [5]Still, the old-fashioned name was unsuitable to the stylish new car that was meant to symbolize a new era in America and contributed greatly to it's lack of sales.

[6]The process by which Ford Motors selected "Edsel" as the name for it's new model is fascinating. [7]The first person to suggest it was R. E. Krafve, the head of Ford's special products division. [8]He thought to honor the name of Edsel Ford, father of the three sons who ran the company. [9]However, Henry II, Benson, and William Clay, the three sons of Edsel, thought it would commercialize their father's name too much and rejected Krafve's suggestion. [10]The choice was then put in the hands of the market research people. [11]They felt that it's some irrational factor in people that makes them buy a particular car, and that its' more logical to look for a name that would reflect the personality, not the mechanism of the car. [12]It's a matter of record that in addition to testing the reaction of thousands of people to 2,000 potential names, David Wallace, director of market research, also hired the poet Marianne Moore to devise some names. [13]It's no surprise that Ford did not accept any of Miss Moore's suggestions: Utopian Turtletop, Intelligent Bullet, and Andante con Moto.

[14]After the list of potential names reached 18,000, it was whittled down to 6,000. [15]Ford then asked the advertising firm that was working

on the list, Foote, Cone, and Belding, to reduce it to ten. [16]The firm's two offices, working independently, came up with two lists of ten. [17]Considering the enormous amount of research, it's not surprising that four of the names appeared on both lists: Corsair, Citation, Pacer, and Ranger. [18]When the executive committee met to make it's decision, the three Ford brothers were away. [19]Ernest Beech decided he did not like any of the names and chose Edsel. [20] Although its true he called Henry II and obtained his approval, the decision was ultimately his own. [21]In two years only 100,000 Edsels were sold.

Chapter **37**
PROOFREADING
THERE AND THEIR

If you write **their**, go to p. 339. If you tend to write **there**, continue here.

---

there

The word **there** is an adverb; it modifies a verb. In some rare instances, **there** is an exclamation or an expletive. It is usually confused with not one but two other words that sound like it.

TESTING THE CORRECTNESS OF *THERE*

a. Locate and circle all examples of **there**.
b. Substitute **here**.
c. If your sentence makes sense, you used **there** correctly; if it no longer makes sense, you should be using one of "sound-alikes" for **there**.

NOTE: The word **here** is substituted for **there** only to test the grammatical correctness of **there**. Their meanings differ, so do not use them interchangeably.

ATTENTION FOCUSING 1*

The word **there** is used correctly in "Expectant Fathers." Circle the 5 instances of the word.

EXPECTANT FATHERS

[1]There is some evidence that expectant fathers frequently experience the same symptoms of pregnancy their wives do. [2]Such extreme empathy

with the expectant mother is called <u>couvade</u>. [3]There were signs of couvade in 90 percent of the 147 expectant fathers included in a recent study. [4]Jacqueline Clinton of the University of Wisconsin-Milwaukee School of Nursing reported that there were many symptoms reported by men that paralleled those of their expectant wives. [5]The men suffered from nausea and insomnia. [6]Their weight increased before the baby's birth and decreased after. [7]There were reports of backaches, irritability, and cravings for particular foods, matching reports of those symptoms by the wives. [8]According to Clinton, men were ashamed of their empathy. [9]In fact, there was evidence that most of the men in the three-year study did not even tell their wives of their symptoms.

REWRITING EXERCISE 1: substituting for *there*

From "Expectant Fathers," rewrite 3 sentences containing **there** and substitute **here.** The sentence should make sense, indicating that you have used **there** correctly.

a. _____

b. _____

c. _____

REWRITING EXERCISE 2: using *here*

To continue testing the effectiveness of substituting **here** for **there,** choose a sentence that contains **their** and write it below, substituting **here.** The sentence should make no sense at all. Put an X through the incorrect form.

_____

REWRITING EXERCISE 3: *there*

From the essay "Expectant Fathers," write below each **there** and the word that follows it.

_____ _____ _____ _____ _____

Notice that **there** is followed by one of the forms of the verb **to be: is, was, are, were.** (Other words that often follow **there** are **has, have,** and **had.**)

> Practice your proofreading skill with PRACTICING PROOFREADING, p. 340.

their

The word **their** is a possessive pronoun (plural). It replaces the possessive form of a plural noun. You would not write: Ballet dancers dance on **ballet dancers'** toes. Instead, you would use the possessive pronoun: Ballet dancers dance on **their** toes.

The word is usually confused with **there** and with **they are** when written as the contraction **they're.** To help eliminate confusion with **they're,** eliminate the use of contractions altogether in formal essays. See also Chapter 29 for contractions.

TESTING THE CORRECTNESS OF *THEIR*

a. Locate and circle all examples of **their.**
b. Substitute **your** or **our.**
c. If your sentence still makes sense, you have used **their** correctly; if the sentence no longer makes sense, determine if you should be using **there.**
d. Also, you might look at the word right after **their.** If you have used **their** correctly, a noun that "belongs" to it or is "possessed" by it is likely to follow.

ATTENTION FOCUSING 2*

The word **their** is used correctly in "Expectant Fathers." Circle the 5 instances of the word.

EXPECTANT FATHERS

[1]There is some evidence that expectant fathers frequently experience the same symptoms of pregnancy their wives do. [2]Such extreme empathy with the expectant mother is called <u>couvade</u>. [3]There were signs of couvade in 90 percent of the 147 expectant fathers included in a recent study. [4]Jacqueline Clinton of the University of Wisconsin-Milwaukee School of Nursing reported that there were many symptoms reported by men that paralleled those of their expectant wives. [5]The men suffered from nausea and insomnia. [6]Their weight increased before the baby's birth and decreased after. [7]There were reports of backaches, irritability, and cravings for particular foods, matching reports of those symptoms by the wives.

[8]According to Clinton, men were ashamed of their empathy. [9]In fact, there was evidence that most of the men in the three-year study did not even tell their wives of their symptoms.

REWRITING EXERCISE 4: substituting for *their*

From the essay "Expectant Fathers," rewrite 3 sentences containing **their,** substituting **your** or **our.** The sentences should make sense, indicating that you have used **their** correctly.

a. _____

b. _____

c. _____

REWRITING EXERCISE 5: using *your* or *our*

To continue testing the effectiveness of substituting **your** or **our** for **their,** choose a sentence containing **there** from the essay "Expectant Fathers" and rewrite it, substituting **your** or **our.** The sentence should make no sense at all. Put an X through the incorrect form.

_____

REWRITING EXERCISE 6: *their*

From the essay "Expectant Fathers," write below each **their** and the word that follows it. Each should be a noun **their** "owns" or "possesses," indicating that you have used **their** correctly.

_____ _____ _____ _____ _____

PRACTICING PROOFREADING:

Circle the 17 instances of **there** and **their** as well as the two starred (*) words. Determine their correctness and correct the 7 that are incorrect.

PAPER

[1]There have been contributions by many different cultures to the development of what we call "paper."

[2]As early as 3,000 B.C., the Egyptians made papyrus from a tall reed that grew there in the marshes of the Nile. [3]Although our word "paper"

comes from the word <u>papyrus</u>, little else does. ⁴There was a brittle quality to papyrus and it turned yellow easily. ⁵Still, there is evidence of its widespread use in all parts of the Mediterranean world, especially Greece and Rome.

⁶About the second century B.C., Greeks in Asia Minor began to make parchment out of animal skins. ⁷There product was intended to rival papyrus. ⁸These rolls of parchment became very popular. ⁹Scribes loved there toughness and there permanence. ¹⁰Their was also more writing space available because both sides could be used. ¹¹Though quite expensive, rolls of parchment became the primary means by which scholars and monks in the ancient world preserved the learning of there age.

¹²"Real" paper was invented by the Chinese in 105 A.D. ¹³Their formula, containing varieties of bark, fibers, and waste, can still be used today. ¹⁴There are sources that actually name the inventor: T'sai Lun, chief enunch of the Emperor Ho Ti. ¹⁵For eight centuries the Chinese kept their manufacture of paper secret. ¹⁶The process was eventually revealed to Arab traders by captured Chinese workmen. ¹⁷To obtain they're* release, the prisoners made paper for their captors. ¹⁸Even though their was continual warfare between Islam and Christianity, paper made its way to the West from the Arabs.

¹⁹The first Europeans to manufacture paper were Italians. ²⁰They produced paper in 1340 in the town of Fabriano. ²¹There were still 100 years before Gutenberg's printing press. ²²In 1800, Matthias Hoops, an Englishman, tried a combination of straw, wood, leaves, and other vegetable matter. ²³There was further improvement on his process by Swedes and Americans, including a chemical process that separated fibers from wood pulp. ²⁴There has been no major change in the details of the process since. ²⁵They're* useful exactly as described more than 600 years ago.

Chapter **38**

PROOFREADING
YOUR AND *YOU'RE*

> If you confuse the two terms, writing **you're** instead of **your**, go to p. 344. If, instead, you usually write **your**, continue here.

your

The word **your** is a possessive pronoun. It replaces the possessive form of a singular (or plural) noun.

Did the hurricane affect **your** area?

TESTING THE CORRECTNESS OF *YOUR*

a. Locate and circle all example of **your**.
b. Substitute **her** or **his** (if singular) or **our** (if plural).
c. If your sentence makes sense, you have used **your** correctly; if the sentence no longer makes sense, you should be using **you are.**
d. Also, look at the word right after **your**. Usually, it will be a noun that "belongs" to it or is "possessed" by it. The presence of such a word right after **your** usually signals that you have used **your** correctly.

NOTE: The words **her, his,** or **our** should be substituted for **your** only to test their grammatical similarity—they are all possessive pronouns. However, their meanings differ, so do not use them interchangeably.

ATTENTION FOCUSING 1*

The word **your** is used correctly in "Blood Pressure." Circle the 15 examples of the word.

BLOOD PRESSURE

[1]The heart is a pump that sends blood throughout your body. [2]When the left ventricle of your heart contracts, it creates a pumping action, forcing blood into your arteries. [3]Your arteries expand to receive the blood, but the muscular lining of the arteries resists this pressure. [4]The resistance squeezes blood out of your arteries into the smaller vessels of your body. [5]"Blood pressure" is the term used to describe the amount of pressure you're creating as a result of your heart's pumping and your arterial walls' resistance. [6]You're at maximum pressure when your left ventricle contracts. [7]This is called "systolic pressure." [8]You're at minimum pressure just before your next heartbeat. [9]This is called "diastolic pressure." [10]If you're a young man, your average systolic pressure is about 120 millimeters as measured by a column of mercury. [11]Your diastolic pressure is about 80 millimeters of mercury. [12]Your doctor is likely to state this as "120/80" or "120 over 80." [13]If you're older, your blood pressure is higher. [14]At age 60, it is about 140/87. [15]If you're active, have a good posture, can relax, and eat right, you can lower your blood pressure.

REWRITING EXERCISE 1: substituting for *your*

From "Blood Pressure," rewrite 3 sentences containing **your** and substitute **her, his,** or **our.** The sentences should make sense, indicating that you have used **your** correctly.

a. _____

b. _____

c. _____

REWRITING EXERCISE 2: using *her, his,* or *our*

To continue testing the effectiveness of substituting **her, his,** or **our** for **your,** choose a sentence that contains **you're** and write it below, substituting one of the other possessive pronouns. The sentence should make no sense at all. Put an X through the incorrect form.

_____

Practice your proofreading skills on pp. 345–346.

you're

The word **you're** is simply the contraction of **you are.**

You're the one that I love. ⟶ **You are** the one that I love.

TESTING THE CORRECTNESS OF *YOU'RE*

a. Circle all examples of **you're.**
b. Rewrite the sentence, writing out the contraction as **you are.**
c. If your sentence makes sense, you used **you're** correctly; if the sentence no longer makes sense, you should be using **your,** the possessive pronoun.

ATTENTION FOCUSING 2*

The word **you're** is used correctly in "Blood Pressure." Circle the 6 examples of the word.

BLOOD PRESSURE

[1]The heart is a pump that sends blood throughout your body. [2]When the left ventricle of your heart contracts, it creates a pumping action, forcing blood into your arteries. [3]Your arteries expand to receive the blood, but the muscular lining of the arteries resist this pressure. [4]The resistance squeezes blood out of your arteries into the smaller vessels of your body. [5]"Blood pressure" is the term used to describe the amount of pressure you're creating as a result of your heart's pumping and your arterial walls' resistance. [6]You're at maximum pressure when your left ventricle contracts. [7]This is called "systolic pressure." [8]You're at minimum pressure just before your next heartbeat. [9]This is called "diastolic pressure." [10]If you're a young man, your average systolic pressure is about 120 millimeters as measured by a column of mercury. [11]Your diastolic pressure is about 80 millimeters of mercury. [12]Your doctor is likely to state this as "120/80" or "120 over 80." [13]If you're older, your blood

pressure is higher. [14]At age 60, it is about 140/87. [15]If you're active, have a good posture, can relax, and eat right, you can lower your blood pressure.

REWRITING EXERCISE 3: substituting for *you're*

From the essay "Blood Pressure," rewrite 3 sentences containing **you're,** and eliminate the contraction by writing it out as **you are.** The sentence should make sense, indicating that you have used **you're** correctly.

a. _____

b. _____

c. _____

REWRITING EXERCISE 4: using *you are*

To continue testing the effectiveness of writing out the complete form of a contraction as a way of testing its correctness, try to "write out" the word **your.** Rewrite a sentence containing **your** from the essay "Blood Pressure" and use **you are** instead of **your.** The sentence should make no sense at all. Put an X through the incorrect form.

_____

PRACTICING PROOFREADING 1

Circle the 19 instances of **your** and **you're** and correct the 7 errors.

TASTE

[1]If you look at your tongue in the mirror, you will see that it is covered with tiny bumps. [2]Your taste buds are located in the walls of these bumps. [3]If you're impressed by the many tastes human beings can experience with those taste buds, think again. [4]Although your a better taster than a whale, your less sensitive than pigs, cows, and antelopes, all of whom have more taste buds than human being do. [5]Your tongue contains only 3,000. [6]A pig's has 5,500, a cow's 35,000, and an antelope's 50,000!

[7]You're tongue, incidentally, has a taste map. [8]The back of you're tongue is more sensitive to bitter tastes, the sides to salty and sour tastes,

and the tip to sweet. [9]The center of you're tongue is a dead zone as far as taste is concerned. [10]You're not likely to taste anything placed there.

[11]Your dependent, however, on more than your taste buds for taste. [12]Your sense of smell has tremendous influence on your sense of taste. [13]If you're deprived of your sense of smell, you have difficulty telling a slice of apple from a slice of potato. [14]Because you're brain is not receiving a message from your nose, it is difficult for it to identify what is in your mouth.

PRACTICING PROOFREADING 2

Circle the 17 instances of **your** and **you're** and correct the 5 errors.

HAIR

[1]Even as you're sitting here reading this, your hair is growing. [2]It grows all the time, though not at the same rate. [3]You're hair grows most slowly at night, whether you're sleeping or not. [4]It grows fastest between 10 and 11 in the morning. [5]It then slows down. [6]As you're leaving work between 4 and 6 in the afternoon, you're hair's growth rate begins to speed up again. [7]Of course, your hair never grows fast enough for you to notice its growth even if your standing in front of the mirror for hours. [8]Although your hair grows only about a half-inch a month, your an amazing hair-producing factory during that month. [9]If instead of individual hairs you could grow a single hair cable, by the end of the year the tip of you're hair would be 37 miles from your scalp. [10]If your're male and blond, you're likely to have finer hair and more hair than if you're female and dark. [11]If you're a red-head, you're the one with the thinnest and coarsest hair.

Chapter 39
PROOFREADING
WHOSE AND WHO'S

> If you confuse the two terms by writing **who's** for both, go to p. 349. If instead you write **whose** for both, continue here.

whose

The word **whose** is the possessive form of **who.** Like all pronouns, it needs no apostrophe to show possession. It is usually followed by a word that "belongs" to it.

Whose ribbon is this?

The word **ribbon** is a noun that "belongs" to **whose.**
Sometimes a descriptive word will come between **whose** and the noun, so look for at least two words after **whose: Whose blue ribbon is this?**

TESTING THE CORRECTNESS OF *WHOSE*

a. Circle all instances of **whose.**
b. Substitute **my, your,** or one of the other possessive pronouns and see if that part of the sentence makes sense.

or

See if the next word is a noun that "belongs" to **whose.**
c. If the sentence meets these conditions, you have used **whose** correctly.
d. If the sentence does not make sense with a possessive pronoun and **whose** is not followed by a word that it "possesses" or "owns," correct it by using **who's.**

NOTE: The words **my, your, his,** or **our** should be substituted for **whose** only to test their grammatical similarity—they are all possessive pronouns. However, their meanings differ, so do not use them interchangeably.

ATTENTION FOCUSING 1*

The word **whose** is used correctly in "Fred." Circle the 6 examples of **whose.**

FRED

[1]For anyone who's named Fred, there are not many namesakes whose lives would make him proud. [2]One television character who's made the name famous is that cartoon caveman, Fred Flintstone. [3]Another is Fred Mertz, the somewhat dimwitted landlord in I Love Lucy. [4]Animals whose owners named them Fred include parrots, frogs, and chimps, not creatures who inspire admiration. [5]Another Fred people remember from TV is Red Skelton's bum who's known as Freddy the Freeloader.

[6]To combat this generally negative public image, there is now a society for people whose name is Fred. [7]Founded by Fred Daniel, the Fred Society has 3,000 card-carrying members, whose intention is to note and fight examples of anti-Fredism. [8]One club member is Fred Hayward who's married to a woman who's refused to name their child Fred. [9]Another is Frederick Crumrine who's compiling a list of all commercials featuring bumbling husbands named Fred.

[10]In the Fred Society's hall of fame are famous people whose name was Fred. [11]They include the composer Chopin, the political philosopher Engels, guitarist Freddie King who's the composer of "Hide Away," and the scientist Curie, whose wife was the famous Madame Curie.

REWRITING EXERCISE 1: substituting for *whose*

Rewrite 3 sentences containing **whose** and substitute **my, her, his,** or **our.** The part of the sentence stating with the new word should make sense, indicating that you have used **whose** correctly.

a. _____

b. _____

c. _____

REWRITING EXERCISE 2: *whose*

From "Fred" write 3 examples of **whose** and the words that follow each:

_____   _____   _____

As you can see, each **whose** is followed by a noun it "owns" or "possesses," showing that you are using the pronoun correctly.

Practice your proofreading skills on pp. 350–352.

---

who's

The word **who's** is a contraction of **who is** or **who has**.

Who's that masked man? ⟶ **Who is** that masked man?

TESTING THE CORRECTNESS OF *WHO'S*

a. Circle all instances of **who's**.
b. Write out each contraction as **who is** or **who has**.
c. If the sentence makes sense, you are using **who's** correctly.
d. If the sentence does not make sense when you write **who's** as **who is**, correct it by using **whose**.

ATTENTION FOCUSING 2*

The word **who's** is used correctly in "Fred." Circle the 6 examples of **who's**.

FRED

[1]For anyone who's named Fred, there are not many namesakes whose lives would make him proud. [2]One television character who's made the name famous is that cartoon caveman, Fred Flintstone. [3]Another is Fred Mertz, the somewhat dimwitted landlord in *I Love Lucy*.

[4]Animals whose owners named them Fred include parrots, frogs, and chimps, not creatures who inspire admiration. [5]Another Fred people remember from TV is Red Skelton's bum who's known as Freddy the Freeloader.

[6]To combat this generally negative public image, there is now a society for people whose name is Fred. [7]Founded by Fred Daniel, the Fred Society has 3,000 card-carrying members, whose intention is to note and fight examples of anti-Fredism. [8]One club member is Fred Hayward who's married to a woman who's refused to name their child Fred. [9]Another is Frederick Crumrine who's compiling a list of all commercials featuring bumbling husbands named Fred.

[10]In the Fred Society's hall of fame are famous people whose name was Fred. [11]They include the composer Chopin, the political philosopher Engels, guitarist Freddie King who's the composer of "Hide Away," and the scientist Curie, whose wife was the famous Madame Curie.

REWRITING EXERCISE 3: substituting for *who's*

From the essay "Fred," rewrite 3 sentences containing **who's,** eliminating the contraction by writing it out as **who is.** The sentences should make sense, indicating that you have used **who's** correctly.

a. _____

b. _____

c. _____

REWRITING EXERCISE 4: using *who is*

To continue testing the effectiveness of writing out the complete form of a contraction as a way of testing its correctness, try to "write out" the word **whose.** Rewrite a sentence containing **whose** from the essay "Fred" and use **who is** instead of **whose.** The sentence should make no sense at all. Put an X through the incorrect form.

PRACTICING PROOFREADING 1

Circle the 13 instances of **who's** and **whose** and correct the 5 errors.

THE SONG AND THE SINGER

[1]A person whose singing is using his voice as if it were a musical instrument.

[2]The vocal cords are important, but other parts of this "instrument" also help determine if a person will have a beautiful singing voice. [3]A person who's vocal cords are longer will have a different general pitch from someone who's cords are shorter, but that does not decide who's voice is better. [4]A person who's a good singer can have the same vocal cords as one who's incapable of carrying a tune. [5]The difference is in the way one person can control those vocal cords and the sixteen muscles that move them. [6]The vocal cords of a singer who's been practicing for years can probably assume all 170 positions possible. [7]Then, to make them vibrate in a certain way, or she must use just the right amount of air and tense his or her vocal cords accordingly.

[8]Other parts of this singing mechanism include the walls: bones, muscles, tissues, and mucous membranes. [9]Again, these might be the same for someone who's a good singer and someone who's not. [10]The better singer, however, will be the one who's "resonating spaces" are superior. [11]A person whose voice is beautiful has resonating spaces inside the windpipe, lungs, oral and nasal cavities, nasal sinuses, and thorax that are shaped like perfect musical instruments. [12]The great singer is the individual whose resonating spaces are exceptional and whose also learned how to control his or her vocal apparatus artistically.

PRACTICING PROOFREADING 2

Circle the 10 instances of **who's** and **whose** and correct the 4 errors.

THE BALD SPOT

[1]The man who's recently noticed a bald spot on top of his head is no longer likely to rush to a dermatologist. [2]It seems that one famous individual after another who's livelihood depends on his looks has decided

that thinning hair is not necessarily a problem. [3]Such well-known actors as Jack Nicholson, Clint Eastwood, Bruce Willis, Bill Murray, and Michael Keaton are staying around even as their hair is leaving. [4]Other people in the public eye who's hair admits to the existence of scalp are Senator John Glenn, singer Phil Collins, and superstar basketball center Kareem Abdul Jabbar.

[5]The man with thinning hair whose still reluctant to hold his head up high can find comfort in a support group. [6]The Bald-Headed Men of America holds annual conventions whose features include a Most Kissable Bald-Headed Man Contest and workshops on confidence building.

[7]Still, for each man who's determined to avoid toupees, weaves, and other coverings, there are many who's baldness remains hidden, waiting for a miracle cure. [8]Though women say they care more about men's shoulders and eyes than their hair, most men remain convinced that, like Samson, their strength lies in their locks. [9]They admire a man like Peter Jennings who's on the evening news nightly, taking a chance that the bright TV lights will reflect off his head or Telly Savalas, who's made a career of his baldness, but deep down they are afraid that they will all look like Woody Allen. [10]According to psychologists, the man claiming to have adjusted to his baldness is just someone who's waiting for a reasonable alternative.

Chapter **40**

PROOFREADING
THEN AND THAN

> If you confuse the two terms, writing **than** for both, go to p. 354. If instead you write **then** for both, continue here.

then

The word **then** is an adverb meaning "at that time" or "after that time."

It turned dark. **Then** the rains came.

TESTING THE CORRECTNESS OF *THEN*

a. Locate and circle all examples of **then.**
b. Substitute **at that time** or **after that time.**
c. If the sentence makes sense, your have used **then** correctly. If the sentence does not make sense, **than** is correct.

ATTENTION FOCUSING 1*

The word **then** is used correctly in "Valentino." Circle the 4 instances of **then.**

VALENTINO

[1]In the eyes of the moviegoing public, there was no greater lover than Rudolph Valentino. [2]But this silent-film star's accomplishments as a lover off screen were less impressive than his performances on screen.

³In 1919, Valentino met and then married Jean Acker, but the marriage did not last the day. ⁴More precisely, the marriage never even began. ⁵When the couple reached the threshold of their room, Jean ran ahead, slammed the door, and then bolted it, leaving Valentino outside.

⁶The beginning of Valentino's second marriage was no more successful than the first. ⁷He married Natacha Rambova before his divorce from Jean Acker was final. ⁸Before he had a chance to be alone with his new bride, Valentino was arrested and charged with bigamy. ⁹Then he had to win his freedom by reassuring the court that the marriage had not yet been consummated. ¹⁰Worse than this initial fiasco were the subsequent months while Valentino and Natacha had to live apart. ¹¹Eventually his divorce was finalized, he remarried, and only then was he granted the opportunity to prove that his exploits on the screen had not been exaggerated.

REWRITING EXERCISE 1: substituting for *then*

From "Valentino," choose 3 sentences with **then** and rewrite them, substituting **at that time** or **after that time**. The sentence should make sense, indicating that you have used **then** correctly.

a. _____

b. _____

c. _____

REWRITING EXERCISE 2: using *at that time* or *after that time*

To continue testing the effectiveness of substituting **at that time** or **after that time** for **then**, choose a sentence with **than** from "Valentino" and substitute one of the phrases for the word **than**. The sentence should make no sense at all. Put an X through the incorrect form.

_____

Practice your proofreading skills on pp. 356–358.

than

The word **than** is used to make comparisons.

A dog's sense of smell is keener **than** a human's.

A dog's mouth is less infectious **than** the mouth of a human being.

NOTE: Do not use **than** with **different.** Correct usage calls for **from** to be used with **different:** Her hat was **different from** the one she wore last year.

TESTING THE CORRECTNESS OF *THAN*

a.   Locate and circle all examples of **than.**
b.   Decide if you are comparing people, actions, things, events, etc. One clue for the presence of comparisons is a word ending in **er** or the word **more** or **less.**

ATTENTION FOCUSING 2*

The word **than** is used correctly in "Valentino." Circle the 4 instances of the word.

VALENTINO

[1]In the eyes of the moviegoing public, there was no greater lover than Rudolph Valentino. [2]But this silent-film star's accomplishments as a lover off screen were less impressive than his performances on screen.

[3]In 1919, Valentino met and then married Jean Acker, but the marriage did not last the day. [4]More precisely, the marriage never even began. [5]When the couple reached the threshold of their room, Jean ran ahead, slammed the door, and then bolted it, leaving Valentino outside.

[6]The beginning of Valentino's second marriage was no more successful than the first. [7]He married Natacha Rambova before his divorce from Jean Acker was final. [8]Before he had a chance to be alone with his new bride, Valentino was arrested and charged with bigamy. [9]Then he had to win his freedom by reassuring the court that the marriage had not yet been consummated. [10]Worse than this initial fiasco were the subsequent months while Valentino and Natacha had to live apart. [11]Eventually his divorce was finalized, he remarried, and only then was he granted the opportunity to prove that his exploits on the screen had not been exaggerated.

REWRITING EXERCISE 3: testing for *than*

Choose 3 sentences with **than** from "Valentino" and determine if they are comparing two things. Write down the word **than** and the comparison word: an **er** word or **more** or **less.**

a. _____

b. _____

c. _____

PRACTICING PROOFREADING 1

Circle the 13 instances of **then** and **than,** and correct the 5 errors.

PENICILLIN

[1]In 1928, the bacteriologist Dr. Alexander Fleming accidentally discovered penicillin, "the wonder drug" against bacterial infection, proving that sometimes it is better to be lucky then good. [2]It then took twelve years before Fleming convinced doctors to try penicillin on human patients, proving that persistent argument can sometimes achieve better results then brilliant argument.

[3]Fleming's discovery came about when he set aside some plates of bacteria. [4]He was trying to isolate a germ culture to further his studies of a pus-forming bacterium. [5]Examining the dishes later, he noticed that mold had grown in them. [6]Then he realized that the mold was dissolving the bacteria. [7]He did not realize right then that he had found a powerful substance that could be used to fight bacterial infections in the human body. [8]Still, true scientist that he was, he decided to investigate, not suspecting that the accidental mold would be infinitely more valuable then the bacteria he had been trying to grow.

[9]He removed a fleck of the mold and then placed it in a protein solution, hoping it would grow. [10]Then he implanted the mold on plates that contained various bacteria. [11]He discovered that some types of bacteria were affected more than others, while some remained unaltered. [12]Then Fleming determined that the health of rabbits and mice injected

with the mold extract was not affected even as the extract was destroying bacteria. [13]Fleming than added penicillin to human blood serum and got the same results.

[14]Although Fleming had thus discovered the most powerful weapon in the fight against bacterial infection, the world remained skeptical. [15]Other bacteriologists remained unconvinced of the usefulness of penicillin or doubted it could be manufactured in more than minute quantities. [16]Than came World War II and with it a great need for antiseptics to treat infected wounds. [17]Dr. Florey, professor of pathology at Oxford's Sir William Dunn School of Pathology, gathered a team of scientists that eventually produced an extract that was still only 5 percent pure penicillin. [18]This work, however, proved that penicillin is effective and eventually led to mass production of the drug.

PRACTICING PROOFREADING 2

Circle the 8 instances of **then** and **than** and correct the 3 errors.

THE SECRET POET

[1]Unknown to her family, Emily Dickinson, the daughter of the treasurer of Amherst College, wrote two kinds of poetry throughout her solitary life. [2]She showed her family some light pieces, but hid from them the poetry that was more serious then the elegies and the nature poems. [3]And because she cared for her privacy more than for fame, she would not allow the world to read any part of her writing. [4]Even the witty notes she wrote to friends would contain the request that the letters be burned rather than allowed to be read by strangers.

[5]The person closer to Emily than anyone else was her sister, Lavinia. [6]Although she was less of a recluse then Emily, Lavinia remained a spinster and took care of her sister. [7]When Emily died in 1896, Lavinia began to burn all letters to Emily, exactly as she had been instructed to do. [8]Than she opened a drawer and found hundreds of poems. [9]Rather than light verse, these were serious poems. [10]Lavinia realized that she had no

instructions to destroy these poems and asked a friend, Mable Loomis Todd, to help her have the poems printed.

[11]Mrs. Todd worked on the haphazard manuscripts for four years. [12]Dickinson's first volume of poetry appeared in 1890 and sold out six editions in five months. [13]A second series appeared in 1891, and then a third in 1896.

Chapter **41**

PROOFREADING
TO AND *TOO*

> If you confuse the two terms by writing **too** for both, go to p. 360. If instead you write **to** for both terms, continue here.

to

The word **to** is (1) a preposition that usually indicates direction (as in **we went to the house**), or the transfer of goods or actions (as in **He gave the book to her**), or (2) part of the infinitive (as in **to go, to walk, to run, to fly**).

TESTING THE CORRECTNESS OF *TO*

a. Circle each **to**.
b. If the word after **to** is an article **(the, a, an),** a possessive pronoun **(my, our),** a verb, or a name, **to** is correct.

ATTENTION FOCUSING 1*

The word **to** is used correctly in "Famous Sayings." Circle the 13 instances of the word.

FAMOUS SAYINGS

1. Early to bed, early to rise, makes a man healthy, wealthy, and wise.

2. To be or not to be, that is the question.

3. The road to hell is paved with good intentions.

4. It's too good to be true.

5. It hurts to be in love.

6. To the victors belong the spoils.

7. That was too close for comfort.

8. Hanging is too good for him.

9. Cleanliness is next to godliness.

10. You can't be too rich or too thin.

11. I want it to be perfect.

12. I drink to your good health.

13. The road of excess leads to the palace of wisdom.

14. No bird soars too high if it soars with its own wings.

15. Fly me to the moon.

16. I like it too.

REWRITING EXERCISE 1: using *to*

Choose 4 examples of **to** from "Famous Sayings" and write them in the spaces below along with the word that follows each. Choose one that is followed by a verb, one by a noun, one by an article, and one by a pronoun.

_____   _____   _____   _____

    Practice your proofreading skills on pp. 362–363.

too

The word **too** is an adverb, used most often with other adverbs in describing an action, as in **He ate too quickly.** It also means **also,** as in **I went to the concert too.**

TESTING THE CORRECTNESS OF *TOO*

a. Circle each **too.**
b. Try either **very** or **also** in place of **too.**
c. If the sentence still makes sense, you have used **too** correctly; if the sentence no longer makes sense, you should be using **to.**
d. Also look at the next word. If it is an adverb or an adjective, you have used **too** correctly.

ATTENTION FOCUSING 2*

The word **too** is used correctly in "Famous Sayings." Circle the 6 instances of the word.

FAMOUS SAYINGS

1. Early to bed, early to rise, makes a man healthy, wealthy, and wise.

2. To be or not to be, that is the question.

3. The road to hell is paved with good intentions.

4. It's too good to be true.

5. It hurts to be in love.

6. To the victors belong the spoils.

7. That was too close for comfort.

8. Hanging is too good for him.

9. Cleanliness is next to godliness.

10. You can't be too rich or too thin.

11. I want it to be perfect.

12. I drink to your good health.

13. The road of excess leads to the palace of wisdom.

14. No bird soars too high if it soars with its own wings.

15. Fly me to the moon.

16. I like it too.

REWRITING EXERCISE 2: substituting for *too*

Choose 3 sentences with **too** from "Famous Sayings." Rewrite them, substituting either **very** or **also**. The sentences should make sense, indicating that you have used **too** correctly.

a. _____

b. _____

c. _____

REWRITING EXERCISE 3: using *very* or *also*

To continue testing the effectiveness of substituting **also** or **very** for **too**, try substituting either word in a sentence from "Famous Sayings" that contains **to**. The sentence should make no sense at all. Put an X through the incorrect form.

_____

REWRITING EXERCISE 4: using *too*

Select 3 sentences with **too** from "Famous Sayings." Write **too** and the very next word. Are the words that follow **too** articles, nouns, pronouns, or verbs?

_____ _____ _____

PRACTICING PROOFREADING 1

Circle the 10 instances of **to** and **too** and correct the 3 errors.

WRONG AGAIN

[1]Joey always thought his friend Herbie was to willing to consider the impossible. [2]He wondered what his friend was trying to do when he found him on his knees beside a large hole in the ground.

[3]"What are you doing now, Herbie?" Joey sighed to his friend.

[4]"Listening to the talking fox in this hole," Herbie answered. [5]"Stick around; maybe he'll talk to you too."

[6]"This is to silly even for you, Herbie. [7]There is no talking fox in there."

[8]Just then, a fox came around from a nearby rock. [9]"Your friend is right, Herbie," he said to the kneeling man. [10]"I've been waiting too, and I haven't heard a fox talk."

[11]"You see, Herbie," said Joey, turning too his friend, "I told you there's no talking fox in that hole."

PRACTICING PROOFREADING 2

Circle the 12 instances of **to** and **too** and correct the 4 errors.

THE NOBEL PRIZES

[1]To win the Nobel Prize is to achieve the highest recognition possible in certain fields. [2]Prizes are given each year to people in the sciences, to a writer, and to people who have helped bring about peace. [3]It is almost to much of an irony that these awards for achievement were established by the man whose invention was responsible for so much destruction.

[4]Alfred Nobel was a Swede who lived from 1833 to 1896. [5]Among his inventions were dynamite and blasting gelatin. [6]A new kind of detonator for explosives was his invention to. [7]Perhaps because he was not to proud of having created these means of destruction, upon his death he willed nine million dollars to a foundation and asked that prizes be awarded to those who made great contributions too world knowledge and peace.

Chapter 42

PROOFREADING
WERE AND *WHERE*

> If you confuse the two terms by writing **where** for both, go to p. 366. If instead you write **were** for both terms, continue here.

were

The word **were** is the past plural form of the verb **to be.**

Africans **were** storytellers long before their appearance in Jamestown.

TESTING FOR THE CORRECTNESS OF *WERE*

a. Circle each **were.**
b. Substitute **are,** the present tense form of **were.**
c. If the sentence makes sense, you have used **were** correctly.
d. If the sentence does not make sense when you substitute **are,** correct it by substituting **where.**

NOTE: Substitutions are suggested only to test the grammatical similarity of words. However, their meanings differ, so do not use them interchangeably.

ATTENTION FOCUSING 1*

The word **were** is used correctly in "Paule Marshall." Circle the 3 instances of the word.

PAULE MARSHALL

[1]Paule Marshall's parents were West Indians who emigrated to the United States from Barbados soon after World War I. [2]They settled in Brooklyn, N.Y., where Paule, by age 10, was already writing sketches and poems. [3]After graduating Phi Beta Kappa from Brooklyn College, Marshall joined the magazine <u>Our World</u>, where she became a feature writer, traveling on assignments to Brazil and the West Indies. [4]Her writing retains the idiom and patterns of Barbados where her parents were born and her experiences in the Caribbean where she traveled so extensively. [5]West Indian and American influences were obvious in her 1959 novel, <u>Brown Girl</u>, and in her 1961 collection of four novellas, <u>Soul Clap Hands and Sing</u>. [6]Some of her stories were first published in the West Indian magazine <u>New World</u>.

REWRITING EXERCISE 1: substituting for *were*

To determine the effectiveness of substituting **are** for **were,** choose three sentences with **were** from "Paule Marshall" and rewrite them with **are.** The sentences should make grammatical sense.

a. _____

b. _____

c. _____

REWRITING EXERCISE 2: using *are*

To continue testing the effectiveness of substituting **are** to determine the accuracy of **were,** try to substitute it for **where** in a sentence taken from "Paule Marshall." The sentence should make no sense at all. Put an X through the incorrect form.

_____

Practice your proofreading skills on pp. 367–368.

where

The word **where** refers to place, location, situation, or position.

In Africa, they lived in a society **where** university life was common.

TESTING THE CORRECTNESS OF *WHERE*

a. Circle each **where.**
b. Substitute **here** or **there** and read the sentence beginning with the substituted word.
c. If the sentence makes sense as it is now, you have used **where** correctly.
d. If **here** or **there** makes no sense, try **were.**

ATTENTION FOCUSING 2*

The word **where** is used correctly in "Paule Marshall." Circle the 4 instances of the word.

PAULE MARSHALL

[1]Paule Marshall's parents were West Indians who emigrated to the United States from Barbados soon after World War I. [2]They settled in Brooklyn, N.Y., where Paule, by age 10, was already writing sketches and poems. [3]After graduating Phi Beta Kappa from Brooklyn College, Marshall joined the magazine Our World, where she became a feature writer, traveling on assignments to Brazil and the West Indies. [4]Her writing retains the idiom and patterns of Barbados where her parents were born and her experiences in the Caribbean where she traveled so extensively. [5]West Indian and American influences were obvious in her 1959 novel, Brown Girl, and in her 1961 collection of four novellas, Soul Clap Hands and Sing. [6]Some of her stories were first published in the West Indian magazine New World.

REWRITING EXERCISE 3: substituting for *where*

To test the effectiveness of using **here** or **there** to determine the accuracy of **where,** select 3 sentences with **where** from "Paule Marshall" and rewrite the sentence from the point where you substitute one or the other for **where.** The sentences should make sense.

a. _____

b. _____

c. _____

REWRITING EXERCISE 4: using *here* or *there*

To continue testing the effectiveness of substituting **here** or **there** for **where,** try to replace **were** with one, choosing a sentence from "Paule Marshall." The sentence should make no sense at all. Put an X through the incorrect form.

_____

PRACTICING PROOFREADING 1

Circle the 10 instances of **were** and **where** and correct the 4 errors.

RICHARD WRIGHT

[1]Richard Wright was born in 1908 on a plantation near Natchez, Mississippi. [2]His early years were spent in Memphis, Tennessee, but, while still a teenager, he went to Chicago were he worked at odd jobs. [3]He was thus one of the many blacks who were part of the mass migration from the South to the North. [4]When he was born, 90 percent of all blacks were living in the South. [5]After they trekked northward, there were four times as many blacks in the North as before. [6]This uprooting and rerooting of his people were important themes in Wright's fiction. [7]His earliest stories were published in the Communist press, but he later diverged sharply from Communist policies. [8]His 1940 novel, <u>Native Son</u>, was the first novel by an American Negro to reach a mass audience. [9]After the publication of <u>Black Boy</u>, an autobiographical account of his childhood and youth, Wright moved to Paris were he lived for about fifteen years and were he died. [10]Although there where fictions and nonfictions by Wright during this final period, critical opinion considers his pre-Paris work as more significant.

PRACTICING PROOFREADING 2

Circle the 10 instances of **were** and **where** and correct the 4 errors.

TRAVELERS FROM SPACE

[1]People who describe seeing "shooting stars" were actually watching meteors fall through our atmosphere were friction, heating their outer layer, causes them to glow. [2]Most such travelers from space are, in fact, no larger than grains of sand and burn completely without landing. [3]Some larger ones survive and become exhibits in museums. [4]But once in a rare while, giant meteors land with great force. [5]The Meteor Crater in Arizona and Gosses Buff in Australia are places were scientists believe meteors crashed a long time ago. [6]More recently, something from outer space came down in 1908 in a remote part of Siberia, where it destroyed a wooded area the size of Rhode Island. [7]Among the many theories offered for the cause of this blast were meteors, exploding spaceships, and a small comet. [8]The advocates of the spaceship theory pointed at trees cut from the area were the blast occurred. [9]After the explosion, the growth rings on many trees were further apart—a sign of faster growth— which some believe could have been caused by the radiation from an exploding spaceship. [10]Most scientists, however, accept the comet theory, which would explain why there was no crater and why there were heat waves and shock waves. [11]As for the growth pattern on the trees, scientists point out that, in any area were more growing room becomes available, trees grow faster. [12]The blast certainly created more space for growth. [13]Whether such visitors are comets or meteors, they are very ancient travelers. [14]They were probably formed during the same time as the sun and the planets.

Chapter **43**

PROOFREADING
LOSE AND *LOOSE*

> If you confuse the two terms by writing **loose** for both, go to p. 370. If instead you write **lose** for both terms, continue here.

lose

The word **lose** is a verb. It should appear with **to;** with the helping verbs **does, did, will, would, can, could, may,** and **might;** and with plural subjects.

A magic number of zero means that a team can **lose** all its remaining games and still finish first.

TESTING THE CORRECTNESS OF *LOSE*

a. Circle each **lose.**
b. Look for **to** or for helping verbs—**can, could, will, would**—before it.

    or

c. Substitute an adjective for **lose.**
d. If the sentence does not make sense when you use a different adjective and the word **to** or another helping verb accompanies **lose,** you have used it correctly.

NOTE: Adjectives should be substituted for each other only to test their grammatical similarity. Clearly, however, their meanings differ, so do not use them interchangeably.

ATTENTION FOCUSING 1*

The word **lose** is used correctly in "Black Sox." Circle the 4 instances of the word.

BLACK SOX

[1]Soon after the 1919 World Series ended, rumors began to circulate that the games had been fixed. [2]Initial comments made light of the idea. [3]Charles Comiskey, owner of the Chicago White Sox, felt that, since some bettors had to lose in order for other bettors to win, the cry of "fix" always goes up. [4]<u>The Sporting News</u> suggested there were loose screws in the heads of professional gamblers, thinking they could destroy the reputation of the game merely because they were crossed.

[5]But the rumors were eventually confirmed as the conspiracy to lose the series became unraveled. [6]Pitchers Eddie Cicotte and Lefty Williams, and Joe Jackson, the famous outfielder, signed confessions. [7]However, because of loose security during a turnover at the Illinois state's attorney's office, the confessions disappeared. [8]When the case came to the courts, the players took back their signed statements that they had been paid to lose the series, and the case was dropped. [9]Despite the fact that the courts had released them, Baseball Commissioner K. M. Landis banned the players from major league parks. [10]To eliminate all loose ends, he also made sure they would lose all opportunities to play even minor league ball.

REWRITING EXERCISE 1: using *lose*

Determine the effectiveness of searching for **to** or a helping verb before **lose** by writing below 4 examples of **lose** from "Black Sox" and the word that precedes each. Try to list at least one **to** and one helping verb.

_____ _____ _____ _____

> Practice your proofreading skills on pp. 372–373.

loose

The word **loose** is an adjective. It describes a noun.

The **loose** jacket made him feel small.

The word **blue** is a more obvious example of an adjective. Notice it fits into the sentence as **loose** does.

The **blue** jacket made him feel small.

TESTING THE CORRECTNESS OF *LOOSE*

a. Circle each **loose.**
b. Substitute a different adjective for **loose**—a color, for example.
c. If the sentence makes sense, you have used **loose** correctly.
d. If the sentence does not make sense (and you also find **to** or a helping word), try **lose.**

ATTENTION FOCUSING 2*

The word **loose** is used correctly in "Black Sox." Circle the 3 instances of the word.

BLACK SOX

[1]Soon after the 1919 World Series ended, rumors began to circulate that the games had been fixed. [2]Initial comments made light of the idea. [3]Charles Comiskey, owner of the Chicago White Sox, felt that, since some bettors had to lose in order for other bettors to win, the cry of "fix" always goes up. [4]<u>The Sporting News</u> suggested there were loose screws in the heads of professional gamblers, thinking they could destroy the reputation of the game merely because they were crossed.

[5]But the rumors were eventually confirmed as the conspiracy to lose the series became unraveled. [6]Pitchers Eddie Cicotte and Lefty Williams, and Joe Jackson, the famous outfielder, signed confessions. [7]However, because of loose security during a turnover at the Illinois state's attorney's office, the confessions disappeared. [8]When the case came to the courts, the players took back their signed statements that they had been paid to lose the series, and the case was dropped. [9]Despite the fact that the courts had released them, Baseball Commissioner, K. M. Landis banned the players from major league parks. [10]To eliminate all loose ends, he also made sure they would lose all opportunities to play even minor league ball.

REWRITING EXERCISE 2: substituting for *loose*

To test the effectiveness of using another adjective instead of **loose** to determine its accuracy, rewrite the sentences from "Black Sox" that use **loose** and substitute a color in each instance.

a. _____

b. _____

c. _____

REWRITING EXERCISE 3: using *another adjective*

To continue testing the effectiveness of substituting another adjective for **loose,** try to substitute one for **lose.** Use a sentence with **lose** from the essay "Black Sox." It should make no sense at all. Put an X through the incorrect form.

_____

PRACTICING PROOFREADING 1

Circle the 7 instances of **lose** and **loose** and correct the 4 errors.

BARBED WIRE

[1]Farmers needed a device that would keep cattle from running lose. [2]The wire fencing in use was simply not adequate. [3]At a country fair in DeKalb, Illinois, in 1873, Joseph Glidden watched a demonstration of an improvement: spiked wooden strips hung along the normal wire fencing. [4]Glidden, himself a farmer with cattle he preferred not to lose, decided he could do better. [5]He twisted short wire barbs onto plain wire and connected these barbs or spikes with wire strips. [6]Once he started mass producing it, he let barbed wire lose upon the West, taming it forever.

[7]To Indians, Glidden's wire was the "devil's rope." [8]Some ranchers preferred to loose cattle than to restrict them from grazing freely. [9]But farmers loved the wire because it kept loose cattle away from their crops. [10]The same cattle that would break easily through the old wire fences would get hopelessly entangled in the barbed wire. [11]Eventually others learned to appreciate Glidden's invention. [12]Once ranchers started using it, they realized they would no longer lose superior cattle to inferior

breeders. [13]They now had a way of keeping them apart. [14]Railroads could now expand into new territory thanks to the barbed wire that kept lose animals from the tracks.

PRACTICING PROOFREADING 2

Circle the 7 instances of **lose** and **loose** and correct the 3 errors.

THE HEARING AID

[1]Alexander Graham Bell set out to help the deaf and ended up connecting the entire world. [2]Unfortunately he could not devise a communication device for people who were destined to loose their hearing. [3]Still, Bell's work in the field inspired Miller Hutchison of New York City to develop a hearing aid. [4]A lose version of the telephone, Hutchison's 1902 device changed sounds into electrical signals. [5]Then, powered by a battery, the device amplified the signals before changing them back into sounds. [6]With the sound now louder, those who had expected to lose the sounds of the world could now hear again. [7]Soon the ear trumpets, held losely in shaking hands, were replaced by electric hearing aids. [8]At first, these were bulky objects, but transistorization has managed not to lose the ability to increase sound even as it reduced the size of the device. [9]Nowadays hearing aids have become so miniaturized that people no longer need to lose sleep over being noticed as wearers. [10]And they are becoming so efficient that people with a hearing loss need have little fear they will lose the sounds of words spoken in a normal tone of voice.

Chapter 44

PROOFREADING OTHER CONFUSING TERMS

Using the proofreading methods you have been practicing throughout:

a. Look specifically for the term you have confused before.
b. After locating each instance of the term, test it for accuracy.
c. Correct terms you have used incorrectly.

To teach yourself to distinguish between confusing terms, learn to associate each term with a word that is similar to it in function. In other words, pair the term with a word that you can substitute for it in a sentence. Substituting a word that has the same function may, of course, change the meaning of the sentence slightly, but it will not alter its grammar. In Chapter 42, for example, a sentence that used **were** still made grammatical sense with **are** even though its time had changed from the past to the present.

This chapter offers alternatives or substitutions for commonly confused terms. When substituted in sentences, these words should help you proofread for the accuracy of each term. When substitution does not work, you can look for other clues to tell the words apart. If substitution (or other clues) reveals that the word you have used is incorrect, try the "sound-alike" or word commonly confused with the term.

accept—You are using **accept** correctly if the sentence still makes sense after you substitute **agree to** or **take.**

  I Draw a line through the sentence that uses **accept** incorrectly.

  a. My parents did not accept the offer for their house.
  b. They were pleased with all details accept the amount of down-payment.

advice—You are using **advice** correctly if the sentence still makes sense after you substitute **suggestion.**

❙ Draw a line through the sentence that uses **advice** incorrectly.

    a. "Take my advice and get married," Jeff said.
    b. "Please don't bother to advice me," John answered.

---

affect—To **affect** is to **act** upon. To remind yourself of how this word is used, think of the **a** in **action** and the **a** in **affect.**

❙ Draw a line through the sentence that uses **affect** incorrectly.

    a. The affect the news had on him was tremendous.
    b. The sound of thunder did not affect his concentration.

---

dessert—As a clue for this word, remember that dessert is something extra or additional you have after dinner. It is the word with the extra or additional **s.**

❙ Draw a line through the sentence that uses **dessert** incorrectly.

    a. Lawrence of Arabia rode camels across the Sahara dessert.
    b. A favorite dessert of his hosts was a dish of figs dipped in honey.

---

every day—If you are unsure about making this one word or two, simply substitute **each** for **every.** If the sentence retains its sense, keep **every** as a separate word.

❙ Draw a line through the sentence that uses **every day** incorrectly.

    a. He rode to school on horseback every day.
    b. His every day clothes underwent a great deal of wear and tear.

---

lay—The verb **lay** means to set or place. In the *present tense*, it should always have an object: something being set down or placed. The **past tense** form of **lay** is **laid.**

❙ Draw a line through the sentence that uses **lay** incorrectly.

    a. I hate to lay there without reading.
    b. Please be careful as you lay the blanket over the back of the chair.

---

number—The clue for the correct use of this word is in its meaning. Think of numbers. If you can **number** a quantity, use **number.** Also, associate this word with few. **(I have a large number of tomatoes; I have few tomatoes.)** If you cannot number a quantity, use **amount** and **little. (I have a large amount of tomato juice; I have little tomato juice.)**

---

our—You are using **our** correctly if you can substitute **your** or **their** for it. Another clue is the word that usually follows **our:** a noun that "belongs" to it.

I Draw a line through the sentence that uses **our** incorrectly.

    a.   We lost our path in the forest.
    b.   The fries our too hot to eat.

---

patients—You can make sure you are using this word correctly by removing the plural **s** ending and testing the sentence for sense. The content should accept one patient if it accepts more than one, while it will reject both if you need the word's sound-alike. This same test is useful for other words ending in the sound-alikes—**nts** and **nce.**

I Draw a line through the sentence that uses **patients** incorrectly.

    a.   The grateful patients wrote letters to the hospital.
    b.   The doctor's patients wore thin.

---

threw—This word is correct if **tossed** can be substituted for it in a sentence.

I Draw a line through the sentence that uses **threw** incorrectly.

    a.   To show his anger, the actor threw plates.
    b.   Some of the fragments flew right threw the window.

---

set—You are using **set** (as a verb) correctly if you can substitute **placed** for it in the sentence.

I Draw a line through the sentence that uses **set** incorrectly.

    a.   We decided to set a while before continuing with the tour.
    b.   An artist set her canvas before our bench and began to draw us.

whether—This word offers a choice. Because it involves a sort of question, associate it with all the other question words in the English language: **what, when, where, which, who, why.** Notice they all begin—as does **whether**—with **wh.**

I Draw a line through the sentence that uses **whether** incorrectly.

    a.   Why is the whether the subject of so much discussion?
    b.   I wonder whether it is worth listening to the meteorology report.

Unit Eight

PROOFREADING FOR SPELLING ERRORS

Many people explain their inability to spell certain words as some sort of mental block—a handicap even—that they can do nothing to correct short of hiring a proofreader. But so-called "bad spellers" misspell only a tiny percentage of the total number of words they use. In addition, when they misspell a word, they tend to misspell the word exactly the same way each time. These oddities of "bad spellers" suggest that they do not lack the ability to spell. When it involves English words, "to spell" means to know that the specific letters in a word are often different from the sounds that they make. In other words, to spell English words correctly, one must know that *most words are not written the way they sound*. And, because even those who think of themselves as bad spellers actually know this truth, they are able to spell correctly the great majority of words that they use.

There are thus no bad spellers. Rather, there are particular people who have difficulty spelling certain specific words or certain types of words. But they do know how to spell. If they did not, they would hardly be able to spell anything correctly, because most words in English are simply not written the way they sound.

Read that line again: "most words are not written the way they sound." Isn't the opposite true? Haven't you been told time and time again to "sound out" a word in the process of spelling it? Weren't you taught how to read (and spell) through the use of phonetics?

Yet such is the nature of the English language that the twenty-six letters in it stand for many more than twenty-six sounds. More important when it comes to "spelling," any sound in the language can be produced by way of many different letters. George Bernard Shaw, the Irish dramatist, mocked this characteristic most efficiently when he demonstrated the "correct" spelling of **fish** as **ghoti**, selecting the **f** sound from the **gh** in **tough,** the **i** from the **o** in **women,** and the **sh** from the **ti** in **station.** Surely you can think of many other instances in which a particular sound can be produced by a great many different letters or combination of letters. The **sh** sound that Shaw found in **ti** can also be produced by **s** in **sure,** by **sh** in **shoot,** by **ch** in **champagne,** and by **ss** in **mission.**

Those of you who did not speak English as your native language must, of course, be fully aware of just how slippery English spelling can be. It makes transcription of nearly every word an adventure, as supposed "rules" give way more often than not to exceptions. Thus, foreign students are the first to realize that learning English spelling is often not a matter of learning rules but an act of memorization, using the brain, the eye, and the hand to learn the shape of each separate word.

Fortunately for them, native speakers of English have long since internalized this fact. That is, they know (even if they cannot articulate it), that the correspondence between sound and spelling is only occasional. Acting on that understanding, native speakers are able to spell correctly 90 percent and more of the words they use, which means spelling them differently from the way they sound if considered letter by letter.

Many misspelled words must therefore be dealt with on an individual basis by the person who has misspelled them. In a curious way, writers "practice" both seeing and writing their incorrectly spelled words, further engraving them in habitual use. To overcome such deeply in-grained errors, you need to practice repeatedly the correct form.

Because misspelling individual words sometimes signals problems with other, similar words, you can eliminate problems with many words by learning a category. Unit VIII, however, focuses on proofreading. Whether you choose to learn the correct spelling by learning rules, by memorizing individual words, or by looking up words as you encounter them, you must first be aware that you have difficulties with a particular pattern. Then you must know how to look for that pattern. Only then can you proceed to correct it. Our emphasis, then, is on locating words.

You are likely to misspell these kinds of words in your essays:

a. any words that you have misspelled before
b. any words that are similar to words you have misspelled before
c. any familiar-sounding words that you have not written very often

Throughout this text you have been told that the key to successful proofreading is knowing what you do not know—in other words, know-ing which grammatical error you are likely to make. The three categories just mentioned attempt to inform you of that. You should take item *c* particularly to heart. The most commonly misspelled word is the word you think you know how to spell. After all, if you need to write **Czecho-slovakia** in an essay, you probably know that you should look it up. But are you likely to look up a common word such as **restaurant?** In fact, you are most likely to misspell ordinary words that you have **met** for the first time with your ears rather than with your eyes.

Begin then by asking yourself what your particular spelling "de-mons" are, based on the three categories mentioned earlier. If your in-structor or a helpful reader tells you that you have made five spelling errors, try to find them on your own. **Circle** ten words that you would be willing to look up because they "fit the profile" of your troublesome spell-ing words. You will be surprised to discover what a good sense you have of the words you are likely to misspell or how quickly you will develop such a sense.

The exercises in Chapter 45 provide practice for locating certain types of words. Chapters 46–49 offer additional strategies and opportu-nities to proofread misspelled words in the four most common patterns: **y** endings, silent **e** endings, doubled consonants, and prefixes. See also Unit VII: Proofreading for Confusing Terms.

Chapter **45**

COMMON SPELLING PATTERNS

ATTENTION FOCUSING 1: endings*

a. Underline in the essay the 20 words that have one of these endings: **ed, er, est, ial, ing, ion.**
b. Write the 20 words below, separating each from its ending.

COURTSHIP RITUALS

[1]A book by Bettyann Kevies, <u>Female of the Species</u> (Harvard University Press, 1986), offers some amusing examples of courtship rituals among animals.

[2]Although animal pairs care about each other's looks, the definition of beauty varies greatly in their world. [3]For the female mandrill, the preferred male is the one with the most beautiful crimson and royal blue facial marking. [4]The female widowbird of Kenya is attracted to the male with the longest tail feathers. [5]But among English moorhens the winner of the mating derby is the shortest and fattest male.

[6]During courtship, many animal Don Juans believe that gifts will get them through the door, so to speak, but once again the nature of the present depends on the nature of the creature. [7]People who live in tiny apartments may understand why a male weaverbird is usually successful when he offers a newly built nest to attract a mother and begin his family. [8]Equally endearing (but only to roadrunners) is the male's gift of a

383

rat to the female, particularly if the rat has first been rendered senseless. [9]Male flies offer elaborate packages of delicacies, counting on the female to be distracted by the fancy wrapping while they make their move. [10]Human beings will recognize the approach of male bullfrogs. [11]They essentially throw a party and croak in chorus, hoping thereby to achieve the desired results.

[12]As far as showing romantic feelings is concerned, all creatures seem to act alike. [13]Horseshoe crabs have long, long, embraces. [14]Lions hug and kiss each other after a separation of only a few hours. [15]And gibbons in love often sing together for the sheer joy of it.

_____ _____ _____ _____ _____

_____ _____ _____ _____ _____

_____ _____ _____ _____ _____

_____ _____

ATTENTION FOCUSING 2: *y* endings*

Imagine that in a previous essay you misspelled the word **happily** by not changing the **y** at the end of **happy** to an **i** before adding **ly.** Now you have to proofread the essay "Courtship Rituals." List 3 words in the essay that you would consider checking in the dictionary because their spelling follows the pattern of your "misspelled" word, **happily.**

_____ _____ _____

For additional work with *y* endings, see Chapter 46.

ATTENTION FOCUSING 3: doubled consonant endings*

Imagine that in a previous essay you misspelled the word **batted** by not doubling the **t** at the end of **bat** before adding **ed.** Now you have to proofread the essay "Courtship Rituals." List 4 words you would check in the dictionary because their pattern is the same as that of **batted.**

_____ _____ _____ _____

For additional work on doubling consonants, see Chapter 47.

ATTENTION FOCUSING 4: silent e endings*

Imagine that in a previous essay you misspelled the word **liking** by not removing the **e** at the end of **like** before adding **ing**, an ending that begins with a vowel. Now you have to proofread the essay "Courtship Rituals." List 6 words you would check because they contain the same spelling situation as **liking**, your "misspelled" word.

_____ _____ _____ _____ _____ _____

> For additional work with silent e endings, see Chapter 48.

ATTENTION FOCUSING 5: silent medial*

Imagine that in a previous essay you misspelled the word **aspirin** by leaving out the **i** in the middle of the word, largely because you didn't really pronounce the sound. Now you have to proofread the essay "Courtship Rituals." Find and list the word that matches the spelling pattern of the word **aspirin**.

ATTENTION FOCUSING 6: *ly* endings*

Imagine that in a previous essay you misspelled the word **conditionally** by leaving out the **al** at the end of **conditional** before adding **ly** because you just do not hear the **al** when you add **ly**. Now you have to proofread the essay "Courtship Rituals." List 4 words ending in **ly** that might match the spelling pattern of the word **conditionally**.

_____ _____ _____ _____

> For additional work with *ly* endings, see Chapter 35.

ATTENTION FOCUSING 7: *ie/ei* words*

Imagine that in a previous essay you misspelled the word **receive** by switching the positions of the **e** and **i**. Now you have to proofread the essay "Courtship Rituals." List 3 words that match the spelling pattern of the word **receive**; that is **ie/ei** appears in the middle of the word.

_____ _____ _____

ATTENTION FOCUSING 8: other endings*

Your misspelled words might also fall into one of the following patterns:

a. **ence/ance** endings: _____ _____ _____

b. **ous/us** endings: _____ _____

c. **cal/cle** endings: _____

d. **able/ible** endings: _____ _____

e. **ence/ent** endings: _____ _____

Select from the following essay, "Swept Away," those words that fit the patterns listed above. In an actual essay you have written, if the error in your misspelled word involves one of these endings, you should check other words with similar patterns.

SWEPT AWAY

[1]Gene Klein, head of security for the Statute of Liberty, was startled to see floating off in the distance one day an enormous duck. [2]It was not so much its appearance near the Staten Island Ferry terminal that was surprising as its apparent helplessness. [3]Ducks, after all, are excellent swimmers.

[4]But this snow-white duck seemed to have difficulty swimming. [5]Klein thought that would be reasonable if its wings had been bound, as is often the case with birds being transported, and the duck had somehow slipped into the water. [6]But upon its emergence from the water, thanks to the efforts of wet-suited Coast Guard swimmers, it become obvious what had made its attempts to stay afloat impossible. [7]Dangling from each wing of the helpless duck was a voodoo doll, fashioned out of fabric and stuffed with beans. [8]Around the neck of each doll was a noose of colored ribbons. [9]Clearly, the duck represented some individual. [10]Its sacrifice was supposed ensure the death of that individual.

[11]The Coast Guard rescued the duck, spoiling the magic. [12]Although he knows he is not being logical, Klein feels that, in saving the duck, he might have saved the life of the intended victim as well.

ATTENTION FOCUSING 9: one word or two*

The frequently used term **a lot** consists of two words. Writing the term as one word is simply incorrect. More problematic are the many compound words that are correct when combined or separated but have different meanings in each instance. We discuss one such term—every day—in Chapter 44. In many other cases, you must simply check your dictionary, because this is one area in which the language is changing, as some words merge, others become hyphenated, and still others are separated.

List below 3 compound words in "Swept Away," 2 of which are hyphenated:

_____   _____   _____

For additional work with prefixes and compounds, see Chapter 49.

Chapter 46

PROOFREADING FOR Y WORDS

REVIEW: the final y pattern

Although there are exceptions to the two rules we offer here, following them should help you spell hundreds of words correctly.

a. If the base word ends in a **vowel** + **y**, there is no change.

toy + ed ⟶ toyed   enjoy + ed ⟶ enjoyed

b. If the base word ends in a **consonant** + **y**, the **y** changes to an **i**, unless the suffix (or ending) already begins with an **i**.

busy + ness ⟶ business   copy + er ⟶ copier
study + ing ⟶ studying

REWRITING EXERCISE: y words*

Using the 2 patterns discussed above, combine the following base words and endings. As most of these words are so-called "nonsense words," ignore the meanings and concentrate on the letter just before the final **y**.

1. cusy + al   _cusial_

2. huzally + ing _____

3. finty + ment   _____

4. grashy + er   _____

5. olly + ous   _____

6. carnify + ed   _____

7. cassowary + es _____

8. chalcedony + es _____

9. zyzyphy + ous _____

10. grundy + ing _____

11. globbuey + ist _____

12. toroy + ally _____

13. voney + s   _____

14. dray + er   _____

388

15. olley + ous _____   **18.** roy + ed _____

16. quay + ing _____   **19.** halley + ous _____

17. cloy + ous _____   **20.** joey + s _____

PROOFREADING STRATEGIES

Look specifically for words with the **y** or **i** near the end of the word, in or near a suffix. Circle those that you are are not sure of. You will not need to circle too many. You are most likely to misspell words you have misspelled before, so look for those first. Especially focus on the endings; some people have difficulties only with particular suffixes: **ing** for example, or **ous**.

PRACTICING PROOFREADING: *y endings*

The selection that follows contains spelling errors involving the endings of **y** words. Find the 15 **y** words and correct the 6 that are misspelled.

WOMEN PIRATES

[1]Among the many pirates who have sailed the seas in the 18th century were a number of women. [2]They handled ships, captained crews, and plundered other vessels. [3]Mary Read, before she ever led a crew, killed the man who was bullying one of her lovers. [4]She ended up on Spanish gallows around 1720. [5]Another of the buccaneer women was Anney Bonney, a shipmate of Mary Read. [6]She was handy with a sword and even livelyier with her tongue. [7]When she was about to be hanged, she told Captain John Rackham, "If you had fought like a man, you need not have been hanged like a dog." [8]But the most famous female pirate of them all was the widow Chang who preyed on ships sailing in Asian waters.

[9]Around 1797, a number of pirate groups joined under the leadership of a man named Ching. [10]The pirates sacked coastal towns so frequently that the pityful inhabitants had to abandon their fishing boats and move inland, taking up agriculture. [11]The imperial authorityes who had ordered this migration were disappointed to find out that they had simply forced the pirates out to sea where they caused even greater havoc.

[12]Incapable of destroying the pirates, they turned to bribery. [13]As Ching readyed himself to accept the emperor's pardon, he was poisoned and his sleepy-eyed wife with the oiled hair, the widow Chang, was elected in his stead.

[14]Thirteen years of plunder followed as Chang carried the pirate hordes to ever greater glory. [15]Historycal accounts tell of extreme cruelty toward victims and extreme severity toward crew. [16]The pirates even defeated an imperial force. [17]Eventually, a second expedition went out to engage Chang. [18]The two navies faced each other, but instead of meeting, waited. [19]Then "balloons" of painted rice paper came flying over from the imperial squadron, carreing stories of a dragon who forgave a fox. [20]The widow finally came to a decision and surrendered. [21]She was pardoned and lived out her days trading in opium.

Chapter **47**
PROOFREADING FOR DOUBLED CONSONANTS

REVIEW: the doubled consonant pattern

The doubled consonant pattern, like any other, has exceptions, but following the rule given here should help you spell thousands of words correctly.

In order to double the final consonant of a word,

a. the word must end in a consonant-vowel-consonant pattern:

commit, but not **comment**; **occur**, but not **circle**

b. and the suffix you add must begin with a vowel:

commit + **ed** ⟶ **committed**, but **commit** + **ment** ⟶ **commitment**

c. and the final syllable must be accented.

REWRITING EXERCISE: doubling final consonants*

a. Circle the words that end in the consonant-vowel-consonant pattern. (Some of them are "nonsense words." Do not be concerned about their meaning. Concentrate on their pattern.)
b. Circle the suffixes that begin with a vowel. (Accented syllables are underlined.)
c. Combine circled words and circled suffixes, doubling the final consonants.

*1. viscin + ing _viscining_

2. ratsan + ing _ratsanning_

3. ompute + ment_____

4. thogif + er _____

5. tho<u>gif</u> + ment_____   13. cup + ing _____

6. trom + ed _____   14. <u>bit</u>ter + ness _____

7. trim + ed _____   15. <u>bat</u>ter + ing _____

8. fit + er _____   16. deme<u>din</u> + ful _____

9. <u>pat</u>tern + ed _____   17. cloy + ing _____

10. grund + ing _____   18. rot + ed _____

11. <u>di</u>rect + ive _____   19. fat + en _____

12. pot + ed _____   20. grab + ing _____

NOTE: The starred (*) word in the exercise—**viscin**—is an example of the exception to the two conditions for doubling. The final syllable of the word <u>vis</u>cin is not accented and thus the consonant does not double.

How To Cope with the Unexpected (1)

The starred (*) word does not meet the requirement that the final syllable be stressed. Therefore, its final consonant is not doubled.

PROOFREADING STRATEGIES

Look at suffixes that begin with vowels. The most frequent is the **ed** ending, used to indicate the past tense and certain adjectives. Other common endings are **er** and **ing.** Circle those words that fit the pattern. Compare those words to other words in which you see the doubled consonants. As always, the word you are most likely to misspell is the word you have misspelled before, so examine your essay for doubled consonant words that appear on your personal list of spelling words. Check the dictionary for the spelling of any that seem wrong. A dictionary will indicate if the final consonant should be doubled when you add a suffix.

PROOFREADING EXERCISE: doubled final consonants

The selection that follows contains spelling errors involving doubled consonants. Find the 4 errors in consonants that have not been doubled or that have been doubled unnecessarily.

LIFE'S SIMPLIFIERS

[1]Can you imagine life without baggies, refrigerators, or toaster ovens? [2]According to an exhibit sponsored by Consumers Union, these are among the items considered milestones by consumers. [3]When they stepped back and considered items around the house they have come to

take for granted, shopers added VCR machines, power mowers, transparent tape, and disposable diapers to their list of items that have affectted their lives and attitudes.

[4]If ownership is any indication of the importance of these items, consider how completely the following have been knited into the fabric of contemporary life. [5]When polled by Appliance Magazine, Americans reported that 99.9 percent of their homes have refrigerators; 92 percent have color TV sets; 70 percent have washing machines; 50 percent electric dryers. [6]All these items were invented within the last fifty years. [7]They have replaced iceboxes and radios, and they have freed people from scrubbing, wringing, and hanging wash.

Chapter **48**

PROOFREADING
THE SILENT *E*

REVIEW: the silent e and suffixes

When you add a suffix beginning with a vowel to a word that ends in a silent **e**, drop the silent **e**.

As you consider the **ed** endings on words such as **distributed** and **bared,** you might wonder about the **ed** rule you have just read. Some textbooks will tell you that words ending in silent **e** receive merely a **d,** rather than an **ed** ending. Not so. The suffix for indicating the past tense (or sometimes an adjective) is **ed,** and that is what you add. The **e** that disappears is the silent one at the end of the word, not one from the **ed** suffix. What is the difference? Not much when both letters are the same, but a great deal when the ending is **ing** or **able,** as in **hate** + **ing** or **love** + **able.** In each instance, the vowel at the end of the word falls away and the suffixes—**ing** and **able**—remain whole.

$$distribute + ed \longrightarrow distributed$$
$$bare + ed \longrightarrow bared$$
$$hate + ed \longrightarrow hated$$
$$hate + ing \longrightarrow hating$$
$$love + able \longrightarrow lovable$$

REWRITING EXERCISE: adding suffixes to silent e endings*

Considering the rule for the silent **e** stated earlier, combine the following base words and endings. Some of the words are "nonsense words." Ignore their meanings and concentrate on their pattern.

1. wate + ing   _Wating_

2. rate + ing   _____

3. compute + er   _____

4. thoge + er   _____

5. thoge + ment   _____

6. trome + able   _____

7. trump + ed _____   14. insure + ance _____

8. fight + er _____   15. envelope + ing_____

9. prate + ing _____   16. develop + er _____

10. like + able _____   17. potato + es _____

11. dare + ing _____   18. rotate + ion _____

12. plain + est _____   19. size + able _____

13. continue + ous_____   *20. manage + able_____

How to Cope with the Unexpected

The starred (*) word does not drop the final **e.** It is an example of the major exception to the silent **e** rule. Words with **c** or **g** before the silent **e** retain the **e.**

manage + able ⟶ manageable
embrace + able ⟶ embraceable

PROOFREADING STRATEGIES

The most frequently used silent **e** suffix is **ed,** indicating the past tense and certain adjectives. Other common endings are **er** and **ing; able** and **ous** appear a bit less frequently. Circle those words that fit this pattern and compare them to others with suffixes beginning in vowels. As always, the words you are most likely to misspell are the words you have misspelled before, so examine your essay for words ending in silent **e** that appear on your personal list of spelling words. Check the dictionary for the spelling of any that seem wrong.

PRACTICING PROOFREADING: suffixes and silent e endings

The selection that follows contains spelling errors involving suffixes and silent **e** endings. Find the 12 silent **e** words that have suffixes attached to them and correct the 6 spelling errors where the silent **e** is retained unnecessarily or removed unnecessarily.

MORE UNFORGETTABLE WILLS

[1]Among the bizarre wills cited by Robert S. Menchin in his <u>Where There's a Will</u> (Farnsworth, 1979), is one that should help all courageous English teachers who argue for preciseion and clarity in language. [2]It

seems that a man wrote in his will that he is leaving "All to Mother." [3]What was to him a straightforward statment proved quite confuseing to everyone else. [4]Apparently he had called both his wife and his mother "Mother," and each felt the estate should belong entirely to her. [5]Many other stories describe the effect of wills on the heirs.

[6]A wealthy nineteenth-century New Yorker, for example, left everything to his nieces and nephews, excludeng only seventy-one pairs of trousers. [7]These, he wrote, had to be sold at a public sale. [8]The sale was held, and the pleased purchasers of the trousers—limited to one to a customer—found $1,000 sewn into a pocket.

[9]Patrick Henry's less famous statement was in his will. [10]Although makeing provisions for his wife's welfare, he specified that the support should end if she remarried. [11]"It would make me unhappy to feel I have worked all my life to support another man's wife," he wrote. [12]His wife remarried anyway.

Chapter 49

PROOFREADING PREFIXES AND COMPOUNDS

REVIEW: joining prefixes and compounds

If two words are combined to form a new word, neither word changes. No endings are dropped, no letters are doubled, no letters changed.

toy + box ⟶ toybox
copy + cat ⟶ copycat
clergy + man ⟶ clergyman

The same holds true when a "prefix" is added to a word. The two terms simply combine:

im + possible ⟶ impossible
dis + satisfied ⟶ dissatisfied

The only spelling problem involving prefixes and compounds lies in the connection itself. Writers sometimes think that prefixes should be attached with hyphens. Other writers are not sure if two words that sound as if they would go together are actually connected, hyphenated, or left separated. In fact, conventions regarding compounds are in a state of flux. Some words are moving from separateness to hyphenation, others to complete unity. Problems arise when two words mean one thing joined and something else separated. Chapter 44 offers suggestions for a group of such words. Keep an up-to-date dictionary handy. It will indicate when words are hyphenated or combined.

REWRITING EXERCISE: prefixes and compounds*

Combine the words or prefixes in the left column with the words in the right column. Retain all letters. Some of the words are "nonsense words." Do not worry about their meaning. Focus on the pattern.

1. dream + boat   *dreamboat*

2. dis + service   _____

3. co + ordinate   _____

4. per + calde   _____

5. folk + lore   _____

6. news + paper   _____

7. mis + spell   _____

8. inter + racial   _____

9. with + heling   _____

10. un + nerving   _____

11. twit + terning   _____

12. out + spoken   _____

13. en + reegen   _____

14. dis + agree   _____

PRACTICING PROOFREADING: prefixes and compounds

Locate in the essay below the 13 words that are compounds, hyphenated words, or begin with a prefix. Correct the 4 that are misspelled at the point where they are correctly or incorrectly connected.

STARTING UP

[1]Reccurring morning headaches should be investigated by a doctor, but various other morning ills can be cured very easily. [2]Do not go back to sleep. [3]Abandon your bedsheets, toss off your nightshirt, and head for the shower.

[4]This is particularly good advice if the symptom is a stuffy nose, especially during wintertime. [5]Dry, heated air and poor ventilation combine to swell mucous membranes in the nose, giving you that stuffed feeling. [6]Taking a shower is a kind of self-diagnosis. [7]If the problem is merely a stuffy nose, the humidity of the warm water will eliminate the stuffiness in a few minutes. [8]For a less everyday but more permanent cure, try a humidifier.

[9]If the stuffed nose is also acompanied by puffy eyes, an allergy might be the culprit. [10]Behind the window-shades, pollen might be lurking. [11]The bedroom rug might have been cleaned with a new cleanser. [12]The cat could have been a nightime visitor.

Unit Nine

THE PARAGRAPH WITHIN THE ESSAY
(a short course in opinion and defense)

Chapter **50**

THE ORGANIZING PROPOSITION

The first day's assignment in a basic writing course:

Recommend yourself for a job or position. (Write about yourself in the third person, as "John" or "Jane Smith," and continue to use "he" or "she" throughout.)

But there was one additional bit of instruction:

Begin your essay by responding to the assignment with a single sentence in which you recommend yourself for a specific job or position.

Here is the way some students began:

Steven Champouillon would make a great bouncer.
I recommend Don Fulcher to be a flight attendant.
Melody Dence is well suited for a job as architect's apprentice.

Why did the instructor insist that students begin their essays by stating their opinion in a single sentence?

In an organized essay, readers should know what comes next. More important, the writer should know what comes next. The instructor insisted on an opening sentence of opinion because he hoped that each of those sentences would not only make its author's opinion clear, but, more important, help point the writer toward what follows: a defense of the opinion.

After all, if others (your readers) are to accept your opinion, you must offer a successful, convincing defense of that opinion. Think of this opening sentence then as a prompt, a pointer, a focus. It is essentially the thesis of your essay, its main idea, the **proposition** of your essay.

You know from previous experience that writing is preceded by various prewriting stages. You might begin by brainstorming—thinking out loud, in a sense—with other students and your instructor until you decide on a topic. Other stages include formulating a position, outlining, **403** and drafting. You might need to read up on your subject or do intensive research. Unquestionably, these and other considerations are essential to the successful writing process. But, just as a learning exercise, try writing immediately, following a **proposition-defense** structure.

The presence of an opinion and the need to defend it will provide you with a structure that will shape your essay. As your writing skills progress, you will have to take on less-structured assignments that require familiarity with the various prewriting stages. For now, however, the text will provide you with an assignment (topic). When you respond to that topic with your opinion, you establish a structure for the rest of the essay.

Once you have declared your opinion—stated a **proposition**—you have, in a sense, organized the rest of your essay. Readers expect to hear why you recommend this individual, or why this individual would be the right person for the job. Because you must know that readers expect you to prove your opinion, you know what to write next—a **defense** of your proposition.

No matter how general the topic is or how bland, if you can formulate an opinion, you can provide a structure for the rest of the essay. You can develop this **argumentative edge** for any topic. Assignments to write about your summer vacation, to describe your room, to compare eating places, or to discuss the sequence of steps in tuning a car can easily fit into the **proposition-defense** structure.

EXERCISE 1: formulating opinions

1. topic: write about your summer vacation
    sample opinion: A vacation in the Poconos was very inexpensive.

    your opinion: _____

2. topic: describe your room or any other room in your house/apartment
    sample opinion: My room does not lend itself to privacy.

    your opinion: _____

3. topic: discuss a restaurant where you have eaten
    sample opinion: Grimaldi's is a typical Italian restaurant.

    your opinion: _____

4. topic: describe a process—how something works or how it should be done
    sample opinion: Tuning a car might seem to require a professional, but, with the right manual and appropriate tools, anyone can do it.

    your opinion: _____

5. topic: talk about how suitable you would be for a particular job/position

sample opinion: Ms. Felder would be an excellent supervisor in your Medical Center.

your opinion: _____

One way of determining if, in fact, you have written a proposition is to see if you can write a statement disagreeing with it.

EXERCISE 2: determining opinion*

Decide if the sentences that follow are opinions by trying to disagree with them. You will find that some are simply statements of fact that contain no opinion. Rewrite those that lack an opinion, giving them an **argumentative edge.** Circle the letter of each sentence that contains an opinion and is thus a **proposition** that needs to be defended. Then disagree with it in the space below.

1. My economics textbook was written by Samuelson.

_____

2. Mickey Mantle was American League MVP in 1956.

_____

3. All official information should be in both English and Spanish.

_____

4. With calculators around, learning math is a waste of school time.

_____

5. MASH has won more Emmys than any other television comedy.

_____

6. The middle child in a family is always at a disadvantage.

_____

7. My father's influence on me has been very positive.

_____

8. Lincoln was president during the Civil War.

_____

9. Chinese uses a special word to indicate time in a sentence.

_____

10. Huey Lewis and the News won the "Most Popular Group" award.

_____

EXERCISE 3: formulating opinions

Write a single statement of opinion—a **proposition**—on ten of these topics:

1. pets _____

2. family size _____

3. your childhood _____

4. food _____

5. a TV show _____

6. sports _____

7. illness _____

8. your job _____

9. rules _____

10. a happy moment _____

11. cooking _____

12. last weekend _____

13. friendship _____

14. inventions _____

15. freedom _____

Obviously, this approach works best when you know enough about a topic to form an opinion on it. By no means should you substitute this quick formula for researching and thinking about your subject matter in actual assignments. But do not hesitate to resort to this formula when you are already familiar with a topic or after you have learned enough about one to take a position. It should work for a variety of writing assignments. If you are asked to write a summary of something you have read, for example, ask yourself: **What is this author trying to prove?** or **What is this author trying to explain?** Your answer to this question is essentially your proposition. Once you have stated what you feel is important to the author, you need to demonstrate—to prove—that the author does, in fact, find this subject important.

Similarly, one way to approach the various rhetorical modes—definition, description, narration, process, even cause and effect—is to present your thesis as a proposition—an argumentative position you need to prove.

As you continue to write, you will eventually be faced with topics about which you cannot immediately form an opinion. But, at this beginning stage, try to take the first major step toward organization by formulating a **proposition.** Once you have stated it, you know eactly what you need to do next: defend your opinion.

Chapter 51 provides some basic ways of defending your proposition.

Chapter 51

THE TWO-PARAGRAPH DEFENSE

The "shape" of the essay-in-progress illustrated here contains room for an **introduction** and an **ending.** In between are two paragraphs of defense. The **proposition** appears as the last sentence of the introduction.

At this point, we are not concerned with the introduction or the ending. You can write those later, when you know exactly how you can use them to help your essay. (See the end of this chapter for various approaches to these two parts of an essay). Thus the essay-in-progress begins with the **proposition** and continues with its **defense.** Keep in mind that this entire process is a short cut, designed to have you write a complete essay on subjects with which you are already familiar. It will be a very basic essay, providing you with a context within which you can utilize your grammatical skills.

This defense consists of two **reasons,** one in each paragraph of defense.

Title

A student's
proposition:

Introduction

Steven Champouillon would make a great
bouncer.

To defend this opinion, the student must come up with two reasons of support, writing each as the first sentence of a paragraph. **407**

The student wrote:

One reason I recommend Steven is that he is physically qualified to be a bouncer.

(Defense 1)

To help emphasize that there are two different paragraphs here, the student was asked to write one reason a few lines below his proposition and the other on the other side of his paper.

Another reason I think Steven would be a fine bouncer is that he has a calm nature.

Defense 2

ending

The student has now basically organized his essay. The next step is to prove the proposition by developing two reasons. One "reason" paragraph will show that Steven has the physical capabilities to be a bouncer; the other that his calm nature qualifies him.

EXERCISE 1: defending with reasons

Offer two reasons in support of each proposition (or take the opposing side and defend that with two reasons). Each of the one-sentence reasons you state would become the topic sentence or main idea for a paragraph. To help remind yourself that you are offering reasons in defense, begin them with the connecting words the student had used: **One reason** and **Another reason**, or **First** and **Second**, or **One** and **In addition**.

1. proposition: All official information should be in both English and Spanish.

    reason 1: _____

    reason 2: _____

2. proposition: The middle child in a family is always at a disadvantage.

    reason 1: _____

    reason 2: _____

3. proposition: The film that won this year's Academy Award for "Best Picture" deserved it.

    reason 1: _____

    reason 2: _____

4. proposition: Limiting sales of liquor to those over 21 is a bad law.

    reason 1: _____

    reason 2: _____

5. proposition: Television advertisements for _____ are very effective.

    reason 1: _____

    reason 2: _____

6. proposition: A major in _____ is a ticket to a comfortable living.

    reason 1: _____

    reason 2: _____

7. proposition: Friendships formed in youth are more significant than those formed later.

    reason 1: _____

    reason 2: _____

8. proposition: The best restaurant in town for a casual meal is _____.

    reason 1: _____

    reason 2: _____

EXERCISE 2: defending with reasons

Rewrite the 8 propositions and reasons you used in EXERCISE 1, leaving out the connecting words at the beginning of each reason. If you are going to use any connecting words, work them into the middle of the reasons somewhere. (The word **also** might be helpful.)

1. proposition: All official information should be in both English and Spanish.

    reason 1: _____

    reason 2: _____

2. proposition: The middle child in a family is always at a disadvantage.

    reason 1: _____

    reason 2: _____

3. proposition: The film that won this year's Academy Award for "Best Picture" deserved it.

    reason 1: _____

    reason 2: _____

4. proposition: Limiting sales of liquor to those over 21 is a bad law.

    reason 1: _____

    reason 2: _____

5. proposition: Television advertisements for _____ are very effective.

    reason 1: _____

    reason 2: _____

6. proposition: A major in _____ is a ticket to a comfortable living.

    reason 1: _____

    reason 2: _____

7. proposition: Friendships formed in youth are more significant than those formed later.

    reason 1: _____

    reason 2: _____

8. proposition: The best restaurant for a casual meal in town is _____.

    reason 1: _____

    reason 2: _____

"TABLE-OF-CONTENTS" SENTENCE

To help develop your defense, try to split each reason into two or three parts. This next sentence is a sort of "table-of-contents" sentence in which you name some specific aspects of the reason.

One way to figure out the specific aspects of your defense is ask **who, what, where,** or **when.** Sometimes you can use the same question to divide both reasons. In any case, write down immediately what aspects of the reason you will be discussing in your paragraph.

To demonstrate how to proceed with the defense, one of Steve Champouillon's paragraphs is worked out in detail. Keep in mind that the second paragraph should follow the same procedure.

The student's proposition:

Introduction

Steven Champouillon would make a great bouncer.

The student's reason:

The student's "table-of-contents" sentence: (The writer asked, "**What** were Steven's physical qualities?")

Steven is physically qualified to be a bouncer. These qualifications consist of his size, strength, and ongoing training.

EXAMPLE 2: "table-of-contents" sentence following reason

proposition: Parents should not use physical force to punish their children.

reason 1: (What kind of physical damage?

Children can suffer permanent physical damage from even mild force. There is great evidence of both external and internal injuries that were caused unintentionally while parents were punishing their children.

reason 2: (When do these scars appear?)

Even if physical damage is not permanent, the emotional damage may be. Emotional scars appear while those punished are still young, and remain as they grow older.

EXERCISE 3: devising "table-of-contents" sentences

Formulate 3 propositions and defend each with 2 reasons. Then split each reason into two (or three) parts, specifying what you will be discussing within each.

1. proposition: _____

   reason 1: _____

   "content": _____

reason 2: _____

"content": _____

2. proposition: _____

reason 1: _____

"content": _____

reason 2: _____

"content": _____

3. proposition: _____

reason 1: _____

"content": _____

reason 2: _____

"content": _____

DEVELOPING THE PARAGRAPH OF DEFENSE

One way to develop the paragraph is to explain each of the two or three parts of your reason, offering illustration and other kinds of support. The work of development can be summed up in the form of the "3E" checklist:

Explanation: Explain Steven's size and its relevance to being a bouncer.

Example: Give an example or illustration.

Evidence: Offer some testimony, expert's opinion, statistics to support your argument.

You need not go through all parts of this process for each of the items in your "table of contents," nor do you always need to follow the Explanation–Example–Evidence format. But, if you construct your paragraph according to this scheme, you will have little difficulty proving your point.

EXAMPLE 1: developing through example

The student's proposition:

> **Introduction**
>
> Steven Champouillon would make a great bouncer.

The student's reason:
The student's table-of-contents" sentence:

explanation of items:

examples of contents:

explanation of relevance of reason:

evidence:

> Steven is physically qualified to be a bouncer. His qualifications consist of his size, strength, and ongoing training. Steve is six feet, six inches tall and weighs 260 pounds. I don't know how much he can lift using weights, but he played defensive guard and wrestled at the University of Iowa. He must have thrown some weight around then! Steven currently keeps in shape by lifting weights and by practicing karate three times a week. A bouncer needs to be bigger and stronger than the customers in a bar, otherwise he couldn't break up any trouble. Steve's physical qualities give him an edge because he is bigger and stronger. He is better equipped to defend himself and to handle others when force is necessary. Fred Rogers, assistant manager of the Sugar Mill, says about Steve, "When push comes to shove, Steve is one of the best bouncers we have ever had."

Steven develops his paragraph by various methods; **example** or **illustration** is probably his most obvious approach. You can also develop your paragraph by one of the other traditional approaches. You might present a **narrative** by way of example or explanation. You might wish to use **comparison and/or contrast** to explain or to present as evidence. You might offer and analyze statistics as part of your development. This process of development has been called **cubing** because it essentially multiplies the original reason many times by explaining it, comparing it, and associating it with similar items. Here are illustrations of two approaches, still using Steve's proposition and reason:

EXAMPLE 2: developing through narration

> Introduction
>
> Steven Champouillon would make a great bouncer.

The student's reason:
The student's "table-of-contents" sentence:

developing through narration:

> Steven is physically qualified to be a bouncer. His qualifications consist of his size and strength. He has displayed both while doing his job as only he knows best at Sugar Mill. Last year, members of the Lancers, a local semi-pro football team, came in to celebrate a victory. When two of the linemen became rowdy with the barmaid, Steve jumped into action. Towering over both of them, he grabbed arms, legs, and anything else his large fists could handle and hustled the 275+ pounders out of there. Once outside, he knocked their heads together until they were quiet. Then he lifted them as if they were cordwood and stacked them in their van. Obviously, he has the size and strength to handle the bouncer chores anywhere.

EXAMPLE 3: developing through comparison/contrast

> Introduction
>
> Steven Champouillon would make a great bouncer.

The student's reason:
The student's "table-of-contents" sentence:
developing through comparison/contrast:

> Steven is physically qualified to be a bouncer. His qualifications consist of his size and strength. Although he has never worked as a bouncer, he has done other work that requires great size and strength. When he worked at Agway Construction, he had to lift and carry 6-foot-long metal pipes used in sewer construction. The pipes were the width of people. If you had seen Steven handling one of these pipes, you could easily imagine him carrying a disorderly person out of a bar. He would pick that person up and encircle him just the way he did those heavy pipes. Can you imagine a person without his strength and reach trying to handle a drunken, uncooperative customer? Those arms and shoulders that handled man-sized pipes that weighed over 200 pounds can manage full-sized people equally well.

Whatever the particular method you use for development, the **proposition and defense** approach should provide a basic organizational scheme, and the **reason + table-of-contents** format provides one effective way of developing your ideas.

Types of Introductions and Endings

Although your reader will read your introduction first and your ending last, you do not need to write your essay in that order. You need to know the content of your essay before you can choose the best type of introduction and ending. Once you have worked out the **body** of the essay, you can decide which of the various approaches in introductions and endings would help make your essay even better.

Introduction

purpose: to inform
    a. define terms that appear in essay
    b. give historical background
    c. give immediate (recent) background
    d. (in longer essays) preview how you will argue your thesis.

purpose: to interest
    e. tell an amusing story or anecdote
    f. connect it to some current event or item of interest

Proposition

First Reason in Support of Proposition

Second Reason in Support of Proposition

Ending

a. offer a solution to a problem described in your essay
b. predict the future of the issue you discussed in your paper
c. call for action regarding your thesis—what can people do if they want to act, find information, protest, or support?
d. complete or add to a story you began in the introduction to provide a "frame" around essay
e. admit to a minor opposition to your argument and refute it
f. briefly mention some minor arguments you did not use in defense
g. (in long essay) summarize the main points of your defense

Remember that the best introductions and endings are those that best fit the essay you have written. If you were trying to prove how "girning" is worthwhile because it improves your mental and physical well-being, your most appropriate way of introducing your thesis would not be to tell an amusing story. Rather, you must define "girning" to enable your audience to follow your argument more easily. Similarly, summarizing your main points in the conclusion of a short two-paragraph essay, will probably not help your cause very much. After all, you have just finished proving your point in greater detail and the information is fresh in your reader's mind. Instead, you would help your essay more by choosing a different type of ending: predicting the future, for example, in an essay that discussed the best VCR or CD currently available. In looking toward future advances, you aid your essay by indirectly pointing out how the VCR or CD you have discussed anticipates these developments.

The next two essays adopt the structure we have discussed in Chapters 50 and 51. They were written at various points during the semester and contain notations by the instructor regarding mechanical errors, noting how they correspond to the chapters in the text. The development in the first essay is primarily by example or illustration; in the second it is by narrative.

NOTE: The essay by Joe Losardo, "My Sister," was written halfway through the semester in a noncredit English composition course. The topic was "controlled" to the extent that it elicited the **'s**, Mr. Losardo's specific area of weakness. After checking for organization and development, he had to pay special attention to possible omissions of the apostrophe by underlining each **s** ending on a noun followed by another noun (see Chapter 30).

MY SISTER

My sister resembles my father's side of the family.

First of all, Theresa resembles the people on her fa-

Chapter 13

ther's side physically. Her facial features and her body structure is completely Losardo. She has high cheekbones and a beauty mark on her left cheek. A few of the women in my family have the same beauty mark and in the same spot. She also has her father's dark hair and very thick eyebrows. In her body structure she is very tall. In fact, she is the tallest girl in her grade. My father was also the tallest in his class when he was Theresa's age. She also has large bones like all the Losardos, but her weight is only medium.

Another way Theresa takes after my father's side is that she has the same coloration that people on that side have. Her skin and her eyes are similar to the skin and eyes of her aunts, uncles, and grandparents on her father's side. Her dark skin coloration is one of her most beautiful features. It is almost like a year-round Coppertone tan. This is very appealing to everyone. The feature of dark skin is a trademark of the Losardo family. Many people who know our family think Theresa is the daughter of our Aunt Beth. This is because their skin color is so similar. The same thing is true of her eyes. Theresa has shiny, dark brown eyes. They are very beautiful. They look just like puppy dog eyes. These are very innocent looking eyes. As I've mentioned before, this is also a trademark feature of the Losardo family.

NOTE: The essay by Don Ambrose was the exit exam for the noncredit course. Because his persistent problem had been the comma splice, he was asked to proofread each comma situation, asking himself if he might need a conjunction to join the sentences (see Chapter 26). Although by departmental standards this was considered a passing essay, the errors in mechanics were called to the student's attention, with suggestions for continued work in the textbook and in the Writing Skills Center.

MY PARADISE

I consider the island of Kawai a paradise.

One thing that makes this island like paradise is the vegetation. Whether it grows wild or not, the vegetation is really lush. I found this out when I recently visited three of the Hawaiian islands. They were all alive with vegetation. We took a bus tour of the island of Kawai and Chapter 47 stoped to have lunch on a cliff that was covered with Chapter 37 beautiful red flowers. As we were eating their, the bus driver spoke about the other growing things. He talked about the "palm trees swaying in the trade winds," and he also said that the the entire island was like a palm tree and "as warm as the red poppies you see here." He explained to us that the rich vegetation was because Ka- Chapter 45 wai recieves more rain in a year than any other place on earth. On the way back to the hotel we passed sugar cane fields, more palm trees, banana trees, and we saw more beautiful flowers. I am sure that Paradise could not have Chapter 40 more or prettier things growing in it then Kawai.

My second reason for thinking of this place as a paradise has to do with the waters that surround the island. They are clear and yet rich in color at the same time. One morning, my wife and I took a walk on the white sands of the beach right after it had rained. Off to my left was the most breath-taking rainbow we had ever seen. The colors were pouring into the ocean, and this was just the beginning. The rainbow made us feel as if the sky was feeding its vibrant colors into the water. The next day we set out on a snorkeling cruise. We reached our destination and set out to discover the colors of a coral reef, and we were struck again by the ocean's colors. We had to be in twenty feet of water, but it was as clear as swimming pool water. The only difference was in all the colors of the tropical fis_h_, re_d_, yello_w_, and black and yellow. Also, the color of the reef itself was breathtaki_ng_, all pin_k_, blac_k, and_ white. Altogeth_er_, the waters that surround the island of Kawai are jumping with color and life. I think that is why I consider it a paradise.

The Instructor's Manual follows a semester's activity and offers additional exercises and answers.

Appendix 1: THE DICTIONARY AS HANDBOOK

The dictionary is not only a handy reference tool for spelling, definitions, pronunciation, and even the origin of words, but also a convenient source for information regarding grammar and usage. As the examples will illustrate, the entries can be extremely helpful for writers.

grass•y (grăs′ē, gräs′ē) *adj.* **-ier, -iest. 1.** Covered with or abounding in grass. **2.** Resembling or suggestive of grass, as in color or odor.

grate¹ (grāt) *v.* **grated, grating, grates.** —*tr.* **1.** To reduce to fragments, shreds, or powder by rubbing against an abrasive surface: *grate cabbage.* **2.** To cause to make a harsh grinding or rasping sound through friction: *grate one's teeth.* **3.** To irritate or annoy persistently. **4.** *Archaic.* To rub or wear away. —*intr.* **1.** To make a harsh rasping sound by or as if by scraping or grinding. **2.** To cause irritation or annoyance. Used with *on: grate on one's nerves.* —*n.* A harsh rasping sound made by scraping or rubbing: *the grate of a key in a lock* [Middle English *graten,* from Old French *grater,* to scrape, from Germanic. See **grat-** in Appendix*]

grate² (grāt) *n.* **1.** A framework of parallel or latticed bars for blocking an opening; a grill: *a grate over a storm sewer.* **2.** Such a framework of metal, used to hold the fuel in a stove, furnace, or fireplace. **3.** A fireplace. **4.** A perforated iron plate or screen for sieving and grading crushed ore. —*tr.v.* **grated, grating, grates.** To equip with a grate. [Middle English, from Old French, grille, from Vulgar Latin *grata* (unattested), variant of Latin *crātis,* frame, wicker basket. See **kert-** in Appendix*]

grate•ful (grāt′fəl) *adj.* **1.** Appreciative of benefits received: thankful. **2.** Expressing gratitude. **3.** Affording pleasure or comfort; agreeable; satisfying: *"he left his home to enjoy the grateful air"* (Ronald Firbank). [From obsolete *grate,* agreeable, thankful, from Latin *grātus,* pleasing, favorable. See **gwere-¹** in Appendix.*] —**grate′ful•ly** *adv.* —**grate′ful•ness** *n.*

grat•er (grā′tər) *n.* **1.** One that grates. **2.** An implement with rough or sharp-edged slits and perforations on which to shred or grate foods.

grat•i•fi•ca•tion (grăt′ə-fi-kā′shən) *n.* **1.** The act of gratifying. **2.** The condition of being gratified; satisfaction; pleasure. **3.** An instance or cause of gratification. **4.** *Archaic.* A reward; gratuity; bonus.

grat•i•fy (grăt′ə-fī′) *tr.v.* **-fied, -fying, -fies. 1.** To please or satisfy: *His achievement gratified his father.* **2.** To indulge; to humor: *"I shall perhaps not a little gratify my own vanity."* (Franklin). **3.** *Archaic.* To requite: to reward. [Middle English *gratifien,* to favor, from Old French, from Latin *grātificārī,* to reward, do favor to, from *grātus,* favorable, pleasurable. See **gwere-¹** in Appendix.*] —**grat′i•fi′er** *n.*

grat•ing¹ (grā′tǐng) *adj.* **1.** Rasping or scraping in sound. **2.** Nerve-racking; irritating. —**grat′ing•ly** *adv.*

grat•ing² (grā′tǐng) *n.* **1.** A grill or network of bars set in a window or door or used as a partition; lattice; grate. **2.** *Physics.* **Diffraction grating** (see).

grat•i•tude (grăt′ə-tōō′, -tyōōd′) *n.* An appreciative awareness and thankfulness, as for kindness shown or something received. [Middle English, from Old French, from Medieval Latin *grātitūdō,* from *grātus,* favorable. See **gratify.**]

gra•tu•i•tous (grə-tōō′ə-təs, -tyōō′ə-təs) *adj.* **1.** Given or granted without return or recompense: unearned. **2.** Given or received without cost or obligation; free; gratis. **3.** Unnecessary or unwarranted; unjustified: *gratuitous criticism.* [Latin *grātuītus,* given as a favor, from *grātus,* favorable, pleasing. See **gratify.**] —**gra•tu′i•tous•ly** *adv.* —**gra•tu′i•tous•ness** *n.*

gra•tu•i•ty (grə-tōō′ə-tē, -tyōō′ə-tē) *n., pl.* **-ties.** A material favor or gift, usually in the form of money, given in return for service; a tip. See Synonyms at **bonus.** [Old French *gratuite,* from Medieval Latin *grātuītās,* present, gift, from Latin *grātuītus.* given free. GRATUITOUS.]

1. *information about endings on verbs:* The **v.** after **grate¹** indicates that, as defined here, the word is a verb. As such, the **v.** is followed immediately by three forms of the verb: the past tense **(grated),** the present participle **(grating),** and the third-person singular **(grates).** Pocket dictionaries, in an attempt to save space, may omit these forms of the verb when they are not unusual. That is, if the verb is "regular," taking **-ed, -ing,** and **-s** to indicate its forms, there will be no listing. However, if the forms are unusual, even pocket dictionaries will list them. As you work on Unit IV: Problems with Verbs (tenses), look to your dictionary for forms of the verb with which you are not familiar.

2. *information about endings on nouns:* The **n.** after **grate²** indicates that the word is now defined as a noun. That there is no listing of the plural form of the word means that it is formed with the addition of an **-s.** Notice that when the plural ending changes the word in any way, as with **gratuity**, the **n.** is followed by **pl.** for plural, and then the special form: **-ties**, indicating that the plural form of **gratuity** is **gratuities.** You may find this information helpful when you work in Unit II: Problems with Nouns and Pronouns.

3. *information about endings on adjectives:* The **adj.** after **grassy** identifies the word as an adjective. As such, the dictionary entry continues with the comparative (**-ier** $\longrightarrow$ grassier) and the superlative (**-iest** $\longrightarrow$ grassiest) forms of the word. By contrast, the absence of this information after the adjective **gratuitous** informs the reader that the comparative form would be **more** and the superlative **most.**

4. *information about other forms of the word:* The end of the entry for the adjective **grateful** lists other words that use **grateful** as their root and identifies the part of speech for each: **gratefully** is an adverb, **gratefulness** a noun.

5. *information about usage:* Because some definitions of a word are less well known than others, or because a word is often confused, a dictionary entry may use the word in a sentence to help demonstrate its use. Notice the sample sentences in the entry for **gratify** and the sample phrases in the entries for **grate¹** and **grate².** You may wish to refer to this function of the dictionary when you work in Unit VII Proofreading for Confusing Terms.

Appendix 2: PRINCIPAL PARTS OF COMMON IRREGULAR VERBS

Present	Past	Past Participle
arise	arose	arisen
be (am, is are)	was, were	been
awake	awoke	awakened
bear	bore	born
bear	bore	borne
beat	beat	beaten
become	became	become
befall	befell	befallen
begin	began	begun
behold	beheld	beheld
bend	bent	bent
bet	bet	bet
bid	bade	bidden
bind	bound	bound
bite	bit	bitten
bleed	bled	bled
blow	blew	blown
break	broke	broken
breed	bred	bred
bring	brought	brought
build	built	built
burn	burnt, burned	burnt, burned
burst	burst	burst
buy	bought	bought
cast	cast	cast
catch	caught	caught
choose	chose	chosen
cling	clung	clung
clothe	clothed, clad	clothed, clad
come	came	come
cost	cost	cost
creep	crept	crept
cut	cut	cut
dare	dared	dared
deal	dealt	dealt
dig	dug	dug
dive	dived (dove)	dived
do	did	done

Present	Past	Past Participle
draw	drew	drawn
dream	dreamed	dreamed
drink	drank	drunk
drive	drove	driven
eat	ate	eaten
fall	fell	fallen
feed	fed	fed
feel	felt	felt
fight	fought	fought
find	found	found
flee	fled	fled
fling	flung	flung
fly	flew	flown
forbear	forbore	forborne
forbid	forbade	forbidden
foresee	foresaw	foreseen
foretell	foretold	foretold
forget	forgot	forgotten
forgive	forgave	forgiven
forsake	forsook	forsaken
freeze	froze	frozen
get	got	got
give	gave	given
go	went	gone
grind	ground	ground
grow	grew	grown
hang	hung	hung
have	had	had
hear	heard	heard
hide	hid	hidden
hit	hit	hit
hold	held	held
hurt	hurt	hurt
keep	kept	kept
kneel	knelt	knelt
knit	knit, knitted	knit, knitted
know	knew	known
lay	laid	laid
lead	led	led
leap	leapt, leaped	leapt, leaped
leave	left	left
lend	lent	lent
let	let	let
lie	lay	lain
light	lit	lit
lose	lost	lost
make	made	made
mean	meant	meant
meet	met	met

Present	Past	Past Participle
mistake	mistook	mistaken
mow	mowed	mown, mowed
pay	paid	paid
put	put	put
quit	quit	quit
raise	raised	raised
read	read	read
rid	rid, ridded	rid, ridded
ride	rode	ridden
ring	rang	rung
rise	rose	risen
run	ran	run
saw	sawed	sawn, sawed
say	said	said
see	saw	seen
seek	sought	sought
sell	sold	sold
send	sent	sent
set	set	set
shake	shook	shaken
shape	shaped	shapen, shaped
shave	shaved	shaven
shed	shed	shed
shine	shone	shone
shoe	shod	shod
shoot	shot	shot
show	showed	shown
shred	shred	shred
shrink	shrank	shrunk
shut	shut	shut
sing	sang	sung
sink	sank	sunk
sit	sat	sat
slay	slew	slain
sleep	slept	slept
slide	slid	slid
sling	slung	slung
slit	slit	slit
smell	smelt, smelled	smelt, smelled
sow	sowed	sown
speak	spoke	spoken
speed	sped	sped
spell	spelled	spelled
spend	spent	spent
spill	spilled	spilled
spin	spun	spun
spit	spat	spit, spat
spoil	spoiled	spoiled
split	split	split

Present	Past	Past Participle
spread	spread	spread
spring	sprang	sprung
stand	stood	stood
steal	stole	stolen
stick	stuck	stuck
sting	stung	stung
stink	stank	stunk
stride	strode	stridden
strike	struck	struck
string	strung	strung
strive	strove, strived	striven, strived
swear	swore	sworn
sweat	sweat, sweated	sweat, sweated
sweep	swept	swept
swell	swelled	swollen, swelled
swim	swam	swum
swing	swung	swung
take	took	taken
teach	taught	taught
tear	tore	torn
tell	told	told
think	thought	thought
throw	threw	thrown
thrust	thrust	thrust
tread	trod	trodden, trod
understand	understood	understood
undertake	undertook	undertaken
undo	undid	undone
uphold	unheld	unheld
upset	upset	upset
wake	woke	woke
wear	wore	worn
weave	wove	woven
wed	wed	wed
weep	wept	wept
wet	wet	wet
win	won	won
wind	wound	wound
withdraw	withdrew	withdrawn
withhold	withheld	withheld
withstand	withstood	withstood
wring	wrung	wrung
write	wrote	written

Appendix 3: ANSWERS TO ATTENTION FOCUSING EXERCISES AND TO REWRITING EXERCISE 1; SELECTIONS FOR REWRITING EXERCISE 2

CHAPTER 1: locating the verb

p. 4: My weight will be over 180. is —→ will be p. 5.: sentence b. will dismiss p. 5: The weight loss has inspired me. inspired. has inspired. inspired.

Practice 1, p. 6

1. were invented 2. opened 3. measured 4. provided 5. kept 6. has taken hold 7. have grown 8. will do

Practice 2, p. 7

1. To 3. to avoid, to change 4. to do 6. to finish, to zip 7. to 8. to decrease, to spend 9. to recover

Practice 3, p. 8

1. sentence 3 (main verb—is able) 2. sentence 4 (has) 3. sentence 7 (are reduced) 4. sentence 8 (serves)

CHAPTER 2: locating the subject

Practice 1, p. 11

2. I 3. The coach 4. What has become a problem? 5. Who think(s) of food all day? I

Practice 2: p. 11

1. *verb*—were invented, *subject*—Drive-in movies 2. opened—Hollingshead and Smith 3. measured—huge screen 4. provided—Watching from cars 5. kept—It 6. has taken hold—the idea 7. have grown—Drive-in restaurants, banks, even churches 8. will do—American drivers

CHAPTER 3: the articles *a/an*

Attention Focusing, p. 19

a + word: 1. a fisherman 3. a bite 4. a small man, a bent back 5. a priest's, a hundred 6. a greenish 8. a second 9. a tattered, a yellowish
an + word: 2. an island 2. an earth hut, an old man 7. an angel's

Rewriting 1, pp. 21

1. An American 2. A Japanese 3. A Greek 4. an Iraqi 5. an Angolan 6. An African 8. an Englishman 9. an American

CHAPTER 4: singular personal pronouns

Attention Focusing, p. 26

referring to Dr. Zaldivar: 1. he 2. He 3. He 4. he 5. his, him 6. he 7. him 8. He 9. he, his /*referring to Sarita:* 6. she 7. her, she 8. she, herself 9. She

Rewriting 1, pp. 28

5. Its 6. Its 7. it, it 8. It 11. its 12. It, it 13. it, its 14. it 15. it, it 16. it 17. its, it, itself

Rewriting 2, pp. 29

(change) 3. They, their 4. They 5. they, their, 7. Their 9. They

Attention Focusing (indefinite) p. 31

a. (1) his (2) He b. (5) He c. (9) He, he (10) His d. (4) each, him (13) Each,

CHAPTER 5: forming plurals

Attention Focusing, p. 37

1. roses—a rose 2. cows—a cow 3. moths—a moth 4. footprints—a footprint, deeds—a deed 5. knives—a knife 6. roosters—a rooster 7. folds—a fold

Rewriting 1, p. 39

1. monkeys, tigers, elephants, cockatoos 2. coyotes 3. raccoons 5. falcons 6. falcons, pigeons

Rewriting 2, p. 39

(change) 1. chicken, pepper 2. tablespoon 3. pinch, pinch 4. cup, cup, cup, onion 5. chicken 6. tablespoon, pinch, pinch 8. (chicken) 9. onion, pepper, can, cup, cup 10. (chicken)

CHAPTER 6: plural pronouns

Attention Focusing, p. 44

referring to **minors** a. (2) their (3) their (4) them (5) They, themselves/b. (8) they (9) them (10) them, *refer to* **gestures**

Rewriting 1, p. 46

1. their 4. They 5. they, themselves, their 7. They, their, their 8. their, they 9. their, they, they 12. They, they 14. their

Rewriting 2, p. 47

(change) 2. it 3. It 4. it, it 5. it, itself 6. it 8. It, it, it, it 9. Its, its, itself 10. creation 11. it

Attention Focusing (indefinite) p. 49

a. many b. many, some, c. wife and child d. criminals e. some, most

CHAPTER 7: pronoun consistency

Attention Focusing, p. 54

first person—6, 8, 8, 9, 10/second person—1, 2/third person—5, 5, 10, 11

Rewriting 1, p. 56

1. people, they 4. people 5. they, they 6. they, they 7. they 8. they, they 9. they, they 10. they, they 11. they, they 12. they, their, they

Rewriting 2, p. 57

(change) 5. We 6. We 7. We, we 8. Our 9. We 10. our

CHAPTER 8: subject-verb agreement (singulars)

Attention Focusing, p. 67

1. a man—knows 2. stubbornness—indicates 3. He—does not consider 4. He—bends 5. A tree—snaps 6. a sailor—slackens 7. A (wise) man—puts 8. He—hears

Rewriting 1, p. 68

1. Mrs. Carton—works, gives 2. She—retouches, she—makes 3. She—performs 5. She—obliges 6. She—has 7. She—obliterates 8. She—turns, she—transforms 9. She—advises 10. She—is

Rewriting 2, p. 69

(subject—verb) 1. Handbook—attempted 2. It—provided 3. One entry—designated 4. Another tidbit—pronounced 5. the book—revealed 6. it—identified 7. It—listed 8. the book—awarded 9. The author—believed

CHAPTER 9: subject-verb agreement (plurals)

Attention Focusing, p. 74

1. we—live (pl.) 2. we—do (pl.) 3. We—live (pl.) 4. Bears—retire (pl.) 5. They—remain (pl.) 6. they—stroll (pl.) 7. Being invisible—does 8. Living (in holes)—does 9. We—hibernate (pl.) 10. we—have (pl.)

Rewriting 1, p. 75

2. the spades—represent 3. they—stand 6. spades—have 7. hearts—symbolize 9. hearts—transform—themselves—cups, they—represent 10. diamonds—evoke—precious gems, they—refer 11. diamonds—have 12. Clubs—look—clubs 14. Clubs—lose

Rewriting 2, p. 76

(change) 1. a female—differentiates—a male 2. a female—performs—she—is *(correct but not necessary to change adjectives)* 3. a female—has 4. a female—ties—a female 6. a woman—receives 7. She—sniffs 8. She—chooses 9. a woman 10. a woman—was

CHAPTER 10: the verb *to be*

Attention Focusing, p. 82

1. Memo—was (sing.) 2. she—was (sing.) 3. roll—was (sing.) 4. three C notes—were (pl.) 6. He and Memo—were (pl.) 8. bookie—was (sing.) 9. eyes—were (pl.) 10. eye—was (sing.), one—was (sing.)

Rewriting 1, p. 83

2. Vesta Tilley—a male impersonator 3. her parents—were, Tilley—was involved 4. She—appeared 5. she—was determined, to her 6. Tilley—was forced 7. she—was so successful, accept her 8. Tilley—was, her soldier 9. She—was convincing 10. Tilley—was often impish 12. Tilley—was 13. she—felt, her, her,

Rewriting 2: p. 84

(change) 1. A dwarf—is 2. My 3. I—am 4. My 5. I—am, I—am 6. I—am—I 7. I—was 8. me 9. I—was 10. I—was 11. I—was—I 12. I 13. I—was—I—I—was 14. I—am, I

CHAPTER 11: intervening elements

ATTENTION FOCUSING, p. 91

1. Research—indicates (S) 2. A job—contributes (S) 3. The professors—think (P) 4. Women—do (P) 5. Fewer cases—were (P) 6. a woman—suffers (S) 7. Appetite loss—occurs (S) 8. two health organizations—have (P) 9. recommendation—was (S) 10. The first step—should (S) 11. The action—forces (S)

Rewriting 1, p. 92

(singular) 3, 6, 10, 11, 12, 13; *(plural)* 5

Rewriting 2, p. 93

intervening phrases in 3, 4, 5, 6, 7, 8, 10, 11, 12, 13

CHAPTER 12: verb before subject

Attention Focusing, p. 103

1. INV—P 2. INV—S 3. INV—S 7. INV—P 9. INV—S

Rewriting 1, p. 104

2. There is an account 3. There was no instance 5. leave as is 7. leave as is 8. Nor was the result 9. leave as is 11. There is no official document

Rewriting 2, p. 105

(change) 5. There is a variation 6. There is . . . an equal amount 7. does a dieter 12. Does a pat of butter 17. There is . . . some benefit 18. There is no opportunity

CHAPTER 13: special problems in agreement

Attention Focusing, p. 115

1. collective noun—singular 3. compound subject—plural 5. indefinite pronoun—singular 7. collective noun—plural 8. title—singular 9. indefinite pronoun—singular 11. compound subject—plural 12. collective noun—singular 13. (could be considered collective noun—singular) 14. indefinite pronoun—plural 15. compound subject—plural

Rewriting 1, p. 116

2. The Searle Company manufactures, has 3. The Searle Company claims 4. It dismisses 5. It does not 6. The Searle Company rejects, its 7. it argues 8. It doubts 9. Its 10. its, the Searle Company claims 12. The Searle Company polices itself 13. The Searle Company 14. The Searle Company, itself 15. The Searle Company is, itself

Rewriting 2, p. 117

(change) 1. Washington, New York, it 2. New York was, Washington 3. New York was, Washington 4. Washington 5. New York was, was unable, Washington from scoring 7. New York was 8. It 9. It 10. New York remains, it

CHAPTER 14: the present tense

Attention Focusing, p. 131

1. buries *(present)* 2. is *(present)* 3. were 4. lived 5. hid 6. kept 7. could 8. do (not) need *(present)* 9. are born *(present)* 10. remains *(present)* 11. covers *(present)*

Rewriting 1, p. 134

1. is 2. sees—resolves 3. makes 4. seems—touches 5. falls 6. caresses—gives 7. clothes—places—hangs 8. places—puts 9. attends 10. stands—prays—calls 11. hears—grants 12. causes 13. returns—goes 14. kisses, is 15. rises 16. blesses 17. uses—uses

Rewriting 2, p. 134

(change) 1. described 2. demonstrated 3. was 4. convinced 5. desired 6. was—forced 7. was—burdened 8. illustrated 9. married—disappeared 10. married—was 11. returned 12. lived—was 13. moved—lived—returned 14. forced 15. gained—was—was 16. encountered 17. repented—resolved 18. escaped—accepted 19. settled

CHAPTER 15: the past tense *(ed)*

Attention Focusing, p. 140

1. turned 2. leaned 3. batted—sprinted 4. grabbed—immobilized—passed 5. pushed, waited 6. merged

Rewriting 1, p. 142

1. looked 2. walked 3. waited—watched 4. continued 5. depended 6. surrounded 7. rested 8. snuggled 9. concealed 10. rested 11. utilized 12. offered—photographed 13. operated 14. registered 15. analyzed—calculated 16. notified 17. placed 18. amounted—switched

Rewriting 2, p. 143

(change) 1. prefers 2. plant 3. fails 4. neglects 5. denies 6. search 7. locate 8. jam—mail 9. selects

CHAPTER 16: the past tense (irregular)

Attention Focusing, p. 148

1. saw (irreg.) 2. turned 3. wore (irreg.) 4. held (irreg.) 5. pointed 6. froze (irreg.) 7. stood (irreg.) 8. felt (irreg.) 9. looked 10. said (irreg.)

Rewriting 1, p. 149

1. was 2. was 3. kept 4. made 5. kept 6. let 7. had 8. were—was 9. set 10. became 11. was—was—flew 12. drew 13. made 14. stuck 15. was 16. said

Rewriting 2, p. 151

(change) 1. will set 2. will take—make 3. will come 4. will become—will break—will go 5. will find—will sell 6. will find 7. will make 8. will leave 9. will send

CHAPTER 17: the future tense

Attention Focusing, p. 157

will shows the future in sentences 1, 4, 5, 6, 8, 9 / *other words that indicate future:* 7. might 10. going to 11. going to

Rewriting 1, p. 159

1. will reject 2. will relax 3. will not use 4. will be 5. will have 6. will just have 7. will be cut 8. will depend, will be 9. will be

CHAPTER 18: the progressives

Attention Focusing, p. 164

1. are expecting (present progressive) 2. are waiting (pres. prog.) 5. was writing (past progressive) 6. was being shaped (past prog.) 10. was struggling (past prog.)

Rewriting, 1, p. 167

1. were washing—were not using 4. were beating and scraping—were making 5. were making 6. were using 8. were importing—were making 10. were not making

Rewriting 2, p. 167

(change) 1. expected, led 2. found 3, got 4. scored—moved 5. scored—combined 6. continue

CHAPTER 19: the perfect tenses

Attention Focusing, p. 172

1. have done 2. have spent 5. has . . . talked / a. (4) had . . . shown b. (7) had quit c. (8) had died

Rewriting 1, p. 175

1. had received 2. had applied 3. had not 4. has landed—have yanked 5. has developed 6. has been 7. has not been 8. had . . . been rejected 9. had tried 11. had been given 12. has declared

Rewriting 2, p. 176

(change) 1. found 2. revealed 3. showed 4. has shown 5. has been 6. existed 7. indicates 9. shows

CHAPTER 20: consistency in tense

Attention Focusing, p. 180

1. is (present) 2. was (past) 3. announced—planned—was criticized (past) 4. came (past) 5. was—started (past) 6. came (past)—capitalizes (present) 7. were followed—(past)—calls (present) 8. followed (past) 9. began—described (past) 10. saw (past)—appears (present) 11. is (present)—will see (future) 12. await (present)

Exercise 1, p. 182

1. present 2. past 3. present 4. present 5. present 6. past 7. future

CHAPTER 21: dependent-word fragments

Attention Focusing, p. 190

1. while 2. before 3. Before 4. that 5. because 6. when 7. that 8. once 9. After 10. as if

Rewriting 1, p. 192

1. if 2. just as 3. if 4. whenever 5. although 6. because

Rewriting 2, p. 193

combine sentences 1 and 2 with **if**, 4 and 5 with **when**, 6 and 7 with **if** or **when**, 9 and 10 with **although**

CHAPTER 22: added-detail fragments

Attention Focusing, p. 198

3. clause after **daikon** 4. clause after **bean sprouts** 5. clause after **tofu** 8. clause after **noodle** 9. phrase after **leaves** 11. clause after **mushrooms** 12. phrase after **kelp** 13. phrase after **mutsu apple**

Rewriting 1, p. 200

combine sentences 3 and 4 with **who**, 5 and 6 with **that**, 8 and 9 with **which**, 11 and 12 with **which**, 14 and 15 with **who**

Rewriting 2, p. 201

begin new sentences with 1. They or Smells 3. It or A skunk 5. It or Earth 7. It or An odor 10. They or Smells

CHAPTER 23: missing-subject fragments

Attention Focusing, p. 206

1. We—people 2. It—*is . . . game.* 3. Cooties—*can . . . time.* 4. child—he or she 5. The child—*may add . . . backs."* 6. Children—*mark . . . Marker.* 7. They—*play . . . playground.* 8. A child—he or she 9. A smart alec—*will watch . . . class.* 10. The next person—everyone

Rewriting 1, p. 209

(Book Review 1) 2. It defines 3. It also points out *(Book Review 2)* 3. The book examines 4. It suggests 5. It traces 6. The book was

Rewriting 2, p. 210

make new sentences out of phrases after these coordinators: 1. and 2. and 3. but 4. and 5. and 6. and

CHAPTER 24: *ing* fragments

Attention Focusing, p. 215

4. phrase beginning with **capping** 5. phrase with **heralding** 6. phrase with **changing** 7. phrase with **making** 8. phrase with **enabling**

Rewriting 2, p. 218

cross out: 2. It 4. Leverage 6. A contract 10. The result 13. The sellers / *make participles out of:* 2. makes 4. uses 6. requires 10. translates 13. lose

CHAPTER 25: *to* fragments

Attention Focusing, p. 223

1. phrase beginning with **to walk** 2. phrase with **to the level** 3. to his left, phrase with **to sight** 6. to the batboy 7. phrase with **to repeat** 8. phrase with **to find** 9. phrase with to **please** 11. to delay the game

Rewriting 1, p. 225

1. To prove herself, Liza often took dares. 3. To see if she could get away with it, she stole something each day from her friends' rooms. 5. To annoy them, Liza continued stealing. 7. To keep her from stealing . . . they grounded her.

Rewriting 2, p. 225

ing phrases following commas in: 2. giving 4. racing . . . or meandering 6. augering 8. pushing 9. imagining

CHAPTER 26: problems with comma splices

Attention Focusing, p. 230

3. **comma** and **but**—new sentence begins with **They** 5. **comma** and **yet**—new sentence begins with **Grapes** 6. **comma** and **and**—new sentence begins with **They** 7. **comma** and **and**—new sentence begins with **Shallow** 8. **comma** and **and**—new sentence begins with **Grapes** 10. **comma** and but—new sentence begins with **The soils**

Rewriting 1, p. 233

1. . . . party, and 3. . . . . place, but 5. . . . shaken, and 9. . . . talk, and 12. . . . tell, but 14. . . . . shake, and

CHAPTER 27: problems with fused sentences

Attention Focusing, p. 239

1. The union called a strike, **but** it had no choice. 2. Trash piles lined the street, **and** some were as high as twenty feet. 3. A state of emergency was declared by the mayor; she had to do it. 4. A settlement was finally reached, **but** the memories remained. 5. **Because** many flies still remain, **I** think that another strike is possible.

Rewriting 1, p. 242

1. . . . sale, but not many people . . . 2. Because the items . . . Forces, they are sold. . . . 3. Although the goods . . . worth, they are *or* . . . worth, but . . . 4. . . . anyway; they . . . 5. . . . equipment, including old TV sets. 6. . . . Africa, but this was . . . 7. . . . DRMA office that is listed *or* office, listed

CHAPTER 28: consistency in phrasing

Attention Focusing, p. 247

2. told me/instructed me 3. Having doubts/not wanting 4. verified/told 5. a coupon book/free service/deep discounts 6. $200 worth/three/a free/twelve 7. equal/lesser 8. some restaurants/other restaurants 9. Health spas/golf clubs/bowling alleys—free games/membership discounts/two-for-one offers 10. coupon book/free camera—camera/coupons—film/development 11. All merchants/the promoter 13. hung up/called

CHAPTER 29: contractions

Attention Focusing, p. 257

2. I am 3. have not 4. they had 5. It is 6. who is 7. I am 8. could have 9. are not 10. What is 11. You are 12. That is

Rewriting 1, p. 258

(change all except **World's, O'Brian,** and **O'Brian's**) 1. World's—there's, O'Brian's 2. O'Brian's 3. he's 4. they're—permit's 5. O'Brian's—they're 6. It's 7. O'Brian—doesn't—hasn't 8. She's—there's 9. O'Brian 11. what's 12. I'll

CHAPTER 30: the possessive 's

Attention Focusing 1, p. 264

1. Gulliver-'s-travels 2. Americans-'X̶—ordeal 3. Brothers-'X̶-fairy tales 4. Nevada-'s-Senator Laxalt 5. horse-'s-mouth 6. brother-'s-keeper 7. Democrats-'X̶-convention 8. television-'s-newest star 9. Tom-'s-Cabin 10. girls-'X̶-gym 11. Mother-'s-Day (Americans, Grimm Brothers, Democrats, and girls are plural.)

Attention Focusing 2, p. 266

1. (one) husband's order 2. (one) Bluebeard's victims 5. (many) Grimm Brothers'X̶ version 6. (many) victims'X̶ lives 7. (one) tale's moral lesson 8. (one) legend's historical foundations 9. (one) Perreault's *Tales* 11. (one) tale's essential elements

Rewriting 1, p. 266

3. it→the tree's green branches 4. its→the tree's branches 5. its→the tree's greenness 6. its→the tree's branches 10. Their→The Christmas trees' 11. their→the Christmas trees'

Rewriting 2, p. 267

change all phrases in **boldface**

CHAPTER 31: capital letters

Attention Focusing, p. 281

1. (3) 2. (3) 3. (1) 4. (3) 5. (3) 6. (3) 7. (1) 8. (4) 9. (1) 10. (2) 11. (1)

Rewriting 1, p. 282

2. One hundred—thirty-three 3. Seven 5. One or A 6. one 7. Two—one or a 9. One or A, five 10. One or A 11. Two—four 12. one half or half 13. Ten

CHAPTER 32: quotation marks

Attention Focusing, p. 290

1. title 2. quotation 3. special sense 4. quotation 5. quotation 6. quotation 7. title 8. title 9. title 10. title

Rewriting 1, p. 292

1. The employer asked, "How long . . . job?" 2. The applicant said, "65 years." 3. The employer asked, "And how old are you?" 4. The applicant said, "45." 5. The employer asked, "How could you . . . old?" 6. The appliant said, "I . . . overtime."

CHAPTER 33: underlining

Attention Focusing, p. 300

1. title 3. title 5. foreign word 6. title—title 8. foreign word—title

Rewriting 1, p. 301

2. <u>Casablanca</u> 3. "Play it again, Sam." 6. "Me Tarzan, you Jane" <u>Tarzan, the Ape Man</u>—<u>Chickadee</u>—<u>The Bank Dick</u> 10. "I never drink wine"—"wine"—<u>Dracula</u>

CHAPTER 34: commas

Attention Focusing, p. 306

1. separates introductory material 2. connects (with **because**) clause to sentence 3. separates items in a series 4. separates parenthetical expression 5. separates introductory material 6. connect (with **and**) two independent clauses 7. separates parenthetical expression 8. separates parenthetical expression 9. connects (with **ing** word, phrase to sentence 10. separates quotation 11. separates quotation

Rewriting 1, p. 309

2. cure the common cold, add strength, and ward off 4. India, Japan, and West Germany 6. lead, cadmium, and mercury 7. anemia, diabetes, and arthritis 8. two small, fragrant, and fresh

CHAPTER 35: Other markers *(ed, er, est,* and *ly)*

Attention Focusing, p. 318

1. silliest—looking 2. sleek-furred—suckling 3. easily—oddest—laying—giving 4. hatching 5. heavily—hunted—relatively—slowly—moving 6. larger 7. webbed—adapted—swimming 8. funnier 9. discovered—considered—living—exhibited 10. stranger

Rewriting 1, p. 321

1. best 2. sooner—busier 3. largest 4. greatest 5. roomier

CHAPTER 36: its and it's

Attention Focusing 1 and 2, pp. 331, 333

its: 1, 5/**it's:** 2, 4, 8, 9, 11

CHAPTER 37: there and their

Attention Focusing 1 and 2, pp. 337, 338

there: 1, 3, 4, 7, 9/**their:** 1, 4, 6, 8, 9

CHAPTER 38: your and you're

Attention Focusing 1 and 2, pp. 342, 344

your: 1, 2 (twice), 3, 4 (twice), 5 (twice), 6, 8, 10, 11, 12, 13, 15
you're: 5, 6, 8, 10, 13, 15

CHAPTER 39: whose and who's

Attention Focusing 1 and 2, pp. 348, 349

whose: 1, 4, 6, 7, 10, 11/**who's:** 1, 2, 5, 8 (**who has**, not **is**), 9, 11

CHAPTER 40: then and than

Attention Focusing 1 and 2, pp. 353, 355

then: 3, 5, 9, 11/**than:** 1, 2, 6, 10

CHAPTER 41: to and too

Attention Focusing 1 and 2, pp. 359, 360

to: 1. (twice), 2. (twice), 3, 5, 6, 9, 11, 12, 13, 15./**too:** 4, 7, 8, 10 (twice), 14, 16.

CHAPTER 42: were and where

Attention Focusing 1 and 2, pp. 364, 366

were: 1, 5, 6/**where:** 2, 3, 4 (twice)

CHAPTER 43: lose and loose

Attention Focusing 1 and 2, pp. 369, 371

lose in sentences 3, 5, 8, 10/**loose** in sentences 4, 7, 10

CHAPTER 44: other confusing terms

correct sentences: accept (a), advice (a), affect (b), dessert (b), every day (a), lay (b), our (a), patients (a), threw (a), set (b), whether (b).

CHAPTER 45: common spelling patterns

Attention Focusing 1, p. 383

1. amusing 2. definition 3, preferred—facial 4. attracted—longest 5. mating—winner—shortest—fattest 8. endearing—rendered 9. counting—detracted—wrapping 11. hoping—desired 12. showing—concerned 14. separation

Attention Focusing 2, p. 384

2. varies 3. beautiful 9. flies—delicacies

Attention Focusing 3, p. 384

3. preferred—fattest—winner—wrapping

Attention Focusing 4, p. 385

1. amusing 2. definition 3. facial 5. mating 11. desired—hoping 14. separation

Attention Focusing 5, p. 385

7. family

Attention Focusing 6, p. 385

2. greatly 7. Equally—newly 8. particularly 11. essentially

Attention Focusing 7, p. 385

1. species 6. believe (10. beings) 11. achieve

Attention Focusing 8, p. 386

a. distance (in 1), appearance (in 2), emergence (in 6) b. enormous (in 1), obvious (in 6) c. logical (in 12) d. reasonable (in 5), impossible (in 6) e. apparent (in 2), excellent (in 3)

Attention Focusing 9, p. 387

4. snow-white 5. somehow 6. wet-suited

CHAPTER 46: y endings

Rewriting 1, p. 388

1. cusial 2. huzallying 3. fintiment 4. grashier 5. ollious 6. carnified 7. cassowaries 8. chalcedonies 9. zyzyphies 10. grundying 11. globbueyist 12. toroyally 13. voneys 14. drayer 15. olleyous 16. quaying 17. cloyous 18. royed 19. halleyous 20. joeys

CHAPTER 47: doubled consonants

Rewriting 1, p. 391

2. rat<u>san</u> + ing→ratsanning 4. thog<u>if</u> + er→thogiffer 6. trom + ed→trommed 7. trim + ed→trimmed 8. $\overline{\text{fit}}$ + er→fitter 12. pot + ed—potted 13. cup + ing→cupping 18. rot + ed→rotted 19. fat + en→fatten 20. grab + ing→grabbing

CHAPTER 48: the silent e

Rewriting 1, p. 394

1. wate + ing→wating 2. rate + ing→rating 3. compute + er→computer 4. thoge + er→thoger 5. thoge + ment→thogement 6. trome + able→tromable 7. trump + ed→trumped 8. fight + er→fighter 9. prate + ing→prating 10. like + able→likable 11. dare + ing→daring 12. plain + est→plainest 13. continue + ous→continuous 14. insure + ance→insurance 15. envelope + ing→enveloping 16. develop + er→developed 17. potato + es→potatoes 18l rotate + ion→rotation 19. size + able→sizable t. manage + able→manageable (exception)

CHAPTER 49: prefixes and compounds

Rewriting 1, p. 397

1. dreamboat 2. disservice 3. coordinate 4. percalde 5. folklore 6. newspaper 7. misspell 8. interracial 9. withheling 10. unnerving 11. twitterning 12, outspoken 13. enreegen 14. disagree

CHAPTER 50: the proposition

Exercise 2, p. 405: (rewritten)

1. My economics textbook, written by Samuelson, deserves (or does not) its wide use in introductory economics courses. 2. Mickey Mantle did not (or did) deserve his selection as MVP in 1956. 5. The Emmy Awards Committee was right (or wrong) to honor <u>MASH</u>. 8. Lincoln was a vigorous (or weak) president during the Civil War. 9. Could be left as is, in order to demonstrate or disprove assertion, or: The Chinese language indicates time in a sentence in a simpler (or more complicated) way than English. 10. Huey Lewis and the News should have (should not have) won the "Most Popular Group" award.

CHAPTER 51: the defense

Exercise 1, p. 408: (sample)

2. a. One disadvantage the middle child faces is a decrease in attention from parents.
   b. A second disadvantage comes from being caught between children; the older one takes advantage of him/her, while the younger one demands too much attention.

APPENDIX 4: DIAGNOSTIC TESTS

DIAGNOSTIC TEST FOR *SKILLS IN SEQUENCE*

DIRECTIONS

Each sentence in the exercise after the sample sentences contains at least one error in standard written English. In each odd-numbered sentence, the error is underlined. Each even-numbered sentence contains errors similar to those underlined in the previous sentence. When you find an error, circle it on the test sheet. Correct the error as you copy the entire sentence alongside. Then circle the correction(s) you have made. Specifically, you will have to change certain verbs, nouns, pronouns, articles, spelling, and/or punctuation marks.

SAMPLE SENTENCES WITH CORRECTIONS

1. When we went riding horses at dawn, the morning fog <u>dampens</u> our hair and made our skin tingle.

   When we went riding horses at dawn, the morning fog (dampened) our hair and made our skin tingle.

2. To our left, we ⬭see patches of wildflowers that seemed to have been shaped into a garden.

   To our left, we (saw) patches of wildflowers that seemed to be shaped into a garden.

3. Our <u>horses</u> breath rose in the ai<u>r</u> and <u>there</u> hooves hardly made a sound in the deep grass.

   Our (horses') breath rose in the air,) and (their) hooves hardly made a sound in the deep grass.

4. We could no longer hear the blare of the hotels loudspeaker and we could pretend we where dreaming.

   We could no longer hear the blare of the (hotel's) loudspeaker(s) and we could pretend we (were) dreaming.

NAME: _____

ID# : _____

DATE: _____

THE EDUCATION OF MALCOLM X (ADAPTED FROM *THE AUTOBIOGRAPHY OF MALCOLM X)*

1. Malcolm X, in his autobiography, <u>describe</u> his life in prison and how frustrated he was at not being able to express himself in <u>writting</u>.

   _____

   _____

   _____

2. He tell in it how on the street he commanded attention when he said something, but in prison, he was an ineffective and an essentialy non-functional writter.

   _____

   _____

   _____

   _____

3. <u>when</u> everyone later heard him speak or saw him on television, <u>they</u> assumed he had <u>went</u> to school far beyond the eighth grade, but this impression, Malcoln X explained, was due entirely to his studies in prison.

   _____

   _____

   _____

   _____

   _____

4. These really began back in Charlestown prison, when a friend had first make him feel envious of their knowledge.

   _____

   _____

   _____

   _____

5. The friend had always taken charge of all <u>conversation</u> he <u>been</u> in, and Malcolm <u>have</u> to try to emulate him.

   _____

   _____

   _____

6. But every book he had pick up had sentences which contained many word he did not recognized.

   _____

   _____

   _____

   _____

7. When he just skipped over those <u>word's</u>, he would end up with little idea of what the book <u>say</u>.

   _____

   _____

   _____

8. So he requested a dictionary from the prison's school, and he spend two day's riffling through it.

_____

_____

_____

9. He <u>realize they</u> contain many more <u>word</u> than he expected.

_____

_____

10. Since he did not know all of the word he needed to know, he just start to copy the first one, along with their definition.

_____

_____

_____

11. In <u>a</u> agonizingly slow_ painstakingly ragged handwriting, <u>hed</u> copy into his tablet everything, on the first page, even the punctuation marks.

_____

_____

_____

12. Then slowly carefully pronouncing each word, he'd read back to himself everything, hed written on an tablet.

_____

_____

_____

13. Looking at his own handwriting, over and over, he <u>red</u> <u>them</u> all.

_____

_____

14. Looking back on them, he remember how time-consuming the work was.

_____

_____

NAME: _____

ID# : _____

DATE: _____

15. Still, it <u>were</u> a <u>begining</u> for Malco<u>lm, he</u> went on to copy the entire dictionary.

_____
_____
_____

16. His knowledge of words began to increase, there was books he could not understand before that now were makeing sense.

_____
_____
_____
_____

17. He knew right <u>their</u> in prison that reading had forever **change a** aspect of his life.

_____
_____

18. Reading, he understand, awakens in people an long dormant craving too be mentally alive.

_____
_____
_____

19. <u>Malcolms</u> stated <u>belief</u> was that his homemade educa<u>tion</u> <u>give</u> him, with every <u>Book</u> that he read, a little bit more sensitivity to the needs of his people.

_____
_____
_____
_____

20. An English Writer once telephoned him from London to ask him where he had receive his education.

_____
_____
_____
_____

21. The answer from Malcolm X was prompt, <u>he</u> said that everything he learned <u>were</u> from "books."

_____
_____
_____

22. Of course, this education from books were not going to lead to a degree, that is the way a college confers a status symbol upon its students.

_____
_____
_____
_____

UNIT I DIAGNOSTIC TEST: LOCATING THE VERB AND ITS SUBJECT

DIRECTIONS

Consider each sentence in the exercise after the sample sentence. In each, underline the main verb(s) and draw a circle around the subject(s). To make reading them easier, the sentences in the exercise have been numbered.

Sample Sentence

Will they in the enjoyment of plenty forget the memory of freedom?
—Thomas Jefferson

Identification of Verb and Subject

Will (they) in the enjoyment of plenty forget the memory of freedom?
—Thomas Jefferson

Remember that each sentence is part of a paragraph.

Proofread carefully!

NAME: _____

ID# : _____

DATE: _____

The paragraph that follows is adapted from Allan Nevin's "The Place of Franklin D. Roosevelt in History," American Heritage (June, 1966).

1. This nation remembers Franklin Delano Roosevelt perhaps more fondly than any other president.

2. Roosevelt made changes that converted a nation of aggressive individualists into a social-minded nation.

3. His most important quality lay in his ability to imbue the American people with a new spiritual strength.

4. He strengthened our best purposes and suppressed our worst instincts.

5. He dealt ably with fifty important issues in a day, making shrewd decisions on each, illustrating his quick, resourceful, and flexible mind.

6. This power to act quickly, shrewdly, and earnestly served the nation well.

7. And there are his unforgettable, spontaneous remarks, such as these uttered on his first days in office.

8. "I never get tired."

9. "This job is a cinch."

10. And to Churchill, "It's fun to be in the same century with you."

11. Yet there did exist criticism.

12. One was that Franklin will, in the light of political realities, refrain from supporting causes he knows to be worthy.

13. Still, when future generations look back on these dire times, they will see Roosevelt's imagination, boldness, and ingenuity.

14. His legacy is that human beings can shape their future for the better.

15. His self-confidence, his enthusiasm, and his happy faculty of obliterating old failures by bold new plans teach us not to be imprisoned by a dead past.

16. In his own words, "The only limit to our realization of tomorrow will be our doubts of today."

UNIT II DIAGNOSTIC TEST: NOUNS AND PRONOUNS (NUMBER AND REFERENCE)

DIRECTIONS

Many of the sentences that follow these samples below contain errors in the use of articles, nouns, and pronouns. No errors exist in other areas. When you see an error, circle it. Correct the error as you rewrite the entire sentence alongside. Circle any changes you have made. If a sentence contains no errors, do not copy it. Simply write "correct" in the space alongside. To make your task easier, the sentences in the exercise have been numbered.

SAMPLE SENTENCES WITH CORRECTIONS

a. My son considers his grandma (a) amazing lady.

My son considers his grandma (an) amazing lady.

b. He picks a dozen (rose) for her each time we visit.

He picks a dozen ros(es) for her each day we visit.

c. Once, a thorn pricked her finger.

Correct

d. (They) hurt until her grandma's kiss took the pain away.

(It) hurt until her grandma's kiss took the pain away.

Remember that each sentence is part of a paragraph.

Proofread carefully!

NAME: _____

ID# : _____

DATE: _____

PASSPORTS

1. With few exception, a passport is required for a United States (U.S.) citizen to enter a foreign country.

_____

_____

_____

2. To travel anywhere in North America, a American (U.S.) citizen is not required to have a passport, but to travel to Central or South America they must obtain passports.

_____

_____

_____

_____

3. Many country in Central and South America require passports of all foreigner.

_____

_____

4. U.S. travelers in all foreign country should carry documentary proof of his U.S. citizenship whether or not passport are required.

_____

_____

_____

5. Every person is required to obtain a individual passport in their name.

_____

_____

6. A child may not be included in his or her parents' passports.

_____

_____

7. Someone 13 year of age or older must appear in person before a agent will accept his or her application.

_____

_____

8. A parent or guardian cannot execute an application for them.

_____

_____

9. In the case of a child aged 12 or younger, a parent may execute their application.

_____

_____

_____

10. Regardless of age, one must apply for a first-time passports in person.

_____

_____

11. When applying, he or she must show evidence of U.S. citizenship.

_____

_____

12. The clerk of any Federal court can accept your application.

_____

_____

13. They will ask to see some personal ID such as your driver's license, a credit card, or a school report card.

_____

_____

14. As a identity document, your passport is valuable.

_____

_____

NAME: _____

ID# : _____

DATE: _____

15. They should be safeguarded to avoid an unnecessary complications when one is traveling in various foreign country.

_____

_____

UNIT III DIAGNOSTIC TEST: PROBLEMS WITH AGREEMENT

DIRECTIONS

Many of the sentences that follow the samples below contain errors in the agreement between subjects and verbs and/or in the agreement between pronouns and the nouns to which they refer (antecedents). No errors exist in other areas. When you see an error, circle it. Correct the error as you rewrite the entire sentence alongside. Circle any changes you have made. If a sentence contains no errors, write "correct" in the space alongside. To make your task easier, the sentences in the exercise have been numbered.

SAMPLE SENTENCES WITH CORRECTIONS

a. California remain one of the nation's favorite vacation sites because of its beaches, mountains, and forests.

California (remains) one of the nation's favorite vacation sites because of its beaches, mountains, and forests.

b. Verdure, defined as "the fresh green color of growing things," are plentiful here, making an environment pleasing to the eyes.

Verdure, defined as "the fresh green color of growing things," (is) plentiful here, making an environment pleasing to the eyes.

c. I loves living here.

I (love) living here.

Remember that each sentence is part of a paragraph.

Proofread carefully!

NAME: _____

ID# : _____

DATE: _____

WHY THE COLOR PURPLE?

1. <u>In Search of Our Mother's Gardens</u> contain Alice Walker's definition of a "womanist" as a black feminist, a feminist of color.

   _____
   _____
   _____

2. The term, derived from a black folk expression of mothers to daughters, refer to a female child who wants to know more and in greater depth than is considered "good" for them.

   _____
   _____
   _____
   _____
   _____

3. There is such terms as "outrageous," "audacious," "courageous," and 'willful" among the words that describes her behavior.

   _____
   _____
   _____
   _____

4. Such qualities is incompatible with "girlish," "frivolous," or "irresponsible" behavior.

   _____
   _____
   _____

5. People who see themselves as womanists appreciates and prefers the emotional flexibility of women.

   _____
   _____
   _____

6. A womanist value tears, the natural counterbalance of laughter, as a sign of strength.

   _____
   _____
   _____

7. A womanist loves music.   _____

8. She love dance.   _____

9. She love the moon.   _____

10. She love the Spirit.   _____

11. She love struggle.   _____

13. She love the Folk.   _____

13. She loves herself, regardless.   _____

14. Love and food and roundness   _____
    completes her loves.   _____

15. "Womanist" are to "femin-   _____
    ist" as purple to lavender.   _____

UNIT IV DIAGNOSTIC TEST: VERB TENSES

DIRECTIONS

Many of the sentences that follow the samples below contain errors in the use of verb forms. No errors exist in other areas. When you see an error, circle it. Correct the error as you rewrite the entire sentence alongside. Circle the corrected word(s). If a sentence contains no errors, write "correct" in the space alongside. To make your task easier, the sentences in the exercise have been numbered.

SAMPLE SENTENCES WITH CORRECTIONS

a. It was many years before I (re-alize) that sarcasm is the protest of the weak.

It was many years before I (realized) sarcasm is the protest of the weak.

b. Until then, I (think) of it as an old, reassuring friend I could turn to in a room full of strangers.

Until then, I (thought) of it as an old, reassuring friend I could turn to in a room full of strangers.

c. I could (of retain) some friends if I had understood this sooner.

I could (have) (retained) some friends if I had understood this sooner.

Remember that each sentence is part of a paragraph.

Proofread carefully!

NAME: _____

ID# : _____

DATE: _____

OCTOBER 31, 1952 (ADAPTED FROM <u>MARKED BY FIRE</u> BY JOYCE CAROL OATES)

1. Whenever winter comes to Oklahoma, the snow fall like chilled confetti out of the sky.

   _____

   _____

2. As the year progresses, the white coldness turns brown and melt, and the birds returned, singing the same hopeful songs.

   _____

   _____

   _____

3. When it was still cold, Mother Barker came to Patience's and rock the baby to sleep.

   _____

   _____

4. That afternoon she had took Abby to her own house to let the tot watch her administer folk medicine to the women wrapped in shawls who had came at her doorstep.

   _____

   _____

   _____

   _____

5. Some days Mother Barker get the child back home just in time for Abby to stand on her own porch.

   _____

   _____

   _____

6. She would be wave as her father came walking home.

   _____

   _____

7. The image that greet Strong was that of a warm, chocolate girl holding on the porch

   _____

   _____

rail in a starched dress with a bow tied in the back and a ribbon dancing on her head.

_____

_____

_____

8. Moonstones sparkle in her dark, black eyes.

_____

9. He think about the velvet interiors of pansies when he saw her smile and said the simple word, "Daddy,"

_____

_____

_____

10. Three months from now, safe inside the Jackson house, in her mother's arms, Abby will again watched the snow fall.

_____

_____

_____

11. By spring, Patience's asafetida bag, strongly aromatic when it was hang around Abby's neck in winter, will of lost its pungency and will be discarded.

_____

_____

_____

_____

12. A cow will have a calf in the ongoing circle of creation.

_____

_____

13. Before long, it be August again.

_____

NAME: _____

ID# : _____

DATE: _____

UNIT V DIAGNOSTIC TEST: PROBLEMS WITH SENTENCE BOUNDARIES

DIRECTIONS

Many of the sentences that follow the samples below contain errors in sentence boundaries. Specifically, there will be fragments and run-ons punctuated as sentences. No errors exist in other areas. When you see an error, circle it. Correct the error as you rewrite the entire sentence alongside. Then circle the word(s) you have corrected. If a sentence contains no error, write "correct" in the space alongside. To make your task easier, the sentences in the exercise have been numbered.

SAMPLE SENTENCES WITH CORRECTIONS

a. The Eternal Road, a play by Max Reinhardt, (that) cut its last act after its opening night.

> The Eternal Road, a play by Max Reinhardt, (○) cut its last act after opening night.

b. In the late 1930s, drama critics had to leave plays by midnigh(○) (if) they did not, they could not make their morning headlines.

> In the late 1930s, drama critics had to leave plays by midnight. (If) they did not, the could not make their morning headlines.

c. When they left at midnight, only three acts of The Eternal Road had been complete(d) (and) they gave the play a rave review without having seen its terrible fourth act.

> When they left at midnight, only three acts of The Eternal Road had been complete(d) and they gave the play a rave review without having seen its terrible fourth act.

d. (Which) is why it was cut.

> (This) is why it was cut.

Remember that each sentence is part of a paragraph.

Proofread carefully!

NAME: _____

ID# _____

DATE: _____

CRITICAL CLOUTS

1. Drama critics and artists do not always duel with words, sometimes they use fists as well.

2. When critic Richard Watts of the <u>Herald Tribune</u> wrote a negative review of a play Jack Kirkland had adapted from Steinbeck's <u>Tortilla Flat</u>.

3. Kirkland was determined to revenge himself.

4. And stormed into Bleeck's Artists and Writers Restaurant on Fortieth Street.

5. Where he knew Watts was having lunch, and knocked Watts' glasses off.

6. Other employees of the <u>Tribune</u> came to Watts' aid, they included Arthur Kuhn, foreman of the press room, and Howard Barnes, a reporter.

7. Henry, the chief bartender, also got into the act he conked Kirkland on the head and tossed him out the door.

8. After Barnes dragged Kirkland back inside.

9. To pummel him with additional punches.

10. The misunderstood playwright almost discovered just how deadly a critic's clout can be.

11. Fortunately, Mr. Bleeck, the owner of the restaurant stepped in.

12. Ordering the hostilities to cease.

13. Also warned that he would no longer serve any "overly" intoxicated persons.

14. Presumably finding ordinary drunks acceptable.

UNIT VI DIAGNOSTIC TEST: PROBLEMS WITH MARKERS

DIRECTIONS

Many of the sentences that follow these samples below contain errors in the use (or absence) of certain markers. When you see such an error in **apostrophes, capitalization, commas, underlining,** or **quotation marks,** circle it. There are no errors in other areas. Correct the error as you copy the entire sentence alongside. Then circle the corrections in your rewritten sentence. If a sentence contains no errors, write "correct" in the space alongside. To make your task easier, the sentences in the paragraph have been itemized.

SAMPLE SENTENCES WITH CORRECTIONS

a. In High School, Justins dictionary lost its cover from so much use, but Justin did'nt care; he scored 800 on the SAT's verbal section.

In High school, Justin's dictionary lost its cover from so much use, but Justin didn't care; he scored 800 on the SAT's verbal section.

b. In College, he received an A in his history 204 class.

In college, he received an A in his History 204 class.

c. "You've made us proud," Justin's pleased mother told him.

"You've made us proud," Justin's pleased mother told him.

Remember that each sentence is part of a paragraph.

Proofread carefully!

NAME: _____

ID# _____

DATE: _____

465

SEEING CELL LIFE

1. This selection, <u>Seeing Cell Life</u>, is adapted from "My life and hard times," a book by James Thurber.

2. One day, Howards biology Professor said cheerily, "Were going to see cells this time arent we?

3. Yes sir, Howard said.

4. Students' to the right and left of him were seeing cells.

5. Whats more they were drawing pictures of cells in their notebooks.

6. Of course Howard did'nt see anything,

7. As I am God's witness, I'll arrange the microscopes lens so that you see cells through it or give up teaching the professor blurted out.

8. with every adjustment of the microscope known to man Howard and his Instructor tried.

9. The one time Howard saw anything but blackness or the familiar milky blur, he saw to his pleasure and amazement a variegated constellation of flecks' specks' and dots'.

_____

_____

_____

_____

10. These he hastily drew.

_____

11. The instructor noting Howards activity came back from an adjoining desk a smile on his lips and his eyebrow's high in hope.

_____

_____

_____

12. Lets see he chirped.

_____

13. After a moments observation he demanded, "what's that"?

_____

_____

14. Thats what I saw Howard said.

_____

15. The instructor bent over and squinted into Howards microscope and then his head snapped up.

_____

_____

_____

NAME: _____

ID# : _____

DATE: _____

16. That's your eye, you idiot, he said.

_____

17. Youve fixed the lens' so that it reflects your own eye.

_____

_____

INDEX